PUTTING ON
THE LIFE OF CHRIST

Volume Two

By

Rayola Kelley

Hidden Manna Publications

Featuring the Following Books:
He Actually Thought It Not Robbery
Revelation of the Cross
In Search of Real Faith
Think on These Things
Follow the Pattern

You can obtain a study reference book to complement your studies of this volume at Gentle Shepherd Ministries' website at www.gentleshepherd.com.

Hidden **M**anna **P**ublications
P.O. Box 3572
Oldtown, ID. 83822
www.gentleshepherd.com

Facebook:
https://www.facebook.com/HiddenMannaPublications/

Dedication

This Volume is dedicated to all of the faithful friends and supporters of Gentle Shepherd Ministries. Through the years there have been numerous supporters, but the following are mentioned as those who have proven faithful to support this ministry through its many changes and challenges.

Nancy Brown
Eva Cole
Chuck and Pearl DeMaris
Larry and Maureen Human
Mike and Carla Kropp
Kit and Kitty Miller
Carrie Seaney
Dale and Donna Spencer

Serving with each of you in the harvest field has been a great honor. May God reward you for your faithful and sacrificial support.

Special Acknowledgment

I want to acknowledge the editing work of
Jo Reaves and Crystal Garvin.

I would also like to thank those who
took time to proofread the
different books in this volume.

Thank you for all of your
commitment and dedication
to see me through this project.

TABLE OF CONTENTS

INTRODUCTION

Putting on the Life of Christ is the second in a series of seven volumes that present diverse themes of the Christian life. The intent of each volume is to compliment and intensify the Gentle Shepherd Ministries Discipleship Course. The groupings of books in Volume Two address the true source behind the Christian life, Jesus Christ.

Christianity is often confused with religious attempts, activities, and associations. However, Christianity points to life. This life is based on the redemption of Jesus Christ, which is to establish reconciliation with God. In the believer's life, this reconciliation is being clearly brought forth through complete identification with the redemptive work and life of Jesus, the sanctifying work of the Spirit, and is distinguished by godliness. In essence, it is actually the very life of Christ being worked in believers as their inward man is changed, their minds transformed, and their outer man conformed to the very image of Christ. The Apostle Paul summarized it best when he instructed each of us as believers to put on the Lord Jesus Christ and we would not give way to the lust of the flesh. However, we cannot put on Christ unless we know Him.

Sadly, there are those who are barren in the knowledge of Jesus. They have an image of Him, but not a living revelation of Him. They have developed some type of understanding about Him, but they have never come to a living knowledge of Him that will enlarge them to explore the heights of His greatness as God and High Priest, and the great depths from which He came to be man in order to ensure our salvation.

Each book in Volume Two reveals the different aspects of Jesus in His deity, humanity, example, and work of redemption. This second volume will inspire you to consider the heights of His deity, explore the depths to which He humbled Himself in His humanity, the mind He displayed in His meekness, and the pattern He left. This pattern enables His people through unfeigned faith to become identified with Him by following Him into the incredible life He has made available.

The first book, *He Actually Thought it Not Robbery* is a beautiful revelation of Jesus. Taken from Philippians 2:5-11, the reader will follow Jesus from eternity into obscurity, and from acceptable servitude all the way to the place of Calvary. It is an incredible journey that will humble and cause awe and worship as Jesus is unveiled in His humanity as He overcame every temptation, and in His deity as He was raised by resurrection power to bring forth new life for those who believe upon Him.

Revelation of the Cross vividly portrays the two crosses presented in the Bible. The first cross points to Jesus' work of redemption. It not only takes us to the depths of the great price He paid for us, but because of it, our precious Lord has been lifted up to great heights, enabling us to see that He is our only solution. Portions of this book have been revised, but the goal remains the same of trying to effectively unveil the cross of Christ hidden in the book of Genesis.

The second cross that is vividly portrayed in this second book of Volume Two is the one each of us as believers must carry to be identified as Jesus' disciples. Such a cross points to the personal cost that, we as His followers, must pay to know Jesus. The information in this book will also allow the reader to discover the meaning and work of the Christian's personal cross in light of Jesus' seven sayings on the cross. The author skillfully paints a picture of how both crosses intertwine to reveal the love, mercy, grace, and plan of God.

In Search of Real Faith is the third book in this volume. As believers, we can only connect the Person of Jesus to the life He has called us to by unfeigned faith. Without faith we will never discover the reality of our Lord. This book has been updated to bring additional valuable insights into what constitutes real faith. It describes the author's own search to discover true faith in the midst of the prevailing worldly unbelief that has often been cleverly disguised by the popular pseudo faiths that have made inroads into Christendom.

You will laugh, cry, and sigh as you follow the author through a maze of discoveries that challenged her perception of God. Each discovery revealed the nature of faith, bringing her to understand and embrace the genuine faith that moves mountains.

The Apostle Paul tells us that our minds must be transformed, rather than conformed to the world. He gives us insight into how to accomplish such a task by bringing all thoughts into captivity to the obedience of Christ. He brings it all together when he instructs us to let the very mind of Christ be formed in us. The fourth book in this volume, *Think on These Things,"* reveals the type of discipline it would take to have such a mind developed in us towards the matters of God. Taken from Philippians 4:8. the author reveals how each quality described in this Scripture will develop the virtues that were clearly present in Jesus' disposition, attitude, and approach.

Jesus commands His disciples to follow Him. Such a command may bring a question mark to some people's mind. Since Jesus is not present in the flesh, how can we follow Him? The Apostle Paul talked about the pattern that was presented even in his own life for us to meditate upon as a means to pursue our life in Christ.

The final book of Volume Two, *Follow the Pattern,* unveils the patterns that were clearly outlined in the Old Testament and revealed in the New Testament. These patterns give valuable insight that believers are able to see, examine, and study in order to understand the godly principles and examples that they should follow to embrace the revelation and life of Jesus for themselves.

Obviously, the books in Volume Two will reveal that our main spiritual search does not have to do with doctrine or religion; rather, it has to do with possessing the real Jesus. He is the essence of our spiritual lives, the sole focus of our faith, the place of sanity for our minds, and the true example for us to follow.

Book One

HE ACTUALLY THOUGHT IT NOT ROBBERY

INTRODUCTION

I have written many books for others, but in this instance, I wrote it for myself. In essence, it is a long love letter to the Lover of my soul, Jesus Christ. It is a book of appreciation to the One who gave it all. It is a small offering of praise to the One who is beyond description.

This book examines Philippians 2:5-11, one of the most powerful revelations of Jesus Christ. I have seen glimpses of this revelation because I constantly refer back to it in my studies, teachings, and preaching.

It is a text that has challenged, matured, and humbled me. Each glimpse has made me appreciate the preciousness of my Lord. Each aspect of the revelation has made me realize how little I comprehend the Lord's love, mercy, grace, and sacrifice.

As I discovered in the text of Philippians, Jesus Christ sacrificed far more than His life. These scriptures showed me an ongoing sacrifice being offered, and through this sacrifice I was able to glean what Christianity is truly all about. It allowed me to see the real example Jesus left for each of us who follow Him.

This example is not offered simply to be pondered in our hearts, but must be lived out in every facet of our lives as Jesus lived it when He came to earth. We are told He is the branch from the root of the lineage of David that came out of the barren wasteland of humanity. He became least in disposition, poor in status, marred by the whips of man, and broken by sin as the Lamb of God. The thing I consider most incredible about the ongoing sacrifice of Jesus was His attitude about it: *He actually thought it not robbery.*

There is so much to grasp in these few Scriptures. I feel I will only scratch the surface, but in so doing, I pray that it will bring about godly changes in my life and yours, and bless you as much as it has blessed me.

Enjoy this incredible, humbling journey.

1

THE MIND OF CHRIST

Let this mind be in you,
which was also in Christ Jesus.
(Philippians 2:5)

Before we can begin to grasp the incredible principles governing the attitude and life of Christ, we must understand the mind of Christ. First of all, we must ask ourselves, what does it mean to have the mind of Christ? We know the mind is comprised of the intellect, thoughts (or feelings), and the will of a person. How do we come to a place where all three areas openly express the disposition of Christ?

The first insight into what it means to possess the mind of Christ is found in the word *"let."* This word implies you are giving way to something. In this case, you are actually giving way to the person of Jesus Christ.

To give way to something involves the will area. You must make a determination that will begin to govern what you will or will not accept. For example, I recently watched a TV magazine. The interviewers were talking to a homosexual who admitted he did not want to accept his sexual preference. He wanted to be what was considered normal to our society, so he sought out various avenues including exorcism *(note, not deliverance)* to subdue his deviant sexual desires because of his religious upbringing.

After listening to this man, I realized he wanted a quick solution that would immediately allow him to stop thinking and feeling the way he did. He was not willing to acknowledge that it was not an inherited trait, but rather perverted thought patterns that he had personally accepted as reality, and then recognizing them as the darkness of lies that originate with Satan. Such a reality became an acceptable preference to him. This man's unwillingness to take responsibility for his perverted thought patterns kept him from experiencing godly deliverance.

This is how people rationalize and justify perverted lifestyles. False images are erected in the chambers of a person's imagination. Instead of distinguishing a false image as a lie, these confused individuals begin to accept it as their identity and lot in life. Such acceptance will allow them to make peace with their screaming consciences and embattled emotions, supposedly confirming their delusion. No wonder Proverbs

23:7 states, "For as he thinketh in his heart, so is he." It is apparent our identity is determined by what we think on.

This is why Paul exhorted followers of Christ to cast down imaginations that are contrary to the character of our holy God, and bring into captivity every thought to the obedience of Christ. The problem with not casting down imaginations is that you will become vain in your conclusions and bring dishonor to God by giving in to perversion. If you do not take responsibility for your thoughts, you will make a decision to not retain God in your knowledge. As a result, God will give you over to a reprobate mind.[1]

A reprobate mind is where the will gives in to the vanity of the mind. This type of mind is carnal or fleshly and, as the Apostle Paul declared in Romans 8:6, such a mind will result in death.

In considering the command to "Let the mind of Christ be your mind," we must acknowledge an exchange has to take place. For instance, I cannot simply choose to put down my carnal mind without having something with which to replace it. I must, therefore, replace my intellect, thoughts, and will with the will, thoughts, and wisdom of Jesus. How do I develop the mind of Christ?

The answer to this question is found in Colossians 3:1-2. This passage tells us we must first seek those things that are above. And, how do we seek those things which are above? The answer is simple: Think on them.

Philippians 4:8-9 tells us,
> Finally brethren, whatsoever things are true, whatsoever things are honest, whatsoever things are just, whatsoever things are pure, whatsoever things are lovely, whatsoever things are of good report; if there be any virtue, and if there be any praise, think on these things. Those things which ye have both learned, and received, and heard, and seen in me, do: and the God of peace shall be with you.

In Philippians 4:8 we see a description of Jesus' character. He is true, just, pure, and lovely. He is a person who not only holds a good report in the hearts of those who love Him, but in the very courts of heaven. He is beyond reproach and deserves our praise.[2] Obviously, we are being instructed not only to think on Jesus, but also to seek Him fervently. Colossians 3:1 confirms this, "Seek those things which are above, where Christ sitteth on the right hand of God."

Have you ever done a study on the position of the right hand? For Christ to be on the right hand of God means He is equal and has the same authority or clout. We know He intercedes for us as our High

---

[1] 2 Corinthians 10:5; Romans 1:21 & 28

[2] If you would like to know more about Philippians 4:8, see the fourth book in this volume entitled, *Think on These Things.*

Priest, which makes Him our Mediator. Psalm 16:11 gives us this beautiful promise, "Thou wilt shew me the path of life: in thy presence is fullness of joy; at thy right hand there are pleasures for evermore." Don't you see? Jesus is the One who represents all our eternal pleasures, and because of being placed in Him, and Him being in us through the presence of the Spirit, we will enjoy such pleasures for ages to come.

The Apostle Paul takes us one step further in Philippians 4:9. He tells us we must put into practice what we have learned, received, and heard. Knowledge without application is void of wisdom. This type of ungodly knowledge operates out of pride that is always in competition with God. Obviously, the result is not being able to retain the knowledge of God.[3] Therefore, Paul is instructing us to put our knowledge into practice in order to ensure that God will remain a reality to us.

The kind of relationship we have with our Lord will determine how open we are to receive from Him. When most of us think about receiving from God, we think in terms of blessings and promises. It is true we receive such gifts from God, but we must also be willing to receive instruction and correction, which are also part of the godly package as well.

A good example of a person who could not properly receive from the Lord is Judas Iscariot. This man sat at the same table as Jesus and fellowshipped with him. He witnessed miracles and partook of untold blessings from the hand of the Father because of Jesus. Yet, the man was ungrateful and ended up betraying the long-awaited Messiah. Why? Because he could not properly receive from Jesus, and as a result he abused his privileges and betrayed the Son of God.

When we receive something from God, we have no rights to it. We must seek His face to know how we are to disperse it among others as Jesus did the few loaves and fish among the 5,000.[4] The things of God have the potential to bless others, ultimately bringing glory to Him.

Finally, we must respond in obedience when we hear God's instruction or else we will find ourselves in opposition to Him. James 1:22-24 puts it best,

> But be ye doers of the word, and not hearers only, deceiving your own selves. For if any be a hearer of the word, and not a doer, he is like unto a man beholding his natural face in a glass: For he beholdeth himself, and goeth his way, and straightway forgetteth what manner of man he was.

The biggest reason Christians fail to develop the attitude of Jesus is because they are not obedient to God's Word. The Scriptures in James tell us if we do not obey the Word of God, we forget what sort of person we really are. We lose perspective and reality. In essence, we are

---

[3] Romans 1:28
[4] John 6:1-14

refusing to bring our mind into submission to the Word of God with the intent of obeying it. It is the Word that serves as our mirror and brings a reality check to our spiritual condition. In the life of Christ, we see He was totally obedient to the Father. His intellect, thoughts, and will were the visible expression of the mind of His Father. If He had not been obedient, we would still be miserably dead in our sins with no real hope or future.

It is amazing how much Christians want the best for their spiritual life, but are not willing to be obedient to what has been established. If you are not obedient to God's Word, you will never experience His peace until you come into line with His will.

Colossians 3:2 then instructs us to, "Set our affection on things above, not on things on the earth." Here Paul is telling us to set or determine to put our affections or feelings on things above. Again, we see that we must make a determination not to give in to fleshly affections, but choose instead to direct all of our emotions and feeling towards Jesus Christ.

You will find that if you set your feelings on Jesus, a transformation will take place in your mind. Transform means, "to change" or "transfigure." It actually involves a change in form, character, and condition. To transfigure something essentially involves reshaping or fashioning something, which will ultimately manifest a new outward appearance.

The Apostle Paul makes this statement in Romans 12:2, "And be not conformed to this world: but be ye transformed by the renewing of your mind, that you may prove what is that good, and acceptable, and perfect will of God." Here Paul is instructing us not to be like, or fashion ourselves according to the world. By giving way to the world, our minds will be molded according to the thought patterns of the world.

Paul also goes on to say, "Be transformed." In other words, bring your mind under the control of God so it will not only be fashioned according to the person of Jesus, but it will become the very expression of His attitude and character.

How are our minds transformed? Paul tells us the change occurs when our minds are actually renewed. Our minds must be renovated, revived, or restored. The only person who can revive our minds is the Holy Spirit. To allow the mind of Christ to be developed in us means we are simply giving way to the work of the Holy Spirit.

In studying Philippians 2:1-4, you will see that Paul actually shows us how this mind will function in our relationship with Jesus and others. You can find this description in verse two, "Fulfil ye my joy, that ye be likeminded, having the same love, being of one accord, of one mind."

To be likeminded implies you have a similar spirit or motivation. To have the mind of Christ means we will be in agreement with Him and that we belong to Him because the same Spirit is motivating us. It is this type of oneness that brings joy to the heart of Jesus, and glory to the Father.

Jesus experienced this oneness with His Father, and His prayer request was simple in regards to His followers. Heeding His words in the correct spirit is vital:

> That they all may be one; as thou, Father, are in me, and I in thee, that they also may be one in us: that the world may believe that thou hast sent me. And the glory which thou gavest me I have given them; that they may be one, even as we are one: I in them, and thou in me, that they may be made perfect in one; and that the world may know that thou hast sent me, and hast loved them, as thou hast loved me (John 17:21-23).

Notice how this oneness will give visible credibility to the real identity of Jesus in this dark, lost, and dying world. The oneness that Jesus is talking about here is not a product of people coming together for moral or religious good. Rather, this oneness is the result of people coming together because they truly love one Person, and that person is Jesus Christ, and they possess a like-spirit, the Holy Spirit.

If you are giving way to the Holy Ghost, the love of God will come forth in both attitude and action. You will be in love with Jesus, and your life will tell it. As the Apostle Paul said in Romans 5:5, "And hope maketh not ashamed; because the love of God is shed abroad in our hearts by the Holy Ghost which is given unto us."

Do you have the mind of Christ, or are your thought patterns a visible expression of the world? To have the mind of Christ is not an option, but a necessity if Christians are going to reach their potential in the kingdom of God.

It is necessary to get to the bottom line on this subject. If you do not have the mind of Christ, you will not be able to follow in His footsteps, which are clearly outlined in Philippians 2. Neither will you be able to experience the full abundance of the Christian life.

2

JESUS IN HIS ORIGINAL FORM

Who, being in the form of God...
(Philippians 2:6a)

"Form" in this scripture means the base or nature of something.[1] To change form implies the idea of adjusting parts or reshaping the nature of something. In this Scripture verse we are given Jesus' identity. It tells us that He was in the form of God. In other words, He is God by nature.

Today there are many cults and New Age beliefs that deny Jesus is God by nature. And yet, the Word is very clear about Jesus' identity. For example, the Apostle John introduces Jesus as God in the first verse of his Gospel, "In the beginning was the Word, and the Word was with God, and the Word was God." We know that this verse is in reference to Jesus Christ as the Apostle John reveals His identity as the Light, Creator, and the Lamb of God in this incredible chapter.

The Apostle Paul gives us this information about Jesus, "For by him were all things created, that are in heaven, and that are in earth, visible and invisible, whether they be thrones, or dominions, or principalities, or powers: all things were created by him, and for him: And he is before all things, and by him all things consist" (Colossians 1:16-17). In these Scriptures Paul identifies Jesus as our Creator, while Genesis 1:1 identifies our Creator as God.

In 1 Timothy 3:16, Paul clearly identifies Jesus as God in the flesh, "And without controversy great is the mystery of godliness: <u>God was manifest in the flesh</u>, justified in the Spirit, seen of angels, preached unto the Gentiles, believed on in the world, received up into glory." (Emphasis added.) The apostle stipulated that the great mystery of God is that He would come in the flesh. The Apostle John declared that only those of the antichrist spirit would deny that Jesus Christ came in the flesh.[2] The reality of Jesus being God Incarnate would be verified by the Spirit, witnessed by the angels, preached as a message of hope unto the Gentiles, believed as truth in the world, and confirmed by Jesus' ascension after His resurrection.

Although the Word is quite clear about the deity of Jesus, many choose to explain it away with human logic, erroneous philosophies of man, and doctrines of demons. Believing the true identity of Jesus

---

[1] Strong's Exhaustive Concordance of the Bible; # 3444
[2] 1 John 4:1-3; 2 John 7

comes down to faith. We either choose to agree with the Word of God by faith in its declarations concerning Jesus or we reject it and walk in unbelief towards God and His record.

The problem with denying that Jesus is God by nature is that a person will never begin to realize the price Jesus paid for our salvation. By downplaying His divine nature, such an individual will ultimately reject His salvation. God's Word constantly verifies and affirms this reality.

The reality of God's presence, work, and purpose in our lives actually guarantees us of our salvation. It is because of God's character that we can trust Him to save us. The Word tells us Jesus is the only way to salvation.[3] In a sense, He is the ladder that connects sinful, insignificant man to his holy God in a living relationship.

We see a type or representation of this ladder in Genesis 28. On his way to his uncle's place, Jacob stopped at Bethel for the night. The meaning behind the name "Bethel" set the tone for Jacob's encounter with God. It means "the house of God." At Bethel, Jacob had a dream. He saw a ladder set upon the earth, and the top of it reached to heaven, and the Lord stood at the top of it. He also noted that the angels of God were ascending and descending upon it.

This is a type of Jesus, who became the ladder that came from heaven to earth. Upon Him alone ascend all of our hopes and prayers, and through Him descend wondrous promises and everlasting life. God Incarnate, how glorious is our Ladder! We will be learning for ages to come how the love of God designed a glorious ladder that required Jesus to descend to earth, which would allow man to ascend and reach heaven.

It was during this dream that the LORD introduced Himself to Jacob. He said in Genesis 28:13, "I am the LORD God of Abraham, thy father." When Jesus walked this earth 2,000 years ago, He was forever introducing Himself as the "I AM."[4] His introduction served as a prelude to heart-stirring invitations and judgments.

> "I am the bread of life: he that cometh to me shall never hunger; and he that believeth on me shall never thirst." "...I am from above...if ye believe not that I am he, ye shall die in your sins." "I am the good shepherd: the good shepherd giveth his life for the sheep." "Verily, Verily, I say unto you, before Abraham was, I am" (John 6:35; 8:23-24, 58; 10:14).

Oh, what a stir Jesus caused! He brought leadership to the lost, rest to the downtrodden, hope to the outcast, and anger to the self-righteous. Men either wanted to worship Him or stone Him. They either wanted to embrace Him as their Messiah or discredit Him by associating Him with the kingdom of darkness.

---

[3] Psalm 27:1; Isaiah 12:2; Acts 4:10-12
[4] Genesis 28:13

For Jacob, his encounter with God brought fear. He sensed His holiness and felt that his meeting with God was a dreadful event instead of a blessing. His response should be a warning to us. He recognized God, and it brought a healthy fear to his soul. To face God without intervention is a frightful experience. The truth is that we will face God in one of two ways. We will face Him within the protection of His grace, or we will encounter His righteousness, judgment, and wrath. How we encounter God on Judgment Day will depend on what we do with His Ladder.

Many different Christs are being presented today, but there is only one God Incarnate. We must recognize the real Jesus for who He is if we expect to come out on the side of God's grace. We must acknowledge that only God could truly provide the acceptable ladder; in fact, He provided Himself, as we will see in the following scriptures in Philippians 2.

We see in Genesis 28:17 that Jacob considered this place a gate to heaven. Jesus said this in John 10:9, "I am the door: by me if any man enter in, he shall be saved, and shall go in and out, and find pasture." Jacob may have encountered what He considered to be the gate to heaven at Bethel, but as Christians, we have encountered the true gate or door to heaven in Jesus Christ. The question is how are we to respond to Jesus?

Jacob gives us a beautiful example of what we must do with Jesus. He took the stone his head had been resting upon, erected it, and poured oil upon it. We know according to Scripture that Jesus is the cornerstone that was erected by God, and anointed by the Holy Spirit, but initially rejected by the builders.[5] This is in reference to a popular legend that was well known by the Jewish people surrounding the construction of the temple of Solomon.

All the stones were shaped and cut to the same size except for one. The builders looked at the unusual stone and concluded that it was useless. They cast it into Kidron Valley, which served as their garbage dump. When they were close to being finished, they noticed they lacked one stone: the cornerstone. As they examined the area, they realized the odd stone they had deemed useless was actually the cornerstone.[6]

Apparently, the cornerstone was designed separately from the rest of the stones. According to the information we have about cornerstones, all other stones or bricks were design to be aligned to the cornerstone. Before the temple could be completed, the builders had to retrieve the cornerstone from the garbage dump.

It was obvious that Jesus Christ had come from a different realm. According to Scripture, there is no beginning to Him for He is the Alpha

---

[5] See 1 Peter 2:6-8.

[6] Lectures On the Book of Acts by H. A. Ironside, 18th Printing, August 1982, pgs. 105-106

and Omega and the Ancient of Days. The Jewish people initially rejected the cornerstone to their spiritual lives. As a result, He became identified with the worst plight and depravity of mankind on the cross, only to be resurrected in power and glory.[7]

Just as Jacob erected the stone or pillar, the resurrected life of Jesus must be erected in the life of man, who is to serve as the temple of the Holy Spirit. It is when the life of Jesus is being developed within the temple of man's life that the anointing will begin to flow freely to others.[8]

Jesus is indeed the cornerstone of man's spiritual life. He was designed before the foundation of the world to make the life of man whole and complete. He stands out because He is God.

This is a thought-provoking statement: If Jesus is not God, we are miserably lost. If He is not God, God's plan would never be carried out on behalf of the world. You might say, "How do you know this?" Because of what happened in Revelation 5. We read that there was a book that needed to be opened in heaven. The angel cried out with a loud voice, "Who is worthy to open the book and to loose the seals thereof?" Verse three tells us there was not a man in heaven, nor in earth, neither under the earth, who was able to open the book.

The writer of Revelation, the Apostle John, claimed he wept much because there was no one worthy to open and read the book. He was finally told by one of the elders to not weep, for the Lion of the tribe of Judah, the Root of David has prevailed to open the book. When John looked to see who the Lion of the tribe of Judah was, he saw a Lamb as it had been slain.

We all know Jesus Christ is the Lion of the tribe of Judah, the Root of David, and the Lamb of God who takes away the sin of the world. But what we must note is that Jesus is no mere man or He would not be able to open the book. Man is wicked and wretched at best, which makes him unacceptable. However, Jesus is God in the flesh, and because He is righteous and without sin, He will be found worthy to open the book.

Likewise, Jesus is the light of the glorious Gospel that is able to penetrate the darkness of man's soul. He is the great I AM and worthy of all worship. He is the Lamb of God who became the ultimate sacrifice for our sin.[9] He is Jesus Christ, God Incarnate.

Do you believe this by faith, or are you rejecting God's provision for your salvation by rejecting the deity of Jesus? As John said in his first epistle,

> Hereby know ye the Spirit of God: Every spirit that confesseth that Jesus Christ is come in the flesh is of God. And every spirit that confesseth not that Jesus Christ is come in the flesh is not of God: and this is that spirit of

---

[7] Revelation 1:8; Daniel 7: 9, 10, 13; 1 Corinthians 15:1-4
[8] 1 Corinthians 3:16
[9] John 1:4-14, 29; 2 Corinthians 4:3-6

antichrist, whereof ye have heard that it should come; and even now already is in the world (1 John 4:2-3).

3

THE IMAGE OF GOD

...thought it not robbery to be equal with God.
(Philippians 2:6b)

In the second part of Philippians 2:6 we see a reference to what we call "the Godhead." We must observe here that even though Jesus was God, He did not think it was robbery when He ceased to be equal with God.

The belief of the Godhead is very controversial. After much study, I have summarized this tenet of faith in the following statement: That within the essence and oneness of the Godhead are three persons: the Father, the Son, and the Holy Spirit. These three persons are co-eternal and co-equal. They are distinct in subsistence, but have the same characteristics or substance. Therefore, the nature of deity of the one true God is manifested in three distinct persons.

People try to understand the Godhead in their own logic. They cannot see mathematically how three persons equal one God. Yet, the Godhead is not a matter of mathematics, but of chemistry. It does not have to do with quantity of something, but with the nature or character of something.

For example, in chemistry we know that two molecules of hydrogen and one of oxygen equal the substance water. Water may manifest itself in different forms such as ice, liquid, or fog, but when you examine the base or nature of any of these substances, you will find it is still water by nature.

This is how the Godhead works. The whole sum of the glory of God has been made apparent through the Father, the Son, and the Holy Spirit. They may come in different forms and have different responsibilities, but they still have the same base nature or characteristics. Therefore, whether you are considering Jesus, regarding the Father, or giving way to the work of the Holy Spirit, you will encounter the characteristics of deity in each person. This is why Romans 1:20 tells us that creation itself verifies the Godhead, and that in the end man will have no excuse for rejecting this established truth.

It is important that when you consider the Godhead you keep in mind it is actually the nature or characteristics of God that identify Him as being the one true God. Paul's reminder to the Galatians about their spiritual state before they encountered the real God confirms this in Galatians 4:8, "Howbeit then, when ye knew not God, ye did service unto them which by **nature** are no gods." (Emphasis added.) Paul is basically telling the Galatians that they were worshipping gods that were not the true God by nature.

We can also find plurality in relationship to the Godhead in scriptures such as Genesis 1:26; 3:22, 11:7, and Isaiah 6:8. According to Ruth Specter Lascelle, Jewish teacher and author, some of the names of God, such as Elohim, Adonai, and El Shaddai, denote plurality as well. These names are consistently used throughout the Bible. For example, Elohim is used 2,500 times, Adonai 90 times; and El Shaddai 48 times.[1]

We also see reference to plurality in Philippians 2:6 as well. Jesus thought it not robbery to be equal with God. Let's just consider this one statement for a moment. If Jesus made up the total sum of the Godhead, how could He cease to be equal to Himself? It is obvious there is more to God than Jesus Christ. In essence this scripture shows us Jesus ceased to be equal to the other two persons of the Godhead. Keep in mind these three persons of the Godhead were enfolded into the all-encompassing glory of deity through complete agreement. These three persons think, move, and act in total agreement in regard to authority, power, and purpose. However, Jesus stepped outside of this order to take on the disposition of a servant in the fashion or shape of a man. In His humanity, He would have a different relationship with the other two Persons of the Godhead. He would become a son to the Father, and a man who needed to be anointed and led by the power of the Spirit. These two relationships would serve as our examples in light to our lives before God.

The truth about the Godhead is not meant to be comprehended by man's mere mind, but to be received as truth by childlike faith. The problem with the idea of the Godhead is not found in the concept itself, but in man's futile attempt to comprehend an infinite God according to his pathetic logic and limited ability to understand something beyond his present dimension.

Man's logic is limited and perverted at best. When it comes to the things of God, the best man's logic can do is make the person a bona fide skeptic towards all of God's simple truths.

Today there are a lot of skeptics in religion. They have erected God into an image that is acceptable to their logic and requires no childlike faith. The end result to such foolishness is that man possesses an idol constructed by his own imagination or devices. Acts 17:29 clearly states, "Forasmuch then as we are the offspring of God, we ought not to think that the Godhead is like unto gold or silver, or stone graven by art and man's devices."

---

[1] Jewish Faith and the New Covenant, pages 62 and 63.

Colossians 2:9 tells us this about Jesus Christ, "For in him dwelleth all the fulness of the Godhead bodily." Keep in mind the term "Godhead" points to deity. In the Person of Jesus is the fullness of deity. Jesus was the complete picture or the visible image or representative of the invisible God in bodily form.[2]

Jesus confirmed this very fact when Philip asked Him to show him the Father. Jesus responded with this statement, "Have I been so long with you, and yet hast thou not known me, Philip? He that hath seen me hath seen the Father; and how sayest thou then, Shew us the Father" (John 14:9).

Jesus was the living, visible expression of God. When Jesus spoke two thousand years ago, man was actually hearing the voice of God. When Jesus touched people, they were feeling the hand of God. When Jesus' eye penetrated the hearts and souls of people, they were actually seeing the heart of God reach out to them.

Another term or title that indicated that Jesus was the visible expression of God is that of the "Son of God." Many cults believe Jesus is the "Son of God," but they do not really understand this term, and end up demeaning the very character of Christ. Many erroneously think that God the Father had something physically to do with Jesus' existence by believing He actually fathered Him. In other words, they believe Jesus did not pre-exist before Bethlehem. According to *Vine's Expository Dictionary of Biblical Words*, the term "Son of God" implies that Jesus is the actual, visible expression of God's character and not His biological offspring.

The Jews clearly understood the term "son." When Jesus referred to the Heavenly Father as His Father, He was stating that He was equal with the Father in nature, status, and authority. To the Jews this was blasphemy because it implied that Jesus was God by nature. As you study Scripture, you will see that Jesus' reference to being the Son of God is what justified the Jewish leaders in their pursuit to crucify Him.[3]

Jesus had three other titles that give us a clear picture of Him as the Son of God. He was the Messiah, God Incarnate, and the Savior of the world. We see that these titles show Jesus' position in relationship to the Godhead as the Messiah, His nature as divine, and His purpose as Savior.[4] In order to understand how Jesus was in fact the Son of God, you have to view Him in light of these other three positions. By combining His position, nature, and purpose, you have the revelation of Jesus as the Son of God.

For example, as the Messiah, the Son of man, He served as the reflection of God's power and anointing in His human form. As deity, He was the visible expression of God's attributes, and as Savior He was the

---

[2] See Colossians 1:15
[3] Luke 23:67-71; John 5:16-18
[4] 1 John 2:21-23; 4:1-3, 14-15

reflection of God's heart of love towards mankind. What an awesome revelation! Within the life of Jesus, the fullness of God's love, character, and power was visibly revealed to mankind.

Today is much like two thousand years ago. Many people miss the reality that God walked among mankind. Even though the world would never be the same after His physical appearance, both then and now, few have truly allowed Him to change their lives.

Like today, some groups of people were threatened by Jesus because He exposed the hypocrisy of their creeds and hearts. Others were insulted because He revealed their complacency and false foundations. In some situations, He actually frightened those who did not want their world challenged with the unexplainable.

It is incredible to think God stood among men, and yet men could not see Him because of their arrogance, prejudices, and fear. How many of us do not see Him today? Oh, we may know He exists, but do we see Him for who He is? Do we know Him for who He is? Or, have we allowed Him to walk by without changing our lives and situations as He did those of His hometown of Nazareth?

Finally, the Scripture tells us He thought it was not robbery to cease to be equal with God. In other words, something was going to change that would cause Him to cease from being like the other two persons of the Godhead.

Hebrews 2:7 gives us this insight, "Thou madest him a little lower than the angels." Now think about this for a moment. Jesus, who is God, did not feel He was being robbed when He was made lower than those He created.[5] If you or I were in a similar situation, we would be crying foul. We would probably throw a big pity party and walk around telling everyone how we were being treated unfairly.

However, in the case of Jesus we see a different attitude and response. He never considered it unfair that He was not equal to God for the first time in His eternal existence. He did not throw a pity party when He was made lower than those who worshipped Him in the courts of heaven. Instead, He willingly embraced it all, giving the impression it was an honor to be demoted in such a way.

Are you beginning to get a small glimpse into the disposition of Jesus? It is obvious that Jesus was not watching out for Himself. It is clear that He had no personal agenda or something to prove. The truth is He did it for you and me. He did not do it because we deserve His intervention. He did it because of God's incredible love towards man. And, when godly love is the motivation, no sacrifice is too great. In fact, it will be a person's good pleasure or honor to offer any required sacrifice.

Love is the secret behind why Jesus counted it as a privilege to come by way of Bethlehem as a babe in a manger and leave by way of a rugged cross as the ultimate sacrifice. This is why the Apostle Paul gave

---

[5] Colossians 1:15-18

this instruction in Philippians 2:3, "Let nothing be done through strife or vainglory; but in lowliness of mind let each esteem others better than themselves." After all, Jesus left us with such a powerful example.

How about you? Are you living in agreement with or in compliance to the example given you? If you are not, it is obvious that you have neither the love of God nor the mind of Christ.

4

HE EMPTIED HIMSELF

But made himself of no reputation...
(Philippians 2:7a)

In our self-serving, self-centered humanity and society, it is hard to imagine what it meant for Christ to empty Himself. First of all, how did He empty Himself? Secondly, what did He empty Himself of?

I believe the answers to these two questions will only be fully revealed in eternity. I also sense as we gain even a slight revelation into this one small section of Scripture, we will be humbled and overwhelmed by the implications of what it is saying.

The initial truth we must recognize up front is that Jesus is the one who made Himself of no reputation. This means to empty oneself of something. In other words, it was His sovereign choice to give up something.

I remember reading the book *In The Footsteps of Jesus* by Bruce Marchiano. Bruce was the one who played Jesus in the Matthew Video Series. One of the incidents that brought a reality check to me surrounded the crucifixion. Mr. Marchiano and the director were ready to make Jesus appear to be an innocent, suffering, mistreated victim. Just before they were about to do the scene, the director approached Bruce and said the Lord had actually told him, "Don't be sorry for Me." Sadly, the suffering, week martyr is how Jesus is being presented in the media, especially in the movie, "*The Passion.*"

It is important for each of us to realize that Jesus was in control of His destiny. He made the choice to walk the route to Calvary. Man did not take his life; rather He offered it up as an offering from God on our behalf. When Jesus went to the cross, He did not go as a victim but as a willing sacrifice. After all, a victim has no rights to choose, but Jesus always had a choice. He could have turned back at any time, but He chose to become the glorious, victorious Lamb of God who would take away our sin.[1] Praise God for His choice and His sacrifice.

---

[1] John 1:29; 10:18

28

In a way, this is true for us. Our choices determine our eternal destiny. Every day we either choose Christ and heaven or we give way to Satan and hell. In order to choose heaven, we must be willing to empty ourselves daily of that which would keep us from realizing our potential in the kingdom of heaven.

On the other hand, the path to hell is broad. A person would only have to make one decision to find himself in the clutches of this tormenting place. This decision is often borne out of the sin of omission where righteousness is omitted in a matter. And, what replaces righteousness towards the character and ways of God?

Complacency is how we justify or qualify our lukewarm attitude and actions towards God. Indifference of this nature results in a person making a decision to reject God's truth, provision, and way in attitude and lifestyle. Since many, out of complacency, give way to the natural man, hell has enlarged its borders to embrace them.[2]

In this Scripture we see Jesus initially made a decision in heaven that would allow Him to pay the necessary price on earth for our salvation. This decision was not a matter of good intentions. In fact, this Scripture implies this decision was of such magnitude that it could not have been spontaneous on His part. We also see in Jesus' physical life on earth that this determination was reinforced on a continual basis until it was fully carried out. Luke 9:51 states, "He stedfastly set his face to go to Jerusalem."

This is a very important lesson for Christians and those who put off salvation. People often postpone making a total decision to love and follow Jesus until they have experienced the attractions of the world. They see themselves as making the right decision when the time comes. Such a conclusion is a false security. The truth is that preparation must take place that will enable a person to stand in uncertain times. Such preparation begins with small steps of obedience that lead to greater feats inspired by abiding faith in God in the midst of great trials.

Another lesson we see from this scripture is that Jesus' decision to empty Himself came from His attitude. In essence, Jesus actually gave way to something that would not benefit Him personally because of His disposition. He surrendered to something contrary to His very person so we could benefit.

People who are self-centered in their attitude will never come to a place where they will yield to anything unless it serves their purpose. They will never consider accepting less unless they get some heroic recognition for it.

This is where we begin to see how contrary the real attitude of Christ is to the self-centered disposition of man. In light of Jesus' disposition, we see how man's pride is exposed for its insidious ways, and his flesh for its unscrupulous practices. We begin to see how hypocritical the heart

---

[2] Isaiah 5:14

of man can be because it is quick to accept delusion, while verbally claiming to love a person by the name of Jesus.

The next question is how did He empty Himself? As we will see in the next scripture, He made an exchange in order to accomplish such a feat. According to my *Webster's New Collegiate Dictionary*, "exchange" is the act of giving or taking one thing in return for another. Jesus gave up His glory as God to take on the disposition of a servant and the form of a man.

The word "glory" means honor, beauty, and majesty.[3] Jesus, as God, gave up that which distinguishes Him as God. He gave up the majesty that would bring Him due honor and praise, as well as the heavenly beauty that would set Him apart from mankind. Jesus did not give up His nature as God, for He could never cease to be who He is. Rather, He gave up His capacity to be God. "Capacity" points to His power and authority as God. In short, He gave up His sovereignty as He ceased to reign as God in His majesty, and became subject to the authority of others.

As I studied this, I had to ask myself, "Why did Jesus have to give up His glory as God?" As I meditated on this provoking thought, the Holy Ghost was gracious enough to remind me of what happened when God appeared to man in His glory. When God met with Moses in the burning bush in Exodus 3 and Joshua in Joshua 5, they were both told to take off their shoes because they were standing on holy ground.

In Exodus 20, we see God speaking to the people of Israel. His majesty was evident as people heard the thundering and noise of the trumpet and saw the lightning and smoke surrounding the mountain. Instead of savoring the moment, the people became afraid and asked Moses to serve as their intercessor between them and God. Now keep in mind that the people of Israel were told that if they touched the mountain they would die. After all, it was holy ground.

We see a total contrast in what happened centuries later. People encountered God in the form of Jesus Christ, but they did not have to take off their shoes. They heard His voice, but they did not become frightened, and they touched Him but did not die. When you consider these events, you begin to gain some insight as to why Jesus as God had to give up His glory.

In two separate incidents, mere man actually witnessed or encountered the implication of Jesus' glory as God. We see the same responses coming from the witnesses as we do from those in the Old Testament who encountered God in His majesty. The first situation occurred on Mount of Transfiguration. Jesus' humanity gave way to His glory as God for a few minutes. The Word of God tells us Jesus' face did shine as the sun and his raiment was white as the light. In the midst of the transfiguration, the voice of the Father was heard. Matthew 17:6 tells

---

[3] Strong's Exhaustive Concordance of the Bible, #1391

30

us the voice caused the three witnesses, Peter, John, and James, to fall on their faces in fear.

The second incident happened in Revelation 1. The Apostle John had a revelation of Jesus' unhindered glory that caused him to fall at Jesus' feet as if he were dead. In other words, it took his breath from him, and he almost fainted from fear. Consider this for a moment. The Apostle John was one of those who were on the Mount of Transfiguration, and the one who laid his head on Jesus' chest the night He was betrayed. Jesus had entrusted His mother to John, and yet when John saw Jesus in His majesty, he practically fainted from fear.

Jesus gave up His glory and became poor for us. The Apostle Paul confirms this in 2 Corinthians 8:9, "For ye know the grace of our Lord Jesus Christ, that, though he was rich, yet for your sakes he became poor, that ye through his poverty might be rich."

It is because of God's grace that Jesus became poor so we could become rich. Being rich does not mean rich according to the world, but rich according to what we can have spiritually in Christ. Today some doctrines teach that if you are a Christian, you should be rich in material goods. According to the Apostle Paul in 1 Timothy 6:3-12, this is a blatant error we must flee from.

Oswald Chambers stated in *Daily Thoughts for Disciples,* that people have become afraid of being poor, and despise anyone who is willing to be poor in order to save his or her life. He goes on to explain that this spiritual poverty means liberation from material attachments, an unbribed soul, indifference, and being able to find value in who we are in Christ, and not what we do or have in this present world. This liberty means we have the right to fling away our life at any moment in an irresponsible fashion.[4]

Jesus made an incredible exchange that meant He acted contrary to His very person. He gave way to something that would not benefit Him. He gave up His glory to take on that which would cause Him to be lower than the angels. He did all of this so we could be spiritually rich.

What does it mean to be spiritually rich? Perhaps James summarizes the real measure of the riches that the citizen of heaven should ultimately value and pursue in this present world in James 2:5. "Hearken, my beloved brethren, Hath not God chosen the poor of this world to be rich in faith and heirs of the kingdom which he hath promised to them that love him?"

Faith is established in us as we follow Jesus. For example, by faith we must follow Jesus' example. He emptied Himself of His glory; therefore, we must empty ourselves of all of our vainglory, or, in other words, our pride. After we empty ourselves, we will be able to make the ultimate exchange.

---

[4] May 21st devotion.

Let us now consider what Jesus actually exchanged for His glory. By understanding it, we will get a glimpse of how much God loved us. We will also begin to sense in a small way just how far He went to reach us in our depravity in order to save us unto eternal glory.

5

THE POSITION

...and took upon him the form of a servant.
(Philippians 2:7b)

To me Philippians 2:6-11 is one of the most powerful summaries of Jesus' journey to Calvary. It gives us a small glimpse as to the price He paid, allowing us to see the choices He made in light of our eternal destination. We also can observe the steps He took that started in eternity and ended on an old rugged cross.

In the last chapter I talked about the fact that Jesus made an exchange. He gave up His glory in order to give way to something else. According to Philippians 2:7, we see Jesus gave up His glory in order to take on the form of a servant. In summation, He adjusted His nature by taking on the disposition of a servant.

What an incredible revelation! Jesus, who is God, became least so you and I could taste the greatness of eternity. Jesus, who deserves service, became a servant so we could become children of the Most High God.

It is important that we realize that Jesus made a decision to accept this lowly position in the courts of heaven long before He executed it on earth in an earthly body. He actually agreed to come into total subjection as a servant in every area of His humanity.[1]

Keep in mind the position of servitude is considered the highest place in the kingdom of God, but among mankind it is considered the lowest rank. Jesus made this contrast clear to His disciples in Matthew 20:25-27:

> Ye know that the princes of the Gentiles exercise dominion over them, and they that are great exercise authority upon them. But it shall not be so among you: but whosoever will be great among you, let him be your minister; and whosoever will be chief among you, let him be your servant.

Charles Spurgeon referred to Jesus as the Servant of servants. This is an awesome insight into the very heart of the example Jesus left for us to follow in spirit and truth. In order for Jesus to be considered a Servant

---

[1] 1 Corinthians 2:7; Revelation 13:8

of servants, He actually became a servant to mankind. The truth is all people are born into servitude, but do not necessarily possess the disposition of a servant. In reality everyone is serving something. They either serve sin, self, or the world, which brings them under the dominion of Satan, or they serve the living God of all creation.

Jesus, who is God, submitted Himself to a position of great servitude. This position was designated in heaven and carried out in the earthly tabernacle of a body. Once again we must realize that Jesus made a choice to take on such a position. He actually made a decision to give up His rights as God to sovereignly reign over His creation. This meant that He gave up His strength and power as God to call the shots. He also gave up His rights as God, and became a living sacrifice for the glory of the Father and to benefit those He came to serve.

Jesus simply gave up that which was normal to Him. He gave up the glories of His heavenly residence. He gave up comfort and conveniences of the sanctuary of His heavenly kingdom. He also gave up His place in the courts of heaven. He gave up His authority and came under the authority of another.

We see this giving manifested in Jesus' humanity as well. As King of kings He had rights to a palace and prestige that would have required even the earthly leaders to pay homage to Him. Instead, we see that He gave up His rights as king in order to live the life of a servant. Jesus confirmed this with these words, "Foxes have holes, and birds of the air have nests; but the Son of man hath nowhere to lay his head" (Luke 9:58).

Jesus' decision and choice are so contrary to the attitude of man. It is hard for arrogant, self-sufficient man to come into submission to something that would never benefit his self-serving agenda. It is hard for stiff-necked humanity to give way to something that would require giving up the comforts and conveniences of life. In fact, it is beyond narrow-minded humans to comprehend how the idea of greatness is measured by becoming the least when they actually strive to become God of their personal domain.

Jesus gave up the normal (heavenly) and took on the contrary (servitude). His actions contradicted the teaching and preference of man. Man may pursue the contrary, but all the time he clings to normalcy. After all, the idea of giving up the normal (rights to self and the world) in order to embrace the contrary (the righteousness of God) is mockery to unregenerate man.

Let me bring the previous thought into focus. It was contrary for Jesus as God to take on the limitations of a servant. It is also contrary for fallen, depraved man to take on God's righteousness. The fact that Jesus stepped through such boundaries to reach you and me so we could be made the righteousness of God shows His power and commitment as God to do the impossible.[2]

Through the years the Lord has allowed me to experience the normal life promoted in America, but I have learned to hold lightly to such comforts and conveniences for they are temporary and belong to Him. If He requires any convenience from me, I must be quick to relinquish it in order to give way to the eternal.

It is amazing to observe how, when Jesus started giving His all in order to obtain our salvation; He never stopped even after He offered Himself as the ultimate sacrifice. He is still in heaven serving as our Priest and point of defense as our Advocate. Oh, how can any of us neglect such a salvation?[3]

Realizing that godly servitude carries a certain attitude with it is also important. Without the right attitude, a servant of God will fall short of service that will glorify God. We see this godly attitude in Christ. He actually described His disposition in Matthew 11:28-30, "Come unto me, all ye that labor and are heavy laden and I will give you rest. Take my yoke upon you, and learn of me: for I am meek and lowly in heart: and ye shall find rest unto your souls. For my yoke is easy and my burden is light." Out of a right disposition, Jesus expressed Himself in an attitude of meekness. The word "meek" implies power or strength under control.

We see the reality of Jesus' attitude of servitude when He walked this earth. As a servant, He gave way to the will, instructions, and authority of the Father. Jesus said this in John 5:30, "I can of mine own self do nothing: as I hear, I judge: and my judgment is just; because I seek not mine own will, but the will of the Father which hath sent me."

We see from this Scripture that Jesus was totally under the authority of the Father. We must also note the Father was the One who sent Him. In other words, Jesus in his humanity did nothing unless the Father ordained it. Keep in mind Jesus was still God, but His strength and power were now in total subjection to the will of the Father.

How many of us would submit all of our power and strength to someone else? How many of us would only respond in controlled strength when given permission to do so, even when faced with suffering and death?

My friend, this is what godly meekness looks like. It only operates within the confines of righteous servitude. It never takes liberty outside of the Master's will, or claims personal rights when circumstances are unfair. It simply means the will, mind, and emotions have come into total subjection to the Master.

Psalm 37:11 and Matthew 5:5 tell us, "The meek shall inherit the earth." I used to meditate on this concept. How can the meek overcome

---

[2] 2 Corinthians 5:21
[3] Hebrews 2:3; 7:24-26; 1 John 2:1

or conquer the earth enough to inherit it? As I considered Jesus' life, I realized that because of His meekness neither was He swayed nor did He become subject to circumstances or earthly persecution that always seemed to follow Him. As a result, He overcame all the claims the world had on His humanity, and conquered Satan and the circumstances that surrounded Him.

This is a very important principle for Christians to understand. It is vital that we bring every area of our lives under the leading of the Holy Spirit. If our strengths are not disciplined properly, we will find ourselves being tossed to and fro by the waves of circumstances and change.[4] Instead of overcoming the world, we will be subdued by it. Instead of conquering our circumstances, we will end up being controlled by them.

Jesus was also lowly. "Lowly" means cast down, humble, and of low degree or estate.[5] Jesus declared that He was lowly in heart. His disposition was felt in every fiber of His being, which produced humility. This low estate allowed Him to prefer you and me to His own well-being. As a result, He gave way to the earthly so we could experience the heavenly.

This attitude is upheld throughout the New Testament. An example of this attitude is found in Romans 12:10, "Be kindly affectioned one to another with brotherly love; in honour preferring one another."

Ephesians 5:21 states, "Submitting yourselves one to another in the fear of God." Godly submission means you are honoring or putting other people's needs above your own. You are actually giving way to that which is worthy or excellent to ensure the best in a matter.

This preference is evidence of godly humility. Many people try to fake this humility, as did the Pharisees in Jesus' time. The piousness of these people was simply outward, but it lacked true love. It was often self-centered; therefore, it fell short of being sacrificial. It displayed itself in religious actions, but was never obedient to the will of God.

Jesus left a precious example. A real servant is an obedient servant. Jesus was obedient in every way to the Father. You and I must be obedient as well to qualify as true servants of God. In fact, we have been given a book of instructions that establishes how we must conduct ourselves in every area of our lives, from attitude to sacrifice.

Let me ask you something: Are you a servant of God? Jesus showed us true servitude in action, and He led the way in example. Are you following in His footsteps?

---

[4] Ephesians 4:13-14
[5] Strong's Exhaustive Concordance of the Bible, #5011

6

THE IDENTITY OF THE MAN, JESUS

...and was made in the likeness of man.
(Philippians 2:7c)

Have you ever thought about how our infinite God combined His eternal state with an earthly, finite state? He actually allowed Himself to be made in the likeness of man while maintaining His eternal attributes of God.

I already discussed what it meant for Jesus to be God, and how He emptied Himself of His sovereignty to take on the form of a servant. However, we need to realize the form of His servitude was visibly expressed in His manhood.

Something else that is important for us to recognize is that Jesus was not made or shaped in the likeness of just any man. He was molded into the likeness of a perfect man. He was an example of the first Adam before he gave way to rebellion in the Garden of Eden.

Scripture confirms the fact Jesus was the second Adam or the second man in 1 Corinthians 15:45. "And so it is written the first man Adam was made a living soul; the last Adam was made a quickening spirit." In considering Jesus, we can actually begin to see man's potential, which was lost in the Garden of Eden.

Oswald Chambers put it best in his teaching found in *Bringing Sons Into Glory* as he explained how Jesus as the second man manifested what the human race is going to be. He is the God-man, the representative of the whole human race in one person. He is not a being with two personalities, but rather He is the Son of God who is the exact expression of Almighty God, and the Son of Man who serves as the presentation of God's normal man. As the Son of God, He reveals what God is like, and as the Son of Man, He serves as a mirror to what the human race will be like at the basis of redemption. This picture points to a perfect oneness between God and man.[1]

In John 16:7-11, we are told that the Holy Spirit has come to reprove the world of sin, righteousness, and judgment. We see how the Holy

---

[1] Bringing Sons Into Glory & Making All Things New; ©1990 by Oswald
Chambers Publication Associations Limited. page 16

Spirit uses the inward conscience of the Law to convict man of sin, but He uses the example of Jesus Christ to reprove the world of unrighteousness. Jesus is the example of what the acceptable, perfect man looks like from within. If we do not have a right heart and attitude, we will fail miserably before God regardless of how righteous we may appear outwardly.

Failure to allow the Holy Spirit to convict us of sin and reprove us of unrighteousness brings us under judgment along with the god of this world. This is why the Holy Spirit always leads us to Christ, who is our mirror regarding our true spiritual condition before God.

1 Corinthians 15:47-49 tells us, "The first man is of the earth, earthy: the second man is the Lord from heaven. As is the earthy, such are they also that are earthy: and as is the heavenly, such are they also that are heavenly. And as we have borne the image of the earthy, we shall also bear the image of the heavenly." In short, Jesus touched pathetic, earth-bound humanity with the heavenly reality of God.

Jesus gave up the heavenly to take on the earthly. Likewise, we must give up the earthly to take on the heavenly. He brought the reality of perfect man to our attention. He is calling us to take on the image of this heavenly Man in spirit and truth. The heavenly Man possesses that which is pure and upright. This Man who has been quickened from above will live forever.[2]

Oswald Chambers put this concept in perspective in *Bringing Sons Into Glory* by pointing out that Jesus came from the outside into the human race, and once a person is born again, the very life of Jesus comes into him or her from the outside. He is a normal man, and in His relationship to God, the devil, sin, and man, we can see the expression in human nature of what Jesus calls "eternal life."[3]

Jesus, the Son of God humbled Himself and became the Son of Man to not only reflect a heavenly man, but a normal man. Jesus came to relate to man in a way that would not only give him a reality check, but also a way to reach his heavenly potential and embrace eternal life.

The title "Son of Man," which Jesus used of Himself throughout the Gospels, holds great significance. According to *Vine's Expository Dictionary of Biblical Words*, the title "Son of Man" is a messianic title. This is brought out when Jesus is referred to as the "Son of David." The title associates Him with both man and the promised Messiah. And, as you study Isaiah's prophesy of the Messiah in Isaiah 9:6, the Messiah is also identified as "The Mighty God."

All of man's hopes and God's promises hinged on the coming of the Messiah, Jesus Christ. He was anointed to heal the brokenhearted, set

---

[2] John 3:3 & 5; Romans 8:29
[3] Page 15

the captive free, and give sight to the blind, and liberty to those who have been bruised by the harsh realities of life.[4]

As man, Jesus was the example of true leadership in the kingdom of God. According to *Vine's Expository,* the title of "Son of Man" went beyond the messianic title to universal headship on the part of One who is man. For example, Jesus is the head of a universal body, the Church. The four creatures found throughout Scripture, the lion, ox, man, and eagle, symbolize His universal leadership.[5]

As the Lion of the tribe of Judah, He became the Lamb of God. As the Lamb, He showed the real strength that comes from authority and power in godly leadership. Such leadership is always expressed in gentleness and meekness. Jesus, as the ox, shows that enduring strength and leadership that comes through the discipline of the yoke and sacrifice that is motivated by godly love.

As the Son of Man, He showed how man must become the crowning glory of God through example. It is important to point out that headship implies leadership by example, not by harsh demands and dictates. Jesus left us with two distinct examples as man. The first example is found in John 13, which we have already discussed in the previous chapter. A man must become a servant of all if he is to become great in leadership.

The second example Jesus left us as man is found in 1 Peter 2:21-22, "For even hereunto were ye called: because Christ also suffered for us, leaving us an example, that ye should follow his steps: Who did no sin, neither was guile found in his mouth." Jesus was without sin, and yet He suffered, leaving us an example.

There are a couple of reasons we must encounter suffering. The first reason we must taste the bitter dregs of suffering is because it works character in us. The Apostle Paul made reference to this in 2 Corinthians 4:17, "For our light affliction, which is but for a moment, worketh for us a far more exceeding and eternal weight of glory."

One of the conditions that will bring suffering to our lives is godliness. The Apostle Paul confirms this in 2 Timothy 3:12, "Yea, and all that will live godly in Christ Jesus shall suffer persecution."

The Apostle Peter takes a person one step further in 1 Peter 2:20, "For what glory is it, if, when ye be buffeted for your faults, ye shall take it patiently? But if, when ye do well, and suffer for it, ye take it patiently, this is acceptable with God."

Godly suffering allows you to become identified with Jesus. This identification will bring glory to God, allowing man to be God's crowning glory in the midst of great despair and darkness. The Apostle Paul put it this way, "But we all, with open face beholding as in a glass the glory of

---

[4] Luke 4:18-19
[5] Ezekiel 1:10; Revelation 4:7

39

the Lord, are changed into the same image from glory to glory, even as by the Spirit of the Lord…if so be that we suffer with him, that we may be also glorified together." [6]

As the eagle, Jesus shows us that godly leadership can only be done in light of a heavenly perspective. Jesus soared above the world because He did the Father's will. He overcame the world because He considered all things in light of eternity. And, because of His type of leadership, He will rule the world as the King of kings.

The Word also tells us that the man Jesus is sitting on the right hand of God. As previously stated, there is much meaning and symbolism in relationship to the right hand, mainly that of authority. We also know scripturally that all pleasures are at the right hand of God. Psalm 16:11 makes this declaration, "Thou wilt shew me the path of life: in thy presence is fulness of joy; at thy right hand there are pleasures for evermore." We know that Jesus is on the right hand of God; therefore, all of our hopes and promises can only be found in Jesus. No wonder the Apostle Paul told us to seek those things above, and to set our affections on that which is in heaven.[7]

Jesus did not give up His manhood after His death on the cross. It is incredible to believe, but Jesus is still totally man. He is in a different body, but He is still man.[8] It has taken me years to realize the significance of Jesus keeping His manhood. I know my understanding of it is still very limited, but it has proven to be humbling and life-changing to me. Jesus needed to keep His manhood to fulfill vital positions and functions in heaven. These positions actually ensure our very salvation.

The foremost position He fills as a man in heaven is that of High Priest. Hebrews 5:1 tells us that the High Priest must be taken from man and 8:1 states, "Now of the things which we have spoken this is the sum: We have such a high priest, who is set on the right hand of the throne of the Majesty in the heavens."

Jesus established an unchangeable priesthood in heaven. As Hebrews 7:25 tells us, "Wherefore he is able also to save them to the uttermost that come unto God by him, seeing he <u>ever</u> <u>liveth</u> to make intercession for them." (Emphasis added.) Think about it. As the Son of Man, Jesus is able to make the intercession for each of us that maintains our salvation. This intercession makes Him our Mediator.

The Apostle Paul made this statement in 1 Timothy 2:5, "For there is one God, and one mediator between God and men, the man Christ Jesus." Once again we must note there is only one mediator. He is identified as the man, Christ Jesus.

---

[6] Romans 8:17c; 2 Corinthians 3:18
[7] Hebrews 8:1; Colossians 3:1-3
[8] John 20:15-17

Jesus does not stand in the gap for us as God, but as man. Meditate on this incredible insight: Jesus has the power to shed His manhood and return back to His original state, but somehow the maintenance of our salvation hinges on His manhood. Once again, we must acknowledge our salvation is so very important to the heart of God. I know we will be spending eternity learning the significance of Jesus as man sitting in the courts of heaven as our High Priest, interceding on our behalf.

Over the years I have caught glimpses of the importance of Jesus' being man in the judgment halls of heaven. We know that to be a good intercessor, you must understand the position of the one you are interceding *for*, as well as understand the mind and heart of the one you are interceding *to*.

Jesus clearly understands both positions. Hebrews 4:15 tells us He was tempted in every way, but yet He did not sin. Jesus' experiences as man allow Him insight into the struggles of humanity. His insight as man not only gives Him a personal understanding, but also gives Him the authority to stand in the gap for each of us. This is why John refers to Jesus as our advocate in 1 John 2:1. He stands in the courts of heaven and becomes our point of defense when we fall into sin and disgrace.

Romans 11:33-34 tells us, "O the depth of the riches both of the wisdom and knowledge of God! How unsearchable are his judgments, and his ways past finding out! For who hath known the mind of the Lord? Or, who hath been his counselor?" No mere man could stand in the place of an advocate for mankind, but Jesus could because He took our place on the cross. He also possesses the wisdom and knowledge of God. He is righteous; therefore, He knows the judgments of God, and has satisfied them as our Advocate. He knows the complete mind and heart of God; therefore, He is able to uphold the righteousness of God, while standing in the gap for us.

Sometimes I have envisioned Jesus serving as my advocate in the courts of heaven. Because He is positioned on the right hand of God, I know He actually has the ear of the Father. In my heart I do not see Him fervently standing up defending me with the skill of a great orator for in sin I stand guilty. I do not see Him pleading for mercy for my wretched soul. Rather, I see Him simply standing and lifting His arms up as silence falls in the judgment hall.

You might be wondering why I could believe such simple actions on Jesus' part could silence the accusers or spectators in heaven. Years ago I realized that heaven was perfect in every way except for a few discrepancies. And, what are those areas of blemish? They are the nail-pierced hands and feet of Jesus. I believe all Jesus has to do to intercede on our behalf is stand up and reveal those nail scars.

These scars remind all of heaven that Jesus paid for our sins, and that redemption was completed on the cross. It verifies that through Jesus' scars He became sin on the cross, and upon our salvation we were made perfect in Him because of His wounds. After all, it was His blood that once ran from those scarred places that cleanses us from all unrighteousness. This very same blood represents a new covenant that brings everlasting life and provides a way into intimate fellowship with God.[9]

As you try to logic out the possibility of Jesus being totally God and totally man in heaven as He was on earth, it becomes too great to comprehend. In His humanity, He could not cease to be God. Apparently, in His glory, He cannot cease to be man. However, in my studies I have concluded that if Jesus had stripped away His manhood, He would have given up His greatest point of mediation on my behalf. As I meditated on this humbling fact, I wondered how I could so easily forget what He has done for me.

I am aware that every time I take communion, I am remembering what Jesus did on the cross. I ask myself, "Do I remember with humility and intensity? Do I remember that Jesus still sits in heaven with the evidence of my own wretchedness, bearing precious scars that will be with Him for eternity?"

How humbling it is to think the one perfect man will remain "physically blemished" to ensure our salvation! It is also sobering to realize His blemishes will overshadow every bit of our imperfection. It is incredible to think how many people shun what Jesus did for them, and heartbreaking to see how many people neglect His salvation.

Let me end this chapter with a challenge. Oswald Chambers has left us with insight about perfection in *Bringing Sons Into Glory.* He stated that we try to enter into Jesus' life by imitation instead of His life entering into us by means of His death.[10] Obviously, this is a wrong approach. His people clearly need to reflect Him, not try to play Him in a world of skepticism and darkness.

---

[9] Zechariah 13:6; John 14:6; 2 Corinthians 5:21; 1 John 1:7; Hebrews 10:10-20
[10] Page 15

7

THE HUMILITY OF CHRIST

*And being found in fashion as
a man he humbled himself.
(Philippians 2:8a)*

Have you ever thought about the humility of Christ? This part of the Scripture tells us that being found in fashion as a man He humbled Himself. As man, Jesus encountered all the limitations of the flesh. He felt hunger and thirst. He knew what it meant to be tired. He felt joy as He embraced a child, and rejoiced as He gave back the dead to the grieving. He felt sorrow over lost mankind and the pain of man's cruelty. He felt both the tearing of His skin and heart. He knew what disgrace felt like as He heard the scorn and mockery of man. He tasted both betrayal and His own blood.

In studying Jesus' life, we see the constant display of Christ's humility. His example should serve as a reality check that will expose our pride in its many forms. His humility goes beyond an outward show of piety to reveal a commitment that reached beyond eternity to grasp the insignificant. For example, the Son of God humbled Himself and embraced the insignificant when He came into this world as a vulnerable child.

In fact, Jesus' allowing Himself to go through the natural process of birth is both miraculous and overwhelming to the finite mind. Jesus allowed Himself to be fashioned as a man. He had given up His capacity as God to take on the form of man. Although His mother was of this earth, He was not from this world. Therefore, He did not inherit the selfish disposition of Adam. He had the disposition of a servant, subjected to His Heavenly Father, and without sin.[1]

Jesus' birth actually caused travail for Mary, His mother. Of course, this travail would pale in comparison to the travail He would experience on a cross to bring eternal life to man.

As an unborn child, He easily could have been aborted if His unwed mother had been stoned according to the Jewish Law because of her untimely pregnancy. From all religious appearances His conception was sinful, not miraculous as the angels had proclaimed. In spite of all the

---

[1] John 3:31; 8:23; Hebrews 4:15

obstacles, Jesus would live for the main purpose of redeeming man from sin's awful consequences so each of us would not have to pay the full penalty of it. His death on the cross appeared as if religion was justified for its rejection of Him, but His resurrection would prove differently.

As a newborn baby, His very presence became a threat to the leader, Herod. This wicked man pursued the child in order to destroy the existence of not just any future leader, but the existence of the ultimate leader.

There are many "Herods" in today's world. They are forever blinded by their desire to be the supreme ruler of their small worlds. They are jealous when it comes to the idea of relinquishing their world to someone who is worthy and greater.

In Herod's blind jealousy, he ended up doing the unspeakable. He sacrificed all the male children in Bethlehem, from newborn to two years old. What a great atrocity! So many innocent children died because of one man's blind obsession. However, Jesus, the Lamb of God, was preserved so that He could become the ultimate sacrifice for all men. [2]

It is humbling to grasp the humility of Christ in just this area of His life on earth. The idea that Jesus came into this world in a natural way as a helpless babe, totally dependent on those around Him, is indescribable. However, His wonderful humility goes beyond the indescribable.

Keep in mind that Jesus came into this world through the door of a dirty manger. Here was God, the Lord of lords, King of kings, surrounded by the residues and odor of animals. In a way, it was symbolic of how one day He would take upon Himself the filth and dirt of all mankind. He would wear the depravity of humanity with great compassion and sorrow. His grace and love were always being extended, but humanity would often remain indifferent to His invitations.

We see how Jesus' humility was visibly represented by the fact that He was always surrounded by the insignificant. His mother was a poor handmaiden, and his adopted father, a carpenter. He was born in an unimportant place called Bethlehem, and He grew up in Nazareth, a place that was often overlooked and ridiculed.

According to *Smith's Bible Dictionary*, people from Nazareth were considered with contempt. Apparently, the Nazarenes spoke with a ruder dialect and were considered less cultivated. They were greatly exposed to heathen influence because Nazareth was located near the well-traveled highway between Egypt and Mesopotamia.

Nazareth, in spite of its location near a popular highway, had a certain measure of seclusion. According to *Reader's Digest's Great People of the Bible and How They Lived*, Nazareth's population was only around 100 residents in Jesus' time. It was also located halfway between the ocean and the Sea of Galilee.

---

[2] Matthew 2:16-18; John 1:29

It was in this place that Jesus submitted Himself to obscurity. The Son of God grew up without any type of notoriety. He lived a quiet life and was known only by those in His small community. This community simply assumed that Jesus was just another member of its small group. The residents had no idea that they were witnessing God in human form. He walked among them and had favor among them, but few would realize that one day they would bow their knees before Him and proclaim Him to be Lord. [3]

As I meditated on Jesus' development into manhood, I could see how Nazareth was an ideal place for His growth. He must have seen, in the passing caravans, people of different nationalities. He witnessed their diversities as well as their similarities. In essence, He witnessed and encountered the activities of the world without becoming part of it.

In the immediate terrain of Nazareth, Jesus was surrounded by ruggedness, which was symbolic of the profession that He was trained in. It is amazing to think how God Incarnate, the Creator of the world, was trained to be a carpenter.

I have no doubt Jesus was an exceptional carpenter. He was a man who could effectively work with His hands. He probably fixed broken plows and cart wheels, mended equipment, and built furniture. I wonder if He ever thought about the day His hands would be used to touch humanity in a way that would forever change its course. He would actually heal broken hearts, mend hopeless lives, and begin to build an eternal kingdom that would abound in the hearts of men.

In this obscurity Jesus was being prepared for a greater feat. As a carpenter, He most likely developed muscles as He wrestled with the wood to conform it to a design or purpose. This rugged profession would prepare Him to endure one of the greatest physical challenges as He found His body being conformed to a wooden cross.

He probably learned how much stress He could put on the wood before it was rendered useless. This may have served as an example to Him as He experienced all the temptations of mankind. He must have realized there were limitations, and that lasting endurance could only be found within the framework of faith and righteousness.

Like Nazareth, which was halfway between the ocean and the Sea of Galilee, Jesus had to be aware that He stood between God's greatness and man's limitations. Because of His position He would be able to accomplish the impossible. He would actually bridge the gap between the powerful and what appeared to be the insignificant. This connection would bring forth rivers of Living Water that would revive the souls of man and bring eternal life to the hopeless and dying.[4]

It is also humbling to consider the one example Jesus left us during this period of obscurity. He was 12 at the time. I am sure you know the

---

[3] Luke 2:51-52; 4:22
[4] John 7:37-39

story, which is found in Luke chapter two. Jesus had traveled with His parents to Jerusalem for the Passover. After the celebration, His parents assumed He was with other family members. They were a day into their journey before they realized Jesus was not among them. He was actually missing.

Imagine how these parents must have felt. A missing child for any length of time brings great dread to the hearts of any responsible, loving parent. Keep in mind Jesus was not just any young boy. God had entrusted Him to Mary and Joseph. It was as though through assumption and neglect these parents had mishandled or misplaced something precious from God.

I know in my Christian life I have mishandled the things of God. I have assumed much about God's will and man's soul. I have neglected the gifts of God because I took for granted the spiritual life that comes by way of God's grace.

This incident also made me wonder if I would notice if Jesus' presence was missing in my life. It is so easy to get caught up with the moments of celebration and life that we quickly leave Jesus behind. It is not unusual to become lost in the bustle of the world so that we are not aware that something precious and vital is absent.

The discovery of Jesus' absence caused His parents to go back to Jerusalem, the place where they had left Him. On the third day they found Him in the temple, sitting in the midst of the doctors, both hearing and asking questions. This timing would serve as a prelude to Him being in the grave for three days, hidden from all, only to be rediscovered alive after His triumphant resurrection.

Luke 2:47 tells us, "And all that heard him were astonished at his understanding and answers." In this Scripture, we see Jesus' wisdom and maturity being evident at a young age. However, it is important to point out that in the Jewish culture a boy steps into manhood at the age of 12. Here we get the first glimpse of Jesus as man. He is among the religious, challenging them with answers that astonish those around Him.

His mother asked Him how He could cause such worry for them. Jesus' answer in Luke 2:49 is simple but profound, "How is it that ye sought me? Wist ye not that I must be about my Father's business?"

As a young man, Jesus is not only aware of His spiritual responsibility and purpose, but He is committed to it all the way. He may have been considered a young man who was exceptional in every way, but He was also obedient to the higher moral law of His Father. This moral law required Him to come into subjection to His parents. Once again we see God Incarnate submitting Himself to the insignificant in Luke 2:51, "And (Jesus) went down with (His parents), and came to Nazareth and was subject unto them." (Parenthesis added.)

I am sure most of us are aware of the fact that many of our children begin to declare their independence during their initial teenage years. When we compare Jesus' reaction, we begin to see how His example should silence all rebellion and cause each of us to adhere to the higher moral law of God.

Recognizing authority in our life is a necessity because it establishes us in righteousness. When you think about it, Jesus could have removed Himself from under His earthly parents' authority with the noble goal to submit to the ultimate authority. After all, He is God and possesses wisdom from above.

The truth is Jesus was submitting to His ultimate authority when He submitted to His earthly parents. Submission to the proper authority is the righteous response of a godly man. It is the evidence of unwavering strength that comes through discipline. Submission, in fact, is the highest form of discipline in the kingdom of God, and is a product of humility that recognizes the importance of that which often seems insignificant. It is often the insignificant points of our lives that develop character and prepare us for future challenges.

I have watched many people fight against coming into godly submission. They consider anything that does not serve their purpose insignificant to the growth and promotion of their lives. They want their way, claiming their independence to seek what they consider a better and more substantial method. What these people do not realize is that godly submission ensures liberty while independence causes bondage and destruction.

As you can see, liberty is not the same as independence. Independence has no real boundaries, but liberty works within boundaries or disciplines that encourage a person to reach his or her highest potential.

The Apostle Paul talked about this discipline which comes out of submission in 1 Corinthians 9:26-27, "I therefore so run, not as uncertainly; so fight I, not as one that beateth the air: But I keep under my body, and bring it into subjection: lest that by any means, when I have preached to others, I myself should be a castaway."

Godly submission results in humility. This type of submission is manifested through the will, emotions, and actions. Jesus showed this submission when He came into subjection to His parents.

Jesus, as our example, shows us that no matter how old we are or what kind of relationship we are in, submission is never out of date in the kingdom of God. It is a godly virtue that is exemplary of righteousness. It is a necessary ingredient when it comes to being about our Father's business.

Do you have the humility of Christ that can be seen in submission to what you might consider to be insignificant?

8

"NOT MY WILL"

...and became obedient.
"Philippians 2:8"

Oswald Chambers pointed out that Jesus will remain a mental abstraction that may be spoken of in terms of culture, poetry, or philosophy, but will have no meaning or power over a person until He becomes incarnate.[1] This has been confirmed by my own personal experience with God.

Before Jesus became a reality to me, God seemed far away and foreboding. It was not until I encountered Jesus in His humanity that I began to consider God in a personal light. He had seemed unreachable until the voice of the Son of God penetrated my heart. He seemed unfeeling until I realized the Son of Man cried over pending judgment and destruction. God, in fact, seemed indifferent to my struggles until Jesus became the Great Physician who came to bring healing to my pathetic, lost soul. He had appeared to be insensitive until I witnessed Jesus as the Lamb of God walking up Calvary with the cross. He also seemed deaf to the plight of all mankind until I realized that as the Man of sorrows His heart was actually broken on the cross for each of us.

Jesus in His fullness as man expressed the fullness of God in love, mercy, and grace. He made God, who seemed so far away, personal to finite and helpless people such as me. While on earth, Jesus revealed the power of God in miracles and deliverance, the will of God on His way to Calvary, and the heart of God on the cross.

We can actually observe the reality of God's heart towards man in the culmination and climax of Jesus' manhood on earth in His final days before the cross. We can see the shadow of the cross becoming more distinct as He came closer to it. After all, the cross was His real destiny. It had simply been a subtle shadow cast throughout the Old Testament, but it was about to become a harsh reality that would reveal the extent of God's love towards mankind and the devastation of sin upon mankind in light of our Creator's holiness.[2]

---

[1] Daily Thoughts for Disciples, August 4
[2] John 3:15-17

In studying Jesus' final days before His crucifixion, I discovered the path He took. It revealed the ultimate purpose of why He came as man. Luke 9:51 tells us that Jesus steadfastly set His face to go to Jerusalem. In other words, Jesus' determination to finish His greatest course as man became more set as the time drew closer to embracing the cross.

According to the Gospel of John, Jesus was at a place called Bethany six days before the Passover. Bethany was located 1½ to 2 miles from Jerusalem on the road from Jericho. Its name means "house of dates" or "house of misery." I believe the real countdown to the cross began here. The timing for Jesus being at this place was significant. This is where He was separated or anointed for His death and burial as the Lamb of God by Mary, the sister of Lazarus. He would become a sacrifice for all sin.[3]

In an article in the February 1999 issue of, "Bible In the News," a valuable rundown of Jesus' last six days before the cross was presented. It caused me to contemplate the countdown to the cross in a way that I have never considered. This publication pointed out that the anointing probably took place on the fifth day before the cross. As pointed out in the article, this would be significant because lambs designated as the Passover lamb were anointed on a Sabbath, five days before the actual Passover.[4] Since Jesus was the complete fulfillment of the Passover Lamb, He would have been anointed on the fifth day as well.

It is important to realize that in order for Jesus to become the Lamb of God, He had to take on the form of a man. As a perfect, sinless man, He could offer Himself up as the true Lamb of God who had clearly been foreshadowed by all of the previous Passover Lambs.

If the time table is correct and Jesus was anointed as the Lamb of God on the fifth day, He was finally acknowledged as King on the fourth day. Instead of presenting Himself as a victorious King, He rode a colt in humility while people took palm branches and went forth to meet him, crying, "Hosanna: Blessed is the King of Israel that cometh in the name of the Lord."[5]

Amazingly, within four days of this event some of the very same people most likely would be yelling, "Crucify Him!" Oh, how fickle we human beings are! How self-centered and self-serving we can prove to be. It is true; at the door of every unbroken and unrepentant man lays incredible treachery against God.[6]

We also see Jesus' tears flow the same day after His triumphant entry into Jerusalem. His status as the greatest of all prophets among mankind had become apparent. His appearance had actually been prophesied in Deuteronomy 18:15-19.

---

[3] John 12:3-7
[4] Exodus 12:3, 5
[5] John 12:12-16
[6] Hosea 6:7

This ecstasy and great distress or sorrow can be found in the life of every servant of God. I know, as a minister, I have experienced both in one day.

As a prophet, Jesus considered the future of Jerusalem. However, His response was not that of a victorious King who was embracing His future residence or kingdom; rather, it was of lament and sorrow as He prophesied its future destruction.[7]

History reveals that Jerusalem is the city that has been sacked most often. According to Ruth Specter Lascelle, Jerusalem has been besieged 47 times and completely brought to the ground 17 times. It is estimated that every 75 years the city of peace has been encompassed by enemy armies, and every 200 years it has been left in ruins.[8]

Right now Jerusalem is at the center of great conflict. Three major religions want to claim this city as their religious capital. Presently, Israel is fighting for its very survival against terrorism. Much of the world is pushing for a Palestinian state to usher in peace. But it will never happen because Jerusalem will be the main obstacle that will prevent all of man's attempts of peace. Ultimately, the city that was ordained and designated by God will become a cup of trembling to the whole world.[9]

Jesus could see the future plight of His precious city. One day He would come as King and reign from it, but until that time, Jerusalem would be at the mercy of fierce and unrelenting Gentiles. These Gentiles would abuse it and ignore the place it holds in the hearts of the Jewish people, and in their future as a nation.[10]

On the third day, Jesus' prophetic office continued as He exhorted the religious leaders, and for the second time in His ministry chased out the merchants and moneychangers from the temple. The number three has an important significance. It represents entirety or completeness. Keep in mind that at the beginning of Jesus' ministry three years earlier, around the same time, He went into the temple and overturned the moneychangers' tables.[11] He had such contempt for those who abused the ordinances of God and took advantage of the religious lives of the less fortunate.

It is possible this second incident implied Jesus' earthly mission (not heavenly ministry) was about to be completed. I often wonder what Jesus would do in some of our modern-day church buildings. Would He throw over the espresso and hotdog stands or maybe knock down booths in the foyers that advertise the latest golf tournament for a so-called charity? Or, through tears, He might condemn the lust that is prevalent in the Christian realm to have bigger, better church buildings

---

[7] Luke 19:41-44

[8] Jewish Faith and The New Covenant, page 34.

[9] Zechariah 12:2-3

[10] Daniel 9:24-27

[11] Mark 11:11-15; John 2:14-17

that offer more entertainment and silly programs in order to attract greater numbers of people, while showing absolutely no regard for the needy. What would He do? Would it cause the same opposition? Due to the opposition His actions caused He went back to Bethany.

On the second day before Passover, Jesus expounded on the events surrounding the end days.[12] Here we see Him as the Great Prophet laying out a prophetic picture for the future. The blueprint was quite clear, but the exact timing was left as a mystery.

On the day before the presentation of the Passover Lamb, Jesus celebrated the Feast of the Unleavened Bread with His disciples. It was a solemn time. Jesus informed the group that one of them would betray Him. What is most amazing to me was how many of them asked Him if they were the guilty party. It was as though they had come to realize the potential of treachery that waited at the doors of their hearts.

Jesus would lift up the bread and declare that it represented His broken body. He would hold up the wine and proclaim it represented His blood, which was symbolic of a new covenant. He would state that it would be their last wine together, "...until that day when I drink it new with you in my Father's kingdom." Isn't it wonderful how Jesus started out with harsh realities, but ended with the promise that one day His followers would feast with Him in the presence of His Father? We now know He was pointing to the wedding supper of the Lamb.[13]

I am sure the disciples had questions about the meaning behind Jesus' declarations. He had told them that He would die, but the reality of it all had eluded them.

Their next stop would be the Garden of Gethsemane. Andrew Murray, in his book, *God's Will: Our Dwelling Place*, made this insightful statement, "Gethsemane! The innermost sanctuary of the life of our Lord and of His great redemption." In some respects, it is even more mysterious than Calvary."[14] Here Jesus would encounter His greatest test as man. In our finite state we are unable to understand the extent of this test, but His Word gives us glimpses that should bring humility and sobriety to our spirits.

In the Garden

It is important to point out that it was in a garden that a man by the name of Adam lost his initial state of innocence. It was in a garden that the gap was established between man and His Creator. It was in a garden that Satan and deception won over truth and righteousness. This first garden was known as Eden or Paradise.

---

[12] Luke 21, note 21:37-38
[13] Matthew 26:28-29; Revelation 19:6-10
[14] Page 46

The second garden, Gethsemane, displayed the opposite contrast. It was known for the olive press that would squeeze the precious oil out of the olives. The first garden was beautiful and perfect, but the second garden was void of such majesty. In the first garden, the first man lost paradise because of disobedience, but in the second garden, the second man reestablished paradise through obedience.

At this time I feel the need to make an important statement. *The battle for souls was lost in the Garden of Eden, but won in the Garden of Gethsemane.* Jesus had to come to a garden as man in order to pass the test that was lost in the Garden of Eden. Here we see the greatest form of obedience. This obedience came out of self-denial that resulted in great suffering. Hebrews 5:8 confirms this, "Though he were a Son, yet learned he obedience by the things which he suffered."

What was the great temptation that brought great suffering to the man Jesus? Was the temptation the cross? Hardly! Jesus came just for the cross. Was it the suffering? No, Jesus reached out to embrace the bitter dregs of man's cruelty and Satan's mockery when He was arrested.

Whatever this great temptation was, He had to contend with fear in His humanity. Hebrews 5:7 confirms this, "Who in the days of his flesh, when he had offered up prayers and supplications with strong crying and tears unto him that was able to save him from death, and was heard in that he feared."

Oswald Chambers believed the great temptation Jesus was facing was not death or suffering, but was the fact that He would be fighting this battle in weak flesh.[15] I tend to agree with him because of what Jesus said to Peter in Matthew 26:41b, "...the spirit indeed is willing, but the flesh is weak."

I believe the Garden of Gethsemane is where we see the great battle of the flesh. Man had lost the battle of the flesh in the Garden of Eden when he partook of the deadly fruit. However, Jesus had to win this battle in spite of unbearable temptation.

Out of obedience Jesus was ready to drink every bit of the bitter cup, but the test would come along the lines of His humanity, not His deity. It would be on the basis of His humanity that He had to pass this test because there would be no second chance. Could He actually make it to the cross after enduring a continual assault on His flesh to become the sin offering, so man could be made in the righteousness of God?[16] He was willing to crawl if need be to die for us, but would His flesh succumb to the unmerciful persecution before the price could be paid in full? His preparation for this time had begun in eternity and He had come so far. Obviously, He could not fail no matter how weak the flesh.

---

[15] Bringing Sons into Glory & Making All Things New; page 123
[16] 2 Corinthians 5:21

Jesus could not allow the physical afflictions to overcome His flesh before He made it to Calvary. He could not allow the cross to silence His cries before He had fulfilled His purpose.

Jesus had two judgments to face before He faced God's judgment on the cross. He had to stand before a self-righteous Sanhedrin Counsel that was bent on crucifying Him. He would next face the judgment of the Roman Political system at a place called Gabbatha. The leaders would treat Him as a hot potato, tossing Him between each other as if He was some form of entertainment. He would face their judgment of indifference, as well as a whipping that could cut a man in half.[17]

Obviously, Satan was playing a big part in Jesus' temptation in the Garden. It was Satan's final chance to throw everything at Jesus. No doubt the liar was bombarding Him with doubts as to whether He would endure to the end or fail to finish the course due to His weak flesh.

We cannot begin to imagine the depth of Jesus' trial in Gethsemane. Hebrews 4:15 tells us He was tempted in all points and yet without sin. In the past I have often viewed His success over temptation in light of His deity. Now I realize He overcame the worst type of temptation as man. He truly became our example.

No matter how weak the flesh, Jesus ultimately knew His destiny was not in the hands of the religious leadership, but in the hands of His Father. He would make a determination to bring His will in line with the Father as He declared, "…thy will be done."[17]

This battle in the Garden became so overwhelming that it brought Jesus to the brink of death. It was so great that an angel came from heaven to minister to Him.[18] He truly became a man of sorrows in the Garden of Gethsemane. He was being crushed like olives are crushed. He was pressed from every side by the incredible weight of the sin of all mankind. In spite of the great struggle, Jesus submitted His flesh under the will of the Father to do with as He pleased as He once again proclaimed, "…nevertheless not my will, but thine, be done" (Luke 22:42b).

Jesus ultimately knew that neither the political system nor the religious leaders had any say over Him. They had been placed in authority for such a time as this.[19] They were limited according to God's plan, and it would not be thwarted in any way.

The account in Matthew 26 shows us that Jesus submitted His will to the Father three times. Keep in mind the world is made up of the lust of the flesh, the pride of life, and lust of the eyes.[20] Each submission showed His willingness to become a sacrificial lamb, ready for the

---

[17] Matthew 26:57-66; 27:1-2
[17] Matthew 26:42
[18] Luke 22:43
[19] John 19:10-11
[20] 1 John 2:15

slaughter, as a means to address the influences of sin upon man, as well as face the three judgments that were before Him.

It is vital to point out that the cross represented the victory of the Son of God, but the Garden is symbolic of the victory wrought by the Son of Man. In a way, Jesus offered a sacrifice in the Garden of Gethsemane. He actually offered His humanity as great drops of sweat, as of blood, fell to the ground.[21] It was as if all the rights and dictates of His manhood were being emptied out on the ground. He was giving way to God's will in the midst of the greatest type of testing.

Perfection was lost in the Garden of Eden by Adam and regained in the Garden of Gethsemane by Jesus. Man's rebellion won out in Eden, but obedience overcame temptation in Gethsemane. Hebrews 5:8-9 give this insight, "Though he were a Son, yet learned he obedience by the things which he suffered. And being made perfect, he became the author of eternal salvation unto all them that obey him."

Adam lost his innocence in the Garden of Eden, but Jesus as the Son of Man was made perfect because He refused to give in to the dictates and fears of the flesh and the temptation of the god of this world, Satan. Instead, He gave way to the will of the Father.

Jesus had won the initial battle for our souls by submitting all of His humanity to the Father. He overcame the weaknesses of the flesh in order to go to Calvary. These are important examples to keep before us. All battles must first be won in our flesh before we can be victorious on the frontlines. In other words, we must deny self before we will be able to pick up our cross to be in the will of God.

So often Christians desire the anointing and power of God over the approval of God. They want to experience all of His blessings, but the battle must be first won in the gardens of the world: self, heart, mind, and the will of man. In every battle there will be choices. We can give in to temptation and lose paradise, or we can submit all to the will of God and overcome.

Jesus had successfully faced the failures of the flesh in light of the judgments wrought by the religions and governments of man. Now He could face the judgment of God for sin on the cross in light of victory.

Since Jesus won the battle of the flesh, He was able to ensure His destiny as the Lamb of God. It was His obedience to the Father's perfect will that established His perfection as man. Such obedience allowed Him to take His next step towards the cross as the perfect, sinless sacrifice.

Believers must realize that they will visit the Garden of Gethsemane throughout their Christian life. They will travel the route of Calvary. They will experience the separation that comes with anointing for God's purpose, and feel the joy of victory as they see Jesus lifted up as King. They will feel the sorrow as they consider the lost souls of men when they bring them warnings of future events that will go unheeded. They

---

[21] Luke 22:44

will know the sweetness of communion, as well as the bitterness of sacrifices, only to be tested in the Garden of Gethsemane where they will feel the crushing press of temptation.

There are two different responses that occur in Gethsemane. A person's response will determine whether he or she will succumb to temptation or complete the course. The first example we have is Jesus Christ. If we come to the garden to be in obedience to God's will, we will experience a breaking and crushing that comes from self-denial. In fact, we will become identified with Jesus, and as a result will be glorified with Him.[22]

The second example is Judas Iscariot. In the Garden of Gethsemane, he ended up betraying the Son of God with a kiss. This second response represents those people who just want to play the religious game. They give Jesus lip service, but their hearts are far from Him.[23] Flesh is still calling the shots while pride is demanding attention and exaltation. They ultimately will betray Jesus in their lifestyles and actions.

Have you been to the Garden of Gethsemane lately? If you have, what was your response? Did you become identified with Jesus by allowing yourself to be crushed, or did you betray Him with a kiss?

---

[22] Romans 8:17
[23] Matthew 15:7-9

9

"IT IS FINISHED!"

...became obedient unto death,
even the death of the cross.
"Philippians 2:8"

It is erroneous to think that Jesus came into this world to be a martyr. In fact, to imply that Jesus came as a martyr is to demean the reason He came. If He had died as a martyr, He would have been dying out of conviction for a principle. In fact, He would have given His life for something worthy or noble.

Jesus Christ did not die for a principle, but rather He died for each of us. He did not die for us because we were worthy of His sacrifice, but He died because we could not change the direction of our eternal, destructive destination. He did not die out of noble reasons; He died because He could do no less due to who He is, God Incarnate.

Oswald Chambers explained that Jesus' death on the cross was not a matter of martyrdom, but was His job description or vocation.[1] The word "vocation" means a work in which one is called. Jesus was ordained to die for you and me. He knew before the foundation of the world the route He would travel to secure our salvation as our sin bearer.

Some Christians give the impression that Jesus went to the cross out of sympathy because He was so good. 2 Corinthians 5:21 clearly states He became sin. This shows us that it was not a matter of sympathy or goodness but one of identification. This identification was necessary in order for Jesus to become a substitute sacrifice for each of us on the cross.

Philippians 2:8 also tells us His death was a matter of obedience. Jesus' whole being had one goal: to obey His Father in heaven. Each step of obedience led Him closer to the cross. As a result of His obedience, He was never out of step. He never took a detour or swayed from the course. He had come for one purpose—to die—and not only would it be an act of obedience, but it would bring glory to the Father.

Scripture clearly declares that as Jesus got closer to the cross, His inclination and determination to reach the cross became greater in order

---

[1] Bringing Sons Into Glory & Making All Things New, pgs. 63 & 69

to fulfill the destiny that had been laid upon Him as Man.[2] Jesus' death as the Lamb of God was the ultimate act of submission and obedience to the will and heart of the Father.

On the cross, man's depravity was exposed and God's love revealed. On the cross mercy and judgment came together to produce grace. On the cross forgiveness won out, paradise was promised, and love reached out in a personal way in the midst of great sorrow and suffering. It was on the cross that thirst represented man's true spiritual condition and showed how bitterness, not comfort, tries to silence its cries. In fact, on the cross the cause for man's deepest spiritual sorrow, that of separation from God, was unveiled.

On the cross we have the representation of man's worst and God's best. We see the love of God overcoming man's hatred. We see arms reaching out to graciously accept acts of gross rejection from men in order to enfold them into the everlasting arms of love.

The cross of Christ brought the greatest darkness, only to give way to the light of glorious resurrection power. The cross caused the earth to shake, only to offer peace to all who would receive its work. It stood as the greatest form of humiliation, defeat, and destruction, only to be exalted as a place of salvation and victory.

I have felt overwhelmed thinking about the cross of Christ. There are not enough words to describe how far the cross of Christ has reached into my soul, how much it has affected my life, and how wondrous it has become to me. I have often meditated on trying to put the cross of Christ into words. I had to ask myself, is there one word that could describe its work? Could any amount of words properly portray the hope it offers, or any one statement explain its eternal affects?

Surprisingly, the answer is "yes." The one word that is able to describe the work of the cross is, *"redemption"*. The hope of this rugged instrument can be summarized in three words, *"It is finished!"* The one statement that could explain its eternal affects can be found in Ephesians 2:16, "And that he might reconcile both unto God in one body by the cross, having slain the enmity thereby...."

Jesus came to redeem hopeless, lost man. Redemption is a term related to money. It means to buy or repurchase something. Did Jesus actually buy something when He went to the cross? 1 Corinthians 6:20 and 7:23 state that each of us has been bought with a price. He bought back our very souls from the jaws of death.

It is clear Jesus paid a debt we could not pay. In other words, we do not have what it takes to make ourselves acceptable to God. Our best is filthy rags, and the most we can give God in our own power is lip service and a prideful self-righteousness that ultimately ends up judging Him.[3]

---

[2] Luke 9:51
[3] Isaiah 64:6

Hebrews 9:22 tells us what kind of tender was used to pay this debt, "And almost all things are by the law purged with blood; and without shedding of blood is no remission." Jesus' blood was the principle payment, while His sufferings and pain could be considered the interest payment.

We have been bought with the blood of Jesus, which serves as a new covenant. This covenant or agreement allows us to enjoy an intimate, personal, childlike relationship with God. It gives us identity, rights, and access to the heart of God. It gives us purpose and direction.

As we can see, Jesus not only went the distance when He went to the cross; He also went the extra mile for us. He not only sacrificed on our behalf, but He became the sacrifice. He not only gave His best; He gave His all. He not only went to the cross; He went to the grave. He was not only resurrected; He ascended to heaven to serve as our High Priest and Intercessor. Jesus not only took the necessary steps to obtain our salvation at Calvary, but He went beyond the cross to heaven to ensure it.[4]

Because Jesus paid the full price for our sins on the cross, the work of redemption was completed. This is why Jesus was able to cry out, "It is finished." In other words, we can do nothing to secure or add to the work of redemption. If we try, we frustrate the grace of God and are giving way to another gospel. It is Jesus alone who saves. To try to add anything to the work of redemption is to make a mockery out of His death and the price He paid.[5] Redemption became a bridge in the spiritual realm. It connected lost man to His loving Creator. This connection is also known as reconciliation. 2 Corinthians 5:18 gives us this insight into reconciliation, "And all things are of God, who hath reconciled us to himself by Jesus Christ, and hath given to us the ministry of reconciliation."

According to *Vine's Expository Dictionary of Biblical Words,* reconciliation is the New Testament term for atonement. The difference between these two words is as obvious as the difference between the Old and New Covenants. Atonement means "covering" while reconciliation goes one step further. It implies that an actual exchange took place.

For example, the blood of animals simply covered a person's sins under the Old Testament, but on the cross Jesus took away our sins by becoming a substitute for us, establishing the New Testament or Covenant. As He became sin (or sin offering), He provided an avenue for us to be made into the righteousness of God. We are no longer just covered; we can now be restored. We no longer have to worry about making other sacrifices because Jesus' sacrifice was sufficient, and we can now walk in liberty before our Lord.[6]

---

[4] Hebrews 7:25
[5] See Galatians 2:16-3:3.
[6] Hebrews 9:12-24; 10:10-22; 1 John 1:7 & 9

This New Covenant means that the common person, including you and me, can now come boldly to the throne of God without fear and personal effort to commune with Him. We can bring every concern, problem, and desire before the One who desires to be our Father, husband, and constant companion.

This New Covenant also means I can enter into a new agreement with God. This agreement is not based on a corporate Law that could neither justify nor make a person righteous. Rather, it is based on grace that justifies and allows a person to stand righteous before God through faith in what Christ accomplished on the cross.[7]

The new agreement can also be found in the type of relationship Jesus is forming with His Body, the Church. It is a marriage relationship.[8] This type of relationship points to one of the most powerful bonds that can exist between two parties. It is a relationship that implies agreement in all three areas of man, the spirit (heart), soul (mind), and body. If the bond is upright, it is unbeatable in quality and unbreakable in strength.

Finally, this new agreement of reconciliation ends in peace. This peace is for real and can only be found when a person has finally made peace with God through Jesus Christ. Matthew 5:9 says it best, "Blessed are the peacemakers: for they shall be called the children of God." We can only be peacemakers because we have spiritual well-being. We can only have spiritual well-being when we have finally entered into the pure relationship as children of the heavenly family, dependent heirs of God.

Reconciliation lies at the heart of the ministry of Christ. Granted, His ministry was motivated by His incredible love. Mercy and grace inspired Him to reach beyond the depths of man's unlimited depravity and despair to bring much-needed hope. Obedience guided each step, commitment each action and compassion allowed Him to rejoice, cry, and die on a cross. But, the truth is that His heart was to reconcile man back to the one true God.[9] This reconciliation results in salvation and restoration.

What Christ accomplished on the cross is miraculous and incredible. This old rugged altar stands as an eternal line that has caused many to stumble in their attempts to avoid or reject its message. It appears to be a foolish fable to those who want to continue to be contrary to God. It has caused much debate, confusion, anger, and sorrow. It requires a decision of agreement or rejection. In the end, it will either save or judge.

There is no doubt that this cruel object stands between life and death. It looms between defeat and victory, and stands tall in the shadows of light and darkness. It serves as a curtain between truth and deception. Even now, more than 20 centuries later, it casts an indisputable shadow over those who reject it, and shines as a star of hope to those who are seeking life, truth, and hope.

---

[7] Ephesians 2:8-10

[8] Ephesians 5:21-33; Revelation 19:7-9

[9] 2 Corinthians 5:18-19; John 14:6

The cross of Christ lies at the core of the greatest story ever told and the revelation of the greatest life that was ever lived. It will remain in the journals of eternity as the ladder that reached heaven, the bridge that closed the great gap between God and man, and an ugly instrument that revealed the glory, power, and love of God in light of sacrifice, suffering, and death.

The question you must ask yourself is what have I done with the cross of Christ? Does it represent a fable or absolute truth? Does it represent foreboding, vanity, sorrow, or great joy? Does it represent the end of Jesus' life or the spiritual birth of your life? Is it a symbol of a useless death or the hope of a new beginning?

Your answer will determine whether Jesus' finished work of redemption on the cross has truly become a reality in your life. Right now, can He make the same declaration about your life as He did on the cross? *"IT...IS...FINISHED!"*

10

EXALTATION

"Wherefore God hath highly exalted him."
Philippians 2:9a

When you travel the route of Calvary with Jesus, you begin to realize how abased Jesus became. You get a small sense of the poverty He experienced for our benefit. For example, as God, He gave up the glories of heaven to become a bondservant. As a servant, He humbled Himself to become a baby. As Creator of all, He came by way of a humble handmaiden and a manger. As a baby, He was at the mercy of fallen humanity. As a boy ready to enter manhood, He was still subjected to His parents. On the day of His water baptism, He submitted Himself to John the Baptist. In the wilderness He came into obedience to the Word of God instead of His needs and rights.

His abasement continued as He walked a narrow path of self-denial during His ministry. As He told one enthusiastic, would-be follower, "Foxes have holes, and birds of the air have nests; but the Son of man hath nowhere to lay his head" (Luke 9:58).

Jesus continued this humble route up to the end of His life. He emptied Himself of the essence of His humanity in Gethsemane and gave up His life on the cross. He was placed in a tomb, while tasting the bitter cup of death, and walked in the midst of the bowels of the earth, preaching to the captives.[1]

Psalm 22:6 describes Jesus' abasement with this prophetic statement, "I am a worm, and no man." Jesus allowed Himself to become a worm in status. Unlike a snake, a worm must accept any abuse given to it because it has no power to fight back. If a snake senses danger, it rises up to protect its existence. This is what self-will does in man. Jesus actually gave up His right to fight back when He became subject to the will of the Father. Like the worm, He accepted the abuse of men that ended in His crucifixion.

Because Jesus allowed Himself to be brought to such depths of depravation, God highly exalted Him. This simply means that Jesus was exalted to the highest place. The Apostle Paul put Jesus' exaltation in

---

[1] Acts 2:27

this perspective in Colossians 2:10, "And ye are complete in him, which is the head of all principality and power."

It is incredible to think how far Jesus abased Himself, only to be exalted to the highest place. This is why the whole essence of Jesus' teaching is that of self-abasement. He is calling His followers to take on the status of a worm. However, before this task can be accomplished, they must humble themselves.

In order to humble ourselves, each of us must become harmless as a dove and innocent as a lamb in the midst of wolves.[2] We ultimately must reach great depths of depravation through self-denial and loss before we will truly realize the heights of God. Andrew Murray said it best, "Just as water ever seeks and fills the lowest place, so the moment God finds you abased and empty, His glory and power flow in."

We must follow the same path of judgments as Jesus did to realize the glory of God. In the Garden of Gethsemane, our humanity will only be poured out as we exchange our will for the will of God. At Gabbatha, our flesh must lose in order for God's perfect plan to have its way. At Golgatha, the total essence of our life (rights and identity) must be offered up in order to possess the life of Jesus.

In short, we must deny self and pick up our cross just as Jesus did. For Jesus, the cross represented death, but ultimately it lifted Him up for the whole world to consider in regards to the matter of one's eternal destination. The cross guaranteed death, but in the end produced resurrected life.

Watchman Nee made this statement about resurrection, "Hence a life which bears the marks of death and yet is alive is called resurrection."[3] Resurrection can only occur when a death has taken place. The purpose of death is to rid a person of the things associated with the first Adam. If there is no death of the old man, then there will be no resurrection of the new and everlasting life.[4]

The cross and resurrection walk hand in hand. It is in death that the cross is able to lift up the humble in power, exalt those who are abased to a place of glory, and bring resurrection power to the lost and hopeless.

The problem with some Christians is that they avoid the cross. They like the idea of it, but refuse to become identified with it. They appreciate the salvation it offers, but stop short of understanding it as a necessary aspect of our Christian life that each of us must personally embrace. They accept the brokenness it wrought in Jesus' body that produced healing, but shun the reality that they must be personally broken as well to experience spiritual wholeness of heart, mind, and soul. They readily embrace the fact that Jesus became a worm in status as He accepted

---

[2] Matthew 10:16; Romans 8:36
[3] Christ the Sum of All Spiritual Things, pg. 27
[4] Romans 6:3-10

man's blows, but refuse to take on a status of a "nobody" so Christ can become a "somebody" in their lives.

The cross was designed to strike fatal blows to the essence of the old disposition of man. This is the only instrument that is able to humble each of us in order to bring us to a place of exaltation. On the cross the flesh dies, pride is silenced and dethroned, rights are crossed out, and earthly identity is lost. As a result, *I* no longer live, but Christ now lives in me. As He lives in me, I am being exalted with Him into high places. In a sense, I have now become an empty shell that can only echo the awesomeness of Christ in His beauty. I am a worthless vessel that has been made valuable because the presence and fragrance of Christ fills my life. In the scheme of things, I have become a "nobody," but in the kingdom of God I am now an heir to a spiritual inheritance that is complete because Jesus is the sum of all spiritual things.[5]

To experience the resurrected life of Christ, I must first be broken. The cross causes brokenness, and each of us must be broken in order for God to put us back together for His use and glory. The cross consumes, and we must become lost in it so we can find our life and identity in Christ. The cross rids us of a past that can now be left buried, vanity that can be sealed up, and worldly pursuits that have lost their attraction in the grave. It is in such an environment that the very light of Jesus' resurrected life becomes a personal reality.

We know that the first four verses in Philippians 2 describe how the attitude of Christ will express itself in our lives. Philippians 2:6-8 describe how a humble, meek attitude expressed itself in Jesus' life. Let us consider the following table on the next page to show how the attitude of Christ manifested itself in His humanity and how it will make itself apparent in the lives of believers.

---

[5] Galatians 2:20; Ephesians 2:6; 2 Corinthians 2:15-16; 4:7; Ephesians 1:9-14

Jesus	Man
Deity: Adjusted His nature to take on a different disposition.	**Humility:** Neglect personal pride through self-denial.
Disposition: He became a servant. He became poor on our behalf.	**Submission:** Lining up to the ways of God to ensure righteousness.
Fashioned: Was shaped as man without sin, became God's sin offering for each of us.	**Death:** Death to self—personal plans, to be made into His righteousness.
Humanity: He became our example of the righteous man.	**Life:** Death allows the life of Jesus to be established in us.
Obedient: Out of obedience He became the sin offering.	**Servant:** It is at this point we will become a true servant of God.

In light of this, is it any wonder that God resists those who hold onto their pride?[6] The proud want the best for their lives but refuse to bend their necks to allow the yoke of the cross to break and discipline them. The conceited want to know about the things of God, but will not allow their own knowledge to become dung in order to know the person of Jesus Christ. The arrogant want to be distinguished in some way by the cross, but will not submit to brokenness because they are unwilling to lose all control and say over their lives. The self-centered want the benefits of Christ, but will not give up their unyielding rights to know the real authority they can have in Him. The self-serving want to be associated with the cross, but do not want to be identified to the life of the cross, which is Christ living alongside, within, and through them. As a result, the proud will be brought down to spiritual ruin and destruction because they lack the resurrected power of Christ's life.

Do you have the mark of death on you? Have you avoided becoming identified with the cross? If you have, God will never be able to exalt you in the life He has prepared for you. As Jesus said in Luke 18:14b, "for every one that exalteth himself shall be abased, and he that humbleth himself shall be exalted."

---

[6] James 4:6

11

OH, WHAT A NAME!

"...are given him a name which is above every name:
That at the name of Jesus every knee should bow..."
Philippians 2:9-10a

What can you say about the name of Jesus? How can you begin to grasp the meaning behind this glorious name? Isaiah 9:6 gives us a special insight into Jesus' name. "For unto us a child is born, unto us a son is given: and the government shall be upon his shoulder: and his **name** shall be called Wonderful, Counselor, the Mighty God, the everlasting Father, the Prince of Peace." (Emphasis added.)

According to *Strong's Exhaustive Concordance,* the word "name" in both Isaiah and Philippians have the same meaning.[1] It indicates a distinct person, but it actually goes one step further to imply this person's mark, and also denotes his or her honor, authority, and character.

It's vital to realize it was the character of Jesus that determined His name, not the other way around. In other words, Jesus did not have to live up to His name like some of us do, but rather His name describes Him. Jesus came into this world with honor as the only begotten Son of God, with authority as the Son of Man, and displaying the character of the spiritual, heavenly man as brought out in 1 Corinthians 15:45-50. In fact, the names in Isaiah accredited to Jesus revealed to the world His identity long before He ever entered into it as a child in the manger. The names in Isaiah can be summarized into one glorious name: **JESUS.**

The first name given to Him is *Wonderful.* Wonderful describes someone who is not only wondrous in every way but is unexplainable. Let's ponder this reality for just a moment. Can any one word paint a picture of Jesus' majesty? Could all the words in the world begin to explain His glory? Of course not! The Apostle Paul called Jesus, God's unspeakable gift.[2] In Revelation 1, we see that John's encounter with Jesus not only overwhelmed him, but he was also overcome by the reality of His Lord.

---

[1] See #8034 and 3686
[2] 2 Corinthians 9:15

Jesus' name should bring such awe to us as we realize that He cannot be explained, comprehended, or worshipped in the manner to which He is worthy. We should always be ready to bow our necks in humility, our knees in submission, and our hearts in adoration to the One who is beyond description.

Obviously, in His wonder, Jesus is beautiful! His beauty is proclaimed by creation, outshines the streets of gold in heaven, and is as immeasurable as the heavens above. How we need to worship Him in spirit and truth![3] Psalm 8:1 and 29:2 say it best, "O LORD our Lord, how excellent is thy name in all the earth! Who hast set thy glory above the heavens?.... Give unto the LORD the glory due unto his name; worship the LORD in the beauty of holiness."

The next name in Isaiah's lineup is *Counselor.* As our Counselor, Jesus serves as our *wisdom.* James 3:17 describes Jesus' attributes as our wisdom. He is first of all pure. In other words, there is no uncleanness in Him. His heart is perfect towards us. His intentions concerning our best are honorable, and are freely given to those who believe, love, and obey Him. His commitment towards our spiritual welfare is of the highest quality. He proved all this when He went to the cross as our substitute.

Since Jesus is pure towards us in every way, we can trust His intervention and counsel in our lives. The problem is that very few trust and regard His counsel; therefore, they never benefit from Him as their Counselor.

The second virtue of His wisdom is that it is peaceable. In other words, He is not aggressive or demanding. As our Counselor, He is meek and humble. His desire is simple; He wants to take the unbearable yokes off our necks and put them on Himself, making our load light. He wants to take our overwhelming burdens and replace them with the light burden of simply trusting and loving Him.

Next, His wisdom is gentle. He is mild in His approach to those who are wounded because He is the great Physician who heals the broken lives and hearts of people. His goal is to bring a sweet fragrance to each of our lives, a healing balm to our souls, and an anointing to our spirits. Song of Solomon 1:3 gives us this special insight, "Because of the savour of thy good ointments thy name is as ointment poured forth, therefore do the virgins love thee."

Jesus is gentle—patient with us in our frailties and longsuffering in our rebellion. After all, He is not willing that any perish but that all come to repentance.[4]

In His infinite wisdom, Jesus can be entreated. He can actually be persuaded because of His love to listen to our greatest concerns, His

---

[3] John 4:24
[4] 2 Peter 3:9

attentiveness to hear the silent cries of our heart, and move heaven and earth to answer our deepest desires.

The persuasion that can entreat Jesus can only occur within two distinct boundaries. First, we must pray in His name. It is important to point out there is no power in the *name* of Jesus, but in the *Person* of Jesus. When we pray in His name, we are praying according to His Person or character.

The Word describes Jesus' body as a veil that was torn. This is symbolic of our right to boldly enter into the Most Holy Place. The Most Holy Place points to intimate communion with God, while the concept of a torn veil reminds us that such communion can only take place through Jesus because of what He accomplished on the cross. We are told in Hebrews 4:16, "Let us therefore come boldly unto the throne of grace that we may obtain mercy, and find grace to help in time of need."

Jesus is the door we must enter into through prayer. To exercise our right we must knock on the door to gain entrance. For example, when I invite someone to my home and they stand outside my door knocking to receive entrance, I know that they are responding to my invitation.

Jesus has sent many invitations forth to those who are His. However, each of us must come and knock on the door He has provided for us to benefit from the life He offers. As the Spirit cries out on His behalf, "Come. And let him that heareth say, Come. And let him that is athirst come. And whosoever will, let him take the water freely" (Revelation 22:17).

Our Lord is also the gate. We must enter through this gate of prayer to embrace a new and rich life. We each must understand that these three entrances represent the facets of Jesus' character. As the veil, He allows us entrance because His blood has bought us; therefore, we have the right to become children of God.

As our door, He gives entrance by way of who He is and must be to us personally. To enter by way of the door shows we are in agreement with Him as our only way, truth, and life. Keep in mind there is only one door, and its entrance is narrow.

The gate means that since we have entered by way of who He is, now we can walk according to His mind, heart, and will for our lives. This is the second qualification to ensure answered prayers: God can only answer prayers according to His will. We cannot understand His will unless we enter by way of the door and pass through the veil.

Many prayers go amiss because they are not done in Jesus, according to His character, and in line with His perfect will. As a result, we miss much godly insight. Keep in mind that it is in our prayer life that the greatest counseling can actually take place.

Jesus' wisdom is full of mercy and good fruits. Let me ask you, have you ever been around an unfeeling counselor? Such a counselor has no patience with your struggles, compassion for your wounds, and no love to cover your faults. These counselors make you feel like a failure before any healing can take place. And, what are the fruits of such meetings? They produce a fleshly response of condemnation and hopelessness.

Jesus knows everything about us. There is not one wound hidden from His sight. He knows every struggle and every failure. Regardless of the challenge, His invitation is the same, "Come to Me just the way you are."

As our counselor, Jesus is not partial. We often fail to recognize this wonderful quality about our committed Counselor. He considers each case individually. He holds up no rulers by which to measure us. He has no favorites that will put us in competition with others. He considers us without conditions or expectations. He sees our potential, desires to work with our failures, heal our wounds, and bring hope to our hearts.

Finally, as our wisdom, He does not possess any hypocrisy. He has no mixture in His commitment, love, and intention for us. He is the same today as He was yesterday and will be tomorrow.[5] He does not say one thing and turn around and do something totally opposite. He does not toy with emotions or flatter anyone with useless words. He is true in every way to what He says, knows, and does.

Next, Isaiah tells us Jesus is to be known as *"The Mighty God."* This tells us that Jesus is God and in His deity He is mighty and strong. "Mighty" implies that He is a Champion of champions.[6] Jesus, as Man, ran the longest race, hit every mark, tackled the greatest enemies, wrestled the most powerful foe, carried the heaviest weight on His shoulders, and jumped the widest gulf in the spiritual realm (the one that existed between life and death).

As mighty, He proved to be the greatest warrior. In fact, the great warrior Joshua took his shoes off in the presence of Jesus. This showed that Joshua recognized the presence of someone who was worthy of all adoration and recognition.[7]

Jesus ultimately proved to be a mighty warrior when He won the war for the souls of man on the cross and in the grave. He subdued the enemy of death and took the power out of sin.[8]

Jesus is also mighty because He is an overcomer. In John 16:33, Jesus declared that He had overcome the world. The world is made up of the lust of the flesh, pride of life, and the lust of the eyes.[9] Jesus overcame the world by subduing His flesh, putting all pride under His feet, and looking upward to keep His focus in the right place instead of around or downward.

---

[5] Hebrews 13:8
[6] Strong's Exhaustive Concordance of the Bible, #1368
[7] Joshua 5:13-15
[8] 1 Corinthians 15:54-57
[9] 1 John 2:15-17

If Jesus overcame all of our enemies in the flesh, won all the battles that raged over our souls on the cross, and endured all the obstacle courses in His humanity in order to win the prize of eternity for you and me, can we do any less? The Apostle John answers that question in 1 John 5:3 and 4. "For whatsoever is born of God overcometh the world: and this is the victory that overcometh the world, even our faith."

It will indeed be glorious when Jesus appears in the eastern skies as the KING OF KINGS, LORD OF LORDS![10] There will be no doubt when He makes this appearance that He is indeed *The Mighty God!*

Isaiah tells us the next name of Jesus is *The Everlasting Father.* Everlasting means "perpetual, ongoing, and eternal". We know that Jesus is eternal because of His deity. In Revelation 1, Jesus stated, "I am Alpha and Omega, the first and the last."

In His confrontation with the Jews, Jesus made this statement in John 8:58, "Verily, verily, I say unto you, before Abraham was, I am." The prophet Daniel called Jesus, "the Ancient of days." Everything about Jesus is eternal. His life in us is ongoing. His ministry on our behalf is perpetual, and His love unending. There are no limits to His mercies for they are new every day, and no boundaries to His grace where sin has once reigned and now has been destroyed by His great work on the cross. He, in fact, is the sum of all spiritual things, and without Him there is nothing that is of eternal value, significant in meaning, substantial in purpose, or important to our spiritual welfare. He is all in all![11]

Jesus is our Father in a wondrous way. It is in the heart of the Godhead to be our Father. A devoted father takes responsibility for the welfare of his children. He protects them like a hen does her chicks, and watches over them as an eagle from a place of authority. His ears are open to their every cry, his heart to their every need, and his arms ready to enfold them in the times of fear and hurt.

It is the heart of God to have this type of relationship with you and me. Each person of the Godhead is committed to ensure this relationship, which has been made available for everyone. Jesus went to the cross to secure our rights as children. The Holy Spirit through conviction and His indwelling presence signifies our adoption. The adoption allows us to know our rights as children of God and to realize the intimacy made available with the Father through Jesus Christ.[12]

Each person of the Godhead also ensures this intimate relationship is maintained. Jesus intercedes for us as the High Priest; the Holy Spirit guides us into all truth and a life that is beyond reproach, while the Father keeps His heart open to embrace us with His presence in the Most Holy place of communion at all times.[13]

---

[10] Matthew 24:27; Revelation 19:11-16
[11] Lamentations 3:22-23; Daniel 7:9; Romans 5:20; Colossians 3:11
[12] Romans 8:14-17
[13] John 14:6, 26; Hebrews 7:24-26

As children of God, we each now have the right to commune with Him. After communion with God, we will come out knowing that God is beyond words. We will become overwhelmed that His face, as reflected in Jesus Christ, is beautiful and beyond description.

The final title in Isaiah is *the Prince of Peace.* Jesus is the sole source of our peace. He gained this title because only by His shed blood on the cross can we now have peace with our Creator.[14] Sin has made mankind an enemy of God, and rebellion has caused lost humanity to reject God's authority in their lives. This conflict has robbed people of peace of mind and causes great turmoil and restlessness in their wandering souls. It literally destroys their spirits, and makes them part of the walking dead who aimlessly travel through this world as vagabonds or fugitives.

As Jesus stated, He came to give peace, not as the world gives, but a peace that is lasting even in the midst of great trials.[15] This peace finds it source in a relationship with God through the second Person of the Godhead.

Jesus is not only the ruler of peace, but He is also the essence of peace. His meekness overcomes aggression, His lowliness silences competition, His humility ends conflicts, and His submission stops adversaries in their tracks. He can bring peace to a weary mind, troubled heart, and hopeless soul. He can still the storms raging in our lives, calm the swells ready to shipwreck us, and halt and defeat any advancement from our enemies.

In logical order, each of Jesus' names in Isaiah leads to the following name and upholds its meaning. For example, Jesus Christ can only be *the Prince of Peace* in our lives when we have been established in that intimate *Father-child* relationship with God.[16]

As Jesus becomes more real to us in this intimate relationship, we will begin to know Him as *The Mighty God* who is our Champion, Warrior, and Overcomer in every area of our life. As His eternal, all-powerful character comes out in victory as God, we will be able to recognize and trust Him as our *Counselor* who actually gave up heaven so He could become identified with us in every way. As His commitment, love, wisdom, and insight penetrate every area of our lives, we will begin to see how *Wonderful* He is, ultimately causing Him to become a priceless gem that we will sacrifice all to possess.

To me it is humbling that Isaiah describes Jesus with five terms. Is it any wonder that the name of *"Jesus"* has only five letters in it? Is this similarity only coincidental? Hardly! The number "five" denotes God's grace.

---

[14] John 14:27; Colossians 1:20
[15] John 14:27
[16] Matthew 5:9

The work of redemption on our behalf and in our lives has been completely wrought by God. This work is motivated by His love, and is an act of total grace on His part. Therefore, we cannot take credit for our salvation, for it is a free gift of God. We cannot take glory for any godliness in our lives because it belongs to God who freely gives it as we humble ourselves and submit to His work. We cannot receive any applause for sanctification in our lives, for only the Spirit can sanctify.[17] The eternal work in us is of God, and the abounding love, which compels us, belongs to Him. Obviously, we are nothing outside of Jesus Christ. His life should be consuming us in such a way that He alone will be left standing.

Has Jesus become *Wonderful, Counselor, The Mighty God, The Everlasting Father, and the Prince of Peace* in your life? Has He become so indescribable to you that the whisper of His very name ends in worship or adoration? Has He become so precious to you that His very name causes your heart to leap with joy, your neck to bend in humility, your knees to fall to the ground, and your arms to reach up not only to touch the hem of His garment, but to be touched by the reality of His majesty or glory?

Is the name *"Jesus"* a magic word to you that you repeat as if a mantra to invoke some response from an unseen force or behind the name is there a real person whom you actually love with all your heart, soul, mind, and might? Do you use the name of *"Jesus"* to display some kind of power play over the demonic world, or does the demonic world shake because you know Him? Is the name of *"Jesus"* a byword you use to appear religious, or the name of the One who is your Lord, Savior, and lover of your soul?

Jesus' name has meaning because of who He is. As already stated, the name *"Jesus"* in and by itself means nothing. It is the Person of Jesus Christ who brings His name meaning. Let us not worship a name, idea, or concept, but rather let us worship Him, the Person, in His unending majesty.

Know this: It is only after we worship our Lord in spirit and truth that we will begin to understand the beauty of His name, and, as His beauty unfolds before our very eyes, we will then be able to declare, *"Jesus, o-o-o-oh what a name!"* Let's praise His holy name!

---

[17] Romans 15:16

12

HE IS LORD!

"And that every tongue should confess
that Jesus Christ is Lord,
to the glory of God the Father."
Philippians 2:11

I have often been overwhelmed and humbled to think that one day every knee shall bow before Jesus. Think about it for a second. Every person who has ever mocked and defied God, every cult leader and each of their members, every atheist and all those who have worshipped Satan, along with Satan and his cohorts, will be brought before the Son of God.

It is possible that we as believers will witness an event that should have taken place on earth in the life of every person. Every stiff neck will bow, every son of Belial will fall to the ground, every wicked leader will be brought low, and every hater of God will be brought humbled before Jesus Christ. It will be at this time we will watch them bow in homage before the King of kings and Lord of lords.

Not only will they bow, but they will also open their mouths. These various mouths which have spoken blasphemies, mocked the things of God, falsely accused His saints as well as cursed His holy character, and used His name in vain will find themselves confessing a truth they had rejected in their hearts and denounced in their natural lives. They will confess that Jesus Christ is **LORD**!

During this time justice will be realized; every persecuted, mocked saint vindicated; and Jesus Christ officially exalted over those who had refused to receive Him into their lives on the basis of who He is. What a glorious time that will be! However, it will also be a sorrowful time as these lost souls begin to realize they really missed it, and are about to reap His wrath.

Matthew 7:21-23 talks about people who will argue with Jesus' rejection of them because they did deeds in His name. However, such deeds that were performed for the doers' own personal vainglory, will not be considered acceptable to God; rather they will be considered a source of iniquity before Him.

Over the years I have met many people who insisted on erroneous beliefs. In one case, a woman became very angry with me when I stepped on her religious idols. I remember thinking that on judgment day she will be repentant and feeling sorry that she chose to disbelieve the evidence and warnings about her idolatrous beliefs. As I was pondering this thought, the Lord revealed to me that this lady will not be repentant on judgment day, but angry that I was right and she was wrong.

It dawned on me that on judgment day there will be no repentance—just tears of self-pity, anger that will be stirred up by the fires of hell, and fear of judgment, but not of God.

I have tried to imagine what it will be like for those who oppose God to find themselves at this place. I am not saying my conclusions are right, but the scenario has posed a thought-provoking picture for me. For example, some of these people actually believed that heaven was a sure thing because they have been decent people. They did not murder or rob. They didn't curse or commit adultery, but they also have never recognized their need for Jesus either. As they begin to see Jesus' nail-pierced hands, they find their miserable fig leaves of self-righteousness falling away, revealing spiritual nakedness and shame. They neglected God's salvation, and now are coming face-to-face with the One who held an insignificant place in their lives. They will probably be surprised that Jesus is unable to declare their names before the Father.[1]

Others will be surprised because they really believed Jesus did not exist. He was an imaginary crutch for the weak and a figment of the imagination to those who clung to Him. The biblical account of Him, in their opinion, was nothing more than a nice fable. Therefore, all that such intellectual individuals were capable of doing was to compare this apparent "myth" to another Santa Claus, tooth fairy, or Easter bunny and nothing more, right? Wrong! Now His very presence will mock and call them fools.[2]

You will see the sons of Belial as well. They worshipped the world, laughed at decency, and clung to pleasure. They refused to give up their immoral lifestyles, drugs. and ungodly pursuits. They hated with a vengeance and took pride in their works of darkness. They were predators within a vulnerable, helpless society. They loved highs, loathed honesty, and hated God. Now they find themselves standing in front of the One they hated. This time they stand in silence, for they have no power to do anything else. In their hearts they still mock Him, and in their minds they are still shaking their fists at Him, but they are about to do something so contrary to their previous lives: They are about to bow before Him.

I must also consider those who became predators among Jesus' flock. They masked their self-serving agendas behind His name. They had been part of the miracles and movements that had actually allowed

---

[1] Hebrew 2:3; Matthew 10:32
[2] Psalm 14:1; Matthew 10:33

them to become a replacement for Jesus in many people's lives. However, in their deluded minds that small fact could not be held against them. They were simply opportunists that gave God's people what they wanted: a magnificent show. They had learned to become professional orators in the midst of these religious people who wanted to have their ears tickled and their flesh fed. Surely, Jesus can't blame them for making a living, even if it was at the expense of His flock, right?[3]

Wrong! These people used God to merchandise the souls of men for their own perverted, self-serving means. They are going to be held accountable to an even higher degree, and something in the air will cause them to tremble in fear. They used Jesus' name like a magic wand, but now they will be face-to-face with Him. The mask they had cleverly hidden behind will now take the shape of a Person who will look into their very souls. Everything will be stripped away from them. Their self-importance will begin to crumble, and their religious works will start to mock them as reality dawns upon them. For years they had seduced people to worship and adore them while they cleverly hid behind Jesus' name and reputation for their own gain. But now they begin to realize the name of Jesus belonged to a real Person. It was this Person who alone was worthy of all worship, and they are about to fall down before Him to take their rightful place—at His feet, while their own devoted followers look on, stunned, fearful, and accusing.[4]

There will also be the evil leaders who supported Satan. They advocated abortions, alternative lifestyles, tyrannical laws, and godless philosophies that would undermine the moral laws of God. They put heavy burdens on His people in the name of tolerance and democracy. In fact, they did everything to destroy the moral fabric of the nations, countries, kingdoms, and families.

They had made plans to bring in the one-world government. They had come so far only to be stopped on some battlefield or in some political arena by an unseen hand. They had gloried in their power, abused their authority, and toyed with lives as if people were nothing more than a cheap commodity.

Now they stand in the presence of One who holds all power and authority. They thought they were the ones in control, but now they begin to realize that they had been nothing more than pawns in the hands of Satan, used to ultimately fulfill the plans of God. He was the One who had the unseen hand that determined their limitations and destruction. He had been in control all along and had actually laughed at their foolish plans.[5]

Jesus Christ is real, and everyone who denied His existence with his or her mouth, lifestyles, or pursuits will face Him in the end. These people will bow and declare that it is Jesus Christ who is Lord. As the

---

[3] 2 Timothy 4:3; Jeremiah 23:23-40; Ezekiel 34:2-7; Matthew 23:12-36
[4] John 2:14-16; 2 Peter 2:3
[5] Psalm 2:1-4

Apostle Paul declared in 1 Corinthians 8:6, He alone holds this title or position.

Most likely when these disloyal subjects declare that Jesus is Lord, they will seal their own fate. It is a known fact that subjects who do not recognize the authority of their King and Lord are traitors. This is an act of high treason that demands death. It is important to realize that when these people proclaim Jesus as Lord, they are also recognizing who He is, and what part He should have played in their lives.

Since Jesus is our Lord, we need to become His bondservants. A bondservant is a servant who serves out of love. In fact a bondservant will abandon a normal life to become a devoted servant to the master.

As Lord, Jesus' deity is once again confirmed. Isaiah 45:21c makes this statement, "Am not I the LORD? And there is no God else beside me; a just God and a Saviour; there is none beside me." Since Jesus is God, He does deserve our worship and adoration. There should not be any divided loyalties in our lives because there is only one true God.

This Scripture also shows us that as our Lord, He is our Savior. He is the only One who can save us. The problem with many Christians is that we see Jesus as our Savior, but not as our Lord. He comes in one package, and we must accept every facet of His character to experience the fullness of His salvation. Keep in mind that it is because Jesus is God that He is able to save us. But, in order for us to possess His life, He must become the Lord of our lives.

As Lord, Jesus is also our Shepherd who has purchased us with His blood; therefore, He owns us. Since we belong to Him, we have no personal rights. Because we are His sheep, He is responsible for our welfare. However, to experience this type of leadership we must follow Him in obedience.

To follow Jesus means we will begin to know Him in an intimate way. As we get to know Him, we will be able to recognize His voice, even among voices of those who are not our real shepherd.

As Lord, Jesus is also our strength and song according to Deuteronomy 15:2. Obviously, Jesus is an abiding place we can run into to find everything we have need of to live a godly life. In fact, Jesus is all in all. He is the sum of all spiritual things.

I was reminded not too long ago that Christians make a mistake in separating God from His abilities and promises. For example, we claim one of God's promises, and then we expect Him to meet us at our need or request. The truth is, Jesus is the essence of the promise we are claiming, and we need to come to Him to realize it.

If we are hungry, He is the bread of Life. If we are thirsty, He is the Giver of Living Water. All we need to do is come, abide in Him, and fellowship with Him to begin to partake of the abundance of His life.[6]

---

[6] John 6:35; 7:37-39; 10:10; 14:13-14; 15:1-8; Hebrews 7:24-26

He is our hope; therefore, if we need hope, all we need to do is simply come to Him. Maybe we need healing; He is the One who heals us, but we first must come to Him. If we need rest, He is our rest. If we need life, He is life. Everything we need to establish our spiritual lives can be found in a relationship with Jesus. Every promise can be realized when we come to Jesus in faith seeking Him. Every prayer can be answered when we come to Jesus, who serves as our door of intercession.[7]

In order to realize all that Jesus has for us, we must come to Him as bondservants. We must make Him our Lord and learn to follow Him into the life He has for us. As a servant, we need not only to serve Him, but also to abide with Him. As Ruth with Boaz, we need to lie at His feet, putting ourselves in His care. We need to get up clinging to Him in expectancy of experiencing every day with the One we love. It is in this type of setting that a servant begins to learn the heart of his or her master. In this type of arena, a servant will become sensitive to the desires of the master. In this type of situation, the relationship can grow into a powerful friendship.[8]

The truth is that Jesus wants us to become His close friends. We can only experience this intimate friendship with Him when we become a recipient of His salvation and a humble servant in His kingdom.

Let me ask you, have you made Jesus your Lord and King, or is He simply just your Savior? Has Jesus become all in all to you, or is He just a name you use for fire insurance? Who is Jesus to you? These are the most important questions you must ask yourself.

Jesus must become everything to you that has been clearly established in the Word. Do not fail this test because your eternal destination will be determined along this line.

My prayer for all of you is that you have already bowed your neck in recognition that you are a sinner in need of a Savior. After you have bowed your neck, I hope you bend your knees before Jesus who is not only your Savior, but who is also God Incarnate, the One who deserves your worship and adoration. After you have bowed your knees in worship, I pray that you have opened your mouth and confessed before the kingdom of darkness and the kingdom of Light that Jesus Christ is **your Lord.** This gives notice to the kingdom of darkness that you are going to serve Jesus, for you now belong to Him. Such a confession will bring praises forth from the kingdom of light as all those around His throne bow before Him in agreement with you.

If you have not done this, you need to before it is too late. It is better to confess Jesus as Lord now, rather than later. Now ensures eternal life, while later could end up mocking you for your foolishness, and branding you as the worst kind of traitor to the King of kings and the Lord of lords.

---

[7] Luke 4:18; John 14:6; Colossians 1:27
[8] Ruth 3:1-12; John 15:15

In Conclusion

This ends the incredible journey we have been taking in this small book. We started out with Jesus Christ giving up His glory to take on the form of a servant and to be fashioned as a man, but who ended being exalted as Lord over all. We followed Jesus from eternity into a manger and up a road to Calvary. We caught glimpses of Him in glory, heard His cries in a garden, and watched Him give up His spirit on a cross. We followed Him through the midst of man's depravity right into the grave, only to discover the ultimate hope of man, Christ Jesus in us, the hope of glory.

We also stood at Bethlehem to rejoice with the angels at His birth, only to wait for Him to emerge after years of obscurity and preparation. We followed Him with expectancy as He walked among humanity and touched the people with power. We marveled at His teachings, cheered over His confrontation with the religious leaders, wept at the cross, and rejoiced at the empty tomb, only to worship at His feet as our risen Lord and Savior.

My, what a journey it has been! I have taken this journey every time I read through one of the Gospels. However, Philippians continues to remind me of something I sometimes miss while reading the account in the Gospels. The Gospels show me how He suffered and died, but Jesus' glorious resurrection always overshadows the tremendous price He paid to obtain our salvation. Philippians reminds me of that price, but it goes one step further.

This epistle actually shows me the great price He paid in light of His attitude. Even though the price was great and entailed more than we could ever comprehend in our lifetime, His attitude about it all says the most about His commitment to each of us. *He actually thought it not robbery* to go from glory to depravity, from worship to mockery, from praise to a cross, from miracles to a grave, from the depths of hell to resurrection power, and from servitude to Lordship. To me this attitude not only tells me of His humility, submission, and obedience, but also of His love, mercy, and grace.

Won't you agree with me now? Oh, what a Lord we have! Let us praise and worship Him in His majesty, beauty, and glory! Let us thank Him for all He accomplished for us yesterday on the cross as Savior, today as our Lord and High Priest, and tomorrow as our Hope of glory! Let us lift Him up in our praises, worship, commitment, love, and life for the whole world to see just <u>how</u> <u>wonderful</u> <u>He is</u>!

Book Two

REVELATION
OF THE
CROSS

INTRODUCTION

The preaching of the cross is the most important message that the Church of Christ should preach and teach. Paul confirmed this very truth in 1 Corinthians 1:18, "For the preaching of the cross is to them that perish foolishness; but unto us which are saved it is the power of God."

The cross brings us back to basic Christianity: sin, repentance, forgiveness, and salvation. In fact, it stands at the heart of the Gospel. Romans 1:16 declares, "For I am not ashamed of the gospel of Christ; for it is the power of God unto salvation to every one that believeth; to the Jew first, and also to the Greek." And, Colossians 1:20-23 tells us the ultimate purpose of the cross: Bringing reconciliation between God and man.

Today the message of the cross is almost treated as foolishness or insignificant in some Christian circles. Why? Is it because the message of the cross reminds us of the great price of suffering and death that was paid for undeserving and depraved man? Does it remind all of us, who are heirs of God's kingdom, of humble beginnings where we all stood equally at the foot of the cross in need of forgiveness and salvation? Is it because it reminds us of a seemingly unpopular message for today's Christians, that of a hard road of self-denial, suffering, and death?

When you think of the cross, what comes to mind? For me, the message of the cross is precious. It is the spiritual stake that gives me security about God's incredible love. It gives me perspective that my hardship in this present age will never outweigh my Lord's sacrifice. It gives me hope in the midst of chaos and failure.

I have observed as a preacher and teacher that the message of the cross has always brought the presence of God into our midst. The Holy Spirit honors any meeting when the cross of Christ is presented in simplicity and without compromise. The reason for His presence is simple; the presentation of the cross always means Jesus will be lifted up in glory. And, if Jesus is lifted up, He will draw all men to Himself resulting in salvation (John 12:32).

This small book is my way of sharing what the Holy Ghost has revealed throughout Scripture about the principle and teachings of the cross. The Word tells us about two crosses: the cross of Christ and the disciple's cross. The principle of both crosses intertwines. The purpose and work of these two crosses will be examined. It is my prayer that as the cross is unveiled to you, you will stand in humility and awe of what it stands for, and what it can accomplish in your life.

1

A PLACE OF DECISION

What can you say about the cross of the Bible that would do it justice? The cross is presented today in many ways. It has been glamorized so much that the simplicity and ruggedness of it has been lost. It has been fashioned into jewelry to wear as an adornment, while few recognize it as a terrible instrument of death. It has been ignored by bloodless cults, perverted by religious cults, and defiled by the kingdom of darkness.

The cross of the Bible serves as a pivot point for all humanity. It separates the Law from grace, divides man's religion from Christianity, and stands between life and death. It is a point of judgment as well as a place of redemption, reconciliation, and resurrection.

When one considers the cross of Jesus, he or she must realize it represents a point of decision that will ultimately determine a person's eternal destination. This scenario can be seen in the life of Jesus. Jesus Christ made a decision to give up heaven and take on the disposition of a servant and the form of man in order to die for us. Even though it was a point of obedience, it required a choice and a decision on His part to become the sacrifice for mankind.[1] He even confirmed His decision to go to the cross when He told His disciples in Matthew 26:53-54, "Thinkest thou that I cannot now pray to my Father, and he shall presently give me more than twelve legions of angels? But how then shall the scriptures be fulfilled, that thus it must be?"

The cross of Christ ultimately brings all men to a point of decision. Because of it, they must choose life to the preference and ways of death. Deuteronomy 30:19 puts this choice in perspective, "I call heaven and earth to record this day against you, that I have set before you life and death, blessing and cursing: therefore, choose life, that both thou and thy seed may live."

---

[1] Philippians 2:5-11

The cross is certainly a witness of God's love and commitment to ensure life and blessings for man. His desire to set man free from the curse of the Law and of death is clearly seen throughout Scripture.[2]

One of the greatest examples of making a choice for life or giving way to the preference of death revolves around another tree that marked a definite crossroad for man. This tree was located in the Garden of Eden. We all know the story of Adam and Eve. What many fail to notice is that in the midst of the Garden, there was not only the tree of knowledge of good and evil, but also the tree of life.[3]

Adam had a choice. He could choose the tree of life or the tree of knowledge of good and evil. The tree of life must not have been as attractive as the tree of knowledge of good and evil. According to Genesis 3:6, the fruit of the tree of knowledge of good and evil appeared to be good for food, pleasing to the eye, and desirable for gaining wisdom.

The choice would be obvious to most onlookers. Choose the tree of knowledge and have it all, right? Except the tree of knowledge represented death, and not life. It meant separation from God, who is the essence of real life. Adam could have chosen the tree of life, but instead, he chose the tree of knowledge of good and evil. He knew the consequences, but he still risked it all.

When we consider the old rugged cross in light of the enticements of the world, we again see the same contrast as the two trees in Eden. The old rugged cross represents suffering and death, while the world, like the tree of knowledge of good and evil, gives a sense of attractive possibilities, but these possibilities will prove to be temporary. The cross represents self-denial, while the world encourages self-satisfaction.

The choice between the world and the cross is as blatant now as it was in the case of the two trees in the garden. Perhaps the cross is not attractive like the world, and represents unpleasant truths. It may not stir up our intellectual arrogance, but it represents real life.

The world and any association with it represent death. It will make you an enemy of God, as well as lead you down a dead-end path that will end in compromise, idolatry, perversion, and spiritual ruin. Your appetites will never be filled, your eyes never satisfied, and your intellectual arrogance will become nothing more than vain philosophies.[4]

Just like Adam, we know the sure choice in regards to life. However, like Adam we can blatantly go the way of death, or like Eve, we can become deluded because our desires and ignorance outweigh the truth. The consequences are the same. We still will ultimately embrace death and not experience a true, full, or complete life. We will be miserable at best and totally deluded at worst.

---

[2] See Romans 3; Galatians 3:10-14; 1 Corinthians 15:53-58
[3] Genesis 2:9
[4] James 4:4; Proverbs 27:20; Colossians 2:8

The choice between life and death will bring a separation in our lives. If we choose life, we will be separated from the consequences and curses of the present world unto everlasting life. If we give way to death, we will be separated from God who is the essence of life, and we will be faced with eternal damnation.

To choose the cross of Christ is the most sensible and intellectual choice a person could make. The proof is all around us. There are many people of the past and present who will testify how the message of the cross not only brought life to them, but also changed their lives in a powerful way.

As Paul said, "...For the preaching of the cross is to them that perish foolishness; but unto us which are saved it is the power of God" (1 Corinthians 1:18). Salvation is a sure bet for those who cling to the cross of Jesus, but it must never lose its importance or excitement. It must always serve as a place of humble beginnings where examination, humility, and submission are automatic responses. This is why Christians must encounter the cross of Christ many times in their Christian walk, knowing that it represents the power of God unto salvation.[5]

Have you made the right decision in regard to your spiritual well-being? If not, you need to choose Christ as Savior and Lord. Have you lost your excitement over the presentation of the cross? If you have, you have most likely left your first love.[6] You need to go back to where you left Jesus and once again become acquainted with the Lover of your soul.

---

[5] Romans 1:16
[6] Revelation 2:1-5

2

THE CHRISTIAN'S ALTAR

Altars served as an important part of worship in the Old Testament. This is why it is important to understand their design and significance. God gave clear instructions about how they were to be constructed. In Exodus 20:25, He gave these instructions concerning a stone altar, "And if thou wilt make me an altar of stone, thou shalt not build it of hewn stone: for if thou lift up thy tool upon it, thou hast polluted it." Here we see that the altar had to be natural. Therefore, if man used personal means to shape the stone in any way, it would be considered a polluted altar.

In the outer court of the tabernacle, there was the Altar of Burnt Offering. This was made of shittim wood and covered with brass.[1] Shittim wood pointed to the humanity of Jesus, while the brass represented judgment upon sin.

Hebrews 13:10 tells us we have an altar before which the priests of the Old Testament had no right to eat. This was in reference to the parts of the certain offerings that the priests were only allowed to eat in the holy place.[2] This verse tells us the Christian's altar is outside of the tabernacle or the religious activities of man's religion. The Living Bible implies this particular altar is the cross of Christ.

The cross of Christ corresponds to the altars of the Old Testament. This altar comes from the earth, and was designed by God for the ultimate sacrifice. Like the sacrifices upon the Altar of Burnt Offering, the judgment of sin came upon Jesus when He was on the wooden cross. Such a place would point to an exchange, where His followers could be made into the righteousness of God.[3]

To understand the significance of both the Old and New Testament altars in the Christian's life and in God's plan, we must first understand what the altars of the Old Testament signified. Altars in the Old Testament served four purposes.

There were altars where commitments, oaths, or covenants were established between God and man or between two parties. Some altars

---

[1] Exodus 27:1-9
[2] Leviticus 6:24-26
[3] 2 Corinthians 5:21

served as memorials or reminders of God's character, greatness, and intervention in the lives of men.[4]

Altars were also places of worship. Both Abraham and Isaac called upon the name of the Lord after building their altars. Such an act implies a sincere desire to meet with God in worship and communion.[5]

Finally, altars were a place of sacrifice. Noah's first act, once out of the ark, was to build an altar and offer sacrifices upon it. Genesis 8:21 tells us the Lord's response to his sacrifice, "And the LORD smelled a sweet savour; and the LORD said in his heart, I will not again curse the ground any more for man's sake; for the imagination of man's heart is evil from his youth; neither will I again smite any more every thing living, as I have done."

Abraham offered sacrifices to God in compliance with His commands in Genesis 15:7-17 and 22. In chapter 22, his willingness to offer his own son, Isaac, was not only a response of obedience, but it was an act of true faith that was reckoned to Abraham as righteousness.[6]

In the Old Testament Tabernacle, sacrifices for sins were made on the Altar of Burnt Offering. These sacrifices made atonement for the sins of Israel. Atonement means, "covering." The blood of innocent animals was a means of covering the sins of Israel. This act was first established for the nation of Israel when God instituted Passover.[7]

It was the blood of the lamb on the doorposts that caused the LORD to pass over the homes of the children of Israel. John the Baptist made reference to both the Old Testament feast and the true Passover Lamb when he made this declaration about Jesus in John 1:29, "Behold the Lamb of God, which taketh away the sin of the world."

Our great and holy God cannot look on sin. A person's sins must, therefore, be covered or taken away. The Bible tells us that the only way God will accept a person is if he or she is hid in Christ. A person's life in Christ serves as the believer's robe and the Spirit of God as the covering. Since Christians are hid in Christ, it is His righteousness that is being established in their lives. This righteousness was purchased by His sacrificial death. If God does not see Christ in a person, then he or she will remain condemned because the individual still stands in filthy rags.[8]

We first get a glimpse of the importance of an acceptable covering in the Garden of Eden. Adam and Eve clothed themselves with fig leaves to cover their shame after disobeying the Lord. This covering was unacceptable to God. Genesis 3:21 states, "Unto Adam also and to his wife did the LORD God make coats of skins, and clothed them."

---

[4] Genesis 12:7; 15:7-21; 33:17-20; Exodus 17:13-16; Joshua 22:10-34
[5] Genesis 12:8; 13:4; 26:25
[6] James 2:21-23
[7] Exodus 12; Leviticus 4:17-21
[8] Isaiah 30:1; 59:2; 64:6: 1 Corinthians 1:30; Colossians 3:3

Here we have the first evidence of a sacrifice that would serve as a covering. The skin that clothed Adam and Eve came from an innocent animal's life. We see right from the beginning, the consequences and solution to man's disobedient act that set the dramatic stage for the sacrifice of the Son of God.

We see a similar contrast between Abel and Cain's sacrifices in Genesis 4. Abel offered God a sacrifice of the firstborn of his livestock, while Cain offered the fruits of the soil. Abel's sacrifice entailed an innocent animal, while Cain's came from the earth. Abel's sacrifice was once removed from the earth, while Cain's was from the fruit of the earth that ultimately was provided by God. Abel's sacrifice involved personal involvement and cost, as well as the blood of an innocent animal being shed, while Cain's came from some personal sweat and toil. However, it is important to point out that all fruit from the land is a product of God blessing the land. Once again, we see God accepting the sacrifice of an animal's life that cost something to the fruit of the land that could bring man undue personal glory. In the end, Cain's jealousy caused him to shed the innocent blood of his own brother.

All acceptable sacrifices pointed to the ultimate sacrifice, Jesus Christ. He was once removed from the earth; therefore, man could not share any personal glory in God's offering. John 1:12-13 confirmed this, "But as many as received him, to them gave he power to become the sons of God, even to them that believe on his name: Which were born, not of blood, nor of the will of the flesh, nor of the will of man, but of God."

His death on the cross and the shedding of His blood would serve as the atonement and redemption for all mankind. This atonement or covering would take on a greater meaning for the believer: Reconciliation with God. It would be complete and final.[9]

When we consider Christ's death on our altar, we see that the cross serves all four purposes as ascribed to the Old Testament altars. It was on the cross that a new covenant or agreement, was established between God and man. This new covenant came by way of the blood of Jesus. Hebrews 9:15 states, "And for this cause he is the mediator of the new testament, that by means of death, for the redemption of the transgressions that were under the first testament, they which are called might receive the promise of eternal inheritance."

This covenant gives believers authority and power. It declares that they belong to God, and their inheritance is eternal. It gives His followers access to all of God's promises and to His throne room. It gives them power to overcome all of the forces of darkness. It makes saints co-laborers and co-heirs with Christ.[10]

---

[9] Hebrews 9:23-28
[10] Hebrews 4:14-16; 7; 10

At every communion service, Christians are reminded of the ultimate price that was paid on the cross. Communion is a memorial service that is used to prepare hearts and minds to enter into fellowship with God. It gives believers hope as they are commanded to observe it until Jesus comes for His Church. It gives them a sense of belonging as the Body is to tarry for one another.[11]

Like the Old Testament altars, the cross stands at the heart of our religious beliefs. It is at the cross that we first come to terms with God about our sinful condition, as well as choose life, rather than giving way to the natural preference of death. It is at the cross that we make a commitment to God, and call upon the name of the Lord to be saved.

The altars of old also served as crossroads for weary sojourners. These altars represented a place where a price was paid and a bit of self was left behind. They also served as places of remembrance in light of future hope, and where an encounter with God occurred that would forever change the lives and courses of men.

The cross has served as a place of solace for me as I sojourn through a world that appears to have no purpose. My walk with God has been challenging, as it has required me to leave bits of myself along the way. However, in the midst of it all, the cross of Christ has helped my focus. As the burdens and entanglements of the world and self fall by the wayside, I am able to catch a glimpse of my God, and of the eternal city which awaits my arrival.

Hebrews 13:12-14 brings this conclusion about the cross of Christ and His sacrifice, "Wherefore Jesus also, that he might sanctify the people with his own blood, suffered without the gate. Let us go forth therefore unto him without the camp, bearing his reproach. For here have we no continuing city, but we seek one to come."

Have you visited your altar lately?

---

[11] 1 Corinthians 11:28, 33

3

A PLACE OF DEVASTATION AND EXALTATION

Jesus made this statement about His death on the cross in John 3:13-15,
And no man hath ascended up to heaven, but he that came down from heaven, even the Son of man which is in heaven. And as Moses lifted up the serpent in the wilderness, even so must the Son of man be lifted up: That whosoever believeth in him should not perish, but have eternal life.

Jesus was making reference to the incident found in Numbers 21:5-8. The children of Israel spoke against God and Moses. God executed judgment by sending fiery serpents among the people. These serpents were poisonous, and many people died from their bites. When the people realized the consequences of their actions, they came to Moses and repented.

Amazingly, God did not remove the serpents like the people requested. Rather, He instructed Moses to make a bronze serpent and lift it up on a pole. God told Moses that if a person was bitten by a serpent, all he or she had to do was look at the bronze snake and he or she would be saved from death.

There is a lot of representation in this situation. The Israelite's rebellion ended in the judgment of the serpent that resulted in death. Sin brings death to the soul that gives in to enticements of the flesh and rebellion of the heart. The bronze snake points to judgment on sin that has the power to destroy the bite of the fiery serpent.

This representation shows us God's choice not to deliver a person from the actual serpent. Rather, He provided deliverance in the midst of death by providing the bronze snake. We know that the bronze serpent represented Jesus who took the sting out of death by becoming sin for us when He was lifted up on the cross. By faith, each individual would have to look to Him for his or her deliverance, just as the children of Israel looked to the bronze serpent.[1]

Just as the exaltation of the bronze serpent came out of devastation and death, so did the exaltation of Christ. Jesus suffered greatly at the hands of His accusers and persecutors. His beard was pulled out. He

---

[1] Romans 6:23; 1 Corinthians 15:55-57

was spit upon, beaten, and humiliated. He was crucified, alone, naked, and destitute before the world. In the midst of His great humiliation, many mocked Him, some mourned Him, and a few recognized Him as the Son of God.[2]

The sin of man has always brought devastation, but God's intervention has always provided a way of deliverance. We see this in the case of Noah. Genesis 6:5-6 describes the condition of the world: "And God saw that the wickedness of man was great in the earth, and that every imagination of the thoughts of his heart was only evil continually. And it repented the LORD that he had made man on the earth, and it grieved him at his heart."

We are told that the LORD decided to wipe out mankind, but Noah found grace or favor in the eyes of the LORD. Genesis 6:9 tells us why Noah found grace, "...Noah was a just man and perfect in his generations, and <u>Noah walked with God.</u>" (Emphasis added.)

Noah was righteous and undefiled by the world. He was considered so in light of his wicked generation. In other words, he was distinct from his generation, and he did not compare, justify, or consider his spiritual status in light of the wickedness that abounded around him.

These righteous attributes were the product of his walk with God. Noah is one of two men who the Bible recorded as walking with God.[3] This implies that he had an intimate relationship with God, and as a result, his family was saved from the wrath that came upon the world. Sadly, Noah and his family only represented eight souls. The number eight symbolizes new beginnings as God brought forth new generations out of the devastation.

This must be true for each of us. In spite of the devastation in our lives due to sin, God can bring forth newness. However, this newness can only occur if we have a growing relationship with our Lord and Savior. Such a relationship will enable us to stand distinct in this world regardless of the wickedness that surrounds us.

Noah was commanded to build an ark. The ark served as a witness of God's willingness to provide a way out for those who would believe and obey. Although the Bible is not clear concerning the exact length of time it took Noah to build the ark, it clearly stood as a silent witness to those who were about to perish in their doomed state. Upon the completion of the ark, and the gathering of all the creatures that would repopulate the world, the LORD shut the door.[4]

It is important to point out that God shut the door. We also see this same scenario in the parable of the ten virgins in Matthew 25. The significance of God closing the door is that man cannot open it. It also points to finality, and serves as a warning that one must be watching,

---

[2] Isaiah 50:6; 53:3-5
[3] Genesis 5:22
[4] Genesis 6:3; 7:16

praying, and ready when God calls a person out of the world and into the ark of safety He has provided.

Noah and his family waited seven days in the ark before the floodwaters were brought forth. 2 Peter 2:5 tells us that Noah's righteousness brought the flood upon the world of the ungodly. God will always provide a contrast between righteousness and wickedness. For this generation, it is Jesus Christ. He stands righteous, and as a result, reveals man's sinful heart, mind, and actions. He also serves as the place of safety for those who will believe the preaching that clearly produces righteousness.

The ark is what is referred to as a type of Jesus Christ. Colossians 3:3 tells us, "For ye are dead, and your life is hid with Christ in God." Just as Noah was hidden safely in the ark, believers are hidden in Christ. Although devastation may abound, those who believe upon Jesus will find safety in Him as the immovable Rock of Ages. He will keep His followers from the wrath of God and the consequences of wickedness.[5]

Like Jesus on the cross, the ark was lifted above the earth. Genesis 7:17 states, "And the flood was forty days upon the earth; and the waters increased, and bare up the ark, and it was lift up above the earth."

Jesus pointed out the importance of Him being lifted up from the earth in John 12:32: "And I, if I be lifted up from the earth, will draw all men unto me."

The ark being lifted up above the earth is not only an awesome picture of Christ being lifted up on the cross, but one must not forget that Noah and his family were inside the ark. This is also a beautiful picture of the believer's position in Christ. Ephesians 2:6 tells us, "And hath raised us up together, and made us sit together in heavenly places in Christ Jesus."

The cross of devastation has served as an entrance to safety for anyone who will come. People who have not entered into the heart of the ark stand condemned and will taste the bitterness of judgment. Like the ark, there is only one way to be spared from the judgment, and that is through the door of the Person of Jesus Christ. Any way or means outside of Jesus points to the broad path of destruction.[6] Only as a person finds his or her heavenly position in the ark of Christ, will he or she be lifted up above the challenges, problems, crises, and judgments of the earth.

In dealing with many Christians, I have noticed that they continue to encounter spiritual devastation and defeat, rather than exaltation and victory. Why? There are two sides to the cross. The backside of the cross is where a person encounters the shadow of the cross. It is in the shadow of the cross that individuals sense the devastation brought upon Jesus because of sin. The problem with this side of the cross is that it

---

[5] Matthew 7:24-28; 1 Thessalonians 5:9
[6] Matthew 7:13-14

can leave a person indifferent to his or her personal sin, and make Christ a noble, suffering martyr.

The front side of the cross is where the reality of the devastation of personal depravity is revealed. This reality usually breaks the individual, bringing forth humility and repentance. Brokenness implies that the person has discovered that there is no goodness in him or her outside of Jesus. Psalm 34:18 states, "The LORD is nigh unto them that are of a broken heart; and saveth such as be of a contrite spirit."

James 4:6-10 tells us how God resists the proud and gives grace to the humble. He will draw near to those who will come near to Him in need. James 4:10 concludes this text of scriptures with this promise, "Humble yourselves in the sight of the Lord, and he shall lift you up."

Christians are lifted up when they become broken and repentant over sin. Out of this brokenness comes a beautiful fragrance that not only reaches God in His glory, but man in his depravity.[7]

The problem with some Christians is they have never moved from the shadow of the cross into the full light of the cross. They are afraid. They sense that if they stand at the foot of the cross and face Jesus, they may lose something of value.

I remember when I finally moved into the light of the cross. For seven years, I had taken many religious detours and finally came to a spiritual dead end. When I realized that I had missed something of value in my spiritual life, I was brought to my knees in repentance.

I learned that I had missed the reality of the cross. Don't get me wrong. I had a real concept of the cross of Christ, but it was founded on sentiment and not reality. My sentiment made me tender towards Jesus, but it brought no real personal sense of God's great cost because the cross had not made its mark on my life. Once I stood in the light of the cross, all my hidden sins, secret motives, and intentions were revealed. It was a reality check that literally broke me.

As I let the full light of Jesus penetrate my being, I recognized that I needed to become identified with Jesus in His sufferings and death. To become identified would require me to embrace the cross in submission and desperation.

Embracing the devastation of the cross in order to become identified with Christ was not a fun experience. However, as I embraced the old rugged cross, I felt myself being lifted up like the ark. For the ark, it was the waters of judgment that lifted it above the earth, but for me, it was the wind of the Holy Spirit who lifted me above the enticements of self and the entanglements of the world.[8] As I felt the precious Wind, I began to experience the beauty and power of my resurrected Lord and Savior.

---

[7] 2 Corinthians 2:14-16
[8] John 3:8

What side of the cross are you on? Do you only sense devastation or do you feel you are being exalted into high places with your Lord? If you have not embraced the cross, I suggest you do so. It may not be pleasant, but it is rewarding. The Apostle Paul put it this way in Romans 6:8 and 8:17; "Now if we be dead with Christ, we believe that we shall also live with him... And if children, then heirs; heirs of God, and joint-heirs with Christ; if so be that we suffer with him, that we may be also glorified together."

4

A PLACE OF EXCHANGE

The cross is also place of exchange. For example, Jesus exchanged the heavenly realm for the earthly realm in order to die on the cross for us. As followers of Christ, we must exchange the earthly for the heavenly to live with Him forever. Such an exchange points to putting off the old life in order to put on the very life or likeness of Christ. These exchanges can be seen throughout Scripture. One of the most well-known Old Testament exchanges came in the life of Abraham.

In Genesis 22, God commanded Abraham to take his son Isaac to the region of Moriah and sacrifice him. Isaac represented both God's promise and blessing to the faithful, spiritual patriarch. But, out of faith, Abraham obeyed. Three days into the journey, Abraham spotted the place in the distance. He secured the already prepared wood on Isaac's back.

When they arrived at their destination, Abraham built an altar. He situated the wood upon the prepared structure, bound Isaac, and then laid him on the altar. As Abraham was ready to plunge the knife into his son, the angel of the LORD called out and stopped Abraham from sacrificing him. As Abraham looked up, he noticed a ram caught in a thicket. The ram became the sacrifice.

Abraham had assured Isaac on his way to the appointed destination that God would provide the sacrifice, and God confirmed Abraham's faith. At the right moment, He made an exchange for the life of Isaac with the life of a ram. This is a beautiful picture of the Heavenly Father and the Son of God. Abraham represented God the Father who was prepared to give up His Son. Placing the wood on the back of Isaac represented the cross that would be put on the back of Jesus.

The difference is Abraham was wonderfully spared from the sorrow of losing his son, but God the Father was not spared that traumatic emotion. Isaac was spared the anguish of death on the altar, but Jesus was not spared from becoming the sacrifice.

The moment the ram became the substitute, Isaac was loosed from the altar and he became a living sacrifice for the glory of God. There were two types of sacrifices in the Old Testament. There were two sacrifices that were made for sin: the sin and trespass offerings. These were considered mandatory sacrifices. Then there were the perpetual

93

sacrifices that were involuntary, such as the burnt, meat, and peace offerings. This is where an offering was made, but fire was applied to the offering and there was smoke or a fragrance that was emitted. This smoke and fragrance served as a sweet savor to God.[1]

These perpetual sacrifices represent the living sacrifice, or the believer in the New Testament. Christ became the mandatory offering, while the Church represents the voluntary sacrifice. As a living sacrifice, Christians are to emit the fragrance of Christ in their lives which will bring glory to God. [2]

Isaac also represented the sinner who is doomed unless someone intervenes. Bound by the cords of various sins, every person deserves to go to the altar of the cross and be sacrificed, but instead, God made the ultimate exchange. He gave His only begotten Son. Romans 5:8 tells us, "But God commendeth his love toward us, in that, while we were yet sinners, Christ died for us."

2 Corinthians 5:21 gives us this information about this exchange, "For he hath made him to be sin for us, who knew no sin; that we might be made the righteousness of God in him." Christ became sin, or a sin offering, so we could be made into the righteousness of God. What an exchange!

Man therefore, must go to the New Testament altar to make the exchange--depravity for the righteousness of God, death for life, and curses for blessings. What a wonderful prospect!

Jesus made this statement in John 3:19; "And this is the condemnation, that light is come into the world, and men loved darkness rather than light, because their deeds were evil." This is a harsh reality. Man would rather remain in the darkness of his depravity than come to the light of God's righteousness. After all, depravity serves the flesh and feeds the pride. It is comfortable, convenient, and pleasurable, especially when it comes to the world's way of doing.

As followers of Christ, we must go to the altar with the main intention of exchanging the old man (depravity) for the new man (Jesus' righteousness).[3] Such an exchange requires a struggle that many Christians avoid. We see this struggle in the life of Jacob.

Jacob left his homeland after he helped his mother to deceive his father into giving him the blessing rather than his brother. Although Jacob rightfully deserved the blessing because his brother, Esau, sold him his birthright, Esau felt Jacob had robbed him of both. Esau devised a plan to kill his brother.[4]

Isaac and Rebekah sent Jacob away to live with her brother, Laban. On his way to his destination, Jacob encountered God at Bethel. It was

---

[1] Leviticus 1-5

[2] Romans 12:1-2; 2 Corinthians 2:15-16

[3] 1 Corinthians 1:30

[4] Genesis 25:31-34; 27:36, 41

here that Jacob made a vow to God. "If God will be with me, and will keep me in this way that I go, and will give me bread to eat, and raiment to put on, So that I come again to my father's house in peace; then shall the LORD be my God" (Genesis 28:20-21).

Twenty years later, Jacob came home. He returned with many blessings. He had two wives, two concubines, 11 sons, one daughter, and much livestock to show for two decades of hard work. On his return journey, Jacob was aware that he was about to meet the man who desired to kill him, his brother. The closer he got to his homeland, the greater was his anxiety.

It was at the fork of Jabbok that Jacob encountered a being. Jabbok means, "emptying" because its waters empty into the Jordan.[5] Jacob was about to fall into the hands of this being and wrestle, as he never had before in order to receive a blessing. The wrestling match took all night. Jacob persisted until he was blessed. Genesis 32:26-28 tells us the rest of the story:

> And he said, Let me go, for the day breaketh. And he said, I will not let thee go except thou bless me. And he said unto him, what is thy name? And he said, Jacob. And he said, thy name shall be called no more Jacob but Israel: for as a prince hast thou power with God and with men, and has prevailed.

For twenty years, Jacob went through a process. Like Jacob, his uncle had also operated in deception. He lied and stole wages from Jacob, but in spite of his uncle's deception, Jacob was fair with him. As a result, God had blessed him for He had given him wisdom concerning how to multiply the livestock he worked with, cared for, and would serve as his wages.[6]

This encounter with God at Jabbok marked both an end and a beginning for Jacob. It was here Jacob needed to make the LORD his God, as he had vowed 20 years previously. After all, God had kept His end of the bargain by keeping Jacob safe and well. He had even blessed Jacob beyond what he had asked for that night long ago.

Now Jacob was coming face-to-face with his past. He was a changed man in so many ways. Like the stream of Jabbok, he had been emptied in many ways, but in this last encounter, it was as if Jacob ceased to be and Israel was unveiled.

Jacob had been emptied of his former ways and brought back to the land that God had promised his grandfather. He had been known as Jacob the "deceiver, supplanter," but after his wrestling match, he came out as Israel, "the prince that prevails with God."

Jacob was now a prince. What an exchange! From a deceiver to an overcomer and a prince, Jacob was a man who was different in

---

[5] Smith's Bible Dictionary; Thomas Nelson Publishers, pg. 273
[6] Genesis 31:2-13

character and in his dealings with others. God personally made that declaration when He changed his name.

In Revelation 2:17, we are told God wants to make a similar exchange for us. "He that hath an ear, let him hear what the Spirit saith unto the churches; To him that overcometh will I give to eat of the hidden manna, and will give him a white stone, and in the stone a new name written which no man knoweth saving he that received it."

Like Jacob, we must overcome our old ways to receive our new name. It is a wrestling match. The Apostle Paul put it this way in 1 Corinthians 9:25-27,

> And every man that striveth for the mastery is temperate in all thigs. Now they do it to obtain a corruptible crown; but we an incorruptible. I therefore so run, not as uncertainly; so fight I, not as one that beateth the air: But I keep under my body, and bring it into subjection: lest that by any means, when I have preached to others, I myself should be a castaway.

The question we must ask ourselves is have we made the exchange? Consider, God made the ultimate exchange on our behalf. How can we do any less in our commitment towards Him?

5

A PLACE OF VICTORY

A person's initial observation about the cross of Jesus is that it is a place of defeat. However, once the person gets past His death and the grave, he or she begins to recognize it as a place of victory. This victory is only obtained when the cross is allowed to do its work in the life of the believer.

The full work of Jesus' cross can be seen in the twelve sons of Jacob. Their names, as well as their lives, prophecies, and blessings bring an incredible revelation of the work and purpose of the old rugged cross.[1] Let us now consider this incredible revelation.

Reuben

Reuben was the first son to be born to Jacob. The name Reuben means, "behold a son." The revelation of the cross begins with beholding a Son, the only begotten Son of God. John 3:16-17 makes this statement about Jesus Christ, "For God so loved the world, that he gave his only begotten Son, that whosoever believeth in him should not perish but have everlasting life. For God sent not his Son into the world to condemn the world; but that the world through him might be saved." Jesus Christ came to this world to save man. He serves as the only mediator between man and God.[2]

In the life of Reuben, we see him standing as the only mediator between his brothers and Joseph when they decided to kill their younger brother. He actually saved the life of his brother even though Joseph was later sold into slavery without Reuben's knowledge.[3]

Genesis 37:29 tells us the reaction of Reuben when he found his brother missing after he was sold as a mere slave. "And Reuben returned unto the pit; and, behold, Joseph was not in the pit; and he rent his clothes." The evil actions of his brothers caused Reuben to tear his clothes.

---

[1] Genesis 29:31; 35:16-17
[2] 1 Timothy 2:5-6
[3] Genesis 37:21

97

We also see a similarity in the life of Jesus. Jesus' body was torn because of the sinful condition of man. Hebrews 10:20 gives us this picture, "By a new and living way, which he hath consecrated for us, through the veil, that is to say, his flesh."

The Apostle Peter made this statement in his first epistle, "Who his own self bare our sins in his own body on the tree, that we, being dead to sins, should live unto righteousness; by whose stripes ye were healed" (1 Peter 2:24).

Unlike Reuben, who could not keep his brother from slavery, Jesus obtained freedom and healing for those in captivity. He came to heal the broken hearted and set the captive free.[4] And, as we have seen in Scripture, His stripes heal us. What a powerful promise!

Healing in this sense can mean physical healing, but mainly it refers to spiritual healing. Jesus confirmed this in Scripture when He made this statement to the Pharisees when they questioned His relationship with tax collectors and sinners, "They that be whole need not a physician, but they that are sick. But go ye and learn what that meaneth, I will have mercy, and not sacrifice: for I am not come to call the righteous, but sinners to repentance" (Matthew 9:12-13).

Reuben represents the sinner as well. He lost his inheritance because he slept with one of his father's concubines. Like Reuben, our best will not cover our worst actions. In fact, our best is as "filthy rags" according to Isaiah 64:6. We all have sinned and fall short of the glory of God, bringing each of us under a curse that will result in the separation of death from our spiritual inheritance.[5]

The death that the Word of God is referring to is spiritual death. This death means a person is separated from God, who is the essence of life, as well as the sum of his or her inheritance. Since God created us to live a full, complete life, spiritual death was never meant to be our inheritance. Therefore, when we come to Christ seeking salvation, we are not only restored and given a full life, but we gain an inheritance of eternal life.[6]

Like Reuben, who became the first born of a great nation, Jesus Christ became the first born of a spiritual kingdom. Colossians 1:15 makes this declaration about Jesus, "Who is the image of the invisible God, the firstborn of every creature."

Romans 8:29 states, "For whom he did foreknow, he also did predestinate to be conformed to the image of his Son, that he might be the firstborn among many brethren."

Jesus described His kingdom in John 18:36, "My kingdom is not of this world: if my kingdom were of this world, then would my servants fight

---

[4] Luke 4:18

[5] Genesis 49:3-4; Romans 3:23; 6:23; Galatians 3:10

[6] Ephesians 1:13-18

that I should not be delivered to the Jews: but now is my kingdom not from hence."

John 1:14 makes this profound statement: "And the Word was made flesh, and dwelt among us, (and we beheld his glory, the glory as of the only begotten of the Father,) full of grace and truth." Have you beheld the only begotten Son of God on the cross? Have His stripes healed you? If you cannot answer these questions with a yes, you need to know Jesus has beheld you, and is waiting patiently for you to come and behold Him so you can experience all He has for you.

Simeon

The second son of Jacob represents the second part of the work of the cross. The name Simeon means "heard or hearing." Hearing points to the Gospel. The Gospel means good news. It is by hearing the good news, believing it in the heart, and confessing that Jesus is Lord that man is saved.[7]

The Apostle Paul defines the Gospel in 1 Corinthians 15:1-4 as being: Christ died for sinners, He was buried, and three days later He rose from the grave. This simple message is the power of God unto salvation.[8] It would seem that most people would be glad to cling to this beautiful message of hope, but 2 Corinthians 4:3-4 tells us there is a problem for man in perceiving the Gospel. "But if our gospel be hid, it is hid to them that are lost: In whom the god of this world hath blinded the minds of them which believe not, lest the light of the glorious gospel of Christ, who is the image of God, should shine unto them."

Satan, the god of this world, ensnares people. They cannot hear clearly or see the true light of the Gospel, which is the Person of Jesus Christ. That is why there are many false Christs being presented to the world today. There are different spirits other than the Holy Spirit motivating man. There are different gospels being preached and false apostles and workmen, masquerading as apostles of Jesus to seduce men into darkness.[9] We get a glimpse of this spiritual bondage in the life of Simeon. Simeon was later bound by Joseph. This happened after Joseph came into power in Egypt. A famine came upon the land, and because of godly wisdom imparted to this powerful new leader, Joseph, Egypt was prepared for the famine.

The famine reached as far as Joseph's family in Canaan. His brothers had to come and ask for supplies from this great leader of Egypt. They, of course, did not recognize their brother, but he recognized them. He took the opportunity to ask them about their father and his youngest brother. Joseph demanded that the next time they came to

---

[7] Romans 10:9-10
[8] Romans 1:16
[9] Galatians 1:6-11; 2 Corinthians 11

Egypt, they had to bring their youngest sibling To ensure they would comply, he bound Simeon before their eyes.[10]

As the youngest and most precious son of Jacob was presented to Joseph at their next meeting, Simeon was restored back to his family. This is a picture of those who are set free from bondage by God's precious Son being presented as the Lamb of God. Before a person comes to Christ, he or she is bound up by sin. Such a person cannot spiritually see or hear. However, when God's most precious Son is allowed to enter the scene through the conviction of the Holy Spirit, the individual is set free and restored.[11]

Another interesting fact about Simeon is that his tribe is missing from among the other tribes when they received blessings from Moses in Deuteronomy 33. I believe that Paul may have explained the absence of Simeon, (hearing) in Romans 11:7-11. We are told God gave Israel a spirit of slumber. As a result, they could not see or hear. This was done so that salvation could come to the Gentiles.

As you study the churches in Revelation 2-3, one of the consistent instructions is, "He that hath an ear, let him hear what the Spirit saith unto the churches."[12] Israel paid a harsh consequence because of unbelief. This unbelief put many of her people into a spiritual slumber, making them incapable of discerning. As I consider the Church in America, I am seeing a lack of discernment. Is God allowing many in the organized Church to come under a slumbering spirit because of unbelief?

Has salvation come to your life because the good news has been made real to you? Romans 10:9-10 tells us, "That if thou shalt confess with thy mouth the Lord Jesus, and shalt believe in thine heart that God hath raised him from the dead, thou shalt be saved. For with the heart man believeth unto righteousness; and with the mouth confession is made unto salvation."

Levi

The name Levi means "joined." Joined means "connection or union." We must ask ourselves, "What brings union between Jesus Christ and man?" The answer is simple: the Holy Spirit.

Jesus said this about the Holy Spirit in John 16:8-11, "And when he is come, he will reprove the world of sin, and of righteousness, and of judgment: Of sin, because they believe not on me; Of righteousness, because I go to my Father, and ye see me no more; Of judgment, because the prince of this world is judged."

---

[10] Genesis 42:24

[11] See John 16:7-13

[12] Revelation 2:7, 11, 17, 29; 3:6, 13, 22

The Holy Spirit was sent into the world to draw men to Jesus by convicting them of their sin in order to see their need for salvation. The Word is quite clear: unless the Father draws a person through the gentle persuasion of the Holy Spirit, there is no hope for salvation. Jesus even admitted to Peter that it was the Father who gave him the revelation about Him being the Christ, the Son of God.[13]

The Holy Spirit also convicts men of righteousness. He does this by pointing to man's only example of righteousness, Jesus Christ. Man often sees himself as being righteous according to the arrogant false "lights" of pride and self-righteousness. However, when Jesus is lifted up as the Christian's true example, His light will cut through such delusion to reveal how far from the mark of righteousness each of us has fallen in our sin. John 15:26 confirms this: "But when the Comforter is come, whom I will send unto you from the Father, even the Spirit of truth, which proceedeth from the Father, he shall testify of me."

The Spirit of God's main responsibility is to lead people to the saving knowledge of Jesus. He not only lifts Jesus up as the solution, but when a person is in search of the truth, He will lead him or her to the real Jesus Christ.

The Holy Spirit not only leads believers in the paths of righteousness, He works righteousness in their lives through sanctification. Romans 15:16 states, "That I should be the minister of Jesus Christ to the Gentiles, ministering the gospel of God, that the offering up of the Gentiles might be acceptable, being sanctified by the Holy Ghost."

The work of the Holy Spirit is to set believers apart as priests by transforming them inwardly. This makes sense since Christians are the temples of the Holy Spirit. It is the Spirit of God residing in saints that fulfills such promises as, "A new heart also will I give you, and a new spirit will I put within you...Who also hath made us able ministers of the new testament; not of the letter, but of the spirit: for the letter killeth, but the spirit giveth life...I will dwell in them; and I will be their God, and they shall be my people." Unlike the Old Testament where the Spirit came down upon man, God's presence is now constantly with His people through the abiding presence of the Holy Spirit in their lives.[14]

When considering Levi, we see a correlation with his descendants and the Christian. The descendants of Levi were set apart to be priests and keepers of the tabernacle.[15] It is interesting to note how, in Genesis 49, Jacob cursed the anger of both Simeon and Levi in the handling of the situation with Shechem and the Hivites. Like these two men, our sinful condition has brought curses upon us, blinded our hearts, and

---

[13] John 6:44-47; Matthew 16:13-20

[14] Ezekiel 36:26; 2 Corinthians 3:6; 6:16; 1 Peter 2:4-5; Revelation 1:6; Romans 12:1-2; 1 Corinthians 6:19-20

[15] Numbers 1:50

caused us to be removed further away from our Heavenly Father's blessings.

Praise God! Jesus became a curse for us and the Holy Spirit was sent to open our spiritual ears so that we can hear.[16] Although the Levites were not allowed to have an earthly inheritance and were dispersed throughout Israel, they were given a heavenly inheritance. Deuteronomy 10:9 states, "Wherefore Levi hath no part nor inheritance with his brethren: the LORD is his inheritance, according as the LORD thy God promised him."

One man lost our spiritual inheritance in the Garden of Eden, but Jesus gained an eternal inheritance for us. Like the Levites, Christians do not have an earthly inheritance, but a heavenly one. Ephesians 1:3; 13-14 tells us,

> Blessed be the God and Father of our Lord Jesus Christ, who hath blessed us with all spiritual blessings in heavenly places in Christ: . . .In whom ye also trusted, after that ye heard the word of truth, the gospel of your salvation in whom also, after that ye believed, ye were sealed with that Holy Spirit of promise, Which is the earnest of our inheritance until the redemption of the purchased possession, unto the praise of his glory.

God placed the Levites in a unique position with a special inheritance. Out of the Levites would come the priests who would stand between man and God, as well as the teachers of the Law. God <u>chose</u> them for this position and responsibility, because they chose the side of God when He executed judgment on Israel's idolatry in the wilderness.[17]

Jesus said this about His followers in John 15:16, "Ye have not chosen me, but I have <u>chosen</u> you, and ordained you, that ye should go and bring forth fruit, and that your fruit should remain: that whatsoever ye shall ask of the Father in my name, he may give it you." (Emphasis added.)

Like the priests of old, Christians are anointed for service as priests, a holy nation, a special or peculiar people who are to stand separate and distinct in this world.[18] 1 John 2:27 states, "But the anointing which ye have received of him abideth in you, and ye need not that any man teach you; but as the same anointing teacheth you of all things, and is truth, and is no lie, and even as it hath taught you, ye shall abide in him."

The third son of Israel is a good representative of the work of the Holy Spirit, the third person of the Godhead in the Christian's life. His goal is not only to bring unity between God and man, but also within the Church. The Apostle Paul said this about this unity in Ephesians 4:3, "Endeavouring to keep the unity of the Spirit in the bond of peace."

---

[16] Galatians 3:13
[17] Exodus 32:26-28
[18] 1 Peter 2:5, 9

The Spirit of God prepares the Christian for death and suffering that comes through the work of the cross. This picture of the Spirit's work gives a clear understanding of the preparation and type of life a Christian should and must be living to make a difference in the world.

As the temple of the Holy Spirit and priests of the most High God, our lives must be seasoned with the virtues of Christ, so that we can be a light in a dark world. We must display His characteristics, so that we are not only set apart from sinful ways, but stand apart from the entanglements of the world.

Right now, are you submitting to the work of the Holy Spirit? If you do not yield yourself to the Spirit's intervention, power, and authority in your life, you will never reach spiritual maturity and victory.

Judah

Judah is the fourth son. His name means "praise or celebrate." The fourth son of Jacob points to sacrifice.

One might wonder why praise or celebration points to sacrifice. There are a few similarities between the people of Israel and the Christian that will enable me to explain the correlation. This comes in light of the celebrations or feasts of the children of Israel. Keep in mind, sacrifices were part of the different celebrations in Israel.

In the Christian life, the sacrifices that are acceptable to God can be found in Hebrews 13:15-16, "By him therefore let us offer the sacrifice of praise to God continually...But to do good and to communicate forget not: for with such sacrifices God is well pleased."

As Christians, we need to offer our lives to God, but this sacrifice is considered our reasonable service.[19] Praise on the other hand, can reach beyond reasonable service, especially when a person offers praise in a time of crisis. This shows his or her confidence and reliance on God's character. Such sacrifice is pleasing to Him.

Praise is a form of rejoicing or celebration. It contains the ingredient of thankfulness that produces both contentment and acceptable service.[20] 1 Thessalonians 5:18 instructs us: "In every thing give thanks: for this is the will of God in Christ Jesus concerning you."

Jacob prophesied this concerning Judah: "Judah, thou art he whom thy brethren shall praise." He proceeds to tell Judah that "the scepter will not depart from you." This is all in reference to Jesus Christ.[21] Jesus, the great Lawgiver, came through the line of Judah. He would end up giving His life on behalf of all men, and become their great intercessor.

---

[19] Romans 12:2
[20] Philippians 4:6-11; Deuteronomy 28:47
[21] Genesis 49:8-11

We actually see this sacrificial and intercessor quality in the life of Judah. It was during the time that the sons of Jacob had to travel a second time to Egypt to request food from Joseph. They knew they could not present themselves to the ruler (Joseph) unless they had Jacob's youngest son, Benjamin, with them. Jacob could not bear sending Benjamin. The idea of losing him as he had lost Joseph was overwhelming and too great to imagine. Benjamin represented a major part of Jacob's life. Jacob could not have known that by being willing to lose his youngest son, he would ultimately receive a double-fold blessing of receiving back both Joseph and Benjamin. To push back Jacob's fear of losing his youngest son, Judah promised his father that he would be personally responsible for Benjamin's welfare for if they did not go, they would all perish.

You may remember the rest of the story. Joseph had his silver cup planted in Benjamin's sack. After the sons of Israel left, Joseph had his men pursue his brothers. When the men caught up to them, they accused the brothers of stealing the valuable article from Joseph. The cup was found among Benjamin's possessions. Needless to say, this brought great distress to his brothers.

Joseph told them the punishment for the crime was that Benjamin would become his slave. It was at this time that Judah interceded on Benjamin's behalf and asked Joseph to make him the slave in his stead. We see Judah willing to make the exchange and the necessary sacrifice to keep his younger brother from slavery, and his father from going into the grave out of great sorrow.[22]

Silver represents "redemption." We know that Jesus went to the cross for us in order to redeem us from slavery and death. He became a man of sorrow, so we could be spared the eternal sorrow of separation from our Heavenly Father. We have this powerful promise, "But this man, because he continueth ever, hath an unchangeable priesthood. Wherefore he is able also to save them to the uttermost that come unto God by him, seeing he ever liveth to make intercession for them" (Hebrews 7:24-25).

Like all men, Judah showed his depraved human side when he participated with his brothers in selling Joseph into slavery, as well as in the incident where he failed to do right by his Canaanite daughter-in-law, Tamara, by giving her his third son to raise up an heir. In the end, she took matters into her own hands, and God blessed her by making her part of the lineage of Jesus.[23] In spite of his wrong decisions, we can witness Judah emerging as a man of honor and victory. The secret to his victory was self-denial and sacrifice.

This is a very important lesson for the believer. There is so much liberty to be gained by becoming a consecrated sacrifice through self-denial. After all, there is no victory without these two godly virtues.

---

[22] Genesis 44
[23] Genesis 38: Matthew 1:3

Let me ask you, are you a victorious Christian? If you are not, it is because you have not denied self and become a sacrifice for God's glory. It is only through denial that one can maintain victory. This denial is expressed in regression or decreasing in light of Jesus in order to progress in a relationship with God. This regression can be clearly traced in the prophecies concerning the rest of Jacob's sons.

6

REGRESSION

The Christian life is about regression for the sake of progression. This is brought out from different angles in Scripture. For example, Jesus said in Matthew 18:3-4, "Verily I say unto you, Except ye be converted, and become as little children, ye shall not enter into the kingdom of heaven. Whosoever therefore shall humble himself as this little child, the same is greatest in the kingdom of heaven."

Jesus clearly shows that a person must regress in a sense to that of child-like faith to enter the kingdom of heaven. This regression is also shown in the Beatitudes in Matthew 5:1-12. You must become poor in spirit, meek in attitude, and pure in heart to see God.

In Matthew 20:25-27, Jesus gives this comparison to His disciples about greatness in His kingdom: "Ye know that the princes of the Gentiles exercise dominion over them, and they that are great exercise authority upon them. But it shall not be so among you: but whosoever will be great among you, let him be your minister; And whosoever will be chief among you, let him be your servant." The victorious life is found in Jesus, but regression is the means to maintain this life. Without regression, it will be business as usual in a world that promotes the exaltation of pride through humanistic philosophies such as self-esteem and survival of the fittest.

As we study the remaining sons of Jacob, we see that this regression is brought out in their names and prophecies. It is an incredible picture of the end product of regression.

Dan is the fifth son of Jacob. His mother was the concubine, Bilhah. It is interesting that beginning with Dan, we do not know much about the character of the rest of the sons of Jacob except for their handling of Joseph. Our insight into their possible character and their potential is discovered through the prophecies of Jacob in Genesis 49 and Moses' blessings of the tribes in Deuteronomy 33.

It is important to realize that the first four sons represent the complete work of the Godhead on behalf of man's salvation. It is also vital to understand that God's grace maintains a person's salvation. In fact, the number five represents grace. The grace of God is made evident at the cross where it is unveiled powerfully, and will maintain believers until they meet their precious Lord face-to-face.

There is another important point that can be made about this apparent regression of Jacob's sons. We actually get a glimpse into the real goal of the cross. The goal of the cross is to bring regression on the part of man in order to allow a progression of Jesus' life to be worked in the lives of His followers. This life is worked in His followers by a process. I cannot help but think about what John the Baptist said of Jesus, "He must increase, but I must decrease" (John 3:30).

How do we decrease? Keep in mind that the work of the cross is to prepare Jesus' followers to decrease, so Christ can become a reality to them. I believe the picture of the next six sons will give you an insight into how the cross will accomplish such a task.

Dan

Dan means "judge." We know this name points to the ultimate judge of all humanity, Jesus. This was confirmed in John 5:22-23, "For the Father judgeth no man, but hath committed all judgment unto the Son: That all men should honour the Son, even as they honour the Father. He that honoureth not the Son honoureth not the Father which hath sent him."

It seems fitting that judgment would follow after sacrifice (Judah). We know that the Judge of the universe experienced judgment when He went to the cross and offered Himself up as a sacrifice. He carried out the judgment pronounced on all sin.

We also know that judgment results in separation. We see this in Matthew 25. The cross of Jesus actually brings a separation between the works of darkness and the children of light. It will bring a distinction between holiness and the defilement of the world. It will result in self-denial to ensure all else comes under the control of the Lord.

It is interesting to note that Jacob prophesied that Dan would judge his people and that he would be a serpent by the way, an adder in the path.[1] The people of Dan have played an insignificant role in the history of Israel. The most famous Danite was Samson, the judge. One of the most notable acts of the Danites in the Bible involved idolatry in Judges 18.

When you study the prophecy of Jacob concerning Dan, you have to wonder if it has yet been fulfilled. Moses stated when he blessed Dan in Deuteronomy 33:22 that he would leap out of Bashan. It has been noted that the tribe of Dan is missing from the 12 tribes of Israel, or the 144,000 that will be called out in Revelation 7.

In his book *Guardians of the Grail,* J. R. Church goes into great detail to show that the tribe of Dan made a leap from the Promised Land to Europe. He maintains that Dan will judge Israel in the person of the forthcoming antichrist. This substitute Messiah will definitely bring a distinct judgment and separation to the people of Israel.

---

[1] Genesis 49:16-18

One of the scriptures that Mr. Church uses to back this belief is found in Amos 5:19, "As if a man did flee from a lion, and a bear met him; or went into the house, and leaned his hand on the wall, and a serpent bit him." In his book *Hidden Prophecy in the Song of Moses,* he points out that the initial symbol of Dan, the snake (a many-headed Hydra) is a symbol used in Revelation to describe the kingdom of the antichrist.

As you study the history and the prophetic implication of the verse in Amos, you can begin to see a double fulfillment of it. For example, it is believed the lion represented Babylon who ruled over Israel around 586 BC. However, it could also be in reference to England, who pushed back the Turks out of Palestine in 1917, and became overseers of Palestine until Israel became a nation in 1948. Babylon is referred to as a lion in Daniel 7:4 and the emblem on England's flag is that of a lion.

The bear represented the old Medo-Persian Empire that ruled over Israel after Babylon. It was under this empire that some Israelites returned to their land in the days of Ezra and Nehemiah to rebuild the temple in Jerusalem.[2] However, some believe it also represents modern-day Russia, who has aided the Arabs with their assaults on Israel. We know that many Jews have exited Russia and at this time, according to some insiders, it is eyeing the many resources of the land of Israel.

This brings us to the snake, or the adder, that will ultimately bite the hand of Israel. Snakes are crafty creatures that try to remain elusive until they are suddenly encountered. When encountered, they will strike. If Dan is the snake that will strike Israel, he will remain illusive until it is time for him to make his sudden appearance. It is upon his appearance that he will strike as a cruel, relentless judge of Israel. If this is correct, this intense strike will come through the antichrist. Only time will tell.

Although the tribe of Dan could produce the antichrist, his name still points to the ultimate judge. Keep in mind, for a counterfeit to exist, there has to be something real. Jesus is the real Christ and the final just Judge. Regardless of what we see coming upon the face of the world, we can be assured that our righteous Judge will return in power and glory.[3] When He does, there will be no doubt in anyone's mind who is Judge, King, Lord, and God.

Meanwhile, make sure you are ready for the appearing of our Lord when He comes for His Church. Keep alert with watchful eyes concerning the events occurring in Israel, and pray with a trusting heart. Prepare for the arrival of the King of kings, emotionally and spiritually. Once you are prepared, then you can do what all people do when they are expecting someone of importance: Look for Him. Or, I should say, in the case of our King, "Then look up, and lift up your heads; for your redemption draweth nigh (Luke 21:28)."

---

[2] Daniel 7:5

[3] Revelation 1 & 19

Naphtali

Once we come to a place of separation in our Christian walk, we find ourselves in a battle that can be fierce. The name Naphtali gives us insight into this battle. His name means "my wrestling."

We are once again reminded of the wrestling match Jacob had at Jabbok in Genesis 32. But, what does the Christian's wrestling match consist of? Jude 3 gives Christians insight into their wrestling match, "Beloved, when I gave all diligence to write unto you, and exhort you that ye should earnestly contend for the faith which was once delivered unto the saints."

Contending for our faith points to a wrestling match. What does it mean to wrestle for our faith? Like Jacob, it means getting self out of the way. Self-sufficiency is the greatest hindrance to the work of God. It will not allow God to be God, and actually produces unbelief in a person's life. Eventually, unbelief can lead to a hard heart.[4]

Jude tells us it is a wrestling match to maintain the pure faith that was first delivered to the saints. According to this epistle and others, real faith has been unmercifully attacked. New doctrines, seducing spirits, and heretics have done their best to destroy what is pure and acceptable to God, especially when it comes to true faith. By undermining real faith, a person's foundation begins to crumble. Confusion sets in and discontentment follows. The person ends up in a deep pit of hopelessness and despair because his or her type of faith has failed to uphold his or her concept of God. This false faith is always confused about God, and eventually He is the one who ends up with a bad rap. Sadly, many have walked away from God because their faith has failed them. They cannot distinguish their faith in faith from their faith in a living, personal, unchanging God.

True faith is about knowing our God, and basing all of our confidence in who He is. Hebrews 11:6 tells us, "But without faith it is impossible to please him: for he that comes to God must believe that he is, and that he is a rewarder of them that diligently seek him." We cannot please God nor can we be saved without this pure faith.

We know this pure faith comes from God. Romans 12:3 states, "For I say, through the grace given unto me, to every man that is among you, not to think of himself more highly than he ought to think; but to think soberly, according as God hath dealt to every man the measure of faith."

When Moses blessed the tribe of Naphtali, he said, "O Naphtali, satisfied with favour, and full with the blessing of the LORD" (Deuteronomy 33:23). Another word for favor is "grace."

Like Naphtali, the Christian abounds in the grace of God. We have this promise in Romans 5:20b, "But where sin abounded, grace did much more abound." We know we are saved by grace through faith in the Lord

---

[4] Hebrews 3

Jesus Christ, and that real faith is counted for righteousness.[5] As you can see, godly faith opens the door of promises and blessings including a better resurrection. (See Hebrews 11:35-40.)

Is your faith in God precious to you? Is it unfeigned? Is it founded on the person of Jesus or does it hinge on circumstances and events? Let me challenge you with 2 Corinthians 13:5: "Examine yourselves, whether ye be in the faith; prove your own selves. Know ye not your own selves, how that Jesus Christ is in you, except ye be reprobates?"

What would examination of your faith reveal?

Gad

Gad means "lucky or fortunate." Christians are a fortunate lot because of the many promises they have available through Jesus Christ. Peter tells us in 2 Peter 1:3-4,

> According as his divine power hath given unto us all things that pertain unto life and godliness, through the knowledge of him that hath called us to glory and virtue: Whereby are given unto us exceeding great and precious promises: that by these ye might be partakers of the divine nature, having escaped the corruption that is in the world through lust.

We have an overcoming power that will allow us to escape the corruption in the world. We have a bright future because of our heavenly inheritance.

Jacob's prophecy concerning Gad states, "Gad, a troop shall overcome him:.." (Genesis 49:19a). This reminds me of what Daniel said about the dreadful beast that will be coming on the scene in the future. This beast has ten horns, and one horn will exalt itself above the others. Many feel this horn will be the antichrist, and Daniel tells how this horn makes war with the saints and prevails against them.[6]

The appearance of defeat is not an unusual scenario in the Christian walk. For example, it looked as if the cross had defeated Christ. All defeat looks hopeless, except God works all things together for good to those who love Him.[7] God has a reason for allowing His saints to go through times of testing, just as He had an eternal purpose for allowing Jesus to die on the cross. Trials and testings have the ability to work the character of Christ in us. The process may not be fun, but the rewards are eternal.

Moses' blessing upon Gad gives us insight into another reason God allowed His people to experience defeat. He states, "Blessed be he that enlargeth Gad" (Deuteronomy 33:20).

---

[5] Ephesians 2:8-10; Romans 4:5

[6] Daniel 7:21

[7] Romans 8:28

Psalm 118:5 gives us insight into the necessity for enlarging our domain or borders, "I called upon the LORD in distress: the LORD answered me, and set me in a large place." In other words, God will set His people free to be all that He wants them to be. However, it will come out of distress, possibly caused by personal defeat.

Victory always occurs at the hand of God. It is not something man can accomplish in his own power. Daniel brings this out in Daniel 7:22. He tells us the saints will be overcomers in the end, "Until the Ancient of days came, and judgment was given to the saints of the most High; and the time came that the saints possessed the kingdom."

We see this victory was imminent for Gad because Jacob finished his prophecy by saying this about Gad, "...but he shall overcome at the last" (Genesis 49:19).

We see in the case of Gad, he will have the best land for himself. When the heads of people assemble, Gad will carry out the LORD'S righteous will and His judgments concerning Israel. This reminds me of how, after the great tribulation, the saints will reign with Christ for a thousand years.[8]

Christians are indeed fortunate. We have an eternal blessing awaiting us. However, the question we must ask is, have we allowed God to enlarge our borders? If we have not, we will most likely find ourselves in a distressful or defeating situation where we will have to cry out to the Victor. He will then set each of us in a large place where we can worship and serve Him freely.

Asher

Asher means "happy." Today, many Americans are searching for happiness. It is amazing how many people have encountered loneliness when they have finally come to the end of what they perceived would bring them happiness, such as relationships, material possessions, and worldly success. However, such a pursuit or emphasis is humanistic; rather than Christ centered.

Where does one find real happiness? We find the answer to this question in the Word of God. The Living Bible paraphrases the word "Blessed" with the word "Happy" in Matthew 5:3-12. This would mean that happiness is not based on our circumstances, but rather on our attitude.

A right attitude always starts with a person recognizing his or her spiritual plight. By coming to terms with personal spiritual poverty, an individual can begin to see his or her need for God. It is this need that leads a person on a spiritual journey that will produce lasting happiness. As people travel this path to find real happiness, they eventually discover

---

[8] Deuteronomy 33:21; Revelation 20:4

it comes out of self-denial, righteousness, mercy, purity, and holiness. This type of life will produce power and anointing.

Unhappiness often occurs because a person is in bondage, due to carrying around various yokes such as selfishness, discontentment, bitterness, and greed. Isaiah 10:27 tells us the anointing breaks the yoke.

As you study Moses' blessing over Asher, you will find oil associated with him. He said, "...and let him dip his foot in oil" (Deuteronomy 33:24). Oil was used to anoint prophets and kings for service.

Oil is also associated with gladness or joy. Psalm 45:7 states, "...thy God, hath anointed thee with the oil of gladness above thy fellows."

In Jacob's prophecy concerning Asher, he made this declaration, "Out of Asher his bread shall be fat, and he shall yield royal dainties" (Genesis 49:20). According to *Strong's Exhaustive Concordance*, fat means "oily, greasy and rich." Richness points to anointing, while dainties mean pleasure and delight. What a beautiful picture of what constitutes lasting happiness.

True happiness comes out of anointing. We are told in 1 John 2:20, "But ye have an unction from the Holy One, and ye know all things." The Holy Spirit in us serves as our power and anointing.[9] He leads us into a relationship with the Father that results in both peace and happiness. Matthew 5:9 tells us, "Blessed are the peacemakers: for they shall be called the children of God."

Like Asher, this anointing makes us part of royalty. 1 Peter 2:9 states, "But ye are a chosen generation, a royal priesthood, an holy nation, a peculiar people; that ye should shew forth the praises of him who hath called you out of darkness into his marvellous light."

We are a blessed people. Proverbs 10:22 tells us, "The blessing of the LORD, it maketh rich, and he addeth no sorrow with it."

Isaiah 3:10 states, "Say ye to the righteous, that it shall be well with him: for they shall eat the fruit of their doings."

A powerful and anointed life will produce fruit. We know there are two types of fruit, the fruit of the Holy Spirit found in Galatians 5:22-23, and the fruit that comes from investing the life of Christ in others.[10]

What do the fruits of your life say about you? Are you carrying an overwhelming yoke or are you enjoying liberty in the Holy Spirit? After all, 2 Corinthians 3:17b tells us, "...and where the Spirit of the Lord is, there is liberty." Do you have freedom because the anointing of the Holy Spirit is real in your life?

---

[9] 1 John 2:27
[10] John 15:16

Issachar

Issachar is the ninth son of Jacob. The number nine can point to the nine gifts of the Spirit, but it is also symbolic of finality.

This path we have been traveling started with the cross (Dan). The cross is meant to bring a separation in our lives. This separation resulted in a wrestling match to obtain faith (Naphtali). This faith brought us to a place where we could understand how fortunate we are, and claim promises to overcome (Gad).

Finally, we came to a place of power and anointing which produces a lasting happiness (Asher). This path has led us to personal regression. Can we now finally come to terms with our proper place in the kingdom of heaven in Issachar? The answer is yes.

Issachar means, "hired." When we finally understand that we are like hired help in the kingdom of God, we will not only develop the right attitude, but we will take our rightful place. The position we are to take in the kingdom of God is that of a servant. As previously stated, the one who becomes a servant to all will become chief in the kingdom of God.[11]

Jacob gave this interesting prophecy about Issachar, "Issachar is a strong ass couching down between two burdens: And he saw that rest was good, and the land that it was pleasant; and bowed his shoulder to bear, and became a servant unto tribute" (Genesis 49:14-15).

A donkey is known as a beast of burden and is associated with obstinacy. Like a donkey, Christians are called to a place of servitude, but are often obstinate in their attitude towards obedience.

Here we see in the case of Issachar, a donkey that is strong, but who is apparently apathetic where his potential is concerned. Instead of striving to reach his potential, he finds a resting-place between two saddlebags or burdens. Complacency can produce a lean animal. We need to consider if our obstinacy is strong, and our spiritual life lean.

Leanness comes to a soul when God gives a person his or her way in a matter. We see this in the case of the children of Israel when they asked for meat. God honored their request, but sent leanness to their soul.[12]

This rawboned donkey simply found his rest between two burdens until he saw what awaited him if he finished the course. Where can a Christian, who has spiritual leanness, find rest for his or her soul?

There are two burdens that are able to bring rest to the soul. They are found in John 4:24. We know these ingredients to be spirit and truth. These two means lead a person into worship. Worship is the door to fellowship with God. It is in the presence of God that spiritual leanness is replaced with the nourishing truth of the Hidden Manna (Jesus) and the

---

[11] Matthew 20:27
[12] Psalm 106:15

refreshing Rivers of Living Water (Holy Spirit). As a person's soul is bathed in the water and nourished by the Bread of Life, a quickening of the spirit takes place. We begin to see the goodness of God that awaits the Christian when he or she enters into an intimate place with God. Man's rest can only be found in God. No wonder Moses told Issachar to rejoice in his tents![13] A tent is a place of abiding rest and communion.

Notice, when the donkey realizes the goodness of the land, he is no longer content with his two burdens. This is when he begins to shoulder them in order to enter into this place of rest. This is true for Christians who finally get past themselves and see what they have in Christ. They cease to go through the mere action of worshipping God, and begin to strive to move into a place of rest and communion.

It is at this point a Christian can become a true servant of Christ. His or her only goal should be to become a bondservant to the Lord of lords. In fact, each Christian is meant to become a co-laborer with God in the harvest field.[14]

Deuteronomy 15:16-18 talks about the servant who decided to serve his master for the rest of his life. The master actually took an awl and thrust it through the servant's ear as a symbol of lifetime ownership. Let me ask you, have you made the same commitment towards Jesus Christ? Does your life symbolize a lifetime commitment or does it show evidence of obstinacy?

If you are obstinate, you will also have leanness in your spirit. It is time to submit to the Lord of lords and discover what true greatness is in the light of godly servitude.

Zebulun

Once we become a servant to our Lord, He will become a dwelling place. Zebulun means "dwelling" and we know Christ is our dwelling place. John 15 tells us Christ is the Vine and we are the branches. We are told to abide or remain in Him in order to bear fruit. This abiding implies we are being obedient to our Lord, allowing Him to bless us and use us for His glory.

Jacob told Zebulun that he would reside by the water and become a haven for ships. All too often, Christians are tossed to and fro by the winds of false doctrines, the lust of the flesh, and the antichrist philosophies of the world. We each need to come to Christ, who is our ark, and allow Him to become a haven for us. [15]

We are also reminded in Colossians 3:3, "For ye are dead, and your life is hid with Christ in God." Notice how we are reckoned dead to self in order to be hidden in Christ, our resting-place. Romans 6:11 confirms

---

[13] John 6:35; 7:37-39; Deuteronomy 33:18
[14] 1 Corinthians 3:5-9
[15] Genesis 49:13; Colossians 3:3

this very thought. It tells us to reckon, or count, ourselves dead. Are you counting yourself dead so you can live for Christ?

Our Christian life begins and ends with Jesus. We started with "Behold a Son" (Reuben) and we end with Jesus as our dwelling place, (Zebulun). Moses said this about Zebulun (dwelling) along with Issachar (the concept of rest), "And of Zebulun he said, Rejoice, Zebulun in thy going out; and, Issachar, in thy tents" (Deuteronomy 33:19).

Jesus, our righteousness, became a sacrifice for us. He is the treasure in an earthen vessel mentioned in 2 Corinthians 4:7. And, the invitation goes out to all of His servants to come and feast on the Hidden Manna and to partake of the Living Water.

Revelation 22:17 gives us this invitation, "And the Spirit and the bride say, Come. And let him that heareth say, Come. And let him that is athirst come. And whosoever will, let him take the water of life freely." Have you really accepted the invitation and partaken of the feast that has been made available through Jesus?

The ten oldest sons of Jacob present a glorious picture of the Christian life from its source and beginnings to coming into an abiding reality of the character of God. However, as with all things in the light of God, there is even more to this picture that we will examine in the last two sons of Jacob.

7

THE LIFE OF THE SON OF GOD

We have been considering the sons of Jacob in light of the victory that came by way of the Son of God, along with the regression that comes from self-denial and the cross. Let us now consider the picture that has been presented thus far by these ten sons of Jacob. It is a picture that will hopefully humble and bless you.

Name	Representation	Result
Reuben	Jesus, Son of God	Revelation
Simeon	The Gospel	Power
Levi	Holy Spirit	Authority / Anointing
Judah	Sacrifice	Preparation
Dan	The Cross	Separation
Naphtali	Faith	Battle
Gad	Righteousness	Blessings
Asher	Godly Attitudes	Identification
Issachar	Servant	Position
Zebulun	Place	Assurance

This brings us to the whole purpose of the cross of Jesus: to bring forth His life in the life of the believer. As you consider the previous table, can you see where there was a subtle exchange occurring spiritually at the point of judgment (Dan)? It is at this point that we actually must exchange the cross of Christ for our own cross.

When Jesus came, He lived, served, and then died on the cross. For you and me to live and effectively serve Jesus, we must first die to self. The purpose of our personal cross is to bring about a daily death that enables us to live unto Christ. This death allows the Holy Spirit to transform our inner man as a means to conform each of us to the image of Christ. It is as the image of Christ is manifested in each follower that he or she will serve as a reflection, or mirror, of his or her Lord to a lost and hopeless world.[1]

The Christian's personal cross will bring him or her to an important stage of his or her spiritual growth. The Christian will begin to realize what he or she has in Christ Jesus.

The last two sons of Jacob give us a very special insight into Jesus and the life He makes available to each of us. Rachel was the mother of Jacob's two youngest sons, Joseph and Benjamin. She had been greatly favored by Jacob. This caused strife and competition with Jacob's other wife, Leah, who was also Rachel's eldest sister. Jacob's favoritism towards Rachel caused God to take pity on Leah. She gave birth to seven of Jacob's children, while Rachel remained barren, envious, and miserable much of the time until the birth of Joseph.[2]

Joseph had to serve as a great point of comfort and joy to Rachel, but the birth of her last son was another story. Interestingly, these last sons serve as a summary of God's incredible revelation of Jesus in the life of Jacob and his sons. These two sons again remind us that our life begins with Jesus and must end with Him.

Joseph's Sons

When Reuben lost the blessing and inheritance of the eldest son, it was passed on to Joseph, the oldest son of the union between Jacob and Rachel. In this example lies a beautiful picture. Jesus gave up the glory of heaven to become a sin offering for us on the cross. He took on the consequences of our sin to ensure spiritual blessings and a lasting inheritance.

Jacob, however, gave Joseph's inheritance to his two sons. This seems to be in compliance with Joseph's name, "May God add."

---

[1] Romans 6; 8:29; 2 Corinthians 3:18; Matthew 5:14-16
[2] Genesis 29-30

According to E. W. Bullinger, the number "twelve" represents governmental perfection.[3] If you add the two sons of Joseph to the remaining eleven sons of Jacob, you end up with thirteen. What was Jacob's intention in giving Joseph's inheritance to his two sons? It is simple, Reuben lost his position as the first son due to sin, and, as stated, it was then passed down to the oldest son of Rachel, Joseph. However, God in His foreknowledge had a plan before the foundation of the world. Levi did not inherit an earthly inheritance with the rest of Israel, and the two sons of Joseph ensured that there were twelve tribes to inherit the Promised Land to maintain perfection in government. Also, keep in mind that the tribe of Dan will be missing from the twelve tribes in Revelation 7. Once again, we see how God is keeping the presentation of governmental perfection of Israel intact.

The two sons of Joseph represent the two types of lives we have available in Christ. Manasseh means, "Who makes to forget" or "God has made me forget." This name points to our sins and how we are cleansed and forgiven because of what Jesus did on the cross. Without forgiveness, restoration would elude us. God forgets our sins and is able to bring healing to our past. Being able to leave our past behind enables us to focus on the eternal life we receive when we believe upon Jesus. Psalm 103:12 gives us this promise, "As far as the east is from the west, so far hath he removed our transgressions from us."

Micah 7:19 tells us, "He will turn again, he will have compassion upon us; he will subdue our iniquities; and thou wilt cast all their sins into the depths of the sea."

Eternal life is a result of God forgiving and forgetting about our sins thanks to the sacrifice of the Lamb of God.[4] How blessed we are to have a God who has a heart of love. He actually provided the sacrifice that would allow Him to fulfill the main desire of His heart: to forgive us of our sins and remember them no more.

Ephraim means, "double fruitfulness." God's desire is to always add to our lives. His heart is not just to see us saved, but for us to have and embrace an abundant life. Even though eternal life is in us through Christ, it is God's heart that we experience a full life even in the midst of earthly struggles.

Jesus made this statement, "...I am come that they might have life, and that they might have it more abundantly" (John 10:10b). The life that Jesus is talking about is a complete life. It is a fruitful life because the Holy Spirit is working the very character of the life of Christ in us. This life is powerful and anointed. It brings joy because it is based on an unchangeable God, and His promises that will never fail.

Through the life and example of Joseph, we do see deliverance or salvation (Manasseh) from death, slavery, and prison. We see exceeding

---

[3] Number in Scripture by E.W. Bullinger, pgs. 253-255
[4] John 1:29

blessings in his life as Joseph was exalted from a place of bondage to a leadership position (Ephraim). We see a man who had so much added to his life by God in the midst of such adversity, that he rejoices in it all because he could see the reason for his years of ordeal: the salvation of his family.[5]

God desires to add much to our life. He is so precious, His love so great, and His grace far reaching. Like a victorious Joseph, humble saints can look back on their various ordeals and declare victory because of the faithfulness of their God to work all things out for those who truly love Him.[6]

How about you? Have you asked God to forgive you of your sin and called upon the Lord to save you? Have you received this forgiveness by faith and chosen to trust Jesus so that you can receive a complete life in Him? If you are truly hid in Him, your life will be complete.[7]

Benjamin

Joseph's sons present a picture of the eternal and abundant life that is found in the sacrifice and life of Jesus, but Benjamin presents a beautiful picture of the complete ministry of Jesus Christ on behalf of His Church. His parents gave Benjamin two different names. His mother, Rachel, gave him a name just before she died while giving him life in Bethlehem. The second name came from his father Jacob, after Rachel's death.[8]

The first name given to him by his mother was Benoni. Benoni means "son of my pain or sorrow." This name points to Jesus on the cross. Isaiah 53:3 tells us that Jesus was a man of sorrows and familiar with suffering. He went through great travail to bring forth His Church. Ultimately, He gave up His life so that the Church could come forth in power and victory.[9]

Jacob changed the name of his new son Benoni to Benjamin. Benjamin means "son of my right hand." This is such an incredible picture. Jesus became a man of sorrow for our sake, but now He sits on the right hand of the Father. He went from a place of devastation to a place of exaltation and authority. He was a Lamb that took away our sins, but now He sits in heaven as our High Priest and advocate.[10]

Jesus died on a cross to redeem us, but now as our High Priest, He sits on the right hand, making intercession for us. This is His way of maintaining our salvation. Hebrews 7:25 confirms this truth, "Wherefore

---

[5] Genesis 50:15-21
[6] Romans 8:28
[7] Colossians 3:1-3
[8] Genesis 35:16-19
[9] John 10:18
[10] Romans 8:34; Colossians 3:1; 1 John 2:1-2

he is able also to save them to the uttermost that come unto God by him seeing he ever liveth to make intercession for them."

Have you made Jesus your Savior as well as your Lord and intercessor? His heart is to save you to the utmost. The question is, are you allowing Him to save you by making Him Lord of your life? It is up to you to make sure your life exhibits your position of being raised up with Christ and seated in the heavenly realms with Him.[11] Obviously, if the work of Jesus on the cross is not a personal reality to you, how would you be able to understand the work your personal cross needs to accomplish in your Christian life?

---

[11] Ephesians 2:6

8

THE COMMAND

The cross of Christ is just the beginning of the path a Christian must walk. It is not enough to come up to the cross of Jesus and embrace it; you must adhere to His call and follow Him all the way into a life of total identification.

To follow Jesus means you must pick up your own personal cross to produce a disciplined life. Such a life means following in the steps of Jesus. This disciplined walk causes one to become totally identified with Jesus in His suffering and death.[1] The Apostle Paul said it best, "That I may know him, and the power of his resurrection, and the fellowship of his sufferings, being made conformable unto his death; If by any means I might attain unto the resurrection of the dead" (Philippians 3:10-11).

The Apostle Paul understood that if he wanted to experience resurrection, he had to first experience the cross and its sufferings. He knew that his personal cross would also bring forth resurrection power in his life. He not only embraced his cross and carried it with intensity, he rejoiced in it.

We often rejoice in Christ's cross because it represents salvation. But, how many of us rejoice in our own cross? We romanticize how Jesus became a sacrifice on the cross, but we fail to recognize that the cross was a brutal instrument, that is, until it comes to picking up our personal cross. We see the glory in the death of our Lord, but we avoid becoming identified with Him in His death. We see the victory in the cross of Jesus, but we cannot see the significance of carrying our own cross.

The cross of Jesus prepares us to carry our personal cross. In fact, the cross of the Christian starts at the point of the complete work of redemption that was secured on the cross by Jesus. What is the purpose of picking up a personal cross since redemption was complete? The disciple's cross actually represents the finished product.

---

[1] 2 Timothy 2:11-12; 1 John 2:6

Philippians 1:6 tells us, "Being confident of this very thing, that he which hath begun a good work in you will perform it until the day of Jesus Christ." God does the work, but He uses our personal cross to work godly qualities into us.

The Apostle Paul could rejoice in his cross because he knew the very life and image of Christ would come forth. He confirmed this in Galatians 2:20, "I am crucified with Christ: nevertheless I live; yet not I, but Christ liveth in me..."

The heart of a Christian only rejoices because of the presence of Christ in his or her life. Nothing will feed the soul, strengthen the spirit, or transform the mind like the reality of Jesus. Nothing smells so sweet, tastes as good, or brings lasting satisfaction to the Christian like the life of Jesus. As Psalm 34:8 declares, "O taste and see that the LORD is good: blessed is the man that trusteth in him."

There is such beauty in the devastation and victory of Jesus' cross, but in our cross there is liberty to experience all that Jesus has for us. There are many Christians in bondage because they will not choose to bear their own cross. There are also Christians who want to get close to Jesus, but not by way of a personal cross. They want to follow Him, but stay on the outer fringes to avoid becoming identified with Him in His sufferings. They want all that He has for them without bearing the cross and paying the price. Sadly, Christians who fail to pay a price will never have the freedom to receive all that their precious Lord has for them. As Romans 8:17-18 states, "And if children, then heirs; heirs of God, and joint-heirs with Christ; if so be that we suffer with him, that we may be also glorified together. For I reckon that the sufferings of this present time are not worthy to be compared with the glory which shall be revealed in us."

I am reminded of how Oswald Chambers talked about the Christian's need to follow Jesus to Jerusalem. He then made this statement, "The saints do not end in crucifixion: by the Lord's grace they end in glory. In the meantime, our watchword is—I, too, go up to Jerusalem."[2]

If believers follow Jesus, He will take them up a hill called "Calvary." There is no way to avoid this destination, but there will be an exchange made: the disciple's cross for Jesus' glory.

The cross of Jesus did not bring Him any glory. He felt the hatred of man as He hung from the cross in destitution and rejection. He was stripped of all dignity, experienced the greatest type of darkness, and cried out in agony. Yet, this rugged instrument brings hope to the Christian.

When the cross of Christ gives way to the personal cross, a person begins to learn godly discipline. Carrying the cross keeps believers from

---

[2] My Utmost For His Highest by Oswald Chambers, © 1963 by Oswald Chambers Publications Association, Ltd.; September 23 devotion.

taking detours, as well as keeps them in step with the yoke of Jesus and their feet on the narrow path. Ultimately, it brings identity and purpose.

Picking up our cross is not an option, but a prerequisite to being a follower of Christ. Matthew 16:24 states, "Then said Jesus unto his disciples, If any man will come after me, let him deny himself, and take up his cross, and follow me." By picking up the cross, believers will find life.

Matthew 10:39 confirms this: "He that findeth his life shall lose it: and he that loseth his life for my sake shall find it." Being willing to lose our life to gain Christ is a basic principle in the kingdom of God. Carrying a personal cross is a command made to every disciple of Jesus. To avoid picking up the cross shows disobedience and unwillingness to become a true disciple of Jesus. This type of disobedience implies Christians will end up taking spiritual detours in their lives because there is no proper discipline to keep them on the narrow path.[3] Such followers of Jesus will become enslaved by Satan's various snares.

In the following chapters, the believer's personal cross will be unveiled. I will explain the results of this cross by combining what Jesus said concerning this personal cross that we must bear with His sayings when He was on His cross.

I believe the seven sayings of Jesus on the cross give us tremendous insight into the disciple's cross. It was humbling for me to realize that the purpose and principle of my personal cross was brought to life by Jesus' example. As His followers, we can gain insight into Jesus' heart and attitude on the cross. We can become identified with His great suffering, but also share in His glory. Like Paul, we will be able to declare, "It is a faithful saying: For if we be dead with him, we shall also live with him: If we suffer, we shall also reign with him..." (2 Timothy 2:11-12). Have you obeyed Christ and picked up your cross? If you haven't, you need to. It means the difference between bondage and liberty, despair and joy, shame and glory.

[3] Matthew 7:13-14

9

FORGIVENESS AND HOPE

The first command Jesus gave His disciples was to deny self. According to *Strong's Concordance,* deny means to "disown or abstain." To put it in simple terms, it means to let go of self and abstain from giving in to its dictates. It is total abandonment.

We see this in Peter's life. The cross of Jesus was fresh in his mind. His denial of the Lord had revealed his humanness. He had come face-to-face with the resurrected Christ and found forgiveness, but he still was lost and confused about the direction he was to walk in. He decided to go fishing and the others followed. Their fishing adventure was unsuccessful, but John recognized Jesus on the shore and declared that the person on shore was the Lord. John 21:7 tells us Peter's reaction, "Now when Simon Peter heard that it was the Lord, he girt his fisher's coat unto him, (for he was naked,) and did cast himself into the sea." This is an example of denying self or total abandonment.

Jesus' first statement from the cross was, "Father, forgive them; for they know not what they do..." (Luke 23:34). Jesus gives us the attitude and response of self-denial: That of forgiveness. Before people can forgive, they must first deny themselves. Self feeds on personal rights and when offended, this carnal entity declares it has the right to be angry and unforgiving. Forgiveness is always a contrary response to this carnal, unmerciful dictator.

Since salvation is established at the cross of Christ, Jesus' cross represents forgiveness to everyone who believes upon Him. Forgiveness produces justification. Romans 5:9-10 tells us, "Much more then, being now justified by his blood, we shall be saved from wrath through him. For if, when we were enemies, we were reconciled to God by the death of his Son, much more, being reconciled, we shall be saved by his life."

Godly forgiveness is at the heart of reconciliation. The Apostle Paul gives us this insight in 2 Corinthians 5:18, "And all things are of God, who hath reconciled us to himself by Jesus Christ, and hath given to us the ministry of reconciliation."

No wonder we have such instructions from Jesus to love our enemies and pray for those who persecute us. We need to forgive others if the Father is going to forgive us. In reference to how many times we are to forgive, Jesus said in Matthew 18:22, "I say not unto thee, Until seven times; but, Until seventy times seven."[1]

Forgiveness is not something we mouth to sound pious. Jesus sincerely meant His request to the Father to forgive those who had put Him on the cross. You need to remember His request for forgiveness was being extended on our behalf. We all helped put Him on the cross, and we can see that His forgiveness was a matter of the heart. This is why He made this statement in Matthew 18:35 in regard to the judgment that will befall those who choose not to forgive, "So likewise shall my heavenly Father do also unto you, if ye from your hearts forgive not every one his brother their trespasses."

Forgiveness is not only necessary for salvation, but for spiritual well-being. Unforgiveness is a product of rebellion because we are commanded to forgive. It eventually turns into bitterness that will defile everything.[2] Bitterness makes a heart hard, and inspires unbelief, causing greater rebellion and disobedience.

This is an example of the cycle of unforgiveness. It serves as an open door for Satan. Therefore, Christians have this instruction in Ephesians 4:26-27, "Be ye angry, and sin not: let not the sun go down upon your wrath: Neither give place to the devil."

Do you have unforgiveness? This question must be personally explored. If you do have unforgiveness, it is obvious that you have not denied yourself.

Unforgiveness will also keep a person from possessing hope. This sin defiles and causes one's conscience to be tarnished, preventing him or her from approaching the throne of God. Hebrews 10:22 says, "Let us draw near with a true heart in full assurance of faith, having our hearts sprinkled from an evil conscience and our bodies washed with pure water."

The beauty of the cross of Christ is that it always serves as a place of great hope. It is at the cross where one can seek forgiveness, cleansing, reconciliation, and restoration by faith. Faith in the character of God allows us the liberty to hope. Hope gives us an eternal perspective. We see this even in the cross of Jesus.

Scripture tells us that Jesus was crucified between two thieves. Once again, we are reminded that the cross brings us to a crossroad where a decision must be made. We also see the contrast and the result of the decision man makes.

The one thief mocked Christ. He told Him, "If thou be Christ, save thyself and us" (Luke 23:39). This man belonged on the cross, but here we see that he wanted God to perform on his behalf. Obviously, he was not interested in the truth. He was angry at his situation, but not

---

[1] Matthew 5:43; 6:14-15
[2] Hebrews 12:15

repentant. He was looking out for his life and not for his soul. Obviously, he was caught up with the present world and indifferent to eternity.

We can see this attitude towards Jesus on the cross in many unbelievers, but how about Christians? Sadly, Christians often display the same attitude toward their own cross. Like this thief, believers can come to the cross of Christ and ask for deliverance, but become angry and resentful when it comes to bearing their own cross. Many want to experience the promises of God, but not at the price of an unmerciful cross.

The other thief knew he belonged on the cross for his deeds. He was repentant and responsible concerning his actions. He was concerned about his soul. Let us consider his response in light of the defiant thief:

> But the other answering rebuked him, saying, Dost not thou fear God, seeing thou art in the same condemnation? And we indeed justly; for we receive the due reward of our deeds: but this man hath done nothing amiss. And He said unto Jesus, Lord, remember me when thou comest into thy kingdom (Luke 23:40-42).

Notice how this thief looked from judgment (the mocking thief) to Jesus to seek mercy and grace. Both the cross of Jesus and our personal cross bring a contrast between judgment and grace, but it also offers hope to the humble.

Jesus confirmed this hope when He said to the thief, "Verily I say unto thee, To day shalt thou be with me in paradise" (Luke 23:43). What a promise! What hope this thief had on the cross! His perspective went from the earth and judgment to Paradise with Jesus.

Jesus gives believers the same hope in John 14:1-3:

> Let not your heart be troubled; ye believe in God, believe also in me. In my Father's house are many mansions: if it were not so, I would have told you. I go to prepare a place for you. And if I go and prepare a place for you, I will come again, and receive you unto myself; that where I am, there ye may be also.

This is our hope, but such hope can only come out of forgiveness and the work of the cross.

Jesus' instructions in Matthew 16:24 reveal that it is not enough to deny yourself, the self life must lose its influence. Such an act of denial is just the beginning. You must pick up the cross if you are going to be with Jesus in Paradise. You must follow as He will lead.

He will lead you beside still waters, up paths of righteousness, and through the valley of the shadow of death right into Paradise.[3] As Peter declared in his second epistle, "Nevertheless we, according to his promise, look for new heavens and a new earth, wherein dwelleth righteousness. Wherefore, beloved, seeing that ye look for such things,

---

[3] Psalm 23

be diligent that ye may be found of him in peace, without spot, and blameless" (2 Peter 3:13-14).

Have you denied yourself and picked up your cross or are you mocking Him? Are you following Jesus or are you testing Him? Are you walking in forgiveness with an eternal perspective or are you bitter? Obviously, forgiveness in the light of the kingdom of God is the essence of finding life, reconciliation, and hope.

10

THE COST OF SEPARATION

The cross implies that there is a cost attached to it. Jesus confirmed this when He made this reference in regards to His cross and discipleship in Luke 14:28: "For which of you, intending to build a tower, sitteth not down first, and counteth the cost, whether he have sufficient to finish it?"

What cost must a person consider before following Jesus? Jesus gave insight to this question while He was on the cross. John 19:25-27 sets up the scene. Jesus' mother stood near the cross, and when Jesus saw His mother Mary, and His disciple John, He said to His mother, "Woman, behold thy son. Then saith he to the disciple, Behold thy mother!" Jesus' mother represented His earthly identity and inheritance. He actually entrusted this earthly association to another, even outside of His earthly family.

Jesus had been separating Himself from His worldly identity long before He entrusted His mother to John, but His mother was to be His last attachment to this world. We see this challenge for separation being presented to those who desired to follow Him in Luke 9:58-62.

First, we see Jesus giving up His right to what we would call a "normal life" in Luke 9:58. His response to the "wannabe" follower is quite shocking to those who want to hold onto a "normal life", while trying to serve Jesus. "Foxes have holes, and birds of the air have nests; but the Son of man hath not where to lay his head."

We see in Jesus' life there was no semblance of a "normal life." I cannot help but hear Jesus' words in Luke 9:25, "For what is man advantaged, if he gain the whole world, and lose himself, or be cast away?"

Jesus not only gave up the "normal life" on earth, but He gave up the glories of heaven so you and I could become rich by obtaining eternal life. The Apostle Paul confirmed this in 2 Corinthians 8:9: "For ye know the grace of our Lord Jesus Christ, that, though he was rich, yet for your sakes he became poor, that ye through his poverty might be rich."

Are we willing to come to a point of becoming poor for the sake of Christ? I hope so because it tells us in Matthew 5:3, "Blessed are the poor in spirit: for theirs is the kingdom of heaven." Poor in this verse implies a "cringing beggar."[1]

---

[1] Strong's Concordance, #4484

Jesus gave us insight into what is really important in Matthew 6:25-33. He also gave us a wonderful promise in Matthew 6:33: "But seek ye first the kingdom of God, and his righteousness; and all these things shall be added unto you."

Jesus told another man to follow Him. The man asked Jesus to first let him go and bury his father. Jesus' reply must have been a bit unsettling. He tells the man, "Let the dead bury their dead: but go thou and preach the kingdom of God" (Luke 9:60). Here we see Jesus separating Himself from the lifeless traditions of the world. The world represents all that is dead and useless. It would seem normal for this man to carry out the cultural practices surrounding a death, but such a ceremony belonged to the world. It was Jesus' way of reminding this man that there were greater matters of importance concerning those who were still alive, but under condemnation.

The world also influences our priorities. Our priorities are usually in line with the world's philosophies and pursuits and not in light of eternity. A young Jesus told his parents in Luke 2:49 after they lost track of Him during the Passover celebration, "How is it that you sought me? Wist ye not that I must be about my Father's business?"

Association with the world not only entangles people, but it entices them to waste valuable time. Such an association makes a person an enemy of God.[2] In this state, people's affections are akin to spiritual adultery, while their priorities constitute idolatry. This is why Paul instructed Christians to, "Set your affection on things above, not on things on the earth" (Colossians 3:2).

Are you committing adultery with the world? Keep in mind, the world will pass away, but those who do the will of God will live forever.[3] As a result, we all need to adopt Paul's attitude towards the world. He tells us in Galatians 6:14b that, "...the world is crucified unto me, and I unto the world."

In Philippians 3:7-8, Paul made this statement in regard to what the world values, "But what things were gain to me, those I counted loss for Christ. Yea doubtless, and I count all things but loss for the excellency of the knowledge of Christ Jesus my Lord: for whom I have suffered the loss of all things, and do count them but dung, that I may win Christ." My prayer is, "Oh, Lord, give each of us this type of attitude towards the world."

In still another incident, a man asked Jesus to allow him to go and say good-bye to his family before following Him. Jesus' statement in Luke 14:26 puts this request in perspective: "If any man come to me and hate not his father, and mother, and wife, and children, and brethren, and sisters, yea, and his own life also, he cannot be my disciple."

---

[2] James 4:4
[3] 1 John 2:17

Jesus is showing us that our love for Him must be much greater than our commitment to family. When Jesus calls people away from family, he often does so because of idolatry or priorities. For example, He called Abraham out of his homeland and away from the influences of family to separate him from that which was idolatrous.[4] Separation in family not only takes place because of idolatry, but because of truth. Jesus confirmed this is Matthew 10:34-35, "Think not that I am come to send peace on earth: I came not to send peace, but a sword. For I am come to set a man at variance against his father, and the daughter against her mother, and the daughter in law against her mother-in-law." Obviously, truth will cause a division among family members. It will not compromise, nor will it ignore that which is wrong, regardless of the type of relationship involved. It will serve as a mirror that brings the contrast of righteousness to a matter, as well as serving as a point of conflict to those who do not love truth.

In some cases, Jesus calls people out of their family because of the priority that is placed on them. Oftentimes, family members can stand in the way of people obeying God.

I have learned to hold lightly to all relationships. Holding tightly to those things that are not beneficial to my life with God will produce bondage. Losing some of my relationships has resulted in great mourning for me, but I know it is part of the price of being separated unto God. I continually remind myself of what Jesus said in Matthew 5:4, "Blessed are they that mourn: for they shall be comforted."

There are great rewards for those who are willing to leave family and follow Jesus. We are told in Matthew 19:29, "And every one that hath forsaken houses, or brethren, or sisters, or father, or mother, or wife, or children, or lands, for my name's sake, shall receive an hundredfold, and shall inherit everlasting life."

Jesus also knew He would not only have a heavenly kingdom, but a heavenly family. This family would have greater worth than an earthly family. He made this statement in regards to this subject, "For whosoever shall do the will of my Father which is in heaven, the same is my brother, and sister, and mother" (Matthew 12:50). Based on your relationship with God right now, would Jesus acknowledge you as one of His family members?

Jesus ended the incredible challenge in Luke 9:62 with the price of true discipleship, "No man, having put his hand to the plough, and looking back, is fit for the kingdom of God." This is a very stern warning. We cannot be casual with this challenge. Lot's wife turned back and was turned into a pillar of salt. We are called to be the salt of the earth that makes a difference, and not a pillar of salt that represents judgment because of disobedience.[5]

---

[4] Joshua 24:2
[5] Genesis 19:26; Matthew 5:13

There will be a separation of some type in your life. For example, sin or disobedience will bring a separation between you and God. We see this in Jesus' fourth statement on the cross in Matthew 27:46, "My God, my God, why hast thou forsaken me?"

It was during this time that Jesus experienced the greatest sorrow of all, that of separation from His Father. It is suspected that this separation happened when Jesus took all of our sins upon Himself. Isaiah 59:2 tells us, "But your iniquities have separated between you and your God, and your sins have hid his face from you, that he will not hear." Isaiah 53:3 called Jesus a man of sorrows. He even mourned in the Garden of Gethsemane and asked the Father to remove the cup of sorrow from Him.[6] Philippians 2:8 says He humbled Himself and became obedient unto death—even the death of the cross. Here we see the essence of meekness and greatness wrapped up in one act. This should not surprise us when we consider Jesus' words in Matthew 5:5, "Blessed are the meek: for they shall inherit the earth."

Jesus, as man, experienced actual separation on the cross from God, the Father, so His people could be separated unto God in righteousness. We do not understand this separation, but it gives us a small glimpse into the despair that plagues man in his present life, as well as in the bowels of hell. However, Jesus' experience on the cross and in the grave reminds Christians of the promise that God will never leave them nor forsake them.[7] What an exchange! Jesus' Church will spend eternity gaining greater understanding of this exchange, only to be humbled and stand in awe of her Lord's everlasting love.

Are you being separated unto God because you are allowing your cross to have its way or are you being separated from God because of sin? Examine yourself and allow the Holy Spirit to search your heart. He will help you to honestly answer the question.

---

[6] Luke 22:42; 2 Corinthians 5:21
[7] Hebrews 13:5-6

11

FROM SUFFERING TO SALVATION

Let us now consider the route our personal cross has brought us. We started out with the command to deny self and bear our cross in light of forgiveness and the promise of Paradise. Here we see the correct perspective in relationship to our response to others on earth, and our hope which is found in heaven.

Next, we come face-to-face with the cost of our cross. We must separate ourselves from the world and our earthly family. And, the place these two sources hold in our life will determine the extent of the cost.

Now we come to the next part of the cross. This part can prove to be the most difficult part to bear—that of suffering. Jesus suffered greatly. In John 19:28, we get a small glimpse into His ordeal when He declared, "I thirst." This statement came after all the scriptures concerning His life, ministry, and suffering were fulfilled.

We know that Jesus' physical thirst was symbolic of the intensity of His suffering. Psalm 22:15 tells us, "My strength is dried up like a potsherd; and my tongue cleaveth to my jaws; and thou hast brought me into the dust of death." There is nothing like physical thirst and its accompanying torment when one has an inability to quench it.

Jesus not only experienced a great thirst because of His physical condition, but He had to drink of the bitter cup of sorrow. We are told He was offered vinegar. According to *Smith's Bible Dictionary*, this beverage consisted of wine and strong drink that had turned sour. This drink represents the bitter cup He was partaking of spiritually for you and me.

Jesus mentioned this cup of sorrow in Matthew 20:22-23. He asked His disciples if they would be willing to drink from the cup He was about to partake of. They answered, "We are able." Jesus' reply was, "Ye shall drink indeed of my cup..." His statement proved they would also have to bear a cross that would cause suffering for them.

Jesus suffered every type of physical wound known to medical science. He actually suffered from five different types of wounds. We know that He was struck and beaten, causing bruising. Isaiah 53:5 tells us: "...he was bruised for our iniquities."

He was flogged. Psalm 129:3 gives us insight into the depth of this whipping: "The plowers plowed upon my back: they made long their furrows."

Isaiah 53:5 tells us how we benefited from His plight: "…with his stripes we are healed."

A crown of thorns was embedded onto His head. It is no wonder that Isaiah 53:2 states He had no form or beauty, and Isaiah 53:3 tells us that the King of kings was despised and not esteemed.

They crucified Him, which meant they pierced his hands and feet with long iron spikes. Psalm 22:16 states, "…they pierced my hands and my feet."

Isaiah 53:4 says, "…yet we did esteem him stricken, smitten of God, and afflicted."

Finally, they pierced His side with a spear. Isaiah 53:5 tells us He was wounded for our transgressions.

Zechariah 12:10b concluded Jesus' suffering with this prophetic event, "…and they shall look upon me whom they have pierced, and they shall mourn for him, as one mourneth for his only son and shall be in bitterness for him, as one that is in bitterness for his firstborn."

Christians who bear their personal cross often experience great suffering. They begin to understand what it means to partake of the cup of sorrow. During this time, believers need to remember that in such suffering, God preserves them. Keep in mind that Jesus experienced five main types of wounds. The number five represents grace. It is the grace of God that keeps His people. The Apostle Paul confirms this in 2 Corinthians 12:8-9: "For this thing I besought the Lord thrice, that it might depart from me. And he said unto me, My grace is sufficient for thee: for my strength is made perfect in weakness."

The cup of suffering and sorrow implies that the process of emptying one's life of self has intensified, and spiritual thirst will be the byproduct. After all, how can a person be thirsty as long as he or she is full of self?

We see in Psalm 42:1-2, the writer understood the need for spiritual thirst. He declared, "As the hart panteth after the water brooks, so panteth my soul after thee, O God. My soul thirsteth for God, for the living God: when shall I come and appear before God?"

No wonder Jesus stated, "Blessed are they which do hunger and thirst after righteousness: for they shall be filled" (Matthew 5:6).

In Matthew 6:33, He gives us this command and promise concerning righteousness, "But seek ye first the kingdom of God, and his righteousness: and all these things shall be added unto you."

Suffering and its constant companion, sorrow, are intended to bring people to a place of spiritual thirst. This place will cause the humbled saint to cry out for God to fill him or her with a greater revelation of Himself. It prepares the longing soul to accept Jesus' invitation found in John 7:37, "If any man thirst, let him come unto me, and drink."

In John 4:14, we are told the importance of this Living Water: "But whosoever drinketh of the water that I shall give him shall never thirst;

but the water that I shall give him shall be in him a well of water springing up into everlasting life."

On His cross, Jesus experienced great thirst so believers could experience the abundance of Living Water that is able to bring forth eternal life. The Christian's personal cross will bring each follower of Christ to a place of great spiritual thirst, so that each believer will seek the Giver of Living Water, and accept His invitation to come.

Victory comes out of suffering that is allowed to have its way in a person's life. The Apostle Paul reminds us in Romans 8:36-37, that although we are accounted as sheep for the slaughter, we are more than conquerors through Jesus. Peter tells us that suffering for the sake of Christ is acceptable to God because it establishes us in our spiritual life.[1] Paul encourages us by reminding us in Romans 8:17 of the reward of sharing in Christ's sufferings, "...that we may be also glorified together."

Suffering is not pleasant for the flesh, but it establishes the spirit of man upon the Rock of Ages, Jesus Christ. Have you been brought to the place of spiritual thirst (emptiness)? If you have, make sure you have accepted Jesus Christ's invitation to come to Him for Living Water. If you have not accepted His invitation, victory will elude you. God cannot fill you and bring you to fullness or completion. This completion is the next step on the road to Calvary.

The Finished Product

Jesus' death on the cross shows the everlasting love, incredible mercy, and unlimited grace of God. Oh, how He loves us! Oh, how He desires for us to know Him and experience the life He has for us! If only we would come and experience the fullness of God which is realized in Jesus.

Jesus' sixth statement helps us to give a sigh of relief. Up to this point, Jesus' suffering has been shrouded in despair, but this one statement gives hope and allows us to reach out in hope.

Before Jesus' statement can have the necessary effect, we must consider the mercy seat upon the Ark of the Covenant that was located in the Holy of Holies. Two angels, whose wings touched, overshadowed the mercy seat. Once a year, atonement was made for the sins of Israel.[2] It was as though judgment and mercy met in the middle to produce grace, while the blood of the sacrifice made atonement for sin.

On the cross of Christ, judgment and mercy once again would meet. But, this time, judgment would be satisfied for good, allowing mercy to reign unchallenged in the backdrop of Jesus' words, "Blessed are the merciful: for they shall obtain mercy" (Matthew 5:7).[4]

---

[1] 1 Peter 2:20; 5:10

[2] Leviticus 16

[4] Hebrews 9:12-15, 21-22; 10:10-20

The three words spoken from the cross at this time would confirm that judgment was satisfied, and mercy would be obtained for those seeking forgiveness and salvation. These words were followed by the fulfillment of all scriptures concerning Jesus' life on earth. They exposed the hypocrisy of religious works, and silenced the demands of all false gods and messiahs. These simple words bring the mercy of God to the forefront, while exalting grace to overshadow the affects of sin. They inspire hope, bring peace, and produce joy.

As I repeat these words, let them remind you of why Christ went to the cross and why we must follow His footsteps up the same path, bearing our cross. John 19:29 tells us that after Jesus declared He was thirsty, the guards lifted up a sponge on a stalk of the hyssop plant soaked with vinegar to Jesus' lips. John 19:30 then tells us, "When Jesus therefore had received the vinegar, he said, It is finished." (Emphasis added.)

Notice how Jesus drank of the bitter cup before making the declaration. All believers know what was finally finished, the work of redemption and deliverance. Even the stalk of hyssop points to another time in the history of Israel when God accomplished a similar feat on behalf of His chosen people. An innocent lamb was sacrificed for Passover. Its blood was then applied to the door posts with hyssop. When the Angel of Death spotted the blood, he passed over the home. God had provided a means of deliverance and protection through the blood of an innocent lamb in the midst of great bondage and judgment.[5]

At the cross of Jesus, the hyssop branch once again pointed us to a sacrifice. Jesus was God's ultimate provision for all mankind. He came to be the Passover Lamb in order to redeem the heirs of salvation. Hebrews 5:8-9 states, "Though he were a Son, yet learned he obedience by the things which he suffered; And being made perfect, he became the author of eternal salvation unto all them that obey him."

Hebrews 9:22 tells us what secured this salvation, "And almost all things are by the law purged with blood; and without shedding of blood is no remission."

Hebrews 10:14 shows us the purpose for Jesus' sacrifice on the cross: "For by one offering he hath perfected for ever them that are sanctified."

This is the complete picture of the finished work of salvation. Our salvation has been secured by the blood of Jesus, and maintained as He establishes us in perfection through the Holy Spirit. Jesus paid the complete price; therefore, nothing can be added. As I have stated many times, Jesus' suffering served as the interest payment and His blood the principle payment, which means the debt created by our sin has been paid in full. Praise God!

---

[5] Exodus 12

It is the heart of God to bring us to perfection or maturity. This perfection can only come by way of the cross. Just as the cross of Christ brought the plan of redemption to completion, our cross will bring us to spiritual maturity.

Romans 9:19-23 talks about God being our Potter. The Apostle Paul tells us that we are nothing more than earthen vessels that contain a great treasure, Jesus Christ. He also declared,

> But we have this treasure in earthen vessels, that the excellency of the power may be of God, and not of us. We are troubled on every side, yet not distressed; we are perplexed, but not in despair; Persecuted, but not forsaken; cast down, but not destroyed; Always bearing about in the body the dying of the Lord Jesus, that the life also of Jesus might be made manifest in our body (2 Corinthians 4:7-10).

Paul is describing the effects of the cross we must bear. It can never destroy us, but it can and will often bring us to the edge of destruction. We must take heart in such times because the work of our cross and the reality of Jesus' cross are designed to bring forth spiritual maturity as the Holy Spirit works the life of Christ in us. This is why Paul could make this statement with assurance, "Being confident of this very thing, that he which hath begun a good work in you will perform it until the day of Jesus Christ" (Philippians 1:6).

It is the Holy Spirit's goal to bring forth the life of Christ in each of us. This goal summarizes the will of God as stated in Romans 8:29, "For whom he did foreknow, he also did predestinate to be conformed to the image of his Son, that he might be the firstborn among many brethren." If the life of Christ is coming forth, unhindered in our lives, Jesus will be lifted up. And, if Jesus is lifted up, He will draw all men unto Himself.[6]

This work of perfection fine-tunes the spiritual quality that will produce the finished product of salvation. This spiritual virtue is known as faith.

Jesus' last statement can be found in Luke 23:46. He shows a total reliance on the Father. Heed His words. "Father, into thy hands I commend my spirit."

Total reliance on God implies unfeigned faith. At the end of this pure faith is salvation. Peter confirmed this in 1 Peter 1:7-9:

> That the trial of your faith being much more precious than of gold that perisheth, though it be tried with fire, might be found unto praise and honour and glory at the appearing of Jesus Christ: Whom having not seen, ye love; in whom, though now ye see him not, yet believing, ye rejoice with joy unspeakable and full of glory: Receiving the end of your faith, even the salvation of your souls.

---

[6] John 12:32

Unfeigned faith is only revealed when self is out of the way. It comes from a heart that displays purity and sincerity. This is why Jesus was able to declare, "Blessed are the pure in heart: for they shall see God" (Matthew 5:8). Child-like faith will bring us to the end of our journey. Remember, the route to Calvary is only wrought in us by the work of the cross.

We are told in 1 John 2:6, "He that saith he abideth in him ought himself also so to walk, even as he walked." Are you walking the course of Calvary? Honestly examine the route of the cross in the following table.

OUR CROSS	JESUS' SAYINGS	OUR RESPONSE	BEATTITUDES
Commanded	Forgiveness	Self-Denial	Preparation
Our Promise	Paradise	Pick up your cross	Poverty
The Cost	Worldly Associations	Willing to lose it all	Mournful
Separation	Desperation Loneliness	Holiness unto God	Meekness
Emptiness	Thirsty	Seeking out Jesus	Righteous
Perfection	Finished	Cross having its way	Mercy
Salvation	Reliance	Obtaining pure faith	Purity

Perhaps your examination shows that you have not denied yourself and picked up your cross. If so, you need to repent, adhere to Christ's command, and begin the trip up to Calvary. Your evaluation could reveal that you started out right, but now you are on a detour. If you are on a detour, go back to where you left your cross. Pick it up and continue on the course.

You may feel weary because your cross has brought you to a point of spiritual exhaustion. You may feel that you do not have what it takes to finish the course. Become like a King David. He was faced with great sorrow and challenges as recorded in 1 Samuel 30. His city had just been destroyed, his family taken captive, and his men were ready to stone him. However, 1 Samuel 30:6 tells us David encouraged himself in the Lord.

There is no choice. The cross is not an option, but a command. You need to respond and do that which is righteous. Deny self, pick up your cross, and follow Jesus to Calvary.

12

RESURRECTION LIFE

There are various aspects of the cross that we have been considering. We know that it represents preparation and victory, and it is the source where redemption was secured. However, the final aspect of it is that the work of the cross would be of no effect if Christ had not risen from the grave.

Peter said this on the day of Pentecost, "He seeing this before spake of the resurrection of Christ, that his soul was not left in hell, neither his flesh did see corruption. This Jesus hath God raised up, whereof we all are witnesses" (Acts 2:31-32).

The Apostle Paul made this declaration in 1 Corinthians 15:14, "And if Christ be not risen, then is our preaching vain, and your faith is also vain." The real victory of the cross is found in the resurrection of Jesus. Jesus knew the cross was not the end when He commended His spirit into His Father's hands, but the beginning.

Resurrection has been the hope of every believer. It is mentioned in the oldest book of the Bible, the book of Job. Job made this declaration in 19:25-27,

> For I know that my redeemer liveth, and that he shall stand
> at the latter day upon the earth: And though after my skin
> worms destroy this body, yet in my flesh shall I see God:
> Whom I shall see for myself, and mine eyes shall behold,
> and not another: though my reins be consumed within me.

The prophet Daniel made this statement in regards to the resurrection in 12:2, "And many of them that sleep in the dust of the earth shall awake, some to everlasting life, and some to shame and everlasting contempt."

Revelation 20:6, 13-14 confirms Daniel's prophetic vision:

> Blessed and holy is he that hath part in the first resurrection:
> on such the second death hath no power, but they shall be
> priests of God and of Christ, and shall reign with him a
> thousand years...And the sea gave up the dead which were
> in it; and death and hell delivered up the dead which were in
> them: and they were judged every man according to their
> works. And death and hell were cast into the lake of fire.
> This is the second death.

What is resurrection life? To understand it, we must consider Jesus Christ. He said in John 11:25, "I am the resurrection, and the life: he that believeth in me, though he were dead, yet shall he live." According to *Strong's Concordance*, resurrection means "to rise to life again or to stand up."[1] For there to be a resurrection, there must be death.

With His death in mind, Jesus made this reference about it in John 12:23-24, "The hour is come, that the Son of man should be glorified. Verily, verily, I say unto you, Except a corn of wheat fall into the ground and die, it abideth alone: but if it die, it bringeth forth much fruit."

Before Christ comes into a person's life, he or she is already dead in his or her trespasses or sins.[2] Once a person believes on Christ, life with resurrection power is placed within him or her through the presence of the Holy Spirit. The Apostle Paul explains the purpose of resurrection power in believers in this way, "Therefore we are buried with him by baptism into death: that like as Christ was raised up from the dead by the glory of the Father, even so we also should walk in newness of life" (Romans 6:4).

Resurrection means a new life coming forth. For a new life to make itself evident in the believer's life, he or she must first put down the old way of life or the "old man." Jesus confirmed this in John 12:25, "He that loveth his life shall lose it; and he that hateth his life in this world shall keep it unto life eternal."

The old man is the sinful, selfish disposition that was passed down from Adam. This disposition is the essence of self, as well as the idea of personal worth and rights. Jesus tells us that we must hate this disposition. By hating it, we can crucify it on a daily basis, along with all of its dictates and rights.

Paul talked about dying daily and told believers to count themselves dead to sin.[3] In Colossians 3:5, he commanded Christians to, "Mortify therefore your members which are upon the earth...."

The Apostle Paul also gives us insight in Galatians 5:16 into the next step believers must take to ensure this old man remains nailed to the cross. "This I say then, Walk in the Spirit, and ye shall not fulfil the lust of the flesh."

2 Corinthians 5:17 tells us we are new creations in Christ, old things are passed away. It is important to understand that positionally believers are new creations. In fact, their lives are hidden in Christ, and they have been positionally raised up with Christ and seated with Him in heavenly realms.[4] Obviously, before Christians can have a new life, old things must pass away. This can only occur if they are dying to the old ways, and striving to know Jesus in order to be like Him.

---

[1] # 386

[2] Ephesians 2:1

[3] Romans 6:11; 1 Corinthians 15:31

[4] Colossians 3:1; Ephesians 2:6

In Romans 13:14, the Apostle Paul instructs followers of Jesus to put on the Lord Jesus Christ. He made this powerful statement in Philippians 3:10-11, "That I may know him, and the power of his resurrection, and the fellowship of his sufferings, being made conformable unto his death; If by any means I might attain unto the resurrection of the dead."

Paul wanted to know the power of resurrection, but he acknowledged that he had to share in Jesus' sufferings, and become like him in death in order to attain it. It is Paul's willingness to become identified with Christ that established the righteousness and life of Christ in him. As Paul declared, "...nevertheless I live; yet not I, but Christ liveth in me" (Galatians 2:20).

There was much Paul understood about His life in Jesus. He called himself the chief of sinners because he understood his depravity. Yet, he experienced Christ's grace as His Lord made him a spiritual giant among men. He recognized the disposition of the old man, but knew what it meant to become a new man in Christ. The apostle described the new creation in detail in Colossians 3:5-10. Paul also understood that the mind had to be renewed for man to change and become new.[5] He realized that the mind could only change as the individual grew in the knowledge of Jesus.

The Apostle Paul was so caught up with Jesus that nothing else mattered to him. He even commented in 2 Corinthians 5:8 that he would prefer to be with the Lord, instead of in his physical body. He was willing to suffer for Jesus' sake because he knew in whom he believed. He had such confidence in Christ that he was ready to be poured out like a drink offering at the end of his life, for he knew his Righteous Judge would reward him, and he would reign with Him.[6]

Paul's life displayed the power of the cross. The cross of Jesus had humbled him, but his personal cross had been the instrument used to mortify the old man in him, so that the new man, Christ, could come forth in resurrection power and glory.

What about you? Have you picked up your cross and allowed it to bring forth the new man? If the new man is missing, then you must consider whether or not you have experienced resurrection power. The raising of the new life in us means the old man is being put to death, allowing the very likeness of Christ to be established in the inner man and ready to come forth in power and glory. As Paul declared, "For if we have been planted together in the likeness of his death, we shall be also in the likeness of his resurrection" (Romans 6:5).

---

[5] Romans 12:1-2; Ephesians 4:23-24
[6] 2 Timothy 1:12; 2:12; 4:6-8

13

A SMALL GLIMPSE

As we come to the end of this spiritual journey from the unveiling of the cross of Jesus in Genesis to its very fulfillment in the Gospels, I hope this small book has unveiled a revelation of God's incredible altar that proved to be challenging, inspiring, and life changing for you. I know this is just a short glimpse of the cross. Although the message and work of the cross are simple, they are also profound. In our frail and limited humanity, we will never grasp the complete work of redemption accomplished on this brutal instrument. In order to comprehend it, we would have to understand the depth of our selfish disposition and the infinite love, power, mercy, and grace of God.

An unknown writer once captured the ministry and death of Christ in this beautiful way:

> He who is the Bread of Life
> began His ministry hungering.
>
> He who is the Water of Life
> ended His ministry thirsting.
>
> He who was weary is our True Rest.
>
> He who paid tribute is the King of kings.
>
> He prayed yet hears our prayers.
>
> He wept but dries our tears.
>
> He was sold for thirty pieces of silver,
> yet redeemed the world.
>
> He was led as a lamb to slaughter,
> but is the good Shepherd.
>
> He died and gave His life, and by dying
> destroyed death for all who believe.

The message and principle of the cross are intertwined throughout the Word of God because they are the power of God unto salvation to everyone who believes. They stand at the heart of salvation, as well as being considered foolishness to those who are perishing.[1]

The Apostle Paul tearfully related how many lived as enemies of the cross of Christ. It is sorrowful beyond description to consider how people reject such love, mercy, and grace, but they do. Paul explained the fruits of these enemies. Their stomach is their god and glory is their shame. Their mind is on earthly things. He then reminded believers how their citizenship is in heaven, and that they should eagerly wait for the return of their Lord and Savior.[2]

Right now, examine your life. Do your attitudes and actions show you are a heavenly citizen or an earthly citizen? If your evaluation reveals that you belong to the world more than to Christ, repent. Allow the following words of Jesus to break you and bring you back to the foot of the cross. Prepare yourself to lose it all in order to gain the only worthwhile possession, the Person of Jesus Christ.

> *For God so loved the world, that he gave his only begotten Son, that whosoever believeth in him should not perish, but have everlasting life.*
>
> *For God sent not his Son into the world to condemn the world; but that the world through him might be saved.*
>
> *He that believeth on him is not condemned but he that believeth not is condemned already, because he hath not believed in the name of the only begotten Son of God.*
>
> *(John 3:16-18)*

---

[1] Romans 1:16; 1 Corinthians 1:18

[2] Philippians 3:18-20

Book Three

IN SEARCH
OF
REAL FAITH

INTRODUCTION

Jesus said in the last part of Luke 18:8, "Nevertheless when the Son of man cometh, shall he find faith on the earth?" Amazingly, Jesus did not ask if He would find religious fervor, works, or beliefs when He came back, but if He would find genuine faith. As various faith movements gain momentum in modern Christendom, this verse is foremost in my mind.

Preachers expound on the subject of faith as if they have been entrusted with "new revelations." Books abound which present endless formulas of how to practice faith, while at the same time, certain "elite" Christians claim to have a corner on it. These individuals are quick to judge those who appear spiritually inferior in their ability to possess this key to "worldly" prosperity.

The question we must ask ourselves is what is true faith? Scriptures reveal that the concept of faith is one doctrine we cannot overlook, nor can we leave its explanation and definition up to mere man. Hebrews 11:6 declares this about God, "...without faith it is impossible to please him." Ephesians 4:5 states there is only one faith, while 1 Peter 1:9 tells us the end of our faith is salvation.

In this small book, I intend to lead the reader on a search to discover true faith by exposing a number of pseudo faiths. How do I know about these false faiths? I have operated within their confines only to find frustration and disillusionment. I toyed with them, only to be let down by each one. I put my trust in their illusive power, only to end up with hot air. God has been gracious to me. He unmasked the futility of each of these pseudo faiths and gently taught me the essence of real faith.

Will this book exhaust this subject? Not hardly! Will it identify all false faiths? Probably not. Will it reveal the necessary formula that activates real faith? Maybe. Is it just another book about faith? I cannot begin to answer that question. You be the judge as you begin to examine yourself to see whether you are in the faith (2 Corinthians 13:5).

1

OPTIONAL FAITH

Walking by faith was one of the desires of my heart. When I heard missionaries and people of great faith expounding on seeing God's miraculous power, I remember thinking that I would have to walk by faith to witness God's greatness in the same way. I recall crying out to God, "God, I want to learn to walk by faith and not by sight."[1]

You need to understand that everything inside of me was sincere. I wanted to really learn what it meant to walk by the mountain-moving faith advocated in Scripture. I desired to see God move in and through my life in a powerful way. I no longer wanted to settle for the minimal or acceptable Christianity that I so often witnessed. I needed to come higher in my life with God to avoid spiritual stagnation.

The opportunity came for me to embark on this faith walk when I was put into full-time ministry. Oh, how excited I was to embark on such a journey! As you can imagine, I was going to learn to walk this supernatural walk. I was about to see God's power on my behalf.

I shared my excitement with my new co-laborer in the Gospel, Jeannette. I remember telling her, "Oh boy this is going to be exciting! I'm going to see God move on our behalf." Jeannette looked at me with shear panic on her face. What her look told me in so many words was, "Rayola, it is not romantic, it is not exciting, it is a hard, narrow path, and it is going to test you as you have never been tested before." Of course, I did not understand her attitude towards my apparent immaturity about this matter. Due to my over-zealous ways and inexperience, I had no idea as to the extent of the hardness of this walk.

My initial steps of faith were quite simple. They were simple because I knew where God wanted me to go and what He wanted me to do. He wanted Jeannette and me to travel from Idaho to Arizona to hold meetings. I was excited about these steps because I knew I was in God's will. Therefore, He would handle any unexpected or overwhelming obstacles. He did not fail me. I actually witnessed God miraculously move on our behalf more than once.

However, what happened after these initial steps was inevitable. The honeymoon I was having with my new walk came to an abrupt halt. Yes, it is very easy to walk by faith when you know where God wants you to

---

[1] 2 Corinthians 5:7

go and what He wants you to do. But what happens when you come to a place where you have no clear direction, and you are not hearing from God? This is exactly what happened to me early in my newfound life.

I discovered I was in a spiritual wilderness. While in this wilderness of spiritual drought, I gained insight as to the rocky road faith leads one. The mountain top experiences are wonderful, but they inevitably lead to the wildernesses of uncertainty, the valleys of confusion, and the plateaus of silence.

The idea of staying in this spiritual wilderness did not appeal to my romantic notions about the powerful Christian life. Nevertheless, I found myself destined to stay in this barren place until God said differently.

What does one do in the wilderness? Basically, you try to figure out what God wants you to do. After all, maybe God made a mistake. Or, possibly He does not realize you are in limbo waiting for His instruction. Maybe, on the other hand, God is speaking, and you cannot hear Him because you feel spiritually inept.

It was in this wilderness that I began to see mountains rise in front of me. One of the most obvious mountains concerned those wretched finances. The bills were starting to mount up. I started to consider my options. If God did not come through for me, I could draw the money out of my savings or tap into one of my IRAs. I reasoned that all was well because I had reliable backups to solve the problem. Hence, I found a temporary peace, but in what?

My trusty backups came in handy, but I discovered I was actually relying on these options to get us out of financial difficulties. One day, it struck me that these options were going to run dry. Then, what would this show me about my faith walk?

The Lord broke through my thoughts. In a gentle, but firm way, He told me, "Rayola, I am not an option, I AM THE SOLUTION! Until you get rid of all of your options and make Me the only solution, you will never understand what it means to walk by faith." It suddenly occurred to me that I was still looking to the world to solve my problems. I was actually relying on the very system that is at enmity with God.[2]

My heart's desire was to put total dependency on God to solve all of my problems, but I had fallen into a subtle trap. Because I could see the worldly options and not God, I simply made God the option and the world's means my solution.

I sat in amazement at my own frailty. God had to become my only solution, making me aware that the world could not even serve as a remote option. I had to somehow change the way I looked at the world in order to bring down my reliance on its importance and significance in my life.

I found myself calling out to God for help. My request was simple. "God I want you to be the solution. I don't know how to get pass these

---

[2] James 4:4

worldly avenues in my life. I don't know how to quit thinking in terms of worldly options in order to really let You become my solution to every challenge in my life." I actually gave God permission to turn the worldly switch off. I knew this would allow me to think only in the terms of God being my solution.

Was it easy to change my way of thinking? No! It was a wrestling match, but God was gracious enough to help me mentally make the switch to where I would not immediately focus on worldly options when confronted with a challenge.

This switch brought me to an intense period of testing. This testing revealed my real level of faith. I found I had none. What I did not realize was that every bit of true faith was a gift from God. He actually gives us a measure of faith as we need it.[3] The distribution of this measure of faith proves the principle we are always hearing concerning our great God. God may never be late on our behalf, but He is rarely ever early. My walk of faith showed me that my God is the I AM, the ever-present God who has all of our lives in full view. He never gets in a hurry nor is He late because He knows what we need and when we need it.

People work from the basis of circumstances that often creates fear that paralyzes or drives. Believers have to remember that God is sitting on the throne, and that He is aware or every aspect of their lives from each hair on their head down to the number of their days on earth.[4]

The day arrived when I came face-to-face with the realization that I lacked the kind of faith that would carry me through a test. We were faced with overdue bills and had no money. I had waited patiently for God to come through, but the days slipped by without any resolution in sight. The frustration began to build up. Here I was looking to God and not the world to solve my problems. What I was met with was DEAD SILENCE!

As frustration bubbled to the surface, I decided to go to the shed to get our daily supply of wood. While standing in the shed, waves of frustration erupted into anger.

For clarity's sake, there will be times of anxiety, doubt, and anger during the fiery test of a person's faith. If anyone gives any other impression, he or she is either lying or have never been at the place of great testing. The issue of faith does not come down to whether a person is going to have times of anxiety and doubt, but what he or she does with these fleshly tormentors. Personally, I have learned to be honest about them before the Lord.

While in the shed, this honesty burst forth loudly before God. I voiced every bit of my frustration and even anger with how He was handling the whole matter. I told Him His Word declares He never fails, but the

---

[3] Romans 12:3
[4] Matthew 10:30; Psalm 139:16

149

present situation implied the contrary. I asked Him, "Why don't you give us $22,000.00?"

In spite of my tantrum, God was gracious with me. I sensed He was quietly waiting for me to get my frustration out so He could speak to my spirit. After words spilled from my lips like ash from a volcano, I stood exhausted and silent. It was at that moment that He quietly answered my question.

"Rayola, if I gave you $22,000.00, you would not learn to trust Me." He then gently reminded me of my heartfelt prayer for Him to teach me to walk by faith and not by sight. I had sensed during my verbal frustration that I was acting like a spoiled child demanding my way. When He actually showed me He was simply honoring my prayer, I felt even lower. I knew I could chastise myself, but I realized His gentle chiding was bringing about a change in attitude that had greater eternal value and was sufficient to bring needed change to my attitude.

Finally, in a subdued voice, I asked Him, "Lord, what do You want me to do?"

Again, in a gentle manner, He answered. "Rayola, ask Me for what you need." What a surprise to ask for the obvious and the practical!

"Lord, I need rent money." Notice how far I had financially come down from my first impulsive, angry request for lots of money. However, I knew right at that moment that God had answered my prayer. I went into the house and made out a deposit slip. I recorded the amount of the one small check we had on hand, but kept the total space blank on the slip. I addressed the envelope to our out-of-state bank and left it unsealed.

We then went to our Post Office. I opened up our Post Office box. In our box were two envelopes. Can you guess what they contained? Within the two envelopes were two checks amounting to our rent. To throw in an extra blessing, one of the checks was from someone we did not personally know.

Later, I pondered my first real lesson on faith. I learned it is not the measure of faith God gives which moves mountains, but the faithfulness of our Great God. And, it is His faithfulness, and not our own, which becomes so precious and real in each fiery test of faith.[5]

I smiled as I thought about my silly request to be bestowed with $22,000.00. In today's world, it would quickly disappear. What was the significance of that figure? Then, I remembered the story of Gideon. Gideon started out with 22,000 men ready for battle, but God weeded this army down to 300 men. It was not the army that brought victory that day to Israel, but God Almighty who showed His might and power.[6] I realized the amount of money I requested and the size of Gideon's initial

---

[5] 1 Peter 1:6-7
[6] Judge 5:6-7

army is the world's solution to the obstacles. I once again recognized my dependency upon the world and not upon God.

It became clear to me why God gave instructions to Israel such as "hamstringing the enemy's horses and burning their chariots."[7] It is easier for God's people to rely upon worldly methods of deliverance and protection than upon God. God's desire is for His people to trust Him with their whole being in all matters.

Godly men such as Joshua and David obeyed God in the area of worldly dependencies, while Solomon accumulated great numbers of horses and chariots for his kingdom.[8] 1 Kings 11:4 makes this reference about Solomon's heart, "...that his wives turned away his heart after other gods: and his heart was not perfect with the LORD his God, as was the heart of David his father."

Solomon's association with the world (foreign wives) and his apparent dependency on its provision and protection led him into blatant idolatry. This is why we read this warning from Jesus in Matthew 6:24, "No man can serve two masters: for either he will hate the one, and love the other; or else he will hold to the one, and despise the other. Ye cannot serve God and mammon."

Another lesson I learned is that the steps of faith are a choice. In my years of walking this hard path, God has brought me to many crossroads. At one crossroad, He actually showed me Lot's plush valleys of Sodom and Gomorrah and the fiery furnace of Shadrach, Meshach, and Abednego.[9] He then told me to choose.

I remembered how Lot became victim to an evil king and his uncle Abraham had to save him. 2 Peter 2:8 tells us Lot was tormented (vexed) in his spirit because of the sin around him. Later on, Lot lost everything including his wife when judgment fell upon these two cities.[10]

In the case of the three Hebrew men who chose the fiery furnace to the sin of committing idolatry, we see an opposite scenario. They did not end up in the furnace alone. There was a fourth figure in their midst. We know this fourth figure to be the Son of God. They were delivered with no evidence of their fiery ordeal. And they, along with their God, were exalted among men.[11]

Needless to say, I have chosen the fiery furnace each time. Have I been gracious about going into the oven? NOT HARDLY! However, I reckoned it was far greater being where the presence of God was than to be surrounded by the world's best and miss Him.

As I studied the people of faith, I could actually see where they chose the path of the unseen. They were aware that God does not want

---

[7] See Joshua 11:6 refer to Deuteronomy 17:16.
[8] Joshua 11:9; 2 Samuel 8:4; 2 Chronicles 9:25
[9] Genesis 13:10; Daniel 3
[10] Genesis 14:19
[11] Daniel 3

any of His people to settle for optional faith in regard to the tangible things of this world. He desires them to find their security in the immovable Rock, Jesus Christ. This precious Rock of the Ages will stand for eternity, while the world will pass away.[12]

What are you putting your faith in right now, Jesus Christ or the things of the world? The world will choke out the Word of God. It will give you a false sense of security and cause you to chase after an earthly retirement rather than eternal rewards. And, when the storms come, which they will, you will fall because you are standing on the ever shifting sands of the world.[13]

The choice is yours.

---

[12] 1 John 2:17
[13] Matthew 7:24-28; 13:22

2

INTROVERTED FAITH

An international evangelist gave us much needed insight about walking by faith. He told us when evangelists share about times of miracles and victories, they rarely discuss the many steps of struggling and preparation that leads to these inspirational and victorious times.

My faith walk has shown me that the different steps of faith can be compared to a baby learning to walk. All babies start out by crawling. As they gain muscle strength, they graduate to pulling themselves up by holding on to a stable object. Solid objects help them take their first steps. These celebrated steps are a form of exercising their weak legs. Beginning steps that eventually lead to walking occur two ways: 1) When the child independently takes a couple of steps as he or she is coaxed by a trustworthy person, and 2) when the child forgets his or her weakness and takes steps to get to a desired destination.

A Christian's spiritual "crawling" experience begins at salvation. It is not enough to be born again, there must be a maturing.[1] This level of maturing will not occur until the person begins to partake of the Word of God.

Roman 10:17 states, "Faith comes by hearing and hearing by the word of God." Christians can only learn to take steps of faith after they begin to cling to the Word of God as their only source of strength. The Word of God begins to establish the Christian on the stable Rock, Jesus Christ, who needs to become his or her main focus for each new step.[2]

A Christian's spiritual legs can only gain momentum when he or she begins to obey what he or she hears.[3] It is possible for Christians to have the cart before the horse. They want God to prove His faithfulness before they obey. God's Word shows that obedience must come first, and then God will show His faithfulness.

We see this principle in many scriptural examples. By faith, Abraham left home and family to go to an unknown place destined by God. In the case of some of the plagues sent against Pharaoh, the Israelites had to obey the commands of Moses to ensure they were spared from the forth-

---

[1] Hebrews 5:11-14

[2] Matthew 16:18

[3] James 1:22-25; 2:14-26

coming judgments. The priests had to step into the Jordan River by faith before the waters parted, allowing all of Israel to cross. Rahab believed the spies and put a scarlet string in the window to save her family. Ruth, the Moabitess, by faith followed Naomi to an unknown place in search of the true God, only to later be exalted among women.[4]

After a person spiritually learns to walk, what comes next? Running of course! Believers must learn to run the race. Paul made reference to this race in 1 Corinthians 9:24-27, Philippians 3:10-14, and 2 Timothy 4:7. The Apostle Paul's statements in the New Testament about running the race gave no allowance for spectators. Christians therefore cannot afford to sit in the stands and watch other believers run this race. All Christians must be in the competition to reach the prize. Paul made this comment in Philippians 3:14, "I press toward the mark for the prize of the high calling of God in Christ Jesus."

At the end of his life, Paul made this declaration in 2 Timothy 4:8a, "Henceforth there is laid up for me a crown of righteousness." Running the Christian race is not based on speed, but endurance. It is a marathon that requires commitment and intense preparation. The course is hard and it spans the duration of the Christian journey through the present age.

The Apostle Paul talked candidly about the right motivation behind his commitment to run the race, as well as the attitude behind the preparation. In 1 Corinthians 9:22-23, he declared he was running the race for the sake of the Gospel. This commitment was upheld at the end of his life when he was able to say, "I have finished the course..."[5]

Paul's attitude was inspired by the eternal blessings before him. This upright attitude enabled him to put to death the flesh to ensure he would not be disqualified from the race. Such a struggle involved a battle that did not last just a season, but required a daily death on his part. We know the end result of the battle Paul fought when he made this declaration in 2 Timothy 4:7, "I have fought a good fight..."[6]

This daily battle involves the flesh. The battle with the flesh encompasses the real test for the Christian runner.[7] If flesh is not put down, true faith cannot be firmly established in the life of a Christian. Hebrews 12:1 puts it best, "...let us lay aside every weight, and the sin which doth so easily beset us, and let us run with patience the race that is set before us."

In my years of running this course, I have had to come face-to-face with the ever-present enemy of the flesh. This enemy is designed to take our eyes, emotions, and attention off of Jesus, and put them on the world. At this point, our flesh becomes our source of strength, inspiration,

---

[4] Hebrew 11:8-10; Exodus 9:13-26; 11; 12; Joshua 3:13-17; 6; Ruth 1
[5] 2 Timothy 4:7
[6] 1 Corinthians 9:27; 15:31
[7] Galatians 5:16-21

and hope. The prophet Jeremiah warned us of the pending destruction of putting confidence in our flesh in Jeremiah 17:5, "Cursed be the man that trusteth in man, and maketh flesh his arm, and whose heart departeth from the LORD."

One of the works of the flesh is the sin of pride. Pride is the most subtle idol in our society today. It sets an individual up with false confidence, while tormenting his or her fragile ego with fears, doubts, and turmoil. Pride competes with God and ultimately declares supremacy over His right to reign in a person's life. If God is not allowed to be God, true faith is reduced to a word only, devoid of power and authority. The Lord has been faithful to bring me face-to-face with this culprit many times.

There was one incident that brought to light the sinister depth of my own pride. I was commissioned by a missionary school to write a discipleship course for the missionaries to teach overseas. I had already started the project upon request of one of the missionaries affiliated with the school. I worked around 15 hours a day, seven days a week for three months to complete the course.

During the writing of the course, my missionary friend became over zealous about the course and started to present it to the other missionaries involved with the school. At the time, I felt the head of the missionary school would not be pleased. However, my concerns went unheeded and were lost in the momentum of her genuine excitement to promote the course. Finally, the day came to present the course to the head of the missionary school. He was receptive and well pleased. A contract was exchanged between us, and we went on our way thinking we had scored a long overdue victory. The next day, it came crashing down around us.

Word got back to him about the early promotion and possible sales of the course to the missionaries. Even though I had informed him in the meeting of our promotion, he instantly became angry. He sent a letter to each missionary instructing each of them to have nothing to do with us or our course.

A week went by before he contacted us. In that week, he made a decision to make us an example by stripping us of our ministry license. Scripturally, the man was in disobedience to true ministry, which is restoration, not restitution. He should have given us a chance to backtrack our actions, but instead, he judged and condemned us without confronting us.

Already exhausted from pushing myself to extremes, I walked out of his office in total despair. I could not understand the absurdity of it all. Supposedly, this was a godly man who harped about ministry always being motivated, surrounded by, and acting in love, but by his actions, he did not demonstrate love, but arrogance and cruelty.

I had to also face the fact that God was trying to warn us about this individual. My co-laborer and I had ignored suspicions about the spirit that was present with this leader, had brought a factor of fear and control to those around him which was contrary to the fruit of the Spirit. His present actions were consistent with the unloving spirit he had displayed at different times. Even though I believe God had spared us from an individual who displayed a cult mentality rather than the love of God, I felt it was all totally unfair.

I immediately went into rebellion and deep depression. I was angry at God for not coming through for us. I had worked so hard. How could He let me down? I refused to read my Bible or pray. I shut down spiritually and emotionally and gave in to self-pity. My perspective became narrower as I focused on self. Eventually, I found myself spiraling downward into a mental mire of hopelessness.

The Lord allowed me the luxury of remaining in my mire for a month. But, after the month, He told me to repent. I will never forget the scene. A seasoned evangelist was staying with us at the time. As we were fellowshipping, the Holy Spirit convicted me of my need to confess my rebellion to her. She graciously listened as I admitted the events of my nightmarish month. After my confession, I realized I was just beginning to climb out of a large pit I had dug for myself.

Looking back on that time, I wished God had pulled my rope sooner. The pit was deep, and it took me a couple of months to climb out of it. In those months, I had to face the wickedness of my own pride. My pride sat on the throne, judging the Judge of the Universe. It had given me rights to falsely accuse God of indifference and unfairness as a means to justify my anger. Perhaps it was my judgmentalism behind my silent accusation towards Him that prompted my Holy God to take a backhoe to the depth of my pride. I was shocked at its unveiling.

The major unveiling came when I was considering some of the people God used in the furtherance of His Gospel. I could see where some were full of pride, while others were novices, trying to be a "somebody" in ministry. I remember presenting my case to God in my "humblest" fashion, which went like this: "Lord, You have invested so much in me. This person has pride, this individual does not have the goods, and this one is nothing more than a religious hypocrite." In my mind, my case was exquisite,

However, when the Lord spoke to me, the case that I had so cleverly developed quickly disintegrated before my eyes. He basically said, "Rayola, I do not need you."

What a shock this statement was to my over-zealous opinion of my spiritual worth. God, not needing me? Like many other servants, I harbored a foolish idea that God needed me to do His bidding, yet Jesus said the stones would cry forth if man did not do so during His triumphant entry. I was then reminded that He could use a donkey if He so deemed necessary.[8]

---

[8] Romans 12:3; 1 Corinthians 10:12; Luke 19:40; Numbers 22:28

I began to see how mere man often thinks the world revolves around him. He wants to control His world, be adored, and worshipped by others. No wonder God resists the proud and hates the prideful look.[9]

As I began to realize the majesty of God, I had to recognize that man is simply a vessel, while our great God is the potter. Who is mere man to assume the Potter needs him when He has the ability to create a new vessel at any time out of insignificant material?[10]

I sat in my chair, smarting from the revelation of God's greatness and my depravity. The reality of His statement burned into my spirit in the silence that followed. He once again broke through my thoughts as brokenness and humility began to enfold my wounded pride. "But, Rayola, I desire to use you."

I was reminded of the cross. The cross is the instrument God uses to prepare His vessels. In fact, we are commanded to pick up our cross daily and follow our Lord.[11] The cross represents separation and death. The Lord gave insight into the first separation that must take place in His servant's life in Matthew 10:37: "He that loveth father or mother more than me is not worthy of me: and he that loveth son or daughter more than me is not worthy of me." He will separate you from your family ties.

Abraham left his family and homeland to travel to the Promised Land. This separation was quite decisive. We see other godly men such as Samuel and John the Baptist being set apart from their families at an early age in order to be prepared and made available for service.[12]

Such family ties often involve idolatry. In my case, my family was tied into a cultic belief. Separation from unscriptural beliefs and the idols they erect can be quite abrupt and drastic for anyone. It is not just a matter of setting self apart from the idols, but it means all loyalties and emotional attachments to them must be severed and replaced with the real things of God. Physical separation can be easy, but spiritual and emotional separation can be quite frightening and difficult. In fact, some people never can quite make the separation. Bondage and condemnation are the results.

This separation continues throughout the Christian walk. Friends, material possessions, and dreams are a few examples of possible weights that must be held lightly and given up quickly when God asks for them.

At times, the loss can become overwhelming. You question the Lord. Why must I lose so much? He will gently remind you how He gave His life for each of us, as well as the specific promise He made to His disciples in Matthew 19:29. "And every one that hath forsaken houses, or brethren, or sisters, or father, or mother, or wife, or children, or lands, for

---

[9] James 4:6; Proverbs 6:16-17

[10] Romans 9:15-21

[11] Luke 9:23

[12] Genesis 12:1; 1 Samuel 2:18-21; Matthew 11:7-12

my name's sake, shall receive an hundredfold, and shall inherit everlasting life."

What is the real purpose of the cross? Is it just to separate us from that which holds no real value, or does it have a greater significance that we must embrace? The answer is yes, it has a greater significance. The goal of the cross is to separate us from personal pride which is defined in one word, "self."

Self is our identity, and so many times, our identity is wrapped up in family, friends, empty possessions, and beliefs. The cross must separate us from those things that determine personal worth according to the world in order for us to gain our true identity that can only be found in Christ. The separation from personal identity requires a death experience. Jesus confirmed this in Matthew 10:39, "He that findeth his life shall lose it: and he that loseth his life for my sake shall find it." What a powerful truth! I had to lose the essence of who I was and who I hoped to be in order to find my life in Christ.

This death experience to self was and continues to be a struggle for me. It requires me to give up my rights to control my world. It calls me to humble my heart before God, submit my will to His way, align my emotions to His heart cry, and allow my mind to be transformed by the Holy Ghost. It means I can no longer rely on my own power, strength, feelings, or conclusions. I must recognize my poverty, mourn my depravity, and become hungry for God's righteousness.[13]

In my struggles with my own cross, I am forever reminded of the cross of Christ. I have learned there are two sides to the cross of Jesus. There is the backside of the cross that casts a shadow and the front of the cross where light permeates the area. Some Christians remain in the shadow of the cross. They have come to the knowledge of their need for salvation by encountering the cross, but have remained a comfortable distance from it.

Other Christians have desired more in their relationship with Christ. They have walked up to the front of the cross and began to realize the ultimate sacrifice of God. They tremble and bow before Love, Grace, and Truth personified. As they sense their hopeless condition, they cry for mercy only to be lifted up to look into the wonderful face of their forgiving Lord. They then begin to boldly embrace this rugged instrument. They start to identify with the sufferings and death of their Lord as never before. They know in so doing, they will gain resurrection power and become identified with Jesus in His glory. They will ultimately both live and reign with Him.[14]

I realize my steps of faith will always lead me back to the cross, to the decision of death to the dictates of my flesh, and the god of self in order to possess the God of the Universe, Jesus. What an experience

---

[13] Roman 12:1 & 2; Zechariah 4:6; Matthew 5:3-6
[14] Colossians 3:10; Romans 8:17; 2 Timothy 11:12

this death to self has been for me! In it all, I found my identity in Christ. I now understand what Colossians 3:3 means. "For ye are dead, and your life is hid with Christ in God." What a revelation of Christ that I have received through it all.

Are you in the race or are you simply being a spectator? When was the last time you chose death and picked up your cross? How long ago did you encounter the cross of Jesus? The way you can test whether you have submitted to the cross recently is how much of the self-life still remains in place without any challenge, conviction, or the mark of death.

3

PIOUS FAITH

Very few Christians have avoided suffering from the effects or consequences of pious faith. This form of faith seems religious and good, as well as having a form of godliness, but it denies the power.[1] People who operate in this faith may be able to impress others with their knowledge of scriptures, but they will lack godly change in their life, as well as prove to be void of godly authority.

A good example of pious faith is the Pharisees. They looked and talked the part of righteous, committed leaders, but Jesus said this about their spiritual condition in Matthew 15:8-9, "This people draweth nigh unto me with their mouth, and honoureth me with their lips; but their heart is far from me. But in vain they do worship me, teaching for doctrines the commandments of men."

It is quite easy to adopt pious faith. I did, early in my Christian walk, and found myself slipping into a religious code of rights and wrongs. I adopted these codes because of the spiritual influences of those around me who actually practiced this self-righteous faith with both skill and ease. I quickly learned how to play the game and talk the talk, which allowed me to join the so-called 'elite" few who appeared to have a corner on God concerning every doctrine and issue. I quickly fell into the endless trap of becoming judgmental towards other Christians who did not live up to my ironclad religious standards.

The Lord allowed me a season of six years to practice this religiosity. During this time, I added biblical knowledge to my already growing conceit. I established my so-called "righteousness" by doing good works that gave the impression I was going beyond the call of duty. I quoted scriptures, defended my beliefs, and used the Bible as an unmerciful sword against anyone who opposed me.

Outwardly, I appeared to be religious, but inwardly, there was a gnawing void growing in my spiritual life. I lost all joy in regard to my salvation as I started to compromise scriptural principles that caused me to become entrapped in sin. This put me in the classification of a genuine hypocrite.

---

[1] 2 Timothy 3:5

I began to realize my self-righteous piety isolated me because I dared not share my struggles or failings with others. Even though many probably saw through my foolishness, I had to keep the appearance of righteousness in the forefront to hide my hypocrisy. Through it all, I sensed something was desperately wrong, but I could not put my finger on it. It was as though I was falling into an endless pit where destruction awaited me. It was just a matter of time.

I did hit bottom and the crash still rings in my ears. I vividly remember the fateful day it happened. I was alone in the house and under a cloud of hopelessness. I knew I had taken a terrible detour in my Christian life, but I had no idea how to get back on track. I sat empty, feeling that I had left something very important behind. I had no joy, no hope, and now, I stood in condemnation without any defense. I was faced with my spiritual condition and I hated it.

To this day, I do not know how it happened, but I fell on my face and began to cry out to God. I felt everything inside of me breaking as a cleansing river of tears washed through my soul. As I laid in brokenness and repentance, something miraculous and beautiful happened. Jesus gently picked me up and took me into the Most Holy Place.

I had heard about this intimate place of fellowship with God, but had never discovered it in my own spiritual life. Prayer, which marked this intimate place, was simply a hard duty to me and not a privilege. Humility that leads to worship served as the entrance to this holy place, but it was far from me because of my self-righteous piety. My need to fellowship with my God in His Holy of Holies had been drowned out by my various religious activities.

Some people come up to the door of this most holy place seeking fellowship, but few ever venture beyond the entrance into the actual room because of fear, pride, and unbelief. Surprisingly, I was in the room, and the reality of it humbled and overwhelmed me.

I will never forget what I found in this special place. I found forgiveness, restoration, and a confirmation that God was going to use me in spite of myself. The joy of my salvation was restored, and hope was resurrected as I realized God is who He says He is.

The excitement was still lingering when I left the room two hours later. I made up my mind to fully serve God, and I wanted to start by telling the world there is indeed a treasure awaiting all who will come. As I ran out the door with new fervor, I felt a gentle hand on my shoulder restraining me. "But Lord, I want to tell others about this place." I could not understand why He restrained me from my new-found mission.

Then I heard the words, "Rayola, first learn who I am." I stopped dead in my tracks. I knew *of* Him and *about* Him, but I realized I did not *know* Him. I was suddenly faced with the missing link in my Christian life. It was Jesus Himself.

As I stood silently before Him, He asked me the next question. "Rayola, what have you done *for* Me?" I had my list, but I knew it lay limp at His feet as a miserable sacrifice.

The next question penetrated my heart. "Rayola, what have you done *with* Me? Have you walked with Me, talked with Me, and supped with Me?" I hung my head in shame.

The Church of Ephesus came to mind. The Christians of this local fellowship had many virtuous qualifications. They worked hard, were persevering, did not tolerate wickedness in their midst, tested those who claimed to be leaders, endured hardships, and were long-suffering. However, Jesus said He had one thing against them. They had left their first love.[2]

I had not only left my first initial love for Jesus, but I had forgotten to fall in love with Him. I simply had substituted an intimate relationship with God Incarnate with religious garb, thereby, never allowing my love for Him to mature.

The invitation was very clear, "Come and sup with Me, Rayola." No more religious games. No more faked righteousness. It was time for me to open the door of my whole heart to my Lord, and let Him come in.

For the next two years, I sat at His table and learned much about the character and ways of Jesus. It was a rewarding time for me, but also a revealing time. My spiritual life was put out on the table for me to examine, and the greatest examination that took place involved unmasking my pious faith, piece by piece.

The first part of my pious faith to be challenged was my self-righteousness. I had acted like I was the spiritual expert, which made me a judge. The Lord reminded me of all the people I had judged in my expertise. I was not examining their fruits or testing their doctrinal foundation, but judging their hearts and call. I had simply judged many because they had not jumped on the bandwagon to support the spiritual causes I had deemed important. I had felt they were spiritually insensitive and actually missing God's calling.

God revealed to me that I was actually judging Him and the work He was doing behind the scenes in people's lives. He showed me that while I was busy judging these individuals, He was actually working in some of their lives to bring about eternal worth. Some of these people were actually where He wanted them to be.

The idea of actually judging God caused me to tremble. I had no idea that self-righteousness reigned supreme along with my religious codes and standards. They all had served as judge and jury. Although all of my religious attempts and notions had an outward appearance of righteousness, the love of God was missing. People were never edified by my cruel, harsh, condemning religious activities.

---

[2] Revelation 2:1-7

I quickly repented of my religious pride. I realized it had served as the motivation behind my pious faith. I asked God to help me beyond the small boundaries of my own righteousness that stood as filthy rags before Him. I then requested Him to fill my heart with His love and compassion. I knew His love would cover a multitude of sins and reveal people's hearts and potential in Christ.[3] He graciously answered my prayer.

The next area He convicted me about was the handling of His Word. My, how smart and clever I thought I had become with the Bible! I knew it well and could use it effectively in any confrontation. I have to admit, I ignored Titus 3:9, "But avoid foolish questions, and genealogies, and contentions, and strivings about the law; for they are unprofitable and vain."

The Lord reminded me that His Word is a sword, and He showed me what I had done with it.[4] I had dissected the Word into various pieces so that I could examine it according to my own perverted, limited understanding. The Lord asked me, "Is this sword capable of being an effective weapon?"

My answer was, "No."

Then I watched Him carefully put the sword back together. He sharpened the blade, brought the beauty back to the handle, and the shine back to the steel. I admired it as He held it, and I wondered what He was going to do with this well designed weapon. The next thing I remember, He took the sword and thrust it through me. It was as though scales came off of my spiritual eyes, and for the first time I was looking into a mirror.

The mirror was the Word of God.[5] I could see how I had abused this powerful weapon. Yes, I had dissected it for knowledge, rather than allowing it to dissect me. Instead of it serving as my instructor, I became a judge over it. Instead of using it as a weapon against Satan, I made it into a hammer to try to pound people into my way of thinking.

I realized I had pursued the letter of the Law rather than the Spirit behind the Word.[6] The result proved to be devastating to my spiritual well-being as the Word had been rendered lifeless and powerless to change my life.

The Lord brought to my mind the purpose behind the Word. The Word was inspired by the Spirit of God to bring much needed correction, reproof, and instruction in righteousness to me. It is in righteousness that a person can be entrusted with the revelation of the Living Word, Jesus Christ.[7]

---

[3] Isaiah 64:6; 1 Peter 4:8
[4] Ephesians 6:17; Hebrews 4:12
[5] James 1:21-25
[6] Romans 7:6; 2 Corinthians 3:6
[7] Galatians 1:12; Ephesians 3:3-4; 2 Timothy 3:16

It is the revelation of the Living Word that brings the written Word to life. I suddenly realized why all my scriptural knowledge had no power to change my life. I had chased after knowledge, rather than seeking to know God. What a subtle exchange it had been! I had exchanged the real thing for images, concepts, and self-exaltation.

This reality struck at my religious pride, but I did not realize that this was the Lord's way of preparing me for the next step. He was about to reveal the source behind my pious faith.

One day I was pondering the sins I had fallen into while I had operated in self-righteous piety. I began to categorize the severity of each sin. As I sat in shame wondering how I could deny my Lord with such actions, He spoke to my spirit. "Rayola, it is all idolatry." His statement surprised me. Idolatry was a lesser sin to me, but I could tell by the intensity of the statement that God did not view idolatry in the same manner.

As I thought about idolatry, the Lord began to parade all of my idols before my eyes. Self-righteousness, knowledge, religious works, spiritual leaders, church affiliation, and doctrine were just a few of the sacred cows that marched proudly in the procession. As all of these idols stood erect, I realized each one had mocked the real things of God. Although some of these things were good, they had subtly become substitutes for Christ's righteousness, wisdom, redemption, holiness, grace, truth, rule, and righteous judgment in my life. Through the unveiling of all my idols, the Lord showed me that I had put faith in the things of God, rather than in the person of God. This false faith was nothing more than idolatrous in nature and practice.

I must confess that it was hard to look at the idols that had served my self-righteousness so well through the years of my endless detours. They also had served my selfish purposes with amazing results. However, I knew one thing, and that is, I wanted the real God. So, I asked Him to bring down all my idols, and down they came. I can still hear it in my spirit as the crash rang throughout the corridors of my soul. When it was all over, the remains laid at the feet of Jesus.

Years later, I am still humbled by the remembrance of this time when I met with Jesus and started supping with Him. I realize that in the first few years of my Christian life I had treated Jesus as if He were simply a concept, an idea, or a force rather than a person. It is because Jesus is a person that I can have an intimate relationship with God.

Every once in awhile, the Holy Spirit reminds me of the privilege I have to commune with my Lord. It is hard to believe that I had made my first years as a Christian so difficult. All that time, He patiently waited for me to realize I had left Him behind, and when I finally turned around, He was right there to lead me into a true relationship with Him.

Are you in bondage to the idols of pious faith? Is the Word dead or alive to you? Have you left your first love? Right now, do you need to turn around to see if you have left Jesus behind? If you have, you need to know that He is waiting for you to come back, open the door of your heart, and begin to sup with Him.

4

EXPEDIENT FAITH

I remember the first time I became aware of practicing expedient faith. My co-laborer in the Gospel, Jeannette, and I were at a very low point in our Christian ministry. We felt as if we were in spiritual straitjackets. This gave us a sense that there was not any room to move or breathe, spiritually or financially.

It appeared as if our ministry was dead in the water. We were in a tight financial situation that hung around our necks like an anchor. Our desires were sincere. All we wanted was to be set free to serve our God in liberty.

As we moved in and out of self-pity, we pleaded our case. "God we cannot handle much more. We have been in this bondage for three years. We are only your handmaidens, but You have promised us You would be our Husband, Father, and constant companion. Lord give us a break because our backs are up against the wall."

This pitiful plea happened on a Saturday night. I remember the day well because the next morning we visited a friend's church. Both Jeannette and I expected something to happen in the service. We both knew in our spirits that God would somehow bring things into perspective.

Immediately following the opening prayer, the pastor turned the podium over to a man. To my surprise, he began the service with a song I had never heard. The song went something like this, "Maybe right now you feel like your back is up against the wall... but remember, His was against the cross."

There is nothing like a jolt of eternal perspective to put you in your proper place. I lost my breath. Did we not just declare the night before that our backs were up against the wall? I suddenly realized how easy it is to foolishly accuse God of not understanding our plight. We tend to forget all of our suffering is menial compared to Jesus' ordeal on the road to Calvary. He was God, but He took on flesh to become identified with mankind. He was King of kings, but He did not have a place to lay His head. He was Lord, but He took on the form of a servant so that everyone that believes could become a child of God. He was tempted in all areas, but He overcame. He was perfect, but He became sin so His followers could be made righteous before God.[1]

In light of Jesus' sufferings, I realized it was now time for me to examine my own heart attitude. Why did I want God to deliver me quickly? Was my back truly against the wall or was I just uncomfortable in my situation? Was I close to being destroyed or was my self-pity working overtime? As I asked these questions, God began to give me a lesson on deliverance.

There are two types of deliverance. One type of deliverance is when you are delivered from something. Salvation is a good example of this type of deliverance. We are delivered from death to life, from darkness to light, and from Satan's rule to the Lordship of Jesus Christ.[2]

The second type of deliverance appears to be the more common of the two types in the faith walk. It is when God delivers you through a situation. Noah was delivered through the flood, the Israelites through the Red Sea, and Shadrach, Meshach, and Abednego through the fiery oven.[3]

I began to understand what Peter meant when he made this observation in his first epistle:

> Wherein ye greatly rejoice, though now for a season, if need be, ye are in heaviness through manifold temptations: That the trial of your faith, being much more precious than of gold that perisheth, though it be tried with fire, might be found unto praise and honour and glory at the appearing of Jesus Christ (1 Peter 1:6-7).

Many people have a misconception about God's deliverance. They feel the greater testimony comes when God expediently delivers someone from a situation. Although this is true in some cases, it does not apply to every situation. Deliverance from or out of a situation establishes a testimony that speaks of what God can do. However, in some cases the greatest testimony is not about what God can do, but who God is. When God delivers us through a situation, He is present. As a person chooses faith in God during such times, he or she discovers God's faithfulness and sustaining power through the trial.

I remember the day I cried out to God about the numerous trials that seemed endless. "God, look how I am trying to serve You, and all I encounter are difficulties. Our car is not working. We are in debt, and do not have any reserves to really fix it without going deeper into debt." The Lord broke through my complaints with Matthew 5:45, "That ye may be the children of your Father which is in heaven: for he maketh his sun to rise on the evil and on the good, and sendeth rain on the just and on the unjust."

---

[1] 2 Peter 1:8-13; Philippians 2:5-11; Hebrews 4:15; 2 Corinthians 5:21

[2] Colossians 1:12-14

[3] Genesis 6-8; Exodus14; Daniel 3

Everyone is faced with trials regardless of their spiritual status. Serving God will not exempt His servant from trying times. In fact, it guarantees more suffering. However, faith in God gives a person confidence that God is using each situation to work something out for his or her spiritual benefit and His glory.[4]

The Lord showed me that if others are to believe His people's faith is real, they must go through situations that make them more pliable in His hands. Believers cannot effectively testify of the beauty and deliverance of God if they have not first experienced it for themselves.[5]

As Peter implied, trials are a means of producing genuine faith in Christians' spiritual lives. In other words, real faith will cost. And, the price for my faith became clear. It involved my flesh. I realized the fiery test of my faith was hard on my flesh. Every time it felt inconvenienced or uncomfortable, it began to cry out for immediate deliverance.

Each time the deliverance did not come in the time or way that was expected, the selfishness of my flesh became visible as it raised its ugly head in false accusation and self-pity. I could see that my flesh wanted to be pampered and adored at all times. It did not like to be inconvenienced or challenged in any way.

The faith walk began to shake every area of my life where the flesh had freely reigned. I found myself not only confronting the flesh, but also disciplining almost all of its appetites. As I came face-to-face with my flesh, I realized I could not simply appease the pride, satisfy the lust of the eyes, and give way to the ongoing demands of my fleshly longings without betraying my life in God.

That day in church, I recognized it was not my back up against the wall; it was my flesh that was being nailed to the cross. The flesh was not about to go graciously to the cross, nor would it remain silent as it was being nailed to it. It would display everything from self-pity to fake nobility. If it could not be exalted, it would become a suffering victim. It never ran out of excuses as it continued to demand that it must live to ensure my very existence. It harbored rights at every point of self-denial and whimpered about inconveniences.

I used to feel condemned when I found myself giving way to the flesh in the major trials that confronted me. I felt like a total failure after throwing my spoiled tantrums before God. Why could I not be meek and trusting in each of these trials? Why did God continue to put up with my whining?

One day, the Lord spoke to my heart about the matter of my flesh. He told me, "Rayola I do not listen to your flesh, but your heart, and your heart is asking me to have My way." The only way I could respond was to thank Him for honoring my heart and not listening to my insidious flesh.

---

[4] 2 Timothy 3:12; Romans 8:28
[5] See 2 Corinthians 1:3-10

The fiery trials of our faith will spiritually stretch us beyond our wildest imagination. There was one incident when I innocently, but impulsively, made a bad decision. Within two months of the decision, the ministry began to reap the consequence for my bad judgment. I began to feel the heat. I speculated that I was at a major breaking point emotionally. I felt I could not take much more of the process. I called out to God and told Him I could not be stretched any further without being destroyed. What happened after that still amazes me. He stretched me some more!

I have to shake my head as I look back to the day I first identified expedient faith in my life. There are many times I have desired to see God deliver me quickly from my plight, and in many cases, I felt I would never survive another day of the intense heat, the overwhelming uncertainty, and the endless maze of trying to survive the test.

My unwillingness to face the test has always brought me to the reality of who sustains and keeps me. In one incident, a good friend prophetically told us we had four more years of intense trials to go through before we would see God's deliverance. I bolted at the thought. I quickly reasoned that we could not survive four more years. We had already gone through three years of tremendous trials. My mind quickly calculated that we would be delivered in our fourth year. Guess what? Our friend gave us that prophesy four years ago to the writing of this book. We have not yet seen God's full deliverance. In fact, we are facing a great trial, but I am STILL HERE!

The real walk of faith involves an intense process. We see this process in the lives of many in the Bible. Abraham waited until he was a hundred years old to see the birth of Isaac. Joseph spent around seventeen years as a servant and prisoner before being exalted in Egypt. Moses was in the wilderness for forty years before he took his rightful place as leader over Israel. Some believe that David spent close to fourteen years dodging Saul in various ways until he was established as king. Jesus spent thirty years in obscurity before His ministry was unveiled. These men all paid a price before they found their rightful place in the kingdom of God.

The questions that must be asked are, "Am I willing to pay the price? Is it worth it all?" Let me give you some insight into this question by referring you to Hebrews 11:39-40, "And these all, having obtained a good report though faith, received not the promise: God having provided some better thing for us, that they without us should not be made perfect." The answer to these questions should be a resounding YES!

My life has never been boring. I have discovered my position in Christ, and through it all the character of Christ is being worked in me. Instead of listening only to people who share about God's greatness, I now share how God has miraculously kept us through all the trials and tribulations. Instead of being on the outskirts of the river of the Holy Spirit who flows freely, I am now in the flow, tasting the sweetness of God.

And through it all, I know that the real prize is at the end of this present life.

What is your heart saying to God? Have you given Him permission to have His way no matter what? Are you tired of being on the outer fringes of the move of God? Take the leap, and be willing to face the fiery trials of your faith as you pay the price of the flesh. Take it from someone who has been there. It is all worth it!

5

OVER-ZEALOUS FAITH

Over-zealous faith comes out of emotional fervor. This emotional fervor can be related to Romans 10:2. "For I bear them record that they have a zeal of God, but not according to knowledge." Although this particular scripture relates to the subject of acceptable righteousness, it can also be used to describe a faith that is based on emotional zeal.

This type of faith comes from the premise of fleshly hype. For instance, as God honors a group of people with His presence, they begin to get excited as they sense Him in their midst. As these people move according to their fleshly excitement, rather than the Spirit of God, they unknowingly step over the line into the fleshly realm. If present, the Spirit at this time will lift, but people continue in their emotional hype, thinking it is the moving of the Spirit of God. From that point, vain imaginations can take over and open the door for Satan to come in and add his form of deception.

During this fleshly time, people try to operate in the gifts of the Spirit. Some get caught up with prophesying, while others try their hand at healing people. By the time it is over, many innocent people, along with those who are on this emotional wave, are often set up for a fall.

God will not honor emotional chaos, and such fervor can cause major damage. There was one incident where a man emotionally felt a leading to go and pray for a man who needed supernatural healing. He felt God was giving him the supernatural faith to speak to this man's paralyzed legs. The man who had been desirous of healing for many years sat silently as the other man prayed for him. It was a big let down for both when the man did not rise from his wheel chair after the heart-felt prayer. Later, the man who prayed for the poor soul was in total confusion. He told me he really did feel God wanted to heal the man. He just could not understand why He didn't.

When I first started to operate in the gifts, I had to learn the difference between the Spirit of God and my flesh. The only way I could learn such a lesson was by stepping over the line and experiencing the consequences of operating in the flesh. One day, I was sharing what I considered some spiritual insights the Lord had given me with a friend. I felt myself being carried away by a deep emotional stirring. I began to go with this so-called "impulsive gut feeling." I later experienced personal disgust when I realized my emotional stirring was not the Spirit of God.

Thank God He is patient with us. I know it is easy to step across the line and begin to operate in the flesh. As a result, I do not assume that everything I see in prayer or perceive in my spiritual times with God is from God. I have learned to test it according to spirit and truth, and if something is true, it will be confirmed. If something is of the wrong spirit, it can be easily identified by asking whether Jesus has truly been lifted up in all of His glory.

In another situation, a woman shared how she had violently lost a loved one. She knew God could raise this precious soul back to life. She justified in her mind why God should do such a miraculous act, and went in to the emergency room where his lifeless body lay. She felt she had sincere faith necessary to raise him and prayed fervently, but all attempts proved to be of no avail. She walked out of the emergency room in shock and disbelief. She admitted she almost turned away from God. After all, where was He? Did He not care, or did He simply turn a deaf ear to her heart-broken cries?

Since over-zealous faith operates from a fleshly point of view, it lacks the most important view, God's perspective. There is an eternal purpose behind everything God allows and does, including miracles. Miracles never inspire true faith; rather they simply confirm one's faith or confidence in God. Miracles will verify God's character as He is true to His Word, His promises, and sincere faith that lines up to His will. Jesus confirmed the eternal perspective of miracles in the raising of Lazarus in John 11:4, "This sickness is not unto death, but for the glory of God, that the Son of God might be glorified thereby."

Hebrews 2:3-4 adds this insight:

> How shall we escape, if we neglect so great salvation; which at the first began to be spoken by the Lord, and was confirmed unto us by them that heard him; God also bearing them witness, both with signs and wonders, and with divers miracles, and gifts of the Holy Ghost, according to his own will?

God uses miracles to bring glory to Himself or to confirm the message of salvation. And, according to Mark 16:17, signs will follow those who believe, to bring such confirmation for their faith.

Some people feel that if God would just show Himself mighty through miracles, many would believe. Scriptures refute this idea. Jesus told a story about the rich man and Lazarus in Luke 16:19-31. Lazarus, a beggar, died and went to paradise while the rich man who knew and ignored Lazarus' plight, died and went to hell. The rich man was in torment and could see Lazarus with Abraham enjoying a blessed time. The rich man called out to Abraham to send Lazarus to warn his five brothers of the impending judgment awaiting them.

> Abraham saith unto him, They have Moses and the prophets; let them hear them. And he said, Nay, father Abraham: but if one went unto them from the dead, they will repent. And he said unto him, If they hear not Moses and

the prophets, neither will they be persuaded, though one rose from the dead (Luke 16:29-31).

Jesus knew that many would witness the resurrection of two men, a man named Lazarus and a man named Jesus Christ. In each case, many tried to destroy the validity of the resurrection or deny these miraculous events.[1] This is why Jesus made this statement to Thomas in John 20:29, "...blessed are they that have not seen, and yet have believed."

Miracles may confirm a truth and inspire a person to greater heights, but miracles will not make the individual stand in light of great trials or change his or her heart. I have witnessed many miracles, but when I am faced with a crisis, it is a choice of faith in light of present events that cause me to remember God's faithfulness, enabling me to endure to the end, and not past miracles. A great example of this truth can be found in the lives of the people of Israel.

The people of Israel witnessed great miracles such as the plagues of Egypt, the parting of the Red Sea, manna from heaven, and water coming forth from a rock, to name a few. When they were faced with the giants of the Promised Land, they forgot the miracles and focused on the giants. As a result of their disobedience and unbelief, a whole generation never entered the Promised Land.[2] Faith comes down to taking God at His Word. True faith declares, "God said it, I choose to believe it." And, the response to such faith will be obedience.

Another problem with over-zealous faith is that it can put God to a foolish test. I have seen people use the promises of God like a magic wand. They figure if they wave the promise of God with enough declaration, He will have to respond according to their claims. In a way, they are demanding that God prove He is God by honoring His Word. The Word, first of all, was inspired to honor and uphold the character of God, not the other way around. The problem with people who operate in this manner is they do not take into consideration God's will or timing.

God is not a liar, and He will uphold His promises, but it will be according to His righteousness and eternal purpose. Over-zealous faith operates in ignorance towards the ways of God; therefore, it lacks real understanding of the character of God. Such faith is often boisterous and insensitive to the real heart of God, thus lacking sacrificial love and failing to be obedient. This type of faith is usually over-confident and tries to force the hand of God without any regard or reverence towards who He is or His will. In a way, it tries to dictate to God, making itself the ultimate authority.

Over-zealous faith actually puts its trust in the idea of faith, making faith a little god. Needless to say, this little god often fails to produce results, leaving a person doubting God's character and love. Individuals

---

[1] John 12:10
[2] Numbers 14

who also operate in this faith will often put the focus on their own righteousness, causing them to focus on self to see if there is some type of sin in their life. They start to put more burdens on themselves. These burdens in turn will require them to perform in a more spiritual manner. What happens when they run out of options? Some lose what little genuine faith remains and will walk away from the one true God.

Genuine faith is based on the character of God, not on His performances. It trusts in the person of God to fulfill promises according to His will, and to carry out all matters according to His eternal perspective. This is why John gives us this insight, "And this is the confidence that we have in him, that, if we ask any thing according to his will, he heareth us" (1 John 5:14).

Some people demonstrate flippancy concerning God's will. They accuse people who choose to trust and surrender to God's will as "faithless". Jesus, our example, prayed according to the Father's will in the garden of Gethsemane. It was not Jesus' will to go to the cross, but it was the Father's will, and He submitted to it.[3]

Do you operate with an over-zealous faith that fails you or makes you look foolish? Do you act in sure confidence because you know your God? This kind of confidence will give you an understanding of the premises He works from regarding His will for your life. Take heed to the promises that follow those who truly know and trust the God of the Bible. Daniel 11:32 states, "...but the people that do know their God shall be strong, and do exploits."

The Apostle Paul made this statement in 2 Timothy 1:12, "... nevertheless I am not ashamed: for I know whom I have believed, and am persuaded that he is able to keep that which I have committed unto him against that day."

1 Peter 1:8-9 makes this powerful declaration, "Whom having not seen, ye love; in whom, though now ye see him not, yet believing, ye rejoice with joy unspeakable and full of glory: Receiving the end of your faith, even the salvation of your souls."

---

[3] Luke 22:39-45

174

6

ASSUMED FAITH

One of the biggest mistakes Christians make is to give way to assumptions about their spiritual life, the spiritual lives of others, and God. For example, some believers assume they can give an account of the hope within them even though they cannot scripturally defend it.[1] Their beliefs are often based on the theology of others, and not on their own scriptural understanding and studies. Because they are not firmly planted on the true Rock, confrontation over scriptural error or beliefs often find them defenseless. This inability to give an account of their hope has caused some to walk away from their faith.

Many Christians assume people who claim to be Christians or attend church, are heirs of salvation without testing their spirit or asking for a testimony.[2] Such an assumption could cost someone his or her soul.

There is a story about a young man who came to church one Sunday morning. He sat away from the rest of the congregation. He did not speak to anyone, nor did any of the people from the church seek him out. He came for the evening service as well, and once again, those of the church ignored him as he sat silently apart from the rest of the congregation. During the service, the young man pulled out a gun and ended his life. He made a final statement, but it was too late for God's people to offer him their reasonable service, showing him Christian kindness and love. What a tragedy as well as a sober reminder of why the Church of Jesus Christ must make a difference.

Many hurting Christian soldiers "fall through the cracks" because believers in the Church assume they are doing okay. These soldiers usually find themselves part of a growing statistic of backsliders who are becoming lost because the Church appears to be uncaring or too judgmental. If a soldier does seek help, he or she risks being shot at more by the self-righteous than by those of the world.

The truth is most Christians are so consumed by their own little worlds that they are often insensitive to the hurts around them. This

---

[1] 1 Peter 3:15
[2] 1 John 4:1

insensitivity is Satan's best weapon as it keeps believers from being the salt of the earth and the light of the world.[3]

Finally, we make a lot of assumptions about our relationship with God. I once heard a sermon that challenged me about this very subject. The pastor took his text from Luke 2:41-51. This incident involved Joseph and Mary accidentally leaving Jesus behind in Jerusalem when He was 12 years old. In the first point of his message, the pastor related how Jesus' parents lost Him in the midst of all the religious practices of the Passover. In his second point, the pastor referred to how they lost Him in the midst of the cultural (worldly) activities of the city. However, his third point is what reached into my very spiritual fiber and jolted me. Joseph and Mary had assumed Jesus was with them as they traveled home. They had no idea they had lost Him until they were a day into their journey.

Real faith is based on the Person of Jesus Christ. If you leave Him behind, you also leave the source of faith behind. I was reminded of how many times I had assumed Christ was with me in a situation, when in fact, I had left Him behind because of all my religious duties and worldly activities. I finally sensed my loss when my tumultuous life began to consume me.

The pastor pointed out how Mary and Joseph first sought the missing Jesus among their relatives, only to find He was not in their midst. After we sense His presence is no longer with us, we tend to seek Him out in church or in the lives of spiritual leaders, only to find that He is not there. Only then, do we realize we must go back to the place where we personally left Him. He is patiently waiting for us to recognize our need for Him to be the source of our life, and return to Him in humility.

Assumptions in my spiritual life have made me ineffective from time to time. One of my assumptions was, since God understands my plight, I do not need to inquire of His intervention. After all, if He really loves me, He will come through for me. This attitude is quite common among Christians, and can cause anything from self-pity and anger to complacency when God does not intervene. I must admit, this attitude not only has tempted me to question God's love, but has brought me close to fainting many times.[4]

Where do we humans get our conclusions about how God should treat us? It usually comes from the world or our own vain imaginations. God is trying to establish a relationship with each of us. The most humbling revelation of Jesus is that He is a person and not just a "force." The goal of Jesus is to lead us into an intimate relationship with the Father.[5]

---

[3] Matthew 5:13-16

[4] Hebrews 12:3

[5] John 14:6

To understand the extent of the relationship that is available to me, all I have to do is think about my stepfather. My mother married him when I was 10 years old. My stepfather wanted to be a daddy and I wanted a daddy. The first statement out of my mouth after they had exchanged wedding vows was, "Welcome to the family, Daddy."

He was not my daddy at that moment, but a year later he had become my daddy in every way possible. He became my protector, my provider, and the one who had to lovingly discipline me for my own good. However, this growing relationship was not one-sided. I wanted to be his daughter, and that required me to submit to his authority in order to enjoy his ever-watchful protection. I learned to trust him in an unwavering way. Because of our love for each other, I found a boldness that allowed me to communicate effectively with him. In all of this, I learned my daddy's heart and became associated with him in a precious way. In fact, I was known as Lester Kelley's daughter, and those who did not know our humble beginnings never suspected we were anything other than biological father and daughter.

This is an example of how Jesus gives us access to the loving Heavenly Father so we can enjoy a relationship with Him. He wants to be our "Daddy."[6] We can enter this relationship because of a simple, childlike faith in Christ Jesus. In fact, Jesus said in Matthew 18:3-5:

> Verily I say unto you, Except ye be converted, and become as little children, ye shall not enter into the kingdom of heaven. Whosoever therefore shall humble himself as this little child, the same is greatest in the kingdom of heaven. And whoso shall receive one such little child in my name receiveth me.

In Luke 18:16-17, Jesus made this statement, "Suffer little children to come unto me, and forbid them not: for of such is the kingdom of God. Verily I say unto you, Whosoever shall not receive the kingdom of God as a little child shall in no wise enter therein."

Childlike faith is not based on assumptions, but on a sincere trust in a loving Father. This type of genuine faith will produce a love that wants to please God. This desire to please God aligns an individual with His will, giving valuable insight as to how to pray according to His will. The result is intimate communication with God. Communication produces faith in the Father's loving character and commitment that allows one to lay hold of a promise and not faint.

James 4:2-3 says, "Ye lust, and have not: ye kill, and desire to have, and cannot obtain: ye fight and war, yet ye have not, because ye ask not. Ye ask, and receive not, because ye ask amiss, that ye may consume it upon your lusts." So many times, people's prayers are inspired by assumptions, comprised of selfish motives, and self-serving pleasures. They are not motivated by a need to get acquainted with the Person of

---

[6] Romans 8:14-17

God or find out what His heart is concerning a matter. In fact, many often treat Him like a genie who offers them an unlimited amount of wishes, instead of a Holy God. When He does not come through for them in the way they expect, they begin to question His love for them, or become resentful or bitter towards Him.

True faith does serve as an active ingredient in an effective prayer life. Jesus confirmed this truth to His disciples in Matthew 17:20, "...for verily I say unto you, If ye have faith as a grain of mustard seed, he shall say unto this mountain, Remove hence to yonder place; and it shall remove; and nothing shall be impossible unto you."

James 1:6-8 made this statement on the subject, "But let him ask in faith, nothing wavering. For he that wavereth is like a wave of the sea driven with the wind and tossed. For let not that man think that he shall receive any thing of the Lord. A double minded man is unstable in all his ways."

Unwavering faith comes out of knowing our God. People learn to trust the Heavenly Father when they take time to enter into a priceless relationship with Him. This growing relationship brings the second perspective into focus.

I remember in my first years of Christianity wondering what I would do for eternity in heaven. I knew heaven was a better option than hell, but would it be boring? After I experienced the presence of God, I had a different opinion of heaven. I realized I wanted to be in His presence all of the time, and heaven represented a place that was filled with His unceasing glory. After all, in His presence, life became new and exciting. I began to understand why His throne was surrounded by the praises of angels and saints, and I knew I wanted to be there in the midst of it all because He is worthy.[7]

The second phase of my faith walk brought me to focus on the eternal perspective. You cannot pay the price of faith or walk by it unless you do so in light of eternity. This was obvious in Abraham's life. Hebrews 11:9-10 states this about Abraham, "By faith he sojourned in the land of promise, as in a strange country, dwelling in tabernacles with Isaac and Jacob, the heirs with him of the same promise: For he looked for a city which hath foundations, whose builder and maker is God."

2 Peter 3:13 gives this promise, "Nevertheless we, according to his promise, look for new heavens and a new earth wherein dwelleth righteousness."

The Lord had finally set the boundaries for my perspective in my incredible faith walk. As I faced these two boundaries, I realized the left boundary is the cross of Jesus, and the right is eternity where Jesus is seated on the right hand of the Father as my High Priest.[8]

---

[7] Revelation 4, 5

[8] Hebrews 8:1

The cross of Jesus reminds me that no challenge or struggle will outweigh the cruel reality of His cross. Like Job, I can declare,

> Though he slay me, yet will I trust in him: but I will maintain mine own ways before him...For I know that my redeemer liveth, and that he shall stand on the latter day upon the earth: And though after my skin worms destroy this body, yet in my flesh shall I see God: Whom I shall see for myself, and mine eyes shall behold, and not another; though my reins be consumed within me (Job 13:15; 19:25-27).

Eternity reminds me where my real hope rests. Colossians 1:27 summarizes the Christian's hope in this fashion, "Christ in you, the hope of glory."

In Colossians 3:1-4, we are given this insight about our eternal perspective:

> If ye then be risen with Christ, seek those things which are above, where Christ sitteth on the right hand of God. Set your affection on things above, not on things on the earth. For ye are dead, and your life is hid with Christ in God. When Christ, who is our life, shall appear, then shall ye also appear with him in glory.

Ephesians 2:6-7 confirms this heavenly view and hope. "And hath raised us up together, and made us sit together in heavenly places in Christ Jesus. That in the ages to come he might shew the exceeding riches of his grace in his kindness toward us through Christ Jesus."

This eternal perspective begins with Christ, His cross, and death only to end with Him in eternal glory. Without the death process, a person cannot truly receive the eternal promises established by redemption. It is submission to not only the cross of Jesus, but one's personal cross that opens him or her up to receive from the loving Heavenly Father.

These two godly perspectives keep the saints' assumptions in check. They cannot assume they are even in the true faith unless they take the time to examine their lives and attitudes in light of Jesus.[9] Christians cannot assume God is in agreement with their direction or prayers unless they first seek His heart and mind. Believers cannot presume their service to God is acceptable until they check out their motivation and His will. Saints cannot suppose they are spiritually on top of a matter until they discern what is really going on around them. They cannot assume someone's spiritual well-being until they care enough to tune in to the Holy Spirit and in to the person's heart cry and need.

Are you operating with assumed faith right now? A good way to test this area is to ask yourself these questions. "Am I angry or resentful towards God? Is my life going anywhere spiritually or am I just playing some religious game to get by? Do I really know God, or am I assuming a lot about Him and His character and will for my life?" Your honest

---

[9] 2 Corinthians 13:5

answers will reveal whether you are settling for assumed faith or experiencing real faith.

7

NOBLE FAITH

In my spiritual walk, "noble faith" has been a major struggle because it is subtle and hard to recognize. After all, it comes across as being so "noble" even though it is quite the opposite. It gives the false appearance of being super spiritual, although it is of the flesh.

God exposed my "noble" faith while in the midst of hopelessness. My faith walk had once again brought me to another place of depression. It appeared that after each challenge I found myself coming full circle to face the same type of dead end of seeing no change or deliverance. And, what came to my mind was the popular saying, "Been there, done that, and now I wear the tee-shirt to prove it." All I could think about was, "What more, God?"

I so wanted to see a complete deliverance. I knew underneath that I could not legitimately complain about God's provision to get us through each trial. I could not forget all of the times He came through for us. For example, there was the time our friend sold her jewelry and gave us the money just in time to help us pay for the trip to Jeannette's grandmother's funeral. Another time, money came in from an unexpected source at the right time, enabling us to go to another state for ministry. Then there was the time we received cash in the mail that supplied us with gas and much needed food for the table.

In the area of protection, I could not forget the incident when our vehicle just happened to overheat right by a turn-off. We were pulling a 25' trailer uphill out of treacherous, steep terrain. Later, we started to make the rest of the climb up the hill. I nervously watched the needle on the heat gauge climb, reflecting the radiator was once again overheating. I told Jeannette to pray. As she prayed, the needle started to go down in the opposite direction. There was also the incident when a heater hose broke on our pickup and God brought a police officer to the rescue that helped fix the problem until we could have it worked on.

There were also the many times God protected us from the elements. We cannot begin to recollect the terrible storms, including forest fires that we missed in our travels, or the dangerous situations we avoided because we made a wrong turn or were lost for a short time. In spite of all this, I again became discouraged.

There is no doubt God held us in His hand, but in my desperation, I wanted to be set free from the bondage, the endless drudgery, and the dead ends. I just wanted to see deliverance much like what Israel experienced when God brought them out of Egypt. But, the same old question tormented me, "Is this too much to ask for, God?"

As I wallowed in my depression, I chided myself. "Why can't you be thankful, Rayola, for what God has done for you? After all, you are to give thanks in all circumstances, and right now, you could offer God a real sacrifice by praising Him for Who He is."[1] All the scriptures I quoted and the discussions I had with myself never seemed to lift the oppressive blanket off my head.

One day, the Lord started to reveal the attitude that lurked beneath my oppressive covering. This attitude said, "This is my lot in life, so I will deal with this situation until God sees fit to deliver me." As I pondered this attitude, I was shocked to see its arrogance. I realized instead of surrendering to God's will, I simply became resigned to settle for the situation. This made my attitude appear noble.

Surrender and resignation are two different acts. "Surrender" is an active word which implies yielding one's self up to a higher and more powerful authority. "Resignation", in this sense, is a form of spiritual retreat. It does not require a good fight, but demands yielding to a situation. Surrender means releasing the burden to God, while resignation "nobly" carries the burden. Surrender produces hope, whereas resignation produces self-pity and complacency.

Since faith is, "being sure of what we hope for and certain of what we do not see," I knew that spiritual resignation was the product of unbelief that harbored resentment. It was clear that such an act of resignation was unacceptable to God,[2] Rather, it encouraged fake nobility that brought honor to the one who was supposedly "graciously suffering" under the hardness of an unfair and uncaring God.

I was surprised at how twisted and warped this "noble" faith was in light of true faith. The realization of the sickness of this faith was reinforced when God brought a man across my path who exemplified it in every possible way.

This man was in a deep depression that was caused by three factors; his terrible past, his unproductive present, and his religious beliefs. This man was contending with a past that haunted him with memories of neglect, prejudices, and compromise. He was a man of many talents, but the present found him working in a menial job. He had no real sound scriptural foundation, and as a result, he was caught up with the teachings of a heretic who warped his perspective about God and Christianity.

This man came to me for ministry. As I ministered to him, I tried to deal with the issues of his past, present, and most of all his relationship with the Father. His attitude towards the Father's love prevented him

---

[1] 1 Thessalonians 5:18; Hebrews 13:15
[2] Hebrews 11:1

from comprehending the Father's commitment to him. He saw the Heavenly Father as aloof and hard. The idea that the Father loved him in a powerful way brought tears to his eyes, but he could not receive it.

His inner struggle made Christianity appear unfair to his unbelieving wife. His wife saw God as harsh rather than loving. In her opinion, God apparently did not really care about the plight of others because He did not seem to notice how hard her husband was struggling in his Christian walk without any results. According to her "suffering" husband, this was the lot God gave him in his life, and he would just have to be gracious about it.

In my last conversation with this man, he was still on the trail of "noble" faith. He told me that God supposedly "showed" him he had to suffer (or do penance) before He could use him. Therefore, he was willing to accept this lot in life no matter how long it lasted.

As I have pointed out, we do go through a process. The goal of this process is not to make us do penance, but to rid us of self, so the character of Christ can be worked in us. This process is not "our terrible lot" in life, but a means by which God's power will come forth through us for His glory. We are not to faint through these tests and trials, but trust Him in every circumstance.[3]

Trust (pure faith) is not a passive word, but an active one. This same trust keeps us pursuing in prayer even though we do not see anything on the horizon. It always results in obedience.[4] Real obedience is not noble, but our reasonable service, the least we can do for our loving, devoted Lord.

As I contended with this man, the Lord reminded me of what He had taught me about "noble" faith. He revealed to me that there was a powerful mindset behind this type of faith.

When the Lord showed me the mindset behind "noble" faith, I was shocked to see how limited it had made me towards God. This mindset did two things to me: First, I often missed God's blessing because it would not comply with my definition of what constituted an acceptable answer. And secondly, if I did recognize His means of deliverance, could I receive it? I realized then that true faith not only produces a response, but it also allowed me to receive from God.

The reality that surprised me the most was that few Christians are able to receive from God. Many feel unworthy; therefore, they are unreceptive towards His many blessings and promises. This mindset is reinforced by the fact that God does not come through the way these people think He should. In the end, they often miss His sovereign move.

The destructive cycle of the mind became clear to me. I could not receive from God because of my mindset about Him. This mindset determined my perception about Him. This perception made God unfair,

---

[3] Isaiah 40:31; Romans 8:28
[4] Luke 18:1-6; James 2:18-20

rather than just. In the end, it made me a victim, rather than an heir of salvation.

In one of our prayer sessions with our pastor at that time, he made this declaration towards Jeannette and me, "We must declare God is not unfair." God is not unfair, but His ways are not our ways, therefore; man cannot easily understand God's ways. [5] Romans 11:33-36 makes this statement:

> O the depth of the riches both of the wisdom and knowledge of God! How unsearchable are his judgments, and his ways past finding out! For who hath known the mind of the Lord? Or who hath been his counsellor? Or who hath first given to him, and it shall be recompensed unto him again? For of him, and through him, and to him, are all things: to whom be glory for ever, Amen.

Do you have "noble" faith? Are you living a surrendered life or have you resigned to settle for your so-called "lot in life?" Do you believe God is unfair or uncaring? Can you receive from God if He did deliver you, or do you have a destructive mindset? Allow the Holy Spirit to illuminate the truth for you, for the truth will make you free.[6]

---

[5] Isaiah 55:8-9
[6] John 8:32

8

ANATOMY OF UNBELIEF

We have been considering different pseudo faiths. These faiths are religious in nature, zealous in response, and sentimental and fickle in attitude. They are also idolatrous as their confidence is in the world, self, religion, others, or even the concept of faith. Since all of these false faiths find their source outside of God, people who operate in them will end up walking in unbelief.

Unbelief is something that every Christian has to confront. For me, I can remember that my biggest spiritual battles have been the result of unbelief wanting to take center stage in my life. I would wrestle against the doubts and accusations against the character and intentions of God that would creep into my thought processes. My desire to trust God would be mocked by the reality that He seemed to be silent in my greatest battles. I would inwardly rage against any conviction to surrender all and simply trust Him.

At times my struggle and even guilt flourished when I had to acknowledge that everything in my flesh resented God for allowing these battles to occur. In my mind I was doing everything in my power to serve Him; therefore, why did He allow it to be so difficult? In such situations, I failed to realize it was my flesh that made it difficult, not faith. It was faith that eventually led me to a place of rest in Christ.

The real battle in the Christian realm is over faith. Unbelief is the natural way of the flesh. It does not want to rely on God to bring each of us through a situation, trust Him in circumstances, have confidence in Him when everything is falling apart, and place all assurance in Him when all seems hopeless. Sadly, we would rather be tormented in unbelief than fling ourselves on God in utter faith to deliver us through or from a situation.

It is important to point out that unbelief is not a matter of people being incapable of believing God or His Word; rather, it is because people refuse to believe. This is the war that truly rages between the flesh and the Spirit. The flesh logics away genuine faith, while the Spirit convicts us of our need to choose to believe God and His Word.[1]

---

[1] John 16:7-13; Galatians 5:16-17

As a minister of the Gospel, the biggest struggle I contend with in Christians is that of unbelief towards God. As already stated in different ways, I understand the battle with unbelief, but I also know where it will lead a person. Unbelief calls God an unreliable liar who does not mean what He says or says what He means. The mocking attitude of unbelief creates an environment that allows wrong spirits to operate, creating a wall of indifference to be erected against the true God of Heaven, along with His Word and His servants. I cannot count the many times I have hit this wall of unbelief. It not only closes the spiritual ears of the individual who is walking in it and perverts what is being said, but it causes slothfulness as it robs life from the very air that is being breathed.

I also cannot begin to count the times that I have had to push through the hindrances of unbelief to bring living water to the thirsty souls of others. Is it any wonder Jesus did not stick around His hometown of Nazareth? He was prevented from ministering because of the people's unbelief.[2] Praise God, He is always faithful to move around the indifferent walls of unbelief and minister to open hearts.

Unbelief is the source behind all rebellion, mockery, and rejection of truth. Unbelief does not reject the idea of God; rather, it rejects trusting God's character and Word as being the absolute source of all truth. It often erects a god that can be understood, and will not require or test a person's faith to believe outside of what is acceptable and worldly. This is how unbelief encourages a pseudo faith, even among those who call themselves Christians.

It is easy to identify unbelief in Christians. It is very touchy. In other words, it can be easily offended. It proves to be unreasonable when challenged, hard-hearted when exposed, and judgmental when it is justifying itself at the expense of truth.

In one incident, a man was challenged to come higher to fulfill his calling. When he actually saw the price he would have to pay, he immediately rejected the idea and went into the darkness of unbelief. Even though this man was given a dream concerning his calling, he did not think God was worth the time or energy. He justified it by trying to fulfill the dream according to his preference. It was obvious this man did not know God. He possessed a religion that was sentimental towards God, but lacked the faith that would trust God's intention towards him, as well as His ability to bring forth the plan He had ordained for him before the foundation of the world.

Another man took pride in his intellectual knowledge. Educated by the humanistic system of the world, he had simply tacked Christ on to his Christian exercises. As his idolatrous knowledge was challenged by the revelation of God, he struggled between anger, mockery, and faith. He liked the "superiority" his so-called "worldly intelligence" gave him. He

---

[2] Mark 6:5-6

trusted in what he knew because he saw it as a means to control his reality. Challenged to trust in a God that could not be seen, dissected, or studied, he often became angry at the prospect of having to count that which was of the world as dung in order to gain Christ. He became frustrated towards the Word of God because the simplicity and life found in its truths often escaped him or exposed the foolishness of his worldly understanding.

This man preferred the world. He did not attempt to hide his contempt for those truths that dared to expose the fallacy of his knowledge or the vanities behind his desire and love for the world. It was clear that he took pride in the fact that he was not trying to be a professional hypocrite in his Christianity.

God in His mercy stepped on the scene to show Himself in a powerful way to this man. However, there was a harsh warning that if this man did not choose the ways of faith and truth, judgment would fall upon him. The man was humbled by the encounter and made some attempts to adjust some of the activities of his life to God.

The Word of God talks about laying aside, putting off, or forgetting that which constitutes the old life and pressing forward to possess the new. Due to this man's love for the world, his unbelief towards God, his skepticism towards the Word of God, and his contempt towards God's servants, this man failed to put off the old in order to embrace the new. His failure to obey caused the struggle between his flesh and the Spirit to escalate, bringing him to a decision.

Like Demas, this man made the decision to go with this present world.[3] In a confrontation with him, his frustration, anger, and mockery hit its peak. He literally screamed for the truth to shut up, and became physical with those who had contended for his soul. That day the light went out in this man. No doubt God has turned him over to his worldly desires. He now tastes the vanity of the world, the mocking arrogance of his knowledge, and the emptiness of his ways. People who have seen him describe his countenance as one who is becoming old and hard.

The difference between him and the first man is that the first man went into a delusion that serves as a false religious light. Such delusion often serves as a form of false security and happiness, blinding this unsuspecting soul to the consequences of his choices. However, the second man is not deluded. He knows underneath that he has rejected the light of truth, and that his future holds nothing but despair and ruin.

Through the years, I have watched many people end up disillusioned with the true God of heaven because they insisted on clinging to their pseudo faiths. Sadly, many of them were no more the wiser about their erroneous and idolatrous concept of faith. Instead of repenting for any self-righteousness or arrogance they may have harbored in regards to

---

[3] 2 Timothy 4:10

the things of self, the world, and heretical beliefs, they become angry with God for not sparing them from being brought low as fools. In the end, they become critical, skeptical, and contrary to the real truths and works of God.

The goals of pseudo faiths are to undermine and replace real faith. Without genuine faith, there is no real rock upon which to stand, withstand, and test all spiritual matters. This is why Jude 3 talks about contending for the faith that was once delivered to the saints.

These pseudo faiths are testing the hearts of God's people to see if they love the truth or if they want Christianity on their terms. Sadly, each of these erroneous faiths have proven that many who call themselves Christians do not fear God or His Word. And, when the Bible reveals their error, they become offended by the truth, as they choose to hide behind pride while clinging to their pseudo faith. Meanwhile, Satan has won the hearts and minds of many people who fall prey to these substitute faiths. These people end up falsely accusing God and mocking the real things of God.

As each person walks according to his or her own version of faith, he or she is walking in unbelief towards God. This is the harsh reality of all pseudo faiths. They create an antichrist environment where everything that is embraced will be a counterfeit of what is real and holy.

The problem with walking in an environment of unbelief is that it will create its own reality. It is important to point out that a person can only put his or her faith in what is real, but pseudo faith is based on imagination and expectations that seem real. Therefore, a reality that is not based on the truth of Jesus Christ will ultimately resist the true Jesus as the truth challenges any of these false faiths. This is where a person will put up a wall against anything that proves contrary to his or her particular philosophy about faith.

As people put up walls against anything that challenges them, they close down whatever spiritual hearing remains to bring the necessary proper contrast. This means that the powerful Word of God will be unable to bring reproof, correction, or instruction.[4] In a way, it is like rendering the sword that dissects and exposes the heart as useless in its ability to bring contrast and correction. Once this occurs, the Word will not be able to become nourishment to the spirit or bring life to its truths and expose any error. Every time truth is rejected, the heart is hardened towards the real Jesus and His truth. This will end in judgment.

Now that a person is walking in unbelief, he or she will develop a certain disposition or attitude towards the things of God. It is important to understand the disposition and the route people travel in unbelief. We have described how to recognize it, but we need to understand its disposition to see how wicked it is before God. In fact, unbelief is found

---

[4] 2 Timothy 3:16-17

at the base of everything that opposes God. Therefore, the next time you are beset by rebellion, fear, idolatry, mockery etc., know you are operating in unbelief.

The core of the disposition of unbelief is arrogance. Arrogance is unable to see any personal error because this attitude causes superiority towards others. This type of environment is void of any humility. As the error of arrogance exalts itself over truth, it will become critical and self-righteous towards anything that does not come into line with its false perception. In the religious realm, such arrogance is nothing more than self-righteousness.

Self-righteousness produces a false light that will delude the person as to his or her spiritual dilemma. This delusion will establish a person upon the shifting sand of his or her pseudo faith. Since all foundations will eventually be shaken, the person's false faith will fail to stand in the storms of life.[5] Due to the arrogance and false light of unbelief, there will be no fear of God or His Word to instill wisdom that is teachable. Without the proper fear, there will be foolishness, blindness, flippancy, or indifference towards truth.

I have dealt with people who claim that if the Word says it, they will believe it. However, as soon as they are challenged with the Word, you often discover a pseudo faith that is mocking towards you, and will reject correction, as it justifies the darkness of unbelief. Such people reveal their hypocrisy and delusion as they adamantly cling to their sacred cows erected by their theology or ignorance.

Since there is no fear of God or fear for His Word, there will be a disposition of disrespect. This will put a person into a very precarious position. A person must have a real sense of accountability towards the Word. But, if the Word cannot discipline him or her, it matters little how much the person might respect the vessel that is being used to challenge him or her. This type of individual will immediately oppose or reject any correction that does not line up to his or her theology. Without the proper respect for the Word, a person can never be called into godly order no matter how close to the truth or far out he or she may be in his or her beliefs.

If a person has no real boundaries outside of religious or personal theology in which to discern or show proper respect for the true servants of God, he or she will have to operate from the basis of presumptions. Presumptions are based on associations, titles, or personal theology. For example, if a person has said the sinner's prayer, goes to church, refers to oneself as a Christian, and possesses a certain theology, he or she presumes that his or her personal religion is okay.

Presumptions cause people to operate from a surface standpoint, rather than from the aspect of fruits. In other words, presumption is

---

[5] Matthew 7:24-27

spiritual ignorance that operates from a fleshly aspect. People, therefore, are judged according to surface matters and not by their fruit. Yet, Jesus stated we can only know people by their fruits.[6]

Presumptions are unable to recognize the real treasures of heaven, which produce the disposition of ingratitude. These people will use the things of God for self-serving reasons, while abusing or neglecting truths or practices that do not support their pseudo faith.

The disposition of unbelief will cause people to become unteachable. They will be condescending towards others because of arrogance. They believe themselves to have it all figured out, and consider those who do not agree as stupid. They will cling to presumptions so they don't have to face the emptiness of their lives. Ultimately, because of fear, they will become unresponsive to challenges towards the vanity ruling their lives.

The manifestation of the disposition of unbelief begins with idolatry. People must put their confidence in something. Sadly, unbelief pretty well stipulates such confidence will not be in the one true God. Therefore, people put their faith in self, knowledge, theology, dynamic leaders, some type of power, or religion.

Idolatry automatically results in people rebelling against God's authority. It causes them to avoid personal accountability by ignoring, explaining or excusing wrong attitudes or actions that would serve as a means of godly warning and discernment.

Rebellion against God manifests itself in mockery towards the things of God. This mockery is a product of a mocking spirit. I have discovered that religious people often mock the things of God. Sadly, unbelief means individuals are walking according to what they see or know and not according to the Word of God. Therefore, they often pass off anything that has to do with the spiritual realm as mythical or metaphoric.

Mocking eventually turns into complacency where the person will not respond to anything spiritual. Since the individual operates from presumptions, there is no need to examine, discern, or test.

The environment of unbelief also leads to an unreceptive heart. An unreceptive heart ties people's hands as far as instructing or warning the individual of future consequences attached to unbelief. Because of the person's arrogance, God will resist him or her, and eventually the person will fall into the judgment of delusion or vanity.[7]

Finally, the disposition of unbelief manifests itself in disobedience. Romans 14:23 clearly states, "…for whatsoever is not of faith is sin." Since a person is unreceptive, he or she will not obey God. This disposition will serve as an open door to Satan. It allows him to come in

---

[6] Matthew 7:16, 20
[7] Proverbs 16:18; 1 Peter 5:5-6

and claim territory, and wherever Satan is oppressing, there will be greater resistance to truth.

A believer cannot afford to assume or presume that his or her faith is genuine unless it leads back to the Jesus of the Bible. The Apostle Paul instructs believers in 2 Corinthians 13:5 to examine themselves to make sure they are in the faith.

Study the following table and see if you are walking in an environment of unbelief. If you are, you need to repent and ask God to give you a measure of faith that will respond in wisdom and obedience, as well as produce spiritual accountability and maturity towards the Word of God.

Disposition	Unbelief	Manifestation
Arrogance	Walking in it	Idolatry
Self-Righteous	Environment	Rebellion
No fear of God	Preference Creates False Reality	Mocking
Disrespect	Resist Truth	Complacent
Presumptions	Put up a Wall	Unreceptive
Ungrateful	Close Down	Disobedient
Unteachable	Hard Heart	Open door to Satan
Will fall God resists	Judgment-- Tied the hands	Unable to warn-- Consequences

9

INGREDIENTS OF FAITH

What is true faith? We all want faith that moves mountains, clings to the Rock, and overcomes the world. However, the different types of faith that most people seem to possess creates greater mountains of doubt while ending up with "rocks of unbelief", crushing them in the form of utter despair. Eventually, they find themselves overcome by the circumstances that surround them.

The Bible implies that real faith is quite simple. For me, I have discovered that it is simple, but hard to embrace. The reason it is hard to embrace is because we so-called "wise and rational beings" have to wade through the unbelief that can be discovered at every level of the soul area, such as in our logic, emotional fervor, personal strength, worldly influences, and fleshly preferences. In fact, it took a lot of wading for me to realize that faith is not about God's people getting matters done for Him, rather it is about God accomplishing great feats in and through the lives of His people.

It is easy to put our faith in something that catches our attention, appeals to our mind, and appeases our affections. However, true faith towards God finds its origins in a person, not a belief, movement, or religious exercise. The Person who must become the focal point and emphasis of our faith is the Lord Jesus Christ. If our faith is not in Him and inspired by His work of redemption, the Apostle Paul stated in 2 Corinthians 13:5 that it will be considered reprobate or worthless.

In his book, "*Finding The Reality of God*," Paris Reidhead stated that faith is the sight of the soul. He identified four types of faith as to what people can actually put their confidence in. There is *head* faith that has an intellectual assent or perception about the matters of God, but such faith is still unable to receive spiritual truths. There is *dead* faith where people put their confidence in rituals, practices, or belief systems, but it is not directed towards the true God of heaven. Such faith can be observed in the many religions that are prevalent in the world. There is the *devil's* faith which is sensual and emotional in its emphasis, but remains hopeless. The devils showed this type of faith towards Jesus when they encountered Him, and admitted who He was. Finally, there is *heart* faith that not only believes, but receives what God has for the person.

It is not unusual to encounter Christians who are confused by what constitutes genuine faith. There is often a mixture concerning biblical application. This means that spiritual truths are not applied to one's life with true faith. For example, people operate in their pseudo faith according to their particular idolatrous emphasis or erroneous take on biblical doctrine, promises, and blessings. This creates a dangerous mixture where the things of God will become illusive because He cannot honor them since faith is not present. Or, the individual will open him or herself up to the supernatural powers of darkness to gain an experience or credibility. Hebrews 4:2 talks about this dangerous mixture, "For unto us was the gospel preached, as well as unto them: but the word preached did not profit them, not being mixed with faith in them that heard it."

Pseudo faiths are humanistic. They find their source in man and his many activities. In fact, in some cases people use their concept of faith as a means to change reality. This is witchcraft, clearly subjecting a person to the devil's type of faith.

On the contrary, real faith can only find its origin in God; therefore, genuine faith comes from God and cannot be found in or conjured up by human means. Romans 12:3 says, "For I say, through the grace given unto me, to every man that is among you, not to think of himself more highly than he ought to think; but to think soberly, according as God hath dealt to every man the measure of faith."

God gives people the measure of faith to take steps of obedience. Obedience is the manifestation of genuine faith.[1] Each step of obedience enables a person to be enlarged with greater measures of faith. Each obedient step brings a person closer to realizing his or her heavenly potential, while learning valuable lessons, embracing real life, partaking of promises, and experiencing blessings.

It is important to point out that faith prepares a person to receive what God has for him or her. This is where a contrast can be observed between pseudo faith and true faith. Pseudo faith is based on unrealistic expectations that man has adopted or developed in regard to God, while genuine faith is based on the person or character of God, allowing God to move in practical and unexpected ways. Sadly, many Christians are not prepared to receive from God because their expectations have them looking elsewhere, instead of right in front of them where God is moving in simple ways. In fact, large numbers of people personally miss the fulfillment of many of God's promises and blessings because of their faulty faith. A good example of this is the people of Israel. They were looking for the Messiah to come as a great conqueror, but instead Jesus came as a servant, who was prepared to be offered up as a Lamb of God. They were looking for political deliverance, not spiritual deliverance.

1 Corinthians 12:9 tells us that the Spirit of God can give a gift of faith for the purpose of edification. The gift of faith is opposite from the measure of faith (which is enlarged with each step of obedience). When

---

[1] Romans 12:3; James 2:14-26

a person is given the gift of faith, it is for the purpose of holding on to a promise until it is fulfilled.

Genuine faith also develops the testimony of a person. It is important at this time to reveal what makes faith great. Great faith is not measured by its size; rather, by the extent of its simplicity, sincerity, and purity. This is brought out by the fact that if you have faith the size of a mustard seed, you can move a mountain.[2] When you consider the size of a mustard seed, you realize that all a person needs to do is choose to believe God about a matter. Such simple belief allows God to be God, and to show Himself in a powerful way.

Since faith allows God to be God, people are assured of encountering God in regards to the issues of life. I have witnessed this in my own life. The battle is the same. Will I step over my logic of what I see and perceive as being reality to choose to believe in God's character and intention towards me? The battle has been intense at times, but once I make the right choice, there is liberty and peace. God brings me to a large place where I can enjoy who He is.

Each encounter with God enlarges a person's testimony about Him. The greatest testimony that will come out of a walk of faith is that *God is faithful* to take something ordinary and make it beneficial, use adversity to build character, and overwhelming circumstances to show Himself mighty.

God's faithfulness has often been the main emphasis in my testimony. As I have already pointed out, God has proved Himself to be faithful in each challenge of life. I am the one who has often become faint in my mind towards the Lord, but He has always proved faithful towards me.

God is faithful and one cannot learn this valuable truth until he or she learns total dependency on God. This dependency occurs when one truly walks by God-centered and God-inspired faith.

Heretical teachings and a weak presentation of the Gospel have undermined genuine faith towards God. The heretical teachings have counterfeited faith that was first delivered to the saints by subtly exalting another faith. The weak gospel that is being presented today lacks the essence of unfeigned faith. It actually puts confidence in a concept of self-worth based on an unrealistic presentation of God's love, rather than in active faith that responds to God's grace in humility and obedience.

As a result, faith rarely graduates from a mere concept to an active response that is actually walked out in the Christian life. Since active faith is missing, God is never allowed to move freely to bring revelations of who He is. This causes people to mistake times of religious zeal or fleshly self-sufficiency as being a form of faith.

---

[2] Matthew 17:20

No person knows the extent of his or her faith until he or she is tested.[3] Clearly, this book has shown how my faith has been tested and found wanting. In the past it has shown where my real dependency rested. This is why the fires of adversity test faith. They unveil each person's level of genuine faith, and the source of his or her confidence. These adversities bring a distinct separation. Some people actually give up on their Christian walk before the test reveals a religion that is absent of genuine faith. They become skeptical and unbelieving towards God while maintaining a religious front. Others are shocked to discover they have no real faith. This can lead to fiery ovens of depression and doubt. Still, there are always a few who have gone through the fiery test of their faith. They discover each time the fire is put to their faith, that it will enlarge the depth of this assurance. They rejoice as they are once again reminded that it is God's desire to increase their faith towards Him.

Even though different aspects of faith have been discussed throughout this book, it is important to bring all the ingredients together to properly confront the many misconceptions that surround this subject. Faith is associated with such words as belief, conviction, trust, and persuasion.

When you consider the word *belief*, you realize it has to do with believing something. As you consider the weak gospel that is being presented today, you can see that this virtue is missing. A person must believe upon the Lord Jesus Christ to be saved. Sadly, most "salvation experiences" are nothing more than mental assent, verbal confession, or a sinner's prayer. Therefore, in the presentation of the Gospel, the active ingredient of "believing" upon the Lord Jesus Christ is totally counterfeited by a religious exercise or adjusted according to personal ignorance towards spiritual matters. If the "believing" is absent, then faith is missing. The Apostle Paul clearly stated that we are saved by grace through faith in what God accomplished through Jesus on the cross.[4]

Keep in mind, faith is active, and when a person initially chooses to believe the Gospel, it will be accompanied with *repentance*. To choose to believe something in light of repentance means to turn from that which would be considered acceptable, wise, and realistic according to one's personal understanding, and to embrace something as truth that is viewed as being contrary, foreign, and foolish. When it comes to the Gospel, I must choose to believe it is true, and turn from my old way of thinking and doing to embrace the new truth that I now should receive by faith.

Consider how the four different types of faith operate according to the following table:

---

[3] 1 Peter 1:5-7
[4] Acts 16:31; Ephesians 2:8-9

Source of Faith	Type of Faith	Point of Reliance	Fruit
Head	Logic	Concept	Skeptical
Dead	Fleshly Inspired	Sentiment	Depression
Devil	Worldly Inspired	Images	State of Unbelief
God (Heart)	Unfeigned Faith	Person of God	Abiding Assurance

Clearly, faith is more than mental assent, some type of fleshly work, or a point of obedience. When you examine sincere faith, you discover that it is a natural response to the revelation of God's grace. This faith goes beyond mental assent and takes root in the heart. We are told we must believe in our heart that Jesus was raised from the grave in order to be saved.[5] "Believing" is active because it is based on heart revelation. This means believing is an active reality that reaches into the very innermost being of a person. In fact, believing something in the heart is the same as declaring that a person knows something is true, and being able to say "amen" or "so be it, for it is so" with confidence.

The *confidence* of true faith will result in submission. It takes sincere confidence to submit to the ways of God. Submission recognizes that the matters of God are perfect; therefore, we can submit to Him as a means of giving way to that which is worthy and far greater than man's limited way of doing something.

Such confidence and submission are not based on blind hope or concepts about God, but on living, verified facts. This type of knowledge results in a response. In other words, such facts will produce change in a person's perception, disposition, and practices. He or she will think and act according to what he or she knows is true. We can see this level of response and change in Jesus' disciples.

---

[5] Romans 10:9-10

Since believing reaches into the depth of our being and embraces our affections, this is where *conviction* comes into the picture. Faith is a deep conviction that is motivated by affections, and ultimately reinforces and directs those affections towards the object of a person's commitment or dedication. This type of conviction, or faith, penetrates every area of a person's life. It points to motivation or being compelled by the evidence of what one knows to be true.

Once again, we see how faith is active. It reacts according to convictions. These convictions produce a deep devotion to God. We see this devotion in Cornelius in Acts 10. Although a Gentile, Acts 10:2 tells us that his devotion to God had three manifestations: 1) He feared God, 2) he showed benevolence towards others, and 3) he prayed always.

Faith is not just an action, but it is also an *attitude*. The fear of God points to an attitude that is expressed in how a person walks before God. This reveals that in faith Cornelius walked carefully and humbly before God. His devotion to God was openly expressed by helping others by way of alms. Alms were often directed towards the stranger, the fatherless, and the widows.

Cornelius prayed always. This part of his life reveals that he constantly sought God. His desire was to know and please the God of Israel which showed the integrity of his faith. As a result, He was truly a man of active faith. His humble walk, his benevolent giving, and his pursuit for God made him open and available to God. God counted Cornelius' righteous acts as a memorial.

God used Cornelius to confirm to Peter that He intended to save the Gentiles when the Holy Spirit came upon this Gentile and those of his household.[6] This was the initial beginning of fulfilling the words of Jesus in John 10:16, "And other sheep I have, which are not of this fold (the Jews): them also I must bring, and they shall hear my voice; and there shall be one-fold, and one shepherd." (Parenthesis added.)

Once a person has conviction that is walked out in obedience, *trust* begins to develop. Trust will result in total *consecration.* Obedience allows God to meet the person in each situation, unveiling His abiding commitment and faithfulness. Each encounter with God's faithfulness causes the trust to go deeper and deeper into the person's being, causing consecration to take place. It confirms what he or she already knows, causing the conviction to grow in greater confidence or abiding trust.

"Trust" is an assured reliance on the character, ability, strength, and truth of someone or something.[7] For the Christian, this trust rests totally on the unchangeable character and ways of God. Reliance of this nature points to a childlike confidence.[8]

---

[6] Acts 10:4-5; 20-35
[7] Webster's New Collegiate Dictionary
[8] Matthew 18:3-5

Genuine faith is also a matter of possessing a right *disposition*. Jesus made three references to this child-like trust in Matthew 18:3-5: 1) One must turn from his or her arrogant, self-sufficient ways and become a child in his or her spiritual walk, 2) a person must take on the disposition of a child; and 3) a childlike walk and disposition will cause one to become great in His kingdom. This childlike quality is necessary to get into the kingdom of God. It means that a Christian must regress in regards to reliance on anything outside of God, and become reliant on Him as his or her only source of life, purpose, and happiness.

This regression involves self-denial to the life that is being presently lived in the flesh and according to pride. It implies total abandonment from any form of self-sufficiency or dependency on the flesh or world to unfeigned dependency on God.[9] Unfeigned dependency is marked by sincerity and purity.

The Apostle Paul commended Timothy for having unfeigned faith. He acknowledged that both Timothy's mother and grandmother had this same type of sincere faith. Faith without hypocrisy allows a person to trust God in greater measure. As he or she becomes more reliant upon God, faith becomes more refined and mature.[10]

As an individual becomes more childlike in his or her reliance upon God, the more he or she will taste the goodness of the Lord.[11] As one tastes the goodness of the Lord, he or she will be even more persuaded in maintaining his or her life before God. Faith is a matter of deep *persuasion* that will not sway from the depth of its conviction, and the assurance of its sincere trust in God's faithfulness. Such persuasion results in the complete selling out to the Lordship of Jesus.

The Apostle Peter was completely persuaded by the reality of Jesus. He assured others in this manner in 1 Peter 1:8, "Whom having not seen, ye love; in whom, though now ye see him not, yet believing, ye rejoice with joy unspeakable and full of glory."

The Apostle John enjoyed an incredible knowledge of Jesus. He made this statement in 1 John 1:1-2:

> That which was from the beginning, which we have heard, which we have seen with our eyes, which we have looked upon, and our hands have handled, of the Word of life; (For the life was manifested, and we have seen it, and bear witness, and shew unto you that eternal life, which was with the Father, and was manifested unto us.)

1 Corinthians 13:13 tells us that faith is one of the virtues that will remain when life as we know it goes by the wayside. It is eternal because it is founded upon and steadfast towards that which is everlasting. The Apostle Paul made reference to the enduring

---

[9] Jeremiah 17:5-8; 2 Corinthians 3:5; 1 Timothy 1:4-5; 1 John 2:15-17

[10] 1 Timothy 1:3-5; 2 Timothy 1:5

[11] Psalm 34:8

persuasion of his faith in Jesus in 2 Timothy 1:12, "For the which cause I also suffer these things: nevertheless I am not ashamed: for I know whom I have believed, and am persuaded that he is able to keep that which I have committed unto him against that day."

The final ingredient of godly faith is *faithfulness.* Faithfulness is one of the ingredients that make up the fruit of the Spirit.[12] This quality points to the state of being trustworthy. In other words, whatever God entrusts to you, you must be faithful to maintain the intent of it in purity and handle it in righteousness. Such faithfulness speaks of endurance, patience, and character.

Christians have been entrusted with four main resources with which to live and uphold the Christian life before God and others: 1) The presence of God through the indwelling of His Holy Spirit, 2) the Word of God, 3) the Gospel; and 4) the authority and power to live the Christian life by faith, as well as teach others to be followers of Jesus.[13] Each Christian will be tested and judged by how he or she handles these four resources.

This brings us to the real test of Christianity. Many Christians equate spiritual success with numbers, gifts, revelations, prestige, or worldly wealth. They see greatness in light of personal exaltation and recognition from others. Jesus refuted such conclusions. He stated the greatest in the kingdom of heaven is the one who serves. Originally, He started out with many disciples, but only eleven remained after His resurrection. Gifts without love will be inconsistent and out of line with God's purpose. Revelations that do not lead back to Jesus are heretical and dangerous. Worldly prestige will cause one to become a spiritual pauper, while worldly riches will become a snare to those who pursue after them.[14]

Psalm 89:1 declares, "I will sing of the mercies of the LORD for ever: with my mouth will I make known thy faithfulness to all generations." For over two decades, I have been on this incredible faith walk. My declaration remains consistent every time I testify of God's abiding presence in my life, "He is faithful!"

The Apostle Paul said this about God's faithfulness in 2 Timothy 2:11-13, "It is a faithful saying: For if we be dead with him, we shall also live with him: If we suffer, we shall also reign with him: if we deny him, he also will deny us: If we believe not, yet he abideth faithful: he cannot deny himself."

In my times of faithlessness before God, I have encountered His faithfulness. In my periods of doubt, I have sensed His abiding presence.

---

[12] Galatians 5:22-23

[13] Matthew 28:18-20; Mark 16:15-16; Romans 1:16; 1 Corinthians 3:16-17;
6:19-20; Ephesians 5:26-27; 6:17; 2 Timothy 2:15; 3:15-17

[14] Matthew 20:25-27; Luke 18:9-14; John 6:60-66; 1 Timothy 6:6-10; 1
Corinthians 13:1-3; Ephesians 3:3-5; 1 Peter 1:13; Revelation 1:1

In my failures, I have been assured that He would not fail me. Through it all, I have been aware of and experienced His trustworthy character and works in various ways. My declaration of His faithfulness remains consistent and strong at each bend, twist, obstacle, or turn I encounter in my walk.

God's faithfulness has produced an abiding confidence in my soul. Obviously, faith is simple in its workings, but profound in light of God's incredible majesty. It finds its roots in a childlike heart. It grows in the midst of personal regression. It is refined in the fires of adversity. It is defined by an ongoing revelation of Jesus Christ. Its enduring powers are revealed in the faithfulness of God.

Consider the following table as to how the different active ingredients of genuine faith will express themselves in and through the life of the believer. Meditate on how each ingredient of faith would address and prove victorious over pseudo faith.

Ingredients	Pseudo Faith	Response Towards God	Fruits	Results
Believing	Optional Faith	Heart Revelation	Repentance	Embrace it as truth
Confidence	Introverted Faith	Giving way to truth	Submission	Inward Change
Conviction	Pious or Expedient Faith	Ensures right motivation or spirit	Deep, abiding devotion	Obedience
Trust	Assumed Faith	Childlike Confidence	Total Consecration	Right Disposition
Persuasion	Noble Faith	Maintaining the Christian Life	Steadfastness	Endurance
Faithfulness	Overzealous Faith	State of being Trustworthy	Abiding Confidence	Integrity

Faith is not a concept, but a reality that can only be experienced as it is walked out in humility and obedience. A greater measure of it is given at the point of obedience, revealed at the place of self-denial and death, and manifested through the childlike disposition of a true servant of God.

As I thought about my declaration of God's faithfulness, I had to ponder His response towards me. He has remained true to His character, but have I been true to Him? After all, faithfulness has to do with affections and allegiance. Are my affections solely directed towards Him? Is my allegiance to Him the epitome of undivided loyalty, adoration, and worship?

Upon meditation of this subject, the words of Jesus in Matthew 25:21 came to mind. "His lord said unto him, Well done, thou good and faithful servant: thou hast been faithful over a few things, I will make thee ruler over many things: enter thou into the joy of thy lord."

In my testimony of God, I can do nothing but declare His faithfulness. However, on judgment day, what will He be able to declare about my level of faithfulness? The answer to that question will rest on the type of faith I possess at the end of my earthly journey.

What type of faith do you possess? Will it be unveiled in the form of faithful and trustworthy service to God or will it be absent, exposing dead works and rebellion? The latter prospect leaves one with these chilling words, "And then will I profess unto them, I never knew you: depart from me, ye that work iniquity" (Matthew 7:23).

10

GENUINE FAITH

In the last couple of chapters, we considered the response, disposition, and ingredients of genuine faith. In this last chapter, we will be considering the complete picture of true, active faith that finds its hope in Christ and its expectation in His many promises.

As already pointed out, people who walk around with a pseudo faith are established on a faulty foundation. If a person has an erroneous faith, it means he or she will have another Jesus. If an individual is wrong about Jesus, he or she will spend eternity paying the consequences.

Although these characteristics have been discussed, it is of grave importance to reiterate the makeup and function of faith that is not only pleasing to God, but can move mountains and end in the salvation of souls.

Real Faith is Based on a Right Perception

Does any follower of Christ have a corner on what constitutes genuine faith? I believe people can understand faith from a childlike perspective, but to have a corner on it would mean he or she would have a corner on God. We know God has no beginning or end, and that He is all-knowing and all-powerful.

The problem is that man tries to corner God by putting Him in an acceptable and understandable package. In other words, people try to bring God down to their pathetic level instead of allowing God to bring them higher in Him. Bringing God down to personal levels broadens the spiritual road people are traveling. We read this warning from Jesus in Matthew 7:13-14, "Enter ye in at the strait gate: for wide is the gate, and broad is the way, that leadeth to destruction, and many there be which go in thereat: Because strait is the gate, and narrow is the way, which leadeth unto life, and few there be that find it."

Jesus tells us few will find the narrow way. Just how does one find the narrow way? Jeremiah 29:13 makes this statement, "And ye shall seek me, and find me, when ye shall search for me with all your heart." Genuine and powerful faith depends on people seeking the true God with their whole heart. By seeking the real God, He will personally meet these individuals and bring them higher in their understanding and revelation of Him.

True faith, therefore, comes down to having a right perception about God. Hebrews 11:6 confirms this, "But without faith it is impossible to please him: for he that comes to God must believe that he is..."

People's perceptions will either let God be God or they will limit Him. A right perception will be based on the Word of God and not on personal conclusions. We are reminded of this sobering fact about limiting God because of a wrong perception in Romans 14:23, "...for whatsoever is not of faith is sin."

In my years of ministry, I have discovered that Christians vary in their understanding of God. Some are in love with their personal concept or idea of God, but not with the God of the Bible. Some people's idea of God, especially the Father, is based on their perception of their own father. If their father was hard and unloving, they transfer that perception upon the Heavenly Father, causing them to hide or avoid the Father. This is why Paul made this declaration in Romans 8:15, "For ye have not received the spirit of bondage again to fear; but ye have received the Spirit of adoption, whereby we cry, Abba, Father."

Other people have a real problem with Jesus. Somehow, the Father seems more approachable, while Jesus is a hard man to yield to. Yet, Jesus plainly stated, "...no man cometh unto the Father, but by me" (John 14:6b).

Romans 10:17 tells us that real faith, "...cometh by hearing, and hearing by the word of God." If a person is not seeking God through the study of His Word and prayer, he or she will not be established on the immovable Rock, Jesus Christ. And, when the storms of life come, he or she will fall.[1]

For example, most people who fall into cults are seeking the real God. Sadly, many look to people to find God. Since they are looking outside of the Bible, those who have a false light will deceive them. This is why the Apostle Paul gave a stern warning in 2 Corinthians 11 about being seduced to believe in another Jesus, gospel, or spirit. He warned that Satan comes as an angel of light, and that there would be false workers, transforming themselves into the apostles who present themselves as ministers of righteousness.

Other people are following God for the wrong reasons. Some are Christians because of the benefits they feel they will get out of being on the right side of the "Big Man" or the "Big Daddy." It is not that they are in love with the person of God, but in what they perceive they will receive from Him. Such motivation falls in the category of 2 Timothy 4:3-4, "For the time will come when they will not endure sound doctrine; but after their own lusts shall they heap to themselves teachers, having itching ears; And they shall turn away their ears from the truth, and shall be turned unto fables."

---

[1] Matthew 7:24-27

The god that people may erect in their hearts is often a god of convenience or comfort. He does not challenge them in their comfort zones nor will he call for separation from anything that might make the flesh or pride uneasy.

The harsh reality is that if we do not get our understanding of God right, we cannot be assured of real faith. He is the only true foundation of our spiritual life, as well as the author and finisher of our faith.[2]

True Faith is a Choice

Faith is not only based on our perception of God, but it is a choice of obedience. Abraham made a choice to obey God and leave his country and his father's house to go to an unknown land.[3] Romans 4:3 states, "Abraham believed God, and it was counted unto him for righteousness." Genuine faith establishes a person in righteousness before God.

Noah obeyed God because of faith, built an ark and was saved. Because of his active faith, he condemned the world and became an heir of righteousness.[4]

By faith, Moses refused to be known as the son of Pharaoh's daughter, and would not even allow himself to enjoy sin for a season. He actually chose to be mistreated along with the people of God. As a result, he became their leader.[5]

By obedient faith, Daniel and his three companions refused to defile themselves by eating the royal food. They were not only miraculously delivered at different times, but were blessed by God.[6]

Hebrews 11:33-35 tells us,
> Who through faith subdued kingdoms, wrought righteousness, obtained promises, stopped the mouths of lions, Quenched the violence of fire, escaped the edge of the sword, out of weakness were made strong, waxed valiant in fight, turned to flight the armies of the aliens. Women received their dead raised to life again....

What an awesome testimony of genuine faith.

Hebrews 12:1 concurs with the fact that we do have a great witness of the power of faith through these saints' examples. It states, "Wherefore seeing we also are compassed about with so great a cloud of witnesses, let us lay aside every weight, and the sin which doth so easily beset us, and let us run with patience the race that is set before us."

---

[2] 1 Corinthians 3:11; Hebrews 12:2
[3] Genesis 12:1-3
[4] Hebrews 11:7
[5] Hebrews 11:24-28
[6] Daniel 1, 3, 6

Much was accomplished and many wonders beheld because of people operating in true faith. But, on the other hand, great trials were experienced as well. Hebrews 11:35-38 goes on to say,

...And others were tortured, not accepting deliverance; that they might obtain a better resurrection: and others had trial of cruel mockings and scourgings, yea, moreover of bonds and imprisonment: They were stoned, they were sawn asunder, were tempted, were slain with the sword: they wandered about in sheepskins and goatskins; being destitute, afflicted, tormented; (Of whom the world was not worthy:) they wandered in deserts, and in mountains, and in dens and caves of the earth.

Obviously, true faith results in godly and sometimes sacrificial responses. These responses of commitment and obedience are our *"reasonable service."*[7] Therefore, genuine faith will ultimately produce obedience to God and His Word, regardless of how much flesh and pride may debate the matter.

We are once again reminded of how James 2:14-26 candidly talks about faith being an active choice. In verse 17, we read, "Even so faith, if it hath not works, is dead, being alone." James pointed to Abraham's willingness to sacrifice Isaac because of his faith. He reminded his readers of the active faith Rahab showed when she hid the spies, possibly putting her life in danger. James 2:24 and 26 concluded the matter by saying, "Ye see then how that by works a man is justified, and not by faith only... For as the body without the spirit is dead, so faith without works is dead also."

Our greatest example, Jesus Christ, confirmed by His actions of going to the cross that genuine faith on our part will express itself in obedience. Philippians 2:8 states, "And being found in fashion as a man, he humbled himself and became obedient unto death, even the death of the cross."

True Faith Finds Its Origin in God's Love

This brings us to the next subject. Genuine faith comes out of real love. The definition of love includes, "Beareth all things, believeth all things, hopeth all things, endureth all things. Charity never faileth" (1 Corinthians 13:7-8a).

Galatians 5:6 states, "For in Jesus Christ neither circumcision availeth any thing, nor uncircumcision; but faith which worketh by love." Therefore, godly love motivates true faith that will faithfully and naturally express itself in obedience.

Genuine faith is part of the fruit of the Spirit found in Galatians 5:22-23. Although the word is often translated as faithfulness on our part, this

---

[7] Romans 12:1

faithfulness is compared to the same response a committed servant would have towards his Lord. This type of commitment is motivated by sincere love. In Matthew 24:45-47, Jesus gives us this insight about what it means to be His faithful servant,

> Who then is a faithful and wise servant, whom his lord hath made ruler over his household, to give them meat in due season? Blessed is that servant, whom his lord when he cometh shall find so doing. Verily I say unto you, That he shall make him ruler over all his goods.

Jesus described such meat as doing the will of the Father. Such eternal meat will not perish. For the committed, obedient servant of Christ, the food is the preaching of the Gospel, and the impartation of the Word to others as a means to make them followers of Christ.[8] Such devoted faithfulness can only come out of true faith.

True Faith Involves a Process

Acts 15:9 made this statement about faith, "And put no difference between us and them, purifying their hearts by faith." The word, "sanctification" can also be used in the place of purify. Sanctification, or the work of holiness, is a setting apart unto God for His use and glory.

Faith will result in sanctification. The walk of faith separates or sets a person apart from sin, the world, and the kingdom of darkness. The steps of faith will take a person to the cross where death and suffering will occur.

Back in 1995, the fiery process of the faith walk was made evident to me in a greater way. My co-laborer, Jeannette, was close to death due to an overly toxic system. Her battle was hard and long. She suffered much, and there was nothing I could do but pray for her.

Meanwhile, my health was not good. I was close to being a diabetic, which caused problems with my blood sugar levels. There was infection in my lymphatic system causing me to be tired and ineffective. My intestinal system also had serious problems. Along with Jeannette, I had to change my diet drastically and get on a strict program of herbs and minerals. Praise God, He had already prepared me to take control over my body two years previously when I fought Candida by changing my diet and taking herbs to combat it.

As I sat in my chair meditating on the hard place we were in, the Lord gave me a vision of what was about to happen to the ministry and us. He showed me that we were in a boat in the eye of a hurricane. I knew the boat was running out of fuel, and I saw myself at the helm, trying to stay away from the full impact of the storm. Since we were running out of gas, I decided to get as far away from the impact of the storm as I could to give us some more valuable time. At that time, I heard

---

[8] Matthew 28:18-20; Mark 16:15-16; John 4:32-24; 6:26-29

the voice of the Lord. He told me, "Rayola, turn around and face the storm." I obeyed, knowing as soon as the storm hit us, that we would go down into the water.

I knew what the vision meant. Since the beginning of the ministry, Jeannette and I had been in the midst of a raging storm. Through a lot of our own strength, we had managed to stay away from the full impact of it, but now, our strength was ebbing away along with our finances. I knew the ministry, Jeannette, and I were heading for a watery grave. As I headed into the storm, I could feel us going down into the water and being consumed.

The Lord gave me the assurance that He would not allow the water to completely destroy us. He reminded me of His words in John 12:24-26:

> Verily, verily, I say unto you, Except a corn of wheat fall into the ground and die, it abideth alone: but if it die, it bringeth forth much fruit. He that loveth his life shall lose it; and he that hateth his life in this world shall keep it unto life eternal. If any man serve me, let him follow me; and where I am, there shall also my servant be: if any man serve me, him will my Father honour.

Jesus made this statement in reference to His death on the cross. He died so we could have life. If we are following Him, He will lead us to the cross, and there, we must lose our present lives in order for more spiritual seeds and fruit to come forth.

The watery grave represented a separation. The purpose of the grave was to bring forth greater anointing and resurrection power out of our lives. What a process!

I have come to the realization that the process often involves obscurity. Obscurity is a hard place when you have ideas of grandeur. In the area of ministry, we have often envisioned standing up in front of crowds of people, but real ministry takes us to prayer closets, into the trenches with lost, hurting people, or simply waiting on the Lord. The test is always the same, "Will I be found faithful wherever God places me? Can I learn to be content in whatever state I find myself? Will I offer the sacrifice of praise no matter what happens?""[9]

This faith walk led us to Houston, Texas. The Lord had begun to dry up our brook in the Seattle area. We sensed in our spirits that it was time to get rid of unnecessary belongings. I have learned that separation from belongings can be quite difficult. It has always amazed me how we cling to silly possessions, and how they cling to us.

During our purging time, the Lord laid on the heart of our friend, Krista, that she would be going with us. So, when the door opened, the

---

[9] Philippians 4:11; Hebrews 13:15

three of us packed up our belongings and started the long six-day journey in a 24-foot moving truck, pulling our car behind.

I had a feeling of great expectancy as we pulled out from the Seattle vicinity. I kept thinking that Houston held the key for raising the ministry up in newness, and getting it out from underneath the oppression it had been experiencing for the past seven years.

On the sixth day, just outside of Houston, we saw a dump truck recklessly pulling off to the side of the road. Suddenly, we noticed something lying in the road. I thought it was a piece of tire, but we found out too late that it was a metal part. I managed to straddle it with the truck, but the car was not as fortunate. The piece hit underneath the car in five places, totally destroying the gas tank. We should have blown up.

The Houston experience proved to fall short of my expectations. Instead of being set free, we found ourselves in greater obscurity. Our car finally fell apart; therefore, we were left in a strange place without a car, friends, or much support. The Lord showed us that He had the three of us right where He wanted us, and He was about to do a deeper work in each of our lives.

Eventually, you quit asking the question, "How long, Lord?" and you begin to ask Him to help you pass the test, to endure to the end. You might say, "Boy, this faith walk is not glamorous." You are right. It is not glamorous, but it is rewarding.

The process brings you closer to God. Obscurity forces you to wait upon Him and listen closely for His voice. The fiery process makes your faith of greater worth than gold. Gold will eventually perish in the fire, but genuine faith will be purified in the fire, for it is eternal. 1 Corinthians 13:13 confirms this characteristic. This chapter declares that when all else ceases, these three virtues remain—faith, hope, and love.

Real Faith Includes a Battle

The Scriptures declare that we are in a spiritual battle. But, what is this battle? Jude 3 gives us a clue about our battle, "Beloved, when I gave all diligence to write unto you of the common salvation, it was needful for me to write unto you, and exhort you that ye should earnestly contend for the faith which was once delivered unto the saints."

The real battle involves our faith. Satan does everything he can to attack our confidence in the character of God. He strives to have us question our God's intentions by subtly exchanging the promises of God's Word for his lies. He brings doubt into our minds about the commitment and love God has for us. He robs us of the joy of our salvation, steals the assurance we have in our God's greatness, and blinds us to the hope that is ever before us. He can be very effective in his devices.

Paul understood the battle quite well. You can see by the sequence of his statement in 2 Timothy 4:7 that the persevering of his faith was his ultimate victory at the end of his life, "I have fought a good fight, I have finished my course, I have kept the faith."

The Apostle Paul also had some instructions about our enemy. In 2 Corinthians 2:11, he made this statement, "Lest Satan should get an advantage of us: for we are not ignorant of his devices." Paul was saying that believers should not be ignorant of Satan's schemes, but in my years of ministry, I have found that many are quite ignorant of his devices.

Jesus said in John 8:44 that Satan has, "no truth in him." Satan's greatest devices are lies. He causes people to focus on self, rather than the love, work, and power of God. This misdirected focus puts the burden of dealing with sin, transforming the mind, and changing direction totally on the person, instead of upon God. If a person does not recognize the deception, he or she will either become self-righteous or feel condemned and depressed.

Another effective weapon that Satan uses comes in the form of people's vain imaginations. The devil weaves his destruction by planting what appear to be logical doubts in a person's mind. These doubts undermine the Word of God and create unbelief and fear.

Many people I have ministered to have been bound up by these vain imaginations. With the help of the Holy Spirit, these fiery darts can easily be exposed, but once they are, the person must choose to believe either the Word of God or Satan. He or she must then strive to allow God to reveal and bring down vain imaginations, and bring all of his or her thoughts into the obedience of Christ.[10]

Another powerful tool of Satan is pride. Pride is a wide open invitation for Satan to come in and have a hey-day with a person's faith. Pride will keep a person from humbling him or herself, and submitting to God, which causes Satan to flee in the face of such humility.[11] Pride that is reigning means Jesus is not Lord. If Jesus is not Lord, then He cannot protect the person. I have witnessed terrible devastation come upon people who will not come under the Lordship of Jesus.

This was made evident in the life of a woman who came to us for help. When I questioned her about her problem, she told me she had many demons. It did not take long to discover that she was telling the truth. After working with this woman in intervals totaling over 30 hours, we finally got down to the fact that she wanted relief from her demons, but not restoration with God through Jesus Christ. She refused to submit to the Lordship of Christ, thus denying herself liberty and setting her

---

[10] 2 Corinthians 10:3-5
[11] James 4:6-10

eternal course. Although we managed to cast out many demons, they started to flood back in because she did not want Jesus.[12]

The last time I spoke with her, she had determined to deliver herself. Her conceit was quite obvious, and her pride about her demonic power was at its height. Her ability to use these powers of darkness to control people gave her much pleasure. However, in the end, I knew Satan had won total rights to her soul and ultimately, he would destroy her.

In another incident, a person became obsessed with being my closest friend. This individual had many problems, but she also had an abundance of pride. She was contrary, sarcastic, spoke crudely, and was always causing trouble. She would strive hard to control and manipulate those around her. It was a constant battle to keep her from stepping over unacceptable boundaries that involved my life and the ministry.

Her obsession turned into a nightmarish situation where Satan began to plague her. She heard voices and accused me of saying things to her I did not say. She mocked the things of God. The one thing I was constantly aware of was her insatiable need for attention and to be a "somebody" in the scheme of things.

In my confrontation with her, I addressed her pride. I told her she needed to repent and that she had to let go of the control by submitting herself to God. The last time I talked to her, she was avoiding repentance. She was considering spiritual warfare, but not looking at her pride or rebellion. She wanted an easy way out without it costing her the ability to control others.

Another powerful avenue is anger. Anger can branch out into other tributaries such as bitterness, resentment, and unforgiveness. The motivations behind its existence and momentum are usually pride or fear. Ephesians 4:25-26 tells us to not let the sun go down on our anger which gives a foothold to Satan.

There was a professing Christian who refused to forgive a person. Although the offense resulted in grave consequences for the one who had been in sin, the person who was offended the most felt she had a right to be angry and unforgiving, giving way to Satan. Eventually, the anger formed a root of bitterness that defiled everything in her life.[13]

Although the Word is quite clear about ungodly attitudes such as anger, this woman ignored the Scriptures, and gave way to the dictates of self. I watched her heart become harder and harder towards God and His instructions. Beware; it's easy to become a "Pharaoh" in heart when you insist on the ways of Satan.[14]

Satan's tactics are easy to understand, but they can take on many disguises. All of these disguises are capable of undermining a person's

---

[12] Matthew 12:43-45
[13] Hebrews 12:15
[14] Exodus 8:32

trust in God and justifying his or her lack of obedience to His Word. As Satan wins with his devices, people begin to fall into a pit of suspicion and unbelief. Their spiritual eyes become blind, their ears deaf, and their spiritual life chaotic.

What about you? Are you fighting a good fight or have you given way to the enemy's devices? A good way to test this area of your life is to ask yourself, "What is my attitude towards God?" If any unbelief, anger, or fear crops up, Satan has managed to weave something into your spiritual life to bring defeat. Humble yourself and cry out to God, for He is faithful to hear you and meet you in your plight.

Coming Around the Mountain... Again

True faith will bring you back around the mountain where you actually started in your walk with Christ. We see this in Peter's life. After Christ died and rose again, we see Peter going back to fishing, his old life. It became obvious to Peter that his old life was as empty as his fishing nets, but he was lost without his Leader. He had come too far to turn back, but he had lost his direction and had no idea where to go or how to start.[15] When Jesus stepped on the scene, we see Peter forsaking all. He jumped into the sea without consideration of life, and swam to shore to speak to His resurrected Lord.

Like Peter, many Christians are brought back around to see the emptiness of their old life. This experience in the Christian life simply proves that the individual is not the same person. Something has happened that has forever changed the person's life and course. There is no attraction, no worldly fruit, or no purpose to the old life. All that presently matters is ensuring the reality of the Person of Jesus.

This lesson became more apparent each time God brought me around the mountain. I realized I valued Jesus more, and that my faith had become more grounded and directed at my blessed Lord who gave it all.

God brought me back around the mountain when He brought us back to Idaho. Idaho was the place where my Christian life and maturity went through the initial growth, failures, testing, and fires. It was here where I determined in my heart to follow Jesus no matter what the cost.

I can remember that long-ago day when I made that decision. I was on the back of a Honda Goldwing 1000 bike, riding up a beautiful, scenic road. I had all the material things I could ask for along with what people would consider worldly security. However, as I was considering all of the material things, I realized they held no real value in light of my real heart desire. I wanted to sell out to God and serve Jesus Christ. I remember saying to God, "If I cannot serve You, take me home right now because nothing makes sense."

---

[15] John 21:1-7

I know now, that was the day I stepped across a line that would forever change the status of my Christian life. Life as I knew it would go up in the air, and even though I would leave with a bit more than Lot had when he left Sodom and Gomorrah, I would not have the desire to look back like Lot's wife. In fact, I have never looked back.

When God began to show me in Houston that He was sending me back to Idaho after a four-year absence from the state, I was reluctant to accept such a thought. I struggled with it because I wanted to go to Georgia, the opposite direction. Eventually, I submitted to God's convicting power.

Coming back to Idaho was a reality check. I was not the same person. It was as if the old life that I lived actually happened to someone else, even though I was aware that it was the old me who had lived it. I no longer cared about the things I used to pursue, because my priorities had changed. As a Christian who had matured in the fire and the flood, I had more confidence in my Lord. I also possessed a sobriety that served as an anchor. My pride had somewhat been replaced by a keen awareness of my own depravity which served as a constant mirror to me.

The Lord even went so far as to bring me back into the place where I had actually grown up, and had my first initial experiences as a new Christian. My hometown represented both victories and failures to me. In fact, I had left in a state of disgrace eight years prior. Now I was invited to speak at a revival meeting. It had not been advertised in the paper and needless to say, a few people who knew me were quite surprised to find out the identity of their mystery speaker.

God had amazingly prepared a table in the presence of former enemies. Exaltation in front of those who formerly held confusing or controversial opinions of you is always humbling and interesting. However, all exaltation of this type is for the sole purpose of glorifying Him. As a saint is lifted up in newness of life, God's work is on visible display. As a result, He is lifted up and glorified in the person's life.

Through it all, I learned that God is faithful. He has brought me through fiery ovens, watery graves, and over mountains. It has been an adventure where self has been exposed, God's character explored, and my Christian life and character enhanced. It has been a rewarding life comprised of surprises. As a result, I live in a state of great expectancy because I know that my God is able to do the impossible. He is able to raise a person out of obscurity, make crooked paths straight, and remove all obstacles.

Since becoming a Christian, have you become a seasoned mountain climber in your faith in God? After each mountain experience, do you find that you are the same person, and are you a more seasoned Christian who appreciates the faithfulness of God? Genuine faith will first bring a person into the depths of the valley in order to bring him or her higher. Therefore, each trek around the mountain will bring an individual higher in Christ.

Restoration

God's heart is restoration; therefore, real faith will result in restoration. However, there cannot be restoration until there is a tearing down. God has been shaking and tearing down all of my foundations in order to build up and restore my life for His purpose.

I have watched God restore my barren wilderness with His beauty. He has turned my obscurity into a greater revelation of Him, and my grave experience into His resurrection life. He has unveiled the marred vessel I was, so I could appreciate the new vessel He was making me into for His glory. [16]

As I look back over my Christian life, the task to shape my life was incredible. I can only compare it to the intensity and power that went into creation. God took something void and without real form, and actually made it into something beautiful with purpose. Each step of faith was designed to lead me down His path, and each detour He orchestrated was to prepare and shape me. His commitment to make my life precious is an expression of His heart, and His ability to make me a new creation is a confirmation of His deity and awesome power.

Just recently, I have been able to enjoy the restoration that He has been bringing to my life. The reason for this enjoyment comes down to the fact that much of myself is now out of the way. Up until recently, I fought His work because I was limited and could not see what He was creating in my life. I could not understand why the process was hard and long. After all, I am only the clay.

The walk of faith has taught me to finally trust my loving Lord and Savior with my life. I have confidence in Him and now I enjoy peace. It is such a relief because much of the fighting and struggle is gone. Restoration has taken place in my life. Health, finances, and spiritual well-being have been and continue to be restored. God is faithful to keep His promises, and will never forsake us. [17]

How about you? Do you need restoration in your life? Begin to take God at His Word. Walk towards Him with the simplicity and sincerity of a child, and He will meet you. Once you encounter Him, you will never be the same because you have met with the God of the Universe who has an everlasting love for you. You can trust Him for He will never fail you no matter how much you may fail Him in your weak humanity. [18]

---

[16] Jeremiah 18:1-6; Romans 9:19-23; 2 Timothy 2:20-21
[17] Hebrews 13:5
[18] 2 Timothy 2:13

Conclusion

I pray I have done the subject of faith some justice. I know there is no real ending to this book. Faith is eternal, and God's faithfulness and intervention on our behalf will continue until we meet Jesus face-to-face. Miracles will occur as our faith allows God to move on our behalf. And, the many priceless lessons around this subject will continue to be reinforced. Those who walk by this eternal virtue will discover a greater measure of the life of Christ as each lesson is reinforced and embraced.

The Word of God tells us there is an end to a person's faith as far as his or her physical journey here. The end of real faith in this life simply stipulates a promise and a new beginning for each of us. Peter tells us what the end of our faith is—the salvation of our souls. As the author and finisher of our faith, Jesus stands at the beginning and the end of the work of redemption. He is Jehovah our Savior, our salvation, and our Lord, and there is none like Him. This is a great consolation for the weary stranger, pilgrim, or Christian soldier. Therefore, each believer can confidently look up in great expectation, for his or her redemption draws near.[19]

---

[19] 1 Peter 1:9; 2:11; Hebrews 12:2; 2 Timothy 2:3; Luke 21:28

Book Four

THINK ON
THESE THINGS

INTRODUCTION

There is a battle going on for the minds and hearts of people. It is an intense battle. After all, who or what controls or influences the minds of individuals will own their affections, devotion, and focus. It will influence their agendas and priorities. Ultimately, it will determine their worldview as to how they view God and life, and what they decide to worship and serve.

Getting a hold of the mind is of the utmost importance. You must get a hold of the mind before you can challenge or influence the affections of the heart. The Word of God brings this out as well. We are told that we faint in our minds, and that our minds need to be transformed. As you study the Word, you will realize that God's Word exposes how people perceive things in order to bring the proper contrast and instruction to change the wrong way of thinking.

The Word of God not only tells us its goal, but it instructs us as to how to change such wrong thinking. It has always been incredible to me to realize the simplicity in the truths of God. You see such simplicity when taking into consideration one Scripture, Philippians 4:8, in which we are told how to change our mind. It comes down to disciplining the mind to think on certain things.

The truths of God are simple, but the carnal mind is not capable of receiving them in simplicity and sincerity. The unregenerate mind will complicate such truths, spiritualize them, adjust them, or change them, but it will not receive them in a right spirit. Obviously, the carnal mind must go through much regression before the mind can progress in a right way of thinking.

This small book is about coming to terms with what it means to develop a right way of thinking. It comes down to developing a right disposition and attitude. It is an upright attitude that ensures a right spirit. And, it is only from a right spirit that the mind can begin to receive, handle, and apply the truths of God in a way in which it can be transformed by the eternal truths of His glorious revelations.

1

THE BATTLE FOR THE MIND

The Word of God is clear that there is a battle for the mind. Hebrews 12:3 tells us that people faint in their minds. Clearly, this is where the battle is lost. For if a person is fainting in his or her mind, he or she is now operating in fear and unbelief, rather than faith in God and confidence in His Word. Revelation 21:8 reminds us that the fearful and unbelieving will end up in the lake of fire.

When you consider the concept of the mind, it is often associated with our brain. Granted, the brain is responsible for our bodily functions. However, the mind in Scripture points to the function of the soul. The soul can be inspired by spirit, but in most cases, its greatest influence comes from the influence of the spirit of the world. The type of spirit a person gives way to will affect how he or she views or reacts to the surrounding world.

Obviously, the mind not only includes the intellect, but it includes all of the senses in which we process the matters of life. In fact, we automatically consider all matters in light of our senses. For example, thinking inspires senses, and senses trigger the thought process. It is from the point of senses that we identify and interpret our environment. We will consider how something affects our hearing, and we evaluate matters as to whether they are attractive to our eyes. We taste something to see if it brings pleasure to our personal preferences. We will consider the fragrance of something to see if it pleases our sense of smell. We also must touch things to experience how it will make us feel. And, we must not forget that sixth sense which puts us in touch with the unseen or supernatural. After all, each sense connects us to the others to bring about certain sensations. It is from the basis of these sensations that we often judge or weigh the matters of life. However, these senses often reveal that we tend to consider everything from a fleshly or soulish perspective.

The Word of God is clear that such a perspective is perverted, and will bring us into opposition to God. Such a state operates in death and walks the broad path to hell. It mocks the things of the Spirit and rejects the simple truths of God.[1]

---

[1] Matthew 7:13-14; Romans 8:7

The key to properly interpreting our environment does not involve weighing matters according to our senses, but disciplining our thinking. Thinking often comes into subjection to our senses, rather than bringing our senses into subjection to our thought process. This can be regularly observed in people as they allow the emotions caused by their senses to determine their reality. Such people appear to be fickle rather than grounded. By bringing senses into subjection to a disciplined mind under the control of the Spirit, a person will be able to properly discern his or her environment, as well as the spirit in operation.

Senses that are not disciplined under the Spirit are not able to give us a fair evaluation concerning life. At this stage, they often become the god we bow down to in regard to how we look at life. They will inspire our attitude towards our Creator God and life. In most cases, undisciplined senses perceive God and the matters of life as being unfair.

By disciplining our thinking, we can bring our senses into the right perspective. As you study the Bible, you realize that our senses are used to judge matters of life. They will determine how we perceive or hear something. Jesus told us to beware of how we hear matters concerning life.[2] To reiterate an important point, when our senses are brought into the proper subjection to the right spirit, they will be used to discern, not judge.

There is a big difference between discerning and judging. Judgment that comes out of the undisciplined senses brings us back to judgmental pride, which is not only the natural motivation of our fleshly, unregenerate state, but it proves to be harsh, unfeeling, and indifferent. Discernment on the other hand, means that our thought process is under the Holy Ghost's leading. We are able to discern the matters of the unseen world around us. The Apostle Paul brings this out in 1 Corinthians 2:13-14:

> Which things also we speak not in the words which man's wisdom teacheth, but which the Holy Ghost teacheth, comparing spiritual things with spiritual. But the natural man receiveth not the things of the Spirit of God: for they are foolishness unto him: neither can he know them, because they are spiritually discerned.

The importance of disciplining our thought process is that in such a state we allow the Spirit of God to transform our mind. This is a must if we are ever going to possess the mind that is sensitive to the Spirit. Transforming the mind also involves changing our senses as to how they interpret a matter. Senses must be disciplined to not *determine* reality, but to come into subjection to the right spirit to *discern* reality. Obviously, our senses must be in subjection to the thought process. The Apostle Paul instructed believers to bring every thought into captivity and into the obedience of Christ.[3]

---

[2] Luke 8:18
[3] Romans 12:2; 2 Corinthians 10:4-5

By bringing our thoughts into subjection to Christ, we can bring all of our senses into submission to the Holy Spirit. Such a practice serves as the means to bring the mind or soul under control. Once the soul is under control, a person will be able to possess his or her soul in patience.[4] "Possessing one's soul in patience" points to owning, acquiring, obtaining, or purchasing his or her soul through the tribulations of life.[5]

It is vital we consider how the mind will be transformed. As already pointed out, the mind must be disciplined. Transformation of the mind implies a complete change. However, to change something, especially that which opposes the present state of affairs, requires going against the grain of a matter before the actual state will begin to change. Hence, enters discipline.

Obviously, for us to go against the grain of our natural influences and responses, we first must discipline our thought process. This means we must cease from being conformed to that which influences our way of thinking. The world initially influences our way of thinking. Therefore, the Apostle Paul instructs us to cease from being conformed to the world's way of thinking.[6]

Being conformed to the world's way of thinking means we are being conditioned or bent towards the influences and persuasions of the world. We will automatically act according to the prevalent persuasion of the age we live in. But, such persuasion brings us under the spirit of the world. The spirit of the world makes us rebellious or contrary to God's way of thinking. As you consider how God looks at such thinking, you cannot help but remember the condition of people in Noah's day. It is recorded that the imaginations of the thoughts of their hearts were continually evil before the Lord.[7]

The finality of this process is that people will not retain knowledge of the true God. They will have no real basis in which to test or discern a matter. In fact, they will possess another god and worship the creation of their own minds. They may perceive that they possess the one true God of the Bible, but they will be strictly operating in delusion and superstition.

In Philippians 4:8, we are told what to think upon to ensure such discipline. As you study this Scripture, you will observe that what we think about will determine our state of mind. For example, if we think on the things of God, our life in Christ will be edified, our soul brought into harmony with His mind, and our spirit will be tuned unto God, thereby, experiencing His peace. If we think on the things of the world, our lusts will be stirred up, our pride tempted, and our rights to the self-life exalted.

---

[4] Luke 21:19

[5] Strong's Exhaustive Concordance, #2932

[6] Romans 12:2

[7] Genesis 6:5; Ephesians 2:2-3

The result can be anything from indifference towards reality, to jealousies, perversion, anger, and disillusionment.

To ensure our mind is transformed, we must understand the thought process. It is not done by the actual brain, but from the aspect of our heart. Our heart condition, or inner environment, will determine how we perceive a matter. Needless to say, the senses are wrapped up with the affections or desires of our heart. Jesus made this statement, "For where your treasure is, there will your heart be also" (Matthew 6:21).

Thinking actually involves five steps. They are as follows: Take inventory (take stock), estimate (examine), count (to know), reason (to come to a conclusion), and reckon (determine it is so). As you consider each step, you will realize that thinking clearly involves a process. However, this thinking process is automatic to each of us; therefore, we do not recognize the steps we take in regard to a matter. Therefore, let us consider how each step works.

The first step we take is an inventory of what we understand. This inventory is necessary because it will bring a much-needed contrast to a matter. Much of the present inventory of what we understand has been taken from various sources such as family, culture, education, religion, and experience. Taking this inventory represents the premise in which we will consider a situation. However, the Word of God warns us that we know in part due to the veil of our flesh.[8] No matter how wise and intelligent our premise may appear, we are still starting from a limited plane of understanding. After all, we can only see in part, the rest we must rightly discern if we are to come to valid conclusions.

After we determine our premise, we must size up or examine what is obvious. This means we must gather up the evidence that is obvious about a matter. Evidence represents the fruit of a situation. What does such fruit say about the environment? The problem with examining the evidence is that it is not always able to tell the whole story. Our estimation of a subject may not be fair since we are only capable of knowing part of the story. Even the best estimation will not reveal the unseen aspect of a situation. Therefore, evidence can prove to be biased and untrustworthy. However, estimation is part of the process of coming to what we consider to be a valid conclusion. In our mind, once the evaluation is found wrong, then our estimation can be changed.

Once we come to the end of estimating a matter, we will feel that we have sufficient evidence to count a matter as being true. "Count" is a mathematical term. It points to a matter always adding up to the same answer. Although our thinking has a tendency to get into a rut, few of us realize that we will always come to the same conclusion, unless we are willing to step outside of what we already perceive as true. We will always conclude that we do have the necessary information to have a right understanding of a situation. This is why Proverbs 16:2 gives us this

---

[8] 1 Corinthians 13:9

warning, "All the ways of a man are clean in his own eyes; but the LORD weigheth the spirits."

Since we have counted our estimation as true, we begin the process of reasoning out the matter. In some cases this reasoning is nothing more than logic. Someone once said God works from logic. This is untrue. Logic begins from a premise of what the person thinks is already true. It is from this premise that he or she will reason with available information with the intent of confirming his or her premise. Therefore, logic does not seek out truth, but will simply confirm its conclusions about a matter.

Reasoning is God's way of bringing a proper contrast to show one what is true. For example, sin is sin, but man has a tendency to logic it away with justification. God, therefore, reasons with each of us about sin by presenting a clear picture of sin in light of His character, Word, and redemption.[9] Reasoning brings us to an understanding that will enable us to agree with God about His conclusion to a matter.

Once we are brought to a conclusion, we reckon or determine that the conclusion is so. In other words, it becomes a matter of truth. At this point we see no reason to debate the subject any longer. However, our conclusions could be nothing more than presumptions that prove to be limiting in perception and stiff-necked when it comes to being wrong or challenged.

The real issue to a matter is that once truth is applied it becomes reality. In most cases conclusions remain theories that sound good, but often prove to be ineffective in practice. This means that they remain a concept that will not stand when tested. Truth will always stand, and will become reality when properly applied to a situation.

This brings us to what can be counted trustworthy. For example, our conclusions will translate into opinions, platitudes, experiences, or truth. Opinions are nothing more than the expression of our overrated ego. We think highly of our conclusions; therefore, they become a matter of pride.[10] In fact, it is not unusual for people to skip one of these steps in their thought process. For example, some people start from their own premise of conceit; therefore, they will skip the first step of even taking inventory. They assume they already have all the necessary information to come to a healthy conclusion. The Apostle Paul gives this warning, "Be of the same mind one toward another. "...Mind not high things, but condescend to men of low estate. Be not wise in your own conceits" (Romans 12:16).

Others actually skip the reasoning part because they perceive that their present feelings or ideas are already revealing the correct conclusion. They conclude that there is no way they can be wrong. However, 1 Corinthians 10:12 gives this warning, "Wherefore let him that

---

[9] Isaiah 1:18

[10] Romans 12:3; Galatians 6:3

thinketh he standeth take heed lest he fall." Obviously, when people skip a step in their thinking process, it is because they have switched from seeking information to operating according to assumptions or presumptions.

When people fail to humble themselves enough to come to a healthy conclusion, they will also fail to arrive at a wise determination. Without the determination, nothing will be done or accomplished. This determination serves as the initiative to put what is considered truth into practice. Often, such people resort to using platitudes when their understanding of a matter fails them. Platitudes, whether religious, scriptural, or made up of worldly wisdom may sound wise, but they often come across as "sounding brass" or a "tinkling cymbal".[11] It is obvious that people who use platitudes are not in step with what is going on. In fact, if religion or Scripture is attached to platitudes, it comes across as being dead-letter, devoid of spirit and life.

When you consider the premise people operate in, and how they often start from assumptions as they develop presumptions about a matter, you begin to understand how biased, dogmatic, and unrealistic opinions and platitudes become. Such people are operating within a limited or faulty premise. Obviously, these people may come out with overrated opinions and unfeeling platitudes that reek with arrogance, indifference. and judgmentalism. However, such conclusions will appear foolish, cruel, and out of touch with reality.

The third premise that people can operate in is that of experience. Experience translates into common sense. Common sense simply means that a person can evaluate a situation from a realistic basis due to experiencing different aspects of life. Instead of remaining clueless and obnoxious about life during trying times, these individuals have actually learned the lessons of life. As a result, they develop a sense about similar incidents. This sense tells the experienced individual why something is probably happening, what is going to happen if matters do not change, and the consequences that will follow. The fact that a person is able to hit the target in different ways reveals that this person is displaying common sense towards a matter. In fact, according to the world's perception common sense is considered wisdom. It is true that common sense reveals wisdom, but it is wisdom that comes from one's ability to be realistic about life, and not from above. Such wisdom is still tainted by earthly limitations, personal preferences, and conceits.[12]

The Word of God actually tells us where experience fits into the scheme of things in Romans 5:3-5. Experience begins with tribulation. Tribulation points to the testing and establishment of character or integrity. It takes character to develop patience.

Many people ask for patience without their character being properly tempered. The work of patience becomes unbearable since these

---

[11] 1 Corinthians 13:1

[12] Compare the two types of wisdoms in James 3:13-18

individuals have no real staying power or endurance. Once patience is in place, it will produce experience. Experience for the Christian is not necessarily developed because of a trying time; rather it is produced once a person endures a time of testing.

Experience includes the beginning of the tribulation, the trying time of tribulation, and the end of the tribulation. It embraces the lessons that are discovered through such trials. Lessons become nuggets of wisdom that can benefit others. As a result, experience is able to comfort others and produce hope. It is through experience that believers encounter the faithfulness of God. Our hope in who God is will give us confidence to stand because we will possess the love of God.

Now as you consider the first three premises in which we may evaluate the matters of life, you will realize opinions are *rarely* applicable to a matter. They will often prove to be foolish and indifferent to what is going on. Platitudes hold some semblance of wisdom, but they can prove to be cruel because they lack substance or personal insight. Therefore, they may prove to be applicable on *occasion*. Experience can prove to be a point of instruction; however, the percentage of hitting the mark is *50%*. Experience is limited because situations vary. As a result, advice that comes from experience must be considered in light of the situation.

However, there is always one premise that will always prove to be applicable, and that is God's truth. Interestingly enough, Philippians 4:8 begins with this very premise. It is important that we consider what it means to think upon that which is true.

2

THE PREMISE

The premise of a matter will not only determine the conclusion of it, but the spirit or intent in which a person approaches a situation. Premise is a person's vantage point from which he or she considers all matters. People may operate within the premise of opinions, platitudes, experiences, or truth, which brings us to the four vantage points from which people will consider the issues of life: the fleshly self-life, the world, Satan, or God. The first three views are assumed vantage points because they lack the ability to gain a realistic view about a matter. We know that the vantage point of self will pervert reality, while the world view will defile reality. Both views point to a person being earthbound to a very limited self-serving view. In fact, people who have these vantage points will eventually dig pits or trenches of hopelessness. Those who consider all matters from the perspective of Satan's view will operate in the darkness of delusion, wickedness, and destruction.

The Apostle Paul clearly established the premise up front for every believer in Philippians 4:8, "Finally brethren whatever things are true...think on these things." According to *Strong's Exhaustive Concordance*, the word "true" means not to conceal a matter.[1] In my *Webster's Dictionary* it points to something that is true as being transparent, faithful, to be in accordance with the actual state of affairs, and to be accurate.

The concept of truth seems simple enough, but in reality, truth is far from the preferable practice for most societies. For America, many live according to fantasies produced by various sources such at Hollywood, the media, and politics. This false reality causes many in America to shun the actual state of affairs. For some cultures, deception is an act that they take much pleasure in for it represents status. For other cultures if lies justify the means, so be it. After all, such matters can be in the name of religion, protection, or political correctness. The harsh reality is that all lies or false realities go back to one source. Jesus identified this source, "Ye are of your father the devil, and the lusts of your father ye will do. He was a murderer from the beginning, and abode not in the

---

[1] # 227

truth, because there is no truth in him. When he speaketh a lie, he speaketh of his own: for he is a liar, and the father of it" (John 8:44).

The question is why do we feel the need to conceal a matter? The answer is simple. The matter is not honorable. For example, if we adjust the truth in any way, it becomes propaganda that intends to seduce while hiding the essence of a real matter. If we effectively change the truth about something, we can influence a person's philosophy. If we can deny truth by debating it away, we can maintain the reality we desire. Obviously, to deviate from truth requires a person to hide the darkness of deception or wicked agenda under some type of cloak or false reality. Isaiah 30:1 makes this statement, "Woe to the rebellious children, saith the LORD, that take counsel, but not of me; and that cover with a covering, but not of my spirit, that they may add sin to sin."

Jesus made this statement in John 15:22, "If I had not come and spoken unto them, they had not had sin: but now they have no cloak for their sin." Cloaks imply that the person is putting on an outward show since there is no real substance behind it. Such an outward show is pretext or pretense. In essence, it is hiding hypocrisy. The Lord stated that He was hated for removing the cloak that hides sin. There are four types of cloaks that people can hide behind. Let us consider how they work.

The first cloak is found in Genesis 3:7. This cloak was nothing more than *fig leaves*. It was used to hide the spiritual nakedness of man. It was man's way of covering up his shame, independence, and separation from God. Although flimsy and appearing non-threatening, it represents fake nobility that hides pride, rebellion, and deceit.

The first man, Adam, wore this cloak. He actually thought he would blend into the scene, and God would not notice that his relationship and status with Him had changed. However, God had to search for him. It was not that God did not know where Adam was; rather, it was Adam who needed to recognize where he was. He was hiding from God. Not only was he hiding from God, but he also was trying to conceal his state of spiritual nakedness. Due to his rebellion, he no longer had a relationship with God. The problem with hiding is that it proves that man wants to hide in the darkness so the light will not reveal his real spiritual state and deeds.

Jesus brought this state out in John 3:19-21:

> And this is the condemnation, that light is come into the world, and men loved darkness rather than light, because their deeds were evil. For everyone that doeth evil hateth the light, neither cometh to the light, lest his deeds should be reproved. But he that doeth truth cometh to the light, that his deeds may be made manifest, that they are wrought in God.

The light of truth reveals sin, and will call us to personal accountability. Most men refuse to come to the light to avoid repentance because they love their wicked deeds. Therefore, when the light comes on, they quickly put on fig leaves to cover their spiritual nakedness, and rush to hide in the shadows of compromise and self-justification.

The second cloak is that of *religion*. The Apostle Paul brings this out in 2 Timothy 3:5, "Having a form of godliness, but denying the power thereof: from such turn away." The religious cloak is a thick cloak. It is very deceptive for it looks good on the outside, but in reality it covers white-washed tombs that are full of dead men's bones and all uncleanness.

The Pharisees of Jesus' day wore this type of cloak. They had religious robes that distinguished them, but did not have lives before God that made their testimonies alive and anointed. They advocated religion without any mercy, sacrifice without any heart, worship that only served as lip service, doctrine that was dead-letter, and a legalistic lifestyle that was hypocritical. [2] These individuals proved by their religious cloaks that what their robes were covering up was the fact that they did not really know God. Therefore, their religious pretense was simply hiding tombs of dead men's religious activities. When the truth exposed their state, they in turn set out to crucify the truth.

The next cloak is found in Matthew 22:11-14. This is a parable about the king who invited all to the wedding. He discovers one man who was not wearing the proper wedding garments. Now keep in mind this man accepted the wedding invitation, but he did not prepare for it. He was an observer, not a participant. In other words, he did not show the proper honor or regard to be part of the celebration.

This man represents those who try to slide by or slide into the kingdom of heaven based on their *personal works and merits* without paying the necessary price to be prepared. Man's best is filthy rags. There is no goodness found in man's flesh and no righteousness in his personal deeds. As a result, Jesus calls us to a life of self-denial and the cross. Such a life points to putting off the old in order to put on the new.[3]

The new is the disposition and life of the Lord Jesus Christ. The Apostle Paul tells us our righteousness is found in Christ. He is the essence of wisdom, righteousness, sanctification, and redemption. By being in Christ, and Christ being in us, He serves as our robe of righteousness. The robe that was placed upon the prodigal son signifies this garment.

The prodigal son came home after being in a pigpen. No doubt he reeked of the filth and odor of the world. However, he came home in an attitude of repentance with the intent to serve in his father's house as a mere servant. His father welcomed him with an embrace, a ring, a robe, and a celebration that involved sacrificing the fatted calf. The father's embrace pointed to salvation; the ring to the Holy Spirit; the robe to the

---

[2] Matthew 9:13; 15:1-9; 23:27: 2 Corinthians 3:6
[3] Isaiah 64:6; Luke 9:23-24; Romans 7:18; Ephesians 4:22-24

righteousness of Christ; the celebration to heaven rejoicing; and the fatted calf to the sacrifice of Jesus.[4] The ring was given to the son, and the robe was placed upon him.

There is no righteousness outside of Jesus. It is by being in Him that we are seen from the throne of God as being righteous. It is His life in us that makes us acceptable to God. This is why the Apostle Paul gave us this instruction in Romans 13:14, "But put you on the Lord Jesus Christ, and make not provision for the flesh, to fulfill the lusts thereof."

The final cloak represents the *best the world* can provide. The Babylonian garment that Achan took in Joshua 7 fittingly represents this cloak. The Babylonian garment represented the glamour, beauty, and enticements of the world. It embodied the spirit of the world, which is nothing more than empty show and pretense.

Sadly, many in the Church are caught up with the robe of the world. They have brought this empty show into the Church through unholy alliances, fleshly worship, and worldly philosophies and practices. Obviously, these people fail to learn the lesson associated with these false cloaks. For Adam, his cloak hid broken fellowship and the judgment of death. For the religious leaders, their robe hid their dead religious works and the greater damnation they were facing. For the wedding guest, the absence of the right garment and the presence of his own cloak singled him out to taste the judgment of hell. For Achan, his cloak not only represented the fact that his presence and that of his family would be completely wiped out from among the living, but it also brought terrible repercussions on all of the children of Israel.

Isaiah 25:7 tells us God will destroy the wicked covering that covers the people and the veil that is spread over all nations. The light will reveal all hidden matters. As Christians we must walk in the light to have all revealed that is not acceptable to God. In fact, all works of darkness must be reproved for the benefit of reconciliation, restoration, and fellowship.[5] We must not allow the darkness of compromise, personal justification, and self-delusion to cover up or justify dishonorable attitudes and practices.

To cover up the fact that we are lacking honorable intentions or actions is our way of setting up a false reality that we want others to believe. God refers to anything that is false as a false way. Psalms 119:104, 128 tells us that we should hate every false way.

The Word of God also confronts what it means to conceal a matter that needs to be brought to the light. Proverbs 28:13 states, "He that covereth his sins shall not prosper, but whoso confesseth and forsaketh them shall have mercy." Clearly, God cannot bless, forgive, or restore those who hold onto their sins. John tells us in his first epistle that those

---

[4] Luke 15:11-32; 1 Corinthians 1:30

[5] Luke 12:2-3; John 3:21; 2 Corinthians 5:8-15; Ephesians 5:8-13; 1 John 1:3-7

who confess their sins will be forgiven and cleansed from all unrighteousness.[6]

Psalm 66:18 tells us that if we regard iniquity in our heart, God will not hear our prayers. Sin erodes authority, power, and confidence before God. It enfolds us in darkness that will cause us to operate in ignorance, delusion, and wickedness. Jesus died on the cross so that we could be delivered from the grave of oppression caused by all darkness of this present age that influences and works in, through, and over our lives.[7] It is a sad state of affairs that man loves his bondage more than he desires liberty to know, love, and be with his Creator for eternity.

As we consider the premise of what is true, we realize it makes a matter transparent. How can one clearly see what is clouded or dark? Without the proper premise, how can one know what to do? Truth rids a matter of all shades of gray and darkness that might cloud the real issues. Nothing can remain hidden as one comes into the light of truth in Christ Jesus.

The reality of spirit and truth establishes a right environment in which the Spirit of God can move, inspire, instruct, and edify. Wherever the Spirit of God is present, He will lead a person to all truth as he or she walks in His leading and guidance. The Spirit will make the things of God more transparent as the truth of Jesus overcomes darkness.

People may not mind that a matter is cleared up by truth, but they fear to be made transparent where the shame of darkness would be exposed. In some cases, it doesn't have to do with sin alone, but with maintaining some semblance of self, dignity, and life on their terms. Those that are hiding dishonorable intentions and actions hide behind cloaks. However, those who are trying to maintain some semblance of self and life are hiding behind walls.

A good example of these walls is found in the incident concerning Jericho.[8] Like this enclosed community, many people are a "closed up city." Sadly, most of humanity is tightly shut up when it comes to God. These unseen walls cause isolation and loneliness for people. Subsequently, no one can come in and no one can leave. These walls begin as a means of protection, but eventually they become dark prisons and tombs.

What do these walls represent to those who stand behind them? First, they give a person a sense of security. However, this security is false. Jericho was a cursed and condemned city, whose walls would not be able to withstand judgment. All walls will eventually come down, allowing the light of God to reveal the lack of faith on the part of the people who are seeking protection behind them. These individuals really do not want the walls to come down. If they are Christians, they are

---

[6] 1 John 1:9

[7] Romans 6:1-12

[8] Joshua 6

failing to remember the example of Rahab and the faith she displayed towards Jehovah God. In Jericho, Rahab was a harlot, but when those walls came down, she was delivered from the judgment on Jericho, and found and embraced a new life. As a result, she became part of the lineage of Jesus.[9] It is only by faith that each of us becomes part of the lineage of the Son of God.

Behind our walls we are subject to the curse and judgment of the Law. We are standing condemned in our filthy rags. It takes faith to allow God to bring down the walls, and to allow His light to penetrate the loneliness of our souls. His light will bring much needed deliverance and healing. Clearly, the light must shine in our souls to make us transparent for our own personal well-being. It is only in a state of transparency before God and His Word that one can be set free to embrace the life God intends for him or her. Jeremiah 29:11 states, "For I know the thoughts that I think toward you, saith the LORD, thoughts of peace, and not of evil, to give you an expected end."

The greatest wall in many people's lives is that of fear. Fear expresses itself in unbelief. The major fear behind most people's fears involves losing control of their lives. Such control is a delusion or an illusion since mere man cannot control the environment around him. However, people maintain a false sense of control because they see it as a means to keep them from being vulnerable to others. Granted, Jesus was aware of the treachery in man and displayed caution, but He never put up a wall. He simply showed discretion or wisdom towards a matter.[10]

Another wall is that of self. We want to maintain the right to self in order to ensure the life we desire or think we deserve. This means holding on to our fragile dignity in the times of failure, our fake nobility in times of sin, and our unrealistic dreams in times of hopelessness. In essence, we are not willing to give up our lifestyles. We are comfortable with our deceitful hearts, our confused minds, and the darkness of our idols. We can maintain the rule of the king of self, that of pride, as it sits on the throne of our hearts. We can indulge the flesh in all of its desires without being called to accountability or discipline.

Obviously, the walls we put up temporarily permit us to have a false sense of security allowing us to believe that we are in control of our reality. However, the truth is we are becoming ensnared into delusion and destruction. Walls simply mean that we can remain ignorant of our impending judgment in spite of the darkness residing in our souls.

The walls must come down, but it takes an act of God. Broken down walls represent either repentance on our part or judgment on God's part. Jesus talked about this very fact in Matthew 21:44, "And whosoever shall

---

[9] Joshua 6:2, 22-26; Matthew 1:5; James 2:25
[10] Hosea 6:7; John 2:23-25; 2 Timothy 1:7

fall on this stone shall be broken; but on whosoever it shall fall, it will grind him to powder."

Jericho means "place of fragrance." This city was a beautiful city that was also known as the "city of Palm Trees". Humanity has the potential to emit a fragrance that will bring conviction to those in rebellion, encouragement to the saints, and serve as a sweet savor to God. However, the walls must come down, the light of the Savior's life must come forth to expose and purge, and the fresh wind of the Holy Spirit must blow freely upon our lives to push back judgment, recreate that which remains, and sanctify what is established for the glory of God.[11]

We are reminded of God's intervention in Jericho. It was a scarlet thread hanging from the window that identified and separated Rahab on the day of God's judgment. We are all Rahabs in one way or the other. We all need God's intervention and personal mark upon our lives. It is Christ hanging on the cross, His cleansing blood flowing downward to every repentant sinner that presently identifies and separates the modern day Rahabs from future impending judgment.

Another aspect of that which is true is that it is faithful to truth. Truth's goal is to bring forth contrast with the intent to bring instruction in the ways of righteousness. However, it takes faith in God and His Word to believe the truth, love it, and be faithful to stand in it, stand for it, and withstand any attack against it. Most people are indoctrinated into a particular point of view to which they are faithful. However, indoctrination does not constitute truth. People are not indoctrinated by the truth; they simply have to believe it. It is upon believing and applying the truth that one discovers the beauty of it. Solomon instructed people to buy the truth and sell it not. The Apostle Paul claimed you could do nothing against the truth, just for it. He also stated that many in the end days will buy a delusion because they would not receive a love for the truth that they might be saved.[12] To love the truth means to love the Person of Jesus Christ.

Truth operates in accordance with the actual state of affairs. Most people do not like the reality of their present lives because they do not serve their purpose. However, God can only meet us in truth and impart His wisdom when we are facing the real state of a matter. Anything outside of what is real is nothing but a delusion or false way. God cannot step out of His character as the great "I AM," the One who serves as the ever-present truth to man, by bowing down to a false reality. He can only meet us at the point of truth.

Once God meets us in truth, He can give us His perspective. It is His perspective that will change our perception of a matter. This is when our reality will change by lining up to the reality of God in a situation. It is only when we have God's perspective that we can start from a correct

---

[11] Genesis 1:2; John 3:8; 7:36-39; Corinthians 2:15-16
[12] Proverbs 23:23; 2 Corinthians 13:8; 2 Thessalonians 2:10-12

premise. This correct premise will ensure that our conclusions to a matter will be accurate since they will be in line with His character and ways.

This is why Jesus said He is the truth. He is not one of the truths—He is the truth. In order to end in wisdom, we must begin with Jesus, who is the essence of truth. To begin with Jesus means to think on Him, His teachings, and His examples. To think on Jesus will ensure that we do not begin the thought process by leaning on our own understanding. We will start by leaning on our knowledge of the Son of God. It is within this knowledge that transparency will exist, sin will be exposed, righteousness exalted to bring contrast, and instruction brought forth in revelation.[13]

Without this premise of truth, we will not be able to come to a wise conclusion about a matter. We will be unable to walk in the Spirit. For only the Holy Spirit can lead us to the fullness of Jesus Christ. Keep in mind, all godly virtues find their source in Jesus Christ, the one sure foundation of all spiritual matters.[14]

How do you begin your thought process? Do you begin from the premise of conceit, doctrine, theology, religion, worldly philosophies, or the Person of Jesus? If you do not start from the right premise, you will end up shipwrecked on the rocks of delusion, disillusionment, despair, destruction, and judgment.[15]

---

[13] Proverbs 3:5-7; John 8:32-36; 14:6; 1 Corinthians 1:30; Philippians 3:8; James 3:17; 2 Peter 1:4-8; 1 John 2:6

[14] 1 Corinthians 3:11

[15] 1 Timothy 1:19

3

THE ENVIRONMENT

We have considered the premise in which all thinking must originate from. The premise of truth will ensure the integrity of a correct environment. The type of spirit in which we will consider a matter is what inspires the type of environment that is present. Environments will either encourage freedom to discover God's perspective and His will about a matter, or they will create a bondage that will spiral one down into the hopeless abyss of darkness, despair, and spiritual ruin.

Environment establishes preferences, agendas, and attitudes. A good example of how environment affects us can be observed when a wrong spirit is in operation. A good illustration of a wrong spirit is a seductive spirit that is mentioned in 1 Timothy 4:1. All wrong spirits operate from the same premise. They work under the dark covering of deception. These spirits will divide people from reality by initially causing confusion about what is true and right. The goal behind this division is to separate individuals from truth in order to close down any discernment they may possess. From the premise of confusion and separation, these spirits will isolate people as a means to cause suspicion towards others, as well as influence or set up the situations that will affect their environment. Ultimately, these spirits will subdue all independent thinking and any discernment through witchcraft, fear, guilt, suspicion, isolation, and depression.

As religious people are seduced into another reality, they will begin to err in how they handle the Word of God. The digression of deviation from the truth will escalate as these individuals begin to err in their interpretation of the Bible and lives. Ultimately the error will manifest itself in an attitude of complacency towards truth. It is in this type of environment that another gospel and a different Jesus can be presented.

As we consider environment, we must personally realize that nothing reveals our inward environment more than our words. We either mean what we say or we prove to be untrustworthy in all that we say. If we start from the premise of truth, we cannot help but be trustworthy in what we advocate or do. However, if we start from the premise of self, we will adjust our words to get desired results, whether they are true or not. Jesus stated that to respond in any other manner than yes or no comes of evil. He also stated that what comes out of the mouth is a manifestation of what is truly in our hearts.[1]

The importance of environment is brought out in Scripture. We see it in the case of God's people, Israel. However, there is one person I want to focus on, Isaac. There was an interesting incident that happened to Isaac in Genesis 26. This chapter begins with a famine. The physical environment often represents the spiritual environment of the people. No doubt there was a spiritual famine that God was about to reveal.

The Lord appeared to Isaac and instructed him not to go down to Egypt. Egypt represented the world. So many people look to and depend on the world to get them through the challenges of life. However, it is association or agreement with the world that will produce unproductive spiritual environments.

Isaac obeyed God. At this point all appeared to be well for him. His obedience was bound to reap him a life of ease. This is how many people perceive Christianity. If they obey God, all should go well for them. However, this is unrealistic. Obedience often results in testing. The test is always the same. Where is a person's reliance?

Rebekah, Isaac's wife, was a beautiful woman. Isaac feared that if the men around him found out that she was his wife, they would kill him. Like his father, Abraham, he decided to tell a little white lie. Such lies seemed harmless enough. However, Abraham's lie brought repercussions on Pharaoh's house, and Abimelech also recognized the possibility of consequences when Isaac's lie was uncovered.[2] God showed His mercy and protection in both situations, but for both Abraham and Isaac it revealed that they did not trust God's intervention in either situation. Granted, Abraham probably had concern about whether God would show protection since he had not consulted Him about going to Egypt. But Isaac knew he was in the will of God. Yet, he did not have the faith to trust God enough to be honest.

It is in this situation that we begin to get some insight into Isaac. Isaac experienced great blessings because of his father, Abraham's, relationship with Jehovah God. This fact was brought out a couple of times. God told Isaac he would bless him for Abraham's sake.[3] Clearly, Isaac knew of God because of Abraham, but there is no indication that he knew God for himself. Sadly, this seems to be the environment of most Christians. God blesses us because of Jesus Christ, but few people know their Lord and Savior for themselves. Their confidence is in their religious associations, doctrines, or ideas of God, but in reality they operate in ignorance towards Him because they do not personally know Him.

---

[1] Matthew 5:37; 15:17-20

[2] Genesis 12:10-20

[3] Genesis 26:4-5, 24

In spite of failing the test God continued to bless Isaac. But, even in the midst of blessings God will allow conflict to enter into our personal worlds to reveal our spiritual need. Isaac experienced this conflict over the wells that his father had previously established.

Water was precious in the land of Canaan. When Isaac tried to uncover the wells dug by his father, the Philistines stopped him. He first dug a well of springing water in the valley, but the herdsmen of Gerar strived with him. He called that particular well, Esek, which means "contention." The Word tells us that contention is a product of pride. Pride is behind all personal battles with others.[4] It causes us to make foolish and unwise decisions.

Isaac did not demand his way with the herdsmen. He dug another well, but found himself involved in another conflict. He called this well Sitnah which means "strife". Strife is also referred to as variance. It is one of the works of the flesh, and those who walk according to the flesh will not inherit the kingdom of God. Proverbs 28:25 tells us that the source of strife is a proud heart. A proud heart points to an unbelieving, hard heart.[5]

Once again Isaac did not demand his right to the well. He departed from the environment of conflict. Pride and the flesh are the two aspects of man's character that will always cause contention and strife. As a result, Jesus instructed His followers to deny self, or deny the pride of the self-life the right to reign, and apply the cross. The cross implies that the flesh is being crucified, stopping it from warring with the Spirit.[6] The reality is that as long as there is conflict, the environment is not conducive to establishing a relationship with God.

Isaac found the environment that would encourage an encounter with God. He dug a third well. This time there was no conflict. Isaac called the well Rehoboth, which means "large or wide places." The psalmist made this observation in Psalm 118:5, "I called upon the LORD in distress: the LORD answered me, and set me in a large place."

A person must be in a large place or a place of liberty before he or she can encounter the Lord. The Apostle Paul revealed where Christians can find such liberty, "Now the Lord is that Spirit: and where the Spirit of the Lord is, there is liberty" (2 Corinthians 3:17).

It is out of the large places that fruit can be produced because life-giving water can flow unhindered. It was from this large place that Isaac was able to go forward in his life before God. It was from here that he went to Beersheba. The name of this place points to "oath and seven". An oath was made at this place between Abraham and Abimelech.

---

[4] Genesis 26:17-19; Proverbs 13:10
[5] Galatians 5:19-21, Hebrews 3:8-9, 19
[6] Luke 9:23-25; Galatians 5:16-18

Seven lambs were exchanged as a witness or token of this oath made between these two men.[7] The number "seven" points to perfection. In this situation, everything was brought to a perfect order.

It was at Beersheba that Jehovah God introduced Himself to Isaac. "...I am the God of Abraham, thy father..." (Genesis 26:24). How the great I AM, the ever-present God of heaven and earth wants to introduce Himself to us! However, there must be an environment in which He can reveal Himself to our hearts. For instance, the environment Jesus wants to meet us in is that of supping or communion. Obviously, it is God's heart that we know Him in an intimate way.[8]

Isaac responded in four ways at Beersheba. He built an altar.[9] An altar represents a memorial or sacrifice. It is where God often met those who were serious about Him. From all appearances, Isaac was serious about doing business with God. His time to ride on the shirttails of his father was now over. It was time for the man, Isaac, to enter into that place of fellowship with God.

Like his father before him, Isaac called upon the name of the Lord.[10] Once again, we see a man seeking God for himself. Calling on the name of the Lord is a way of appealing to His character, and to obtain His mercy and grace. It is a way of acknowledging who He is, Lord, Ruler, and God over all. It is a place of humility. After all, he was seeking God, rather than God seeking for him. This is also the key to salvation. Romans 10:13 states, "For whosoever shall call upon the name of the Lord shall be saved."

Isaac's next move was to pitch a tent. His action pointed to "abiding." It is not enough to encounter God; we must abide where He reveals Himself to us. It is in the abiding that we develop a relationship with our God. The Apostle John relates this to abiding in the eternal Vine of Jesus.[11] It is in the place of abiding that we will grow in the knowledge of our God. Our faith will be firmly established in our Lord, His promises confirmed, and our lives in Him revealed and made fruitful.

Isaac's final act in this incident was to have his servants dig another well. Keep in mind the main point of conflict and life surrounded water. The Holy Spirit represents the rivers of Living Water to every Christian. When a person receives Jesus as Lord and Savior, he or she becomes part of an everlasting covenant. The Holy Spirit is given as a seal. His responsibility is to bring us to perfection in our Christian walk.[12]

---

[7] Genesis 21:22-34
[8] Genesis 26:24; Revelation 3:20
[9] Genesis 26:25
[10] Genesis 21:33
[11] John 15:1-8; 1 John 2:6
[12] John 7:36-39; Romans 8:10-17; Ephesians 1:13; Titus 3:5; Hebrews 13:20

No doubt it was during this time that Jehovah God became Isaac's God. We have verification of this fact in the life of Jacob. While Isaac's son, Jacob was on his way to his uncle's place, He encountered God. God introduced Himself in this way: "...I am the LORD God of Abraham, thy father, and <u>the God</u> of Isaac:..." (Genesis 28:13). (Emphasis added.)

The final result of Isaac establishing a relationship with his God was that of peace. Jesus said, "Blessed are the peacemakers: for they shall be called the children of God" (Matthew 5:9). Peace is associated with those who know their God. We see in the case of Isaac that his identification to Jehovah God caused his enemies to make peace with him.[13]

Obviously, we need a right environment to encourage and ensure a right relationship with God. Therefore, what do we need to think upon to encourage such an environment where there is liberty to move forward, God is free to reveal Himself, the altar of our hearts are upheld, the character of God is honored, the abiding presence of our Lord is a reality, and the Living Water is flowing freely? The Apostle Paul gives us the necessary ingredient, "Finally, brethren, whatever things are honest...think on these things." "Honest" means honorable, free from fraud or deception, and marked by integrity.

God can only work in an environment that is honest. A right environment points to a clean conscience in all matters. Such a conscience comes from a willingness to live honestly.[14] To think on that which is honest is to think on and do that which is honorable. Many people are into nobility, but few understand what it means to be honorable. Although there are similarities between these terms, the fruits of these characteristics can be quite different. Nobility is man's attempt to be noble or attain to some type of sainthood or status such as being an aristocrat or being in a high position. In most cases nobility ends up becoming a pride trip. However, honorable has to do with privilege, credibility, respect, uprightness, and conduct.[15]

People who are honorable know how to honor or respect others. Such individuals in the kingdom of God know how to humble themselves in preference to others.[16] They do not assume their position; rather they recognize their life before God as a privilege that must not be taken lightly. Their intention towards others is sincere.

Sincere intentions mean that an individual will not be treacherous in his or her dealings. Hosea 6:7 states, "But they like men have

---

[13] Genesis 26:26-31

[14] Hebrews 13:18

[15] Meanings of the different virtues ascribed to in Philippians 4:8 were taken from two sources: Strong's Exhaustive Concordance and Webster's New Collegiate Dictionary.

[16] Romans 12:10

transgressed the covenant: there have they dealt treacherously against me." Obviously, those who do not honor God will deal treacherously against God. This is true for anyone who is not honorable. Such individuals will commit fraud in all they say and do against even those who are close to them, encouraging an environment of distrust and deception. Instead of being marked by integrity, they will be identified as individuals who are untrustworthy. Therefore, the Apostle Paul instructed believers to walk honestly before men, provide those things that are honorable to both God and men, and not to return evil for evil or commit fraud.[17]

Our honest walk must be obvious in all areas of our lives. We not only must be honest with those of the household of faith, but we must be honorable in all of our activities with those who are outside of our faith. Being honorable will avoid bringing a reproach upon Christ, the Gospel, and our testimony. The beauty about being honest is it allows us to inherit the promise that we will lack nothing in our lives. This does not mean that all of our desires will be realized, but that we will have a satisfying life before God. The Apostle Paul related this life to leading a quiet and peaceable life in all godliness and honesty, for this is what proves to be good and acceptable in the sight of God, our Savior.[18]

This brings us to the source of an environment is which honesty is clearly established in all matters. King David was an honorable man. Granted, he showed tremendous dishonor in the case of Bathsheba and her husband. However, when confronted, he did not remain a fool in his sin, but rather, he humbled himself, sought God, confessed his iniquity, and asked for mercy.[17] His response revealed a man whose life was marked by integrity or character.

1 Kings 9:4 tells us the source of David's integrity, "And if thou wilt walk before me, as David thy father walked, in the integrity of heart, and in uprightness, to do according to all that I have commanded thee, and wilt keep my statues and my judgments." Integrity comes from a heart that is honorable.

Jesus talked about such a heart in Luke 8:15. An honest and good heart represents good ground or a proper environment. After hearing the word, such a heart will not only keep it, but will also bring forth the fruit of it in patience. Patience on our part points to the longsuffering of the Spirit and it is the only way a person can possess his or her soul. Patience or long-suffering speaks of the fruit of the Spirit, as well as valuable experience that will be fully realized in the glorious hope of our Lord and Savior.[18]

---

[17] Romans 12:17; 13:13-14; 2 Corinthians 8:21; 1 Thessalonians 4:6-7

[18] 1 Thessalonians 4:12; 1 Timothy 2:2-3

[17] Psalm 51

[18] Luke 21:19; Romans 5:3-5; Galatians 5:22-23

As we study the thought process, one cannot help but notice that if a person starts from the premise of truth, he or she cannot help but operate from an environment that is honest and honorable. Such an environment will produce the necessary character to stand upright before God and others. As you will see, each step in the thought process will produce the next virtue.

How is your heart condition? What does your inner environment say about your life before God? As Christians, it is vital we examine such matters to ensure that our conclusions about a matter will honor the One who walked according to the environment of humility. As a result, He was led to Calvary where He died on the cross for us, and secured our hope for a glorious future.

4

THE ESSENCE OF CHARACTER

The premise of truth will set up an environment where matters can be handled in an honest or honorable way. Clearly, this will allow truth to have its way in a situation. Such an environment becomes a breeding ground in which integrity or character can be properly established. Such character will express itself in upright deeds and practices.

The proper expression of character is important to understand. Most people perceive themselves as doing the best they can, when in reality they are often failing to do what is right. When you consider their reasoning, you will realize their best is based on what they are willing to do, but in such selfishness, there is no real consideration for what is right in light of those who may be involved with or affected by these self-serving people's lives and deeds.

For example, there was a situation where a man brought a large dog into a subdivision. Obviously, the dog needed a lot of room and a certain type of attention to bring out its potential. Although this man claimed he had done all the research concerning this dog, he really did not understand the dog's needs of adequate space, exercise, and training. Needless to say, this dog liked to visit the neighbor's yard, which caused conflict. Frustration grew as this man's neighbor did not see the problem of the visiting dog being honestly dealt with. Finally, the frustration hit its peek when the dog came over during a barbeque. The neighbor bluntly told the man to keep his dog home. The man became insulted by the neighbor's bluntness. After all, he was "trying" to control the dog.

As you consider the dog's owner and his handling of matters, it is obvious that he had no consideration for his dog or his neighbors. Granted, few of us initially understand the commitment and responsibility that surround issues such as pets. However, this dog owner did not have the character to face the problems that confronted him. It was as if those around him had to accept his reality of doing what he considered was enough, even though it was clearly a matter of personal convenience on his part, regardless of the infringement others were experiencing because of his immature and irresponsible decision. In this man's mind, the neighbors were to accept the miserable bone he threw at them so he could maintain his irresponsible fantasy about his overrated ability as a dog handler.

When this man was being called to accountability, he failed to show any character. In fact, his response to accountability revealed treachery.

Character will take responsibility and show maturity in facing the real issues. The dog owner simply copped an attitude of self-pity, anger, and that of being an innocent victim, while making the neighbors out to be the bad, unreasonable culprits in the situation.

In my observation of such matters, I realized why Isaiah 64:6 states that man's best is filthy rags before God. As I considered this man's best towards his dog and neighbors, I could see where his best was self-serving, as well as maintaining a false reality about his personal character and level of maturity. Obviously, righteousness is missing where man's best is concerned. After all, man's best is not about being right or doing right in a matter, it is about coming out on top without paying the price that is required to be responsible and sacrificial if necessary.

As we consider character, we must realize people are not born with it, and that even the right environment cannot ensure that it will exist in a person. Character is actually formed in a person's very way of thinking and being. When a person has character, right attitudes and actions will naturally manifest themselves in his or her lifestyle.

The problem with most people is that they fail to develop character. Due to their selfish disposition, they prefer an environment that serves their selfishness. Such preference for self causes them to justify treachery in their practices. Of course, such treachery translates into hypocrisy when it becomes a matter of God and religion.

This brings us to our way of thinking. If the environment is right, what must we think on to maintain an honorable environment that will maintain the integrity of truth and be devoid of the treachery of hypocrisy? The apostle Paul gave us the key to this answer in Philippians 4:8, "Finally, brethren whatsoever things…are just…think on these things." To be just, one must be innocent in his or her thought process. Innocence will possess joy due to godly influences, as well as conduct itself in the ways of righteousness. Such conduct will translate into being morally upright.

The Word of God clearly reveals that we love and serve a just God. In this arena "just" translates into justice or upright judgments towards a matter. Judgments point to decisions or determinations. Are our decisions or determinations "just" to ensure that we will be morally upright in our practices? After all, our God is just or morally upright in His ways. That is why He is clearly distinguished as being perfect in His ways.

In fact, the opposite of being morally upright is that of iniquity. When people fail to be morally upright in their practices, it reveals that they have iniquity or moral deviation in their character. Moral deviation can be traced back to pride, which is not only idolatrous and self-serving, but foolish and treacherous.

Justice requires perfection in one's character. However, perfection in a Christian's life manifests itself in spiritual maturity or coming to age in one's spiritual walk.

The Apostle John talked about the different levels of maturity in his first epistle. These levels are children, young men, and fathers. We already know that there is no male or female in God's kingdom. When He created Adam and Eve, He called them man.[1] With this in mind, we must realize that the term "young men" also refers to "young women", and the term fathers includes mothers who possess the same level of spiritual maturity.

As you study the children of God, they are distinguished by the love of the Father. They have been born into the kingdom of God. As a result, they have been given a new heart that is inclined towards God and a new spirit that is sensitive to His leading. Clearly, they have been set apart by the new birth experience, and the process of maturing in Jesus has begun.[2]

The next level of maturity is that of being young men and women in God's kingdom. These people are those who are overcoming Satan with the Word of God. Such people are distinguished by the Word of God taking root in their spirits. The Word of God could not have such a place in these people's lives unless they were learning to walk as Jesus walked, in obedience to the Father's purpose, in the spirit of love, and in the joy of His truths. Ultimately, such people will overcome the world.[3]

Mature Christians do not have the intense battles with the flesh, for it is more natural for them to walk according to the Spirit. These mature saints do not walk in insecurity for they know their place in God's kingdom. These people's walk is distinguished by the fact that they know God. The God they know is the God who has been in existence from the very beginning. It is because God serves as these people's source of strength that they stand strong in their faith, immovable in their testimonies, and sure of their future glory with their Lord and Savior.[4]

As you consider these three levels of maturity, you will find that children are learning to overcome the influence of the world as they grow in their relationship with the Father. The young people are becoming soldiers as they learn how to overcome Satan with the Word. The fathers and mothers have overcome the flesh as they have become crucified to the world, and as a result, have gained authority over Satan.

The reason these three levels of maturity were mentioned is because "just character" will be revealed in those who have come of full age. Justice will be the natural response of those who have come to maturity in their spiritual lives. These individuals will be void of treachery. They will have anointing and power, and the ability to make just judgments. Wisdom will restrain them, love will motivate them, joy will abide in them, and righteousness will season all they do.

---

[1] Genesis 5:1-2; Galatians 3:26-29; 1 John 2:12-14

[2] Ezekiel 36:26-27; John 1:12; 3:3, 1 John 2:12-14; 3:1-3, 9-10

[3] Philippians 2:1-8; 1 John 1:4; 2:6; 3:4-8; 5:2-5

[4] Romans 8:12-14: 1 John 1:12-14

The question is how does one develop such character in his or her way of thinking and being? You must go back to the meaning of what is just.

The Word tells us that the just shall live by faith. In light of faith, the concept of just becomes a state. In other words, we stand justified because of the redemption of Christ. Justified implies you come to God just as you are to receive forgiveness of sin. Forgiveness is a pardon that places you in a state of innocence where righteousness can be realized in your life.[5]

However, we are not talking about a state. We are talking about character that is just in every way. How does thinking on that which is "just" develop character? Once again, we are reminded of the meaning of just.

A person must start from the point of innocence. In other words, he or she holds no pre-conceived notions about a matter. As stated, individuals who begin from a point of judgment will come out with the same conclusions, regardless of the case presented to them. Just judgments find their source in God's premise, while blind judgments are the product of selfishness and pride. Therefore, to be just in our way of thinking we must start from a point of innocence. Innocence is a frame of reference where a person has no real knowledge or opinions concerning a matter. Such an individual is able to actually approach a matter without having any prejudicial opinions. People who operate from the basis of innocence are without guile or cunning. It is from the point of innocence that separation or discernment will occur. In other words, a person will be able to properly wade through a matter to ensure that a just or fair conclusion is arrived at. Such a person will be able to discern the intent from the words, actions, or results.

It is important to point out that to think on that which is just is motivated by the concept of practicing what is just, or in other words, always handling a matter in a just or fair way. It is the handling of a matter that will separate the just from those who are truly practicing evil in their dealings.[6]

Sadly enough, when justice is missing in a situation, then oppression, depression, despair, and anger reign. This can be observed when unjust judges sit on the benches of the land. Injustice placates wickedness and oppresses righteousness. It can be bought, influenced, and flattered. It is unpredictable and treacherous, as it will harbor and promote personal agendas. Such judgment causes despair among those who see that it is biased. In the end, such injustice will cause chaos as it exalts wickedness and mocks and opposes righteousness.

For this reason, Christians must realize that they must be just in all areas, because failure to do so leads to bondage and despair. As

---

[5] Romans 1:17; 3:24-26; 5:1, 18
[6] Matthew 1:19; 5:45; 13:49

believers, we must be marked by separation from the world's biased judgments and separated unto God to ensure that which is just in our lives, homes, businesses, and churches.

Once a just conclusion is arrived at, a person will be able to be righteous in his or her actions. Such actions will reveal an upright disposition. An upright disposition will not be present if one is being self-serving in his or her thought process.

To be just in our thinking does not mean we will execute judgment against others.[7] Rather, it means we will be just in our character. Character not only means making just judgments about a situation, but being just in practice regardless of circumstances. Just judgments and practices also point to being morally upright before God and beneficial to those around you.

Such character will cause others to show respect. After all, they can trust you to be fair. They will seek you out concerning important matters, they will believe your words, and trust your judgments.

Let us now consider what will encourage us to think in a just way. We must not forget our God is just in His judgments, ways, and dealings.[8] He does not step outside of His character regardless of what is going on. Therefore, we must consider His character and examples.

God's commandments are just.[9] Obviously, we must not only consider His character, examples, and commandments to make just conclusions, but we must line up to His character in attitude, submit to His example, and obey His commandments to ensure that we are just in our practices towards others. Psalm 119:11 states," Thy word have I hid in mine heart, that I might not sin against thee." Obviously, being just in our conclusions and practices will require discipline that will only be evident when character is formed in our inner disposition.

How is the essence of your character? Is it being manifested in just conclusions and practices or is it being revealed through harsh, unrealistic, and indifferent judgments? Do you desire to be just or do you demand justice from others based on personal offense? Such manifestations will determine if you are truly thinking on those things which are just in character and practices.

---

[7] Luke 14:14; Romans 12:17-21

[8] John 5:30; Revelation 15:3-4

[9] Romans 7:12

5

THE APPROACH

We have started with the premise of truth to ensure an honorable environment in which just character will be upheld. Now that we have these virtues in order, we can now approach a situation in a way that will ensure godliness and acceptable service before God. The Apostle Paul tells us what we need to think on to approach life in a right way, "Finally, brethren, whatsoever things...are pure...think on these things."

The word "pure" presents an interesting perspective. When we think of pure, we think of a child that has not yet been tainted by the harsh realities of this present life or the world, or we think of fresh snow that has not become scarred or muddied by man's footprints. These are two good examples of the concept of purity. The meaning of this word is in agreement with these concepts. It means to "be clean from defilement, clear of compromise, spotless in content, and chaste in practice".

We know that one must be pure in heart to see God. In other words, a person must approach God from a place of purity in order to perceive Him in a right way. The first thing we learn about approaching a matter in purity is that we must have a pure heart. We are also told that the end of the commandments is love that comes out of a pure heart. Obviously, such a heart points to a right spirit. Therefore, a pure heart means that a person will approach matters with pure motives (right spirit), and in a state of purity (clean conscience) to ensure he or she will not defile the matters of God in his or her life or in others. [1]

Titus 1:15 tells us, to the pure all things are pure, but to the defiled all things are perverted. The type of mind we hold will often serve as a filter in which we regard things. For example, if you start from a perverted source, you will not end up with a pure perspective. You must start from the point of purity to ensure you will approach a matter in a pure way. Otherwise, you will not be able to trust your conclusions. In fact, you can be assured that your conclusions will be perverted and untrustworthy. However, how many of us start from the wrong source?

The heart represents the issues of life.[2] Jesus brought this out in Matthew 15:18-19, "But those things which proceed out of the mouth come forth from the heart; and they defile the man. For out of the heart

---

[1] Matthew 5:8; 1 Timothy 1:5
[2] Proverbs 4:23

proceed evil thoughts, murders, adulteries, fornications, thefts, false witness, blasphemies." Obviously, to think on that which is pure, one must start from a pure heart. Only a pure heart can ensure that matters will be regarded in a clear, concise manner.

Most people approach a matter from a stony heart that is very much deceptive as to the extent of its wicked ways.[3] Such a heart points to a heart that is full of self. People with stony hearts approach life from a selfish, unrealistic, or ignorant perspective. For example, if they are considering a matter from a selfish point of view, they will not only adjust a matter to bow down to their selfishness, but they will destroy any purity that might be present, thus creating an environment that is self-absorbed, self-centered, or self-serving. Needless to say, such an approach creates a defiled or perverted conscience towards the matters of life.

If people approach a matter from an unrealistic perspective, they will be dealing in fantasy. As a result, purity will be tainted by sentimentality that is often the byproduct of such fantasy, especially in the area of religion. For instance, people are often caught up with their sentimental point of view of God and religion. They swing from one religious fantasy, hope, and experience to the next. They perceive such fantasy as being pure, when in fact it is delusional.

The other approach is that of ignorance. This ignorance is confused with innocence. People pride themselves on how "innocent" they are about a situation, when in fact it is not a point of innocence, but a point of choosing to remain ignorant about a matter.[4] After all, if a person is truly educated, he or she is now responsible for what is known. Not only is the person responsible for what he or she knows, but also, he or she will be held accountable.

An irresponsible attitude often points to slothfulness. People who possess this attitude do not want to bother with putting the time or energy in to address their ignorance. Hence, enters the choice to remain ignorant, while claiming such ignorance as being innocent. Such claims are sinister and wicked. Therefore, ignorance will pervert purity.

As you can see, a defiled heart will produce perversion in different ways. Individuals cannot and will not see the true God of the Bible from this perspective. They will not have a pure conscience to even be able to approach God about matters that concern them. Hebrews 10:22 brings this out, "Let us draw near with a true heart in full assurance of faith, having our hearts sprinkled from an evil conscience, and our bodies washed with pure water."

The real source of purity will always be traced back to God. There is nothing pure outside of the character, ways, and reality of God. James 1:17 tells us His wisdom is pure. Clearly, if we are thinking on that which

---

[3] Jeremiah 17:9-10; Ezekiel 36:26

[4] Hosea 4:6

is pure, then we will be approaching it from the perspective of the wisdom that comes from above. Such wisdom will bring clarity to a situation. Is it any wonder that many people are in constant confusion since most wisdom is based on the world's perverted presentation of what constitutes life?

Many people hide from God behind religious fig-leaves, self-righteous cloaks, and pious masks. Even though they expound on the things of God, there is no power, authority, or real fruit in any of it. As you get more involved with their lives, you begin to see that there is confusion. As the confusion is torn away, you can begin to identify perversion, revealing that a pure heart is missing.

Peter explained the pure heart in this way in 1 Peter 1:22, "Seeing that ye have purified your souls in obeying the truth through the Spirit unto unfeigned love of the brethren, see that ye love one another with a pure heart fervently." First, we see the premise of truth. We purify our souls by obeying the truth. However, the integrity of truth can only be maintained through the Spirit. Such maintenance can only be wrought by being led by the Spirit in all spiritual matters.[5]

There are many people who religiously obey the different requirements of religion, but they are not purifying their souls because their hearts and deeds are not in line with truth and being established in and through the Spirit. Remember, all purity will lead back to God. Purity is maintained as it remains within the boundaries of truth and of the Spirit of God. It is not enough to obey religious aspects if the integrity of truth and the Spirit of God are missing.

Once we line all matters up to the truth and Spirit of God, we will have the type of love that will be pure or without hypocrisy towards others. Godly love is the manifestation of a right attitude. In this case, the love of God comes from the state of lowliness and an attitude of meekness. The Apostle Paul described such an attitude as displaying the mind of Christ. Jesus said of this love that it would identify us as His disciples.[6] The Apostle Paul gave us this exhortation in Romans 12:9-10, "Let love be without dissimulation. Abhor that which is evil; cleave to that which is good. Be kindly affectioned one to another with brotherly love; in honour preferring one another."

The main problem that is identified when people are lacking a pure heart is that their vision for others is clearly missing. They are so caught up with their perverted perceptions, limited worlds, and self-absorbed ways, that they have no real concern for others. In fact, people with needs will be considered a grave intrusion, people who are different will be seen as unworthy, and those who are lost will be seen as deserving their lot in life. It takes a pure heart to have a pure vision, and a pure vision to have a right perspective and attitude towards people.

---

[5] Romans 8:8-14; Galatians 5:16-18
[6] Matthew 11:28-29; John 13:34-35; Philippians 2:5

James confirms this in James 1:27, "Pure religion and undefiled before God and the Father is this, To visit the fatherless and widows in their affliction, and to keep himself unspotted from the world." James summarized pure religion. It manifests itself in two ways: how we treat others and the type of relationship we have with the world.

God is aware of those who are at the mercy of the society they live in. They are not necessarily at the mercy of society because of bad decisions, but because of life in general. It is not a widow's fault she is widow, nor is it a child's fault that he or she is missing a parent, such as a father. Such people are in their situations because of circumstances beyond their control.

As people of God, we have a responsibility towards such people. Sadly, most people trip over those who fall into this category. However, such people are a true test to Christianity. And, if we fail the test, it is because we do not have a pure heart and a pure vision towards people. Without such purity, we often put those who are victims of life in greater oppression. God has some tough warnings concerning such oppression. The greatest warning can be found in Exodus 22:22-24, "Ye shall not afflict any widow, or fatherless child. If thou afflict them in any wise, and they cry at all unto me, I will surely hear their cry; And my wrath shall wax hot, and I will kill you with the sword; and your wives shall be widows, and your children fatherless."

You can see this warning actually carried out in the case of Sodom. When we hear the word "Sodom" we think of the moral deviation that was taking place within its boundaries. But the abominations were not limited to unnatural sexual preferences and practices. Consider what else was going on, "Behold this was the iniquity of thy sister Sodom, pride, fulness of bread, and abundance of idleness were in her and in her daughters, neither did she strengthen the hand of the poor and needy. And they were haughty, and committed abomination before me: therefore I took them away as I saw good" (Ezekiel 16:49-50).

Sodom was a place of abundance, but it did not use that abundance to help the poor or needy. Due to its abundance, it was idle. There is no greater breeding ground for moral deviation and people exploring the evil fantasies of their wicked imaginations than during times of idleness. It was haughty in its practices. In other words, it defied God in its exploitation of abnormal practices such as homosexuality. In fact, America easily falls into this same category. God dealt with Sodom as He saw fit. It was with complete and total destruction. Wisdom would heed such warnings, but man in his foolish state becomes more defiant against God, rather than display pure wisdom from above.

The next aspect of defilement has to do with our involvement with the world. Friendship with the world causes us to come into an unholy agreement. Such an agreement is considered spiritual harlotry, and puts us in opposition against God.[7]

James tells us pure religion involves keeping ourselves unspotted from the world. Clearly, this instruction reminds us to beware of what we expose ourselves to. The more exposed we become to the world, the more indifferent we become to the things of God. The world perverts the things of God by its spirit. It redefines righteousness with its godless philosophies. It mocks godliness with it politically correct presentations. It does away with God's truths with its psychology. It educates or indoctrinates away any real moral obligations with humanistic philosophies. As a result, it has made people religious about matters, but godless in their pursuits.[8]

Exposure to the world makes Christians spiritually dull. It causes them to become lukewarm in their lives and service before God.[9] In other words, the unholy ceases to be profane. The attitude that is adopted at this point is that the unholy is no big deal and "we" can handle it. However, the truth is many Christians are being conditioned by the world. The result is that the professing Church no longer holds a sober view of sin, holiness, and godliness; instead, much of it maintains a worldly view of tolerance about matters that will send people to hell.

The more Christians become exposed to the world, the more their worldview will change. Their conscience will eventually become seared, and they will lose all their ability to discern. Such a frightening reality brings us to the opposite side of the issue. We must not allow ourselves to be exposed to the world in its idolatrous, harlotry ways, but we must ensure influences that will establish a pure perspective.

To ensure godly influences, believers must expose themselves to the Word of God with a pure heart and conscience. To ensure a pure heart and conscience with the Word of God, we must choose to love it and cease from partaking of sin. Exposing ourselves to, downplaying, or agreeing with sin in any capacity is partaking of it. We are told to keep ourselves pure by not partaking of sin.[10] Peter tells us what to partake of in 2 Peter 1:4, "Whereby are given unto us exceedingly great and precious promises: that by these ye might be partakers of the divine nature, having escaped the corruption that is in the world through lust."

As believers we are to partake of Jesus' divine nature. In short, this means we are to believe Him and His words. By believing the whole essence of who Jesus is and what He did for us, we can actually partake of Him through His precious promises. However, notice how we have escaped the corruption that is experienced in this world through the lust of our flesh. It is faith in Christ and obedience to the Word that will allow us to experience the fulfillment of His promises. Such an obedient walk

---

[7] 2 Corinthians 6:14-18; James 4:4

[8] John 8:44; 2 Corinthians 4:3-4; Ephesians 2:1-2; Colossians 2:8

[9] Revelation 3:14-19

[10] Psalm 119:140; 1 Timothy 5:22

will also ensure that the avenue of temptation will be closed down. As a result, we will escape the corruption that is alive and well in this present world.

God's Word is the key to this great escape. His words are pure. They have been proven and tried. As a result, they are able to wash, cleanse, and sanctify us, presenting us without spot, a chaste bride that will bring our loving Lord and Savior honor. They have the ability to create the very purity that eludes many in their search for what is real, honorable, and sincere. They have the power to cause us to flee the unholy, separate from the defiled, and desire that which is acceptable to God.[11]

To give place to the Word of God's powerful influence, we must meditate on it. This means we must chew on it until we have received the necessary spiritual nutritional value from it to ensure spiritual growth. And then, we must chew on it some more. Clearly, this is how purity is established in our lives. By thinking on the Word, we will approach and consider all matters from this immovable point of truth. There is nothing purer and more powerful than the Word of God when it comes to changing our way of thinking about the real issues confronting life.[12]

Sadly, the diet of the world has caused many of us to lose our spiritual edge. We have gotten away from the center of our holy God, causing our understanding and ways to become tainted and impure. I have felt that impurity in my life many times. I have cried out for God to put the fire to me and separate that which is pure from the dross of self and the world. I truly have desired what is pure, but desire is not enough. I must become pure in heart, mind, and body. I must be cleansed in every area with the fire of His Spirit and the water of His Word. And, sometimes when the purging of my soul caused spiritual leanness, I have cried out like Isaiah, "...Woe is me! for I am undone; because I am a man of unclean lips, and I dwell in the midst of a people of unclean lips: for mine eyes have seen the King, the LORD of hosts" (Isaiah 6:5).

In my desire for this purity, I have been reminded of Isaiah 1:18, "Come now, And let us reason together, saith the LORD: though your sins be as scarlet, they shall be as white as snow; though they be red like crimson, they shall be as wool." God wants to reason with us about sin, that which is unholy, and destructive to our souls. He wants to make us pure once again. However, we must recognize our sin, and realize only He can cleanse us, and make us pure. He will cleanse our sins with His blood, He will wash us from the influences of our unholy alliances with His Word, and He will submerge us in the current of His Living Water (His Spirit) to ensure we are sanctified, set apart for His use and purpose.[13]

---

[11] Psalm 12:6-7; 119:11; John 17:17; Ephesians 5:26-27; 1 Peter 1:23-25
[12] Psalm 119:15, 23, 48, 78, 97, 99, 148; Hebrews 4:12
[13] Acts 1:4-5; Ephesians 5:26-27; Titus 3:5; 1 John 1:7-9

Do you desire purity? It is not enough to desire it; each of us must become pure in heart. We must be able to approach everything from a point of purity to ensure that we will have the mind of Christ, a mind that will be lowly in disposition, meek in attitude, and harmless or undefiled in spirit.

6

THE ATTITUDE

Christianity becomes a matter of religion for most people. However, Christianity is a life that must be walked out. This life will become an expression of the One we love, serve, and worship. Such an expression will be manifested through our disposition. However, it is a person's attitude that will reveal his or her real disposition, as well as serve as a reflection of the soul. Thus, Jesus stated that we will know people by their fruits.[1] Fruits not only involve our conduct, but the attitude in which we do something.

Obviously, as you follow Jesus in His life, He will verify the fact that fruits involve conduct as well as attitude. You will realize as you study His life, it is not just a matter of what He said or what He did, but it is the attitude in which it was expressed. Jesus said this of His attitude, "Take my yoke upon you, and learn of me; for I am meek and lowly in heart: and ye shall find rest unto your souls" (Matthew 11:29).

Jesus was lowly in disposition. His humble disposition was expressed by His attitude of meekness. Meekness reveals that the person is under control. For Jesus, it meant that He was a servant to the Father's will and sensitive to the leading of the Holy Spirit.[2] Jesus, as man, did nothing outside of these two boundaries.

It is within the boundaries of this type of disposition that a person will be susceptible to the things of God. However, such a disposition will only be established by learning of Jesus. It means putting on the Lord Jesus in thinking, practice, and conduct.[3] As we consider what we must think upon, we will realize that we must first learn of Jesus to develop His mind or disposition. To learn of Jesus, we must begin with who He is. It is the Person of Jesus who must serve as the essence of truth.

As already pointed out, truth must serve as our premise. As we respond in an honest way to truth, we will develop the character to be just in our ways and judgments. As character is developed, we will become purer in our approach towards the things of God.

The purer we become in our life in regards to God, the more our attitude will express or reflect the reality of Christ. This brings us to the

---

[1] Matthew 7:16-20
[2] Luke 3:22; 4:1, 18-19
[3] Romans 13:14

type of attitude we will express. The Apostle Paul gives us insight into the attitude that will reflect Christ in Philippians 4:8, "Finally brethren, whatever things are...lovely...think on these things."

"Lovely" implies having a friendly, acceptable, lovable attitude that displays a moral character or ideal as to the worth or excellence of something to those who encounter it. Such an attitude will be delightful because it will express the beauty or glory of God, and will manifest itself in one's countenance, revealing harmony with the heart, mind, and Spirit of God.

One of Jesus' names is Wonderful. "Wonderful" means a marvelous thing.[4] The Son of God would also be known as Counselor, The Mighty God, The everlasting Father, and The Prince of Peace. However, what would identify Him would be the fact that His very countenance would reveal His wonderful character. He is indeed wonderful in every way. Even flesh would not be able to hide the wonder of His incredible character. He was a friend to sinners and an acceptable sacrifice of God. He revealed the love of God through compassion, and was sinless, proving to be worthy as a sacrifice. He was a delightful gift from heaven, and the beauty of His grace and truth reveal that He was in complete harmony with the Father.[5]

We catch glimpses of Jesus' loveliness in other ways. In the Song of Solomon, there is a beautiful revelation of Him. We receive this insight into Him in 5:16, "His mouth is most sweet: yea, he is altogether lovely. This is my beloved, and this is my friend, O daughters of Jerusalem." We will be spending eternity discovering the loveliness of our Lord and Savior.

However, can people see the loveliness of our Lord and Savior in our countenance? What will people see when they witness the loveliness of Jesus? They will see truth and encounter honesty that manifests itself in honorable practices. They will see purity in how one approaches a matter. They will see harmony.

It was said of David and Jonathan that they were lovely in their lives and in their death, they were not divided. These two men's souls were knitted in agreement. Clearly, loveliness possesses a strength that cannot be measured. These two men were lovely due to their relationship. They had agreement that was true, honest, just, and pure. Their greatest agreement came at the point of God and His righteousness.

Jonathan was in line to be king, but he knew that God had chosen David as king. The lovely part about Jonathan is that he gave way to God's plan. Loveliness is clearly seen by how these individuals lived, as well as the type of relationship they had, not only with God, but also with others. Jonathan preferred David to himself and blessed him. David said

---

[4] Strong's Exhaustive Concordance of the Bible, # 6382
[5] Isaiah 9:6; John 1:14-17; 10:30; 2 Corinthians 9:15; Revelation 5:12-14

of Jonathan that he was mighty and very pleasant. He declared that Jonathan's love for him was wonderful, surpassing the love of women.[6] Obviously, our true character will prove to be lovely to those who are pure, or it will reveal darkness to all who encounter us.

We see this same loveliness in the life of John the Baptist towards Jesus Christ. John was the voice in the wilderness. However, the voice in the wilderness gave way to the Word who became flesh. He decreased so that Jesus would increase. Such loveliness shows a disposition of lowliness, and an attitude of meekness.[7]

Consider what Jesus said about John the Baptist. He acknowledged that many people came to John, but not because of His clothes or appearance, but because of his message.[8] Jesus then made this statement, "Verily I say unto you, Among them that are born of women there hath not risen a greater than John the Baptist: notwithstanding, he that is least in the kingdom of heaven is greater than he" (Matthew 11:11).

Obviously, John had the right disposition that truly represented the One he was preparing the way for. However, Jesus said that if a person had humility, he or she could be considered greater than John in the kingdom of God. Real Christianity reflects the mind of Jesus in every situation. In fact, the Apostle Paul tells us we should be reflecting Jesus in our lives.[9] There are many times I have told those under my leadership that I do not want to see them, I want to see Jesus in them. After all, they cannot save anyone. They cannot give any lost soul hope, and they cannot get anyone to heaven who may follow them. Only Jesus can save, give hope, and lead people into heaven.

This brings us to Jesus' mind. How lovely He was when He silently went to the cross on our behalf. How lovely He was when He laid down His life for us. How lovely He was when He gave way to death and the grave, so we could receive the fullness of His life. This is the essence of loveliness. It is always willing to give way to that which is worthy and excellent. It is in such greatness that loveliness can be beheld. It is in such greatness that the beauty of heaven will come forth in grave darkness.

In Ezekiel 33:31-33, the prophet is being told by God that the words he speaks will be lovely to the ears of his hearers, but the hearers will fail to adhere to them. Truth is always lovely to the ears of those who are lean in spirit, but they will not produce loveliness in an individual unless they are applied. Ultimately, such words will judge those who fail to respond.

---

[6] 2 Samuel 1:23-26; Ecclesiastes 4:9-12
[7] Matthew 3:3:1-4; John 3:30
[8] Matthew 11:7-15
[9] 2 Corinthians 3:18

The things of God are lovely. They are pleasant to the soul, satisfying to the spirit, and glorious in practice, but few practice God's words, ways, and examples. This brings us to possessing a lovely countenance. To have the countenance or reflection of Jesus, we must expose ourselves to Him. We must know His mind, obey His instructions, and walk according to His examples. Such practices will develop Jesus' mind or disposition in matters concerning life.

Constant exposure to the Person of Jesus will result in abiding in Him. He is the Vine we are the branches.[10] We must reach deep into His person and character to take of His disposition and life. We must seek greater revelations of Him so that the light from His life will reveal His glory through us in greater measure.

Abiding in Jesus will ensure us that we will walk or live according to His yoke.[11] The yoke of Christ is easy because it simply requires us to love Him with all of our hearts, minds, souls, and strength. His yoke disciplines us. In other words, the yoke of His love disciplines us in how we express His love to others. Such love will always be expressed in meekness. God's love is lovely or delightful, but it requires us to be lovely in our execution of it. Towards the lost, it will show long-suffering. Towards the fearful, it will show patience. Towards those who are angry it will show temperance, and to those who are insecure, it will show faith. To those who are anxious, it will display peace, and to those who are hurting, it will extend compassion.

What does your countenance say about you? For Cain, it revealed that sin was at the door of his heart, waiting to entrap him. For Jacob, Laban's countenance told him that he no was longer supportive of him. For Moses, it told the people of Israel that he had been in the presence of God. David's countenance spoke of his character and life in the inner chambers with God. Nehemiah's countenance told the king that something was amiss in his life. Solomon tells us that it is a merry heart that makes a cheerful countenance. We are told that the countenance of Jesus in His resurrection was like that of lightening, and in John's revelation of Him, His countenance was as the sun shining in its strength.[12]

Obviously, our countenance reveals much about our inner life with God. If we truly experience fellowship with God, our countenance will reflect his glory. If we come more into agreement with the world, we will reflect its false glory. If we come into agreement with any aspect of man, we will reflect his fading glory. Therefore, what glory is being reflected in your countenance?

---

[10] John 15:1-8

[11] 1 John 2:6

[12] Genesis 4:6-7; 31:1-2; Exodus 34:29; 1 Samuel 16:12; 17:42; Nehemiah 2:2; Proverbs 15:13; Matthew 28:3; Revelation 1:16

7

GODLY CONDUCT

As we consider the thought process, we cannot help but notice how it will influence our perception and our conclusions. Ultimately, it will determine our frame of reference.

Frame of reference will establish how a person processes information. It will influence the spirit in which a person regards a matter, producing the attitude in which he or she will approach a situation. How this person approaches a situation will create the fruit, revealing the state of his or her inward disposition. This fruit will manifest itself in the person's attitude and conduct.

We all have our ideas about conduct. Conduct, however, becomes the truest expression of who a person is becoming before God. This expression will manifest itself in the manner in which a person will act, carry something out, or manage a situation. Conduct shows us the spiritual conduit a person is connected to, as well as the moral principles that he or she adheres to.

Most people think of conduct in terms of what they do. As you can see, conduct is determined more by what a person is influenced by. For example, the Bible talks about evil company corrupting good manners.[1] Once again we must conclude that our conduct is an expression of what truly is influencing our way of thinking.

This brings us back to our thinking process. To ensure godly conduct, we must begin from the premise of truth. Truth must operate in an honorable environment to ensure just character. Upright character will approach all matters from the point of purity. As individuals walk out these virtues in their lives, they will reflect a lovely countenance that will express itself in godly conduct. Godliness is something that will be evident because it is what believers will exercise if they are being obedient to the truth in the right spirit.[2] Therefore, conduct serves as a living testimony or witness as to what each of us believe, love, and serve.

As you consider godly conduct, you will realize that such conduct finds its source in God, its instruction in His Word, its example in Jesus

---

[1] 1 Corinthians 15:33
[2] 1 Timothy 4:7-8

Christ, and its power in the presence and moving of the Holy Spirit. This is why the Apostle Peter made this statement in 2 Peter 1:3, "According as his divine power hath given unto us all things that pertain unto life and godliness, through the knowledge of him that hath called us to glory and virtue." (Emphasis added.)

If our lives are connected to God, then we will become an expression of what is godly. Godliness is expressed in a couple of ways: through contentment and good works.

The Apostle Paul made this statement in 1 Timothy 6:6, "But godliness with contentment is great gain." As you consider contentment, you must realize it is a preference. Contentment comes down to a proper attitude about life regardless of the state of circumstances. In other words, I choose to be satisfied in my present state. The Apostle Paul stated that he had to learn to be content in whatever state he found himself.[3] Notice how Paul learned contentment. It became his preferred attitude as he encountered the different aspects of life. This means he actually practiced contentment by being satisfied.

Satisfaction comes out of gratitude. The problem with most Christians in America in regard to their conduct is that they lack genuine gratitude. They are moody because they are dissatisfied. They are complaining because they are miserable in their ungrateful state. They are touchy because they are full of self. They are unhappy because they have an ungodly attitude. As a result, they are treacherous and unpredictable, as they swing between anger and self-pity.

The core of all dissatisfaction is a matter of unbelief. People who are dissatisfied do not trust God with their lives. If their personal worlds do not bow down to them, placate their foolishness, appease their pride, honor their very presence, and exalt their desires, they become mean-spirited and unreasonable.

Such a spirit is a product of unbelief. Unbelief refuses to trust God's character and ways; therefore, it will not allow God to reign. It will become dissatisfied with life, walk in indifference towards God, and display rebellion towards righteousness.

Contentment is the preferred attitude behind all godliness, but good works are the visible evidence of it. The Apostle Paul made this statement in Titus 2:14, "Who gave himself for us, that he might redeem us from all iniquity, and purify unto himself a peculiar people, zealous of good works."

Most people assume that God will accept any form of good works. Such a concept is incorrect. Good works can be considered reprobate or useless.[4] The quality of good works is not based on the action, but on the inward environment of the vessel. Obviously, Titus 2:14 confirmed that a

---

[3] Philippians 4:11
[4] Titus 1:15-16

person must be purified unto God before his or her works can become acceptable or sacrificial to God.

For a vessel to be clean from within, a person must have a right attitude. Good works are a manifestation of a person's attitude. If a person wants to honor God because He is satisfying, then the works will be offered in a right spirit. However, if a person offers good works out of a self-serving attitude or one that is resentful, it defiles the works, making them reprobate before God.

Works must find their source in faith that will be considered righteous to God. If I do a deed on the basis of faith, because it is right before God and beneficial to others, it will be accounted to me as righteousness. After all, it takes faith to believe that God would accept deeds that are based on His holy character, His eternal Word, His righteous ways, and His heart towards others. Such faith is wrought by the love of God. Galatians 5:6 states, "For in Jesus Christ neither circumcision availeth any thing, nor uncircumcision; but faith which worketh by love."

Works that come out of godly conduct are clearly motivated by the love of God, distinguished by their purity, and established by genuine faith. Faith of this nature advocates righteousness in all that is being done.

Genuine faith serves as a witness to God's character, goodness, power, and majesty. Ultimately, faith that walks in total disregard to the things of the world, in complete reliance upon God, and in total abandonment of servitude, devotion, and love to God will cause the person to not only walk contrary to the present world, but it will raise him or her above any identification or association with it.[5] Hebrews 11:38-40 summarizes such an individual in this way, "(Of whom the world was not worthy:) they wandered in deserts, and in mountains, and in dens and caves of the earth. And these all, having obtained a good report through faith, received not the promise: God having provided some better thing for us, that they without us should not be made perfect."

Since the preference of contentment and the visible evidence of godly conduct are being identified as expressing true faith, we must now come to terms with how this attitude and acceptable works will be established and maintained in our thinking process. The Scriptures in Hebrews 11 gave us insight into what it will take to establish right thinking in the area of conduct. However, the Apostle Paul once again brings this to the light in Philippians 4:8, "Finally, brethren...whatever things are of good report...think on these things."

The concept of good report points to being well spoken of, reputable, and producing praiseworthy character. Thinking on that which would be of a good report, would ultimately reveal the type of conduct or behavior that is unacceptable. Environments that produce gossip, slander, or seeds of discord would be unacceptable. For example, when people

---

[5] 2 Corinthians 5:6-10; Hebrews 11:1-2

think about the business of others, it rarely ends in a good report. When people think on the character flaws that offend their rigid standards, their self-righteousness raises its head in unmerciful judgment and condemnation. In fact, if people would think on that which would establish what is praiseworthy, there would not be so much backbiting and division in the Body of Christ.

Let us consider those things that would end in a good report. In Acts 6:1-3, the new Church found the beginning of division due to the fact some needs were being neglected in the Body. To avoid a division, seven men were chosen to serve the needs of the Body. They had to be of honest report. In other words, their character had to be impeccable.

To incur an honest report, one must have a good name that will identify or associate him or her to such character. Solomon stated that a good name is rather to be chosen than great riches. [6] Sadly, most people compromise their reputation, good name, and character by being treacherous with their words and dealings. Often questionable practices are done in the name of jobs, security, and success. However, the reason for such compromise is to gain the riches of this world. To have a good name and honest character, individuals must be trustworthy in all they say and do. There should be no doubt as to their conduct because they have proved to be true to their word, and consistent in being honest about dealing with matters on every level in their lives.

As you study those who were considered as being of good report, you will realize God was able to honor them. The reason for this is because a person cannot be of good report unless he or she serves the true God of heaven. Granted, such a person can be honest, but being of good report identifies you to the One who is considered good. Such goodness is strictly attached to God. It points to a life that is beneficial because of God's goodness being manifested in practices. This life is expressed by conduct that cannot be reputed in its motive, intention, and practice.

This is confirmed in Acts 6. The seven men did not only have honorable reputations, but they were full of the Holy Ghost and wisdom from above.[7] Clearly, these heavenly influences distinguished these men in their attitudes, mannerisms, and practices. Obviously, the eternal and heavenly were the source behind the conduct of these believers. As a result, those who knew or witnessed their conduct could easily identify them as fitting the necessary qualifications to minister to the needs of those in the new Church.

Another such man that was of good report was Cornelius. It was said of this Roman Centurion that He was just or righteous. He feared the God of heaven, and was of good report among all the nation of the Jews. Obviously, the fact that Cornelius was just reveals that he was upright in

---

[6] Proverbs 22:1
[7] Acts 6:3

all of his dealings. He feared God. Fearing God reveals an attitude that walks in sobriety before God and His people. Sobriety is opposite of foolishness and silliness. As a result, Cornelius was of good report among the Jews, and became one of the first Gentile believers of Jesus Christ.[8]

Ananias was another man who was of good report.[9] Ananias was a devout man. In other words, he was devoted to Jehovah God. Devotion to God during the establishment of the new Church was expressed in a person's life by observing the intent and practice of the Law. Since Ananias was such a man, the Jews respected him in his community. However, the greatest sign of trust came from God. He entrusted the blind Paul, known as Saul, to this man. As a result, he became part of Paul's testimony of how Jesus met him on the road to Damascus, blinded him by His glorious light, and then led him to the man, Ananias, who had been prepared by the Lord to minister the life of Jesus to the future apostle.

It is hard to find conduct among Christians that has not been compromised by the world, tarnished by dead-letter religion, and made worthless by unabated spirituality that is influenced by the kingdom of darkness. Much of the conduct that can be observed is silly, hyper, and unrealistic. To trace its influence, one cannot help but conclude that it is anything but godly.

Clearly, there is a mixture. And, when you consider this mixture, you discover that faith towards the true God is definitely missing.[10] Of course, the mixture varies according to the influence that is in operation. If a person is influenced by doctrines of demons, he or she will adjust the truth, making him or her religious, critical, and unpredictable to that which would challenge his or her concept of truth. If an individual is being influenced by the enticements of the world, he or she will be indifferent and critical to the move and work of the Spirit, thereby, making truth dead-letter. If a person is being influenced by idolatry, he or she will pervert all truth, creating a different god and spiritual reality.

As believers, we must examine our conduct to see if its source is God, its authority is the Word, and its inspiration is the Holy Spirit. If our conduct does not identify us to God, then we must conclude that something is terribly amiss in our lives. Such a conclusion must bring us back to our way of thinking. If godly conduct is missing in our lives, so will be the witness or a good report in regard to our lifestyles.

What are we thinking upon? Our outward conduct will expose our thinking process. It will lead us back to our premise, our inward environment, the quality of our character, our type of approach, and our attitude.

---

[8] Acts 10:22
[9] Acts 22:12-16
[10] Hebrews 4:2-3; 6:1

Right now consider what your conduct is saying about your life before God.

***

As we consider this thought process in Philippians 4:8, a wonderful picture immerges. Let us now consider this picture before we continue on in our journey to understand how the mind is influenced by how one thinks upon the matters of life.

Consider the following table:

Manifestation	The Area that will Be Affected	The Virtue
Spirit	Premise	True
Words	Environment	Honest
Deeds	Character	Just
Service	Approach	Pure
Reflection	Attitude	Lovely
Visible Witness	Conduct	Good Report

The thought process clearly shows the mind and influence of Jesus. It is all about connecting with our different environments in order to interact with them according to spirit and truth. Interacting with our environment is of the utmost importance. It will allow us to properly discern it. Discerning is necessary if we are going to be effective in ministering before God and to others.

8

THE EXCELLENT SACRIFICE

We have been considering the thought process. To have the mind of Christ is not an option, it is commanded. We must have the mind of Christ to come into subjection to the Father's will and give way to the Spirit of God in submission to His leading.

Since Jesus is the truth, His whole premise as man was perfect in every way. He was in subjection to the Father's will, making Him honest in all that He did. As a result, He ensured an honorable environment that was trustworthy to those who encountered Him in sincerity.

Jesus was just in all of His dealings. He tells us in John 5:27 that the Father had, "...given him authority to execute judgment also, because he is the Son of man."

He is also pure. The Apostle Peter put it in this perspective, "Who did no sin, neither was guile found in his mouth" (1 Peter 2:22).

We already established that Jesus was lovely in every way. His character was beyond description, His ways were honorable, His disposition lowly, His attitude was meek, and He was under the control of the Holy Spirit. As a result, He was a man of good report. His accusers could not find any fault in His conduct, and He was crucified because He was who He said He was, the Son of God.

As we consider the character of Christ, we would quickly point out that He was the Son of God. But we must remember that He possessed this mind and character as man, not in light of being the Son of God. Oswald Chambers stated that Jesus Christ was the only man considered normal in the kingdom of God.[1] Adam failed to reach his potential due to rebellion, marring his potential, as well as all mankind. God brought contrast through His Son. Jesus not only represents the person we can all be in light of God, but He also reveals what the normal man was intended to be before the fall of Adam.

As man, Jesus' perfection did not come from His deity, but through suffering. His disposition did not come from His glory as God, but from His submission as man. His attitude did not come because of His greatness; rather it came because He abased Himself in every way.

---

[1] Bringing Sons Into Glory & Making All Things New: Oswald Chambers; © 1990 by Oswald Chambers; Publications Associated Limited, pg. 116

Jesus became the man He did because He chose to. You can follow Jesus' choices from the glory of heaven to His obedience to His earthly parents, right into obscurity. You can follow Him into the wilderness as the Spirit leads Him there. You can catch glimpses of Him praying, seeking the will of His Father.[2] Ultimately, it will lead you to the Garden of Gethsemane, and His words, "…nevertheless not my will, but thine, be done" (Luke 22:42).

Jesus serves as our example as man, but not in light of Him being the Son of God. We need to cease from excusing ourselves from having the mind of Christ. We need to realize that if we are born again of the Spirit and the water (the Word of God) we can develop the life and mind of Christ in us. However, it is a choice—as to what we decide to think upon. It is a discipline—as to how we will perceive the matters of life around us. It a point of development—as to what will determine the influences, preferences, agendas, and priorities behind our thought process.

The truth of the matter is we all want to control the world around us. However, the only point of say and control we have come down to the type of individual we become. Sadly, most of us shy away from this reality. We want to believe that our environment and its influence determine our disposition, attitude, and conduct. It is sad to think that man wants to take control of his world, and dictate how it must be, but he does not want to take responsibility for how he thinks, feels, acts, and conducts the affairs of his life.

The man Jesus is the truth about how man can become godly. He reveals how man must think, how he must be, and what he must strive to become in this present world.

As you consider Paul's instruction in Philippians 4:8, you realize He is really telling us what it means to have the mind of Christ. We have to put on the Lord Jesus.[3] It begins by having His mind. This means, we are obtaining His disposition and attitude. As His disposition is established in us and His attitude developed in us, then His life will come forth.

What is the key to ensuring that we do not put on some religious cloak that gives the impression we partially have the mind of Christ, or that we even occasionally display it in certain situations? In other words, how can I make sure we are not faking His mind? In reality, we either have His mind or we don't. However, people can deceive themselves about such matters.

In Philippians 4:8, the Apostle Paul gives us insight into the inspiration or springboard to ensure the integrity of our complete thought process. Consider his words, "…if there be any virtue, and if there be any praise, think on these things." Each aspect of our thought process must

---

[2] Luke 2:51; 4:1; 2 Corinthians 8:9; Philippians 2:6-11; Hebrews 5:8-9
[3] Romans 13:14

be considered in light of whether it is virtuous, and whether it will result in praise.

"Virtue" points to that which is excellent. That which is excellent speaks of qualities that express themselves in strength or courage. Strength used in the right way is commendable, while courage ensures the quality of a matter. When you take the concept of virtue as a point of inspiration, you will realize that each part of our thinking process will be distinguished by the trait of excellence. Truth is proven to be excellent when it is honorable. Honesty will show itself courageous when it is just. The characteristic of being just will convey strength when it is pure. Purity will prove to be excellent when it is manifested in loveliness. Loveliness will prove to be virtuous when it is expressed as being of good report.

Virtue must be evident in every aspect of our thinking. Since it represents what is excellent, it will automatically adjust our focus heavenward. This is the only source or place of excellence. After all, you cannot find virtue in the flesh, the practices of the world, and the workings of the kingdom of darkness. Only that which is of God, inspired by eternity, and contains a touch of heaven can possess the excellence of His majesty, the strength of His character, and the courage to love sacrificially. In essence, this virtue can only exist when the attitude or mind of Christ is applied or is present in our thinking.

The Apostle Peter tells us that we have been called to glory and virtue. You cannot encounter glory without experiencing the excellence of God's character and greatness. In fact, we are to add the quality of virtue to our faith. This virtue will find its origin in diligence that will enable faith to become virtuous. Without virtue, faith will not possess the integrity to remain pure, the strength to stand on the truth, and the courage to go on when all of hell comes against it.[4]

Faith must display the excellent character that only comes when one is established on the foundation of Jesus Christ, lining up to His character, and walking according to His example. The key to this character can be found in the life of Daniel. He had an excellent spirit. He showed his spirit and life through faith that was exemplary in conduct.[5]

Once faith is adorned with virtue, then knowledge can be added in a right spirit. Knowledge that contains the reality of Jesus will express itself in temperance, rather than pride.[6]

Temperance will manifest itself in patience. Since patience produces experience, it will be conveyed in godliness. Godliness will in turn show benevolence to others. If these qualities abound in us, we will not be barren in the knowledge of our Lord Jesus Christ.[7]

---

[4] 2 Peter 1:3, 5
[5] Daniel 6:3
[6] 1 Corinthians 8:1-2
[7] Romans 5:3-5; 2 Peter 1:8

Once again, we are reminded that our thought process must take on the disposition and attitude of Christ. If we take on the mind of Christ, our perspective will be eternal, our understanding will possess revelation, and our practices will be godly and practical. Clearly, such a mind is focused heavenward upon the One who deserves worship and glory.

This brings us to the excellent sacrifice that will come out of those things that are virtuous. The Apostle Paul instructs us to offer our bodies as a living sacrifice, which is our reasonable service.[8] Such a sacrifice will avail our lives before God in such a way that we will discover His good, acceptable, and perfect will. It is important to realize that reasonable service points to worship that will bring glory to God.

Everything we do as believers, must serve as a point of worship. Wherever there is true worship, one will find sacrifice. The Apostle Peter tells us that since we make up a priesthood, we are to offer spiritual sacrifices. Clearly, these sacrifices are to be seen by God, and not man.[9]

This brings us to the excellent sacrifice that will come out of those things that are virtuous. Keep in mind that such a sacrifice will serve as a point of worship. It will bring honor and glory to God. Hebrews 13:15 gives us this insight about such a spiritual sacrifice, "By him therefore let us offer the sacrifice of praise to God continually, that is, the fruit of our lips giving thanks to his name."

As you consider the thought process that the Apostle Paul is talking about in Philippians 4:8, it will ultimately lift you above this world as you consider the reality of our Lord. Therefore, if the thought process does not take you beyond self, this present world, and ungodly influences, you will never be able to offer the sacrifice of praise.

Acceptable praise can only occur when the mind finally reaches up into the very heights of God. Praise soars in the reality of God. A person's perspective is being totally consumed by the One who sits in the array of all of His glory and majesty in the heavenlies. Such a mind not only honors God before man, but will also distinguish a person's commitment and love for God, thereby, bringing glory to Him. However, the mind can never get off of the runway if it is weighed down by the demands of this present world. It cannot leave the hangers as long as people hold on to self. It cannot get beyond the burdens of life if it is focused on matters that are not eternal.

Hence, enters the attitude of gratitude. The mind that is being established in Philippians 4:8 has the liberty to see the life that is being produced. Such a life can only result in a thankful heart. This heart will rejoice in truth, desire honesty, value that which is just, cling to that which is pure, seek that which is lovely, and surround itself with that which maintains a good report.

---

[8] Romans 12:1-2
[9] 1 Peter 2:5

Clearly, such a heart, mind, and life are God's plan, God's desire, and God's doing. A thankful heart allows the soul of man to explore the impossible, the incredible, and the eternal. Such a heart allows a person to enjoy God. People who have learned to enjoy God have a heart that is overflowing with His benevolence and a soul that is satisfied in every way. Out of such an environment will come forth the fruit of the lips–lips that will be full of praise. Such praise will commend God's faithfulness, declare confidence in His immutable ways, and will express approval in regard to His benevolent intervention on His peoples' behalf.

Obviously, it is only as the mind humbly gives way to the Spirit, that the soul rises up in thankfulness, in earnest expectation, and in worship, that the lips will sing true praises to God. This is the excellent sacrifice that God is worthy of. Praise lifts up the mind of man to honor God. As the mind reaches upward to encounter God in His glory, God will receive the sacrifice. And, it is such a sacrifice that God not only deserves but also desires from each of us. It is within such exaltation that God will inhabit the praises of His people.[10]

God's presence encourages communion. It is within the environment of fellowship that hearts are enlarged to receive, minds are expanded to consider, and lives are changed for His glory.

Sadly, we make God too small in our minds. It is only as our heart is enlarged by His greatness, and our soul is challenged as it becomes disillusioned by the vanity of this present world, that we by faith can dare to explore the unseen and the eternal aspects of our great God. It is in our discovery of our God that we become thankful and learn what it means to praise Him.

Today praise has been replaced with emotional hype, worship with sensationalism, and communion with supernatural experiences. However, God is not in it. Such practices are idolatrous in nature. The fruits are obvious. Men's lives remain unchanged, as they become silly, unpredictable, and arrogant over their religious experiences. The biggest fruit of their lives is the point of their affections. They are in love with their experiences, gifts, personal prophecies, and the concept of the moving of the Holy Ghost, but they are not in love with Jesus, nor do they have genuine love for others.[11]

The religious camps of today are producing militants who are drunk with causes, but who do not know the real voice of Jesus Christ. They are producing religious zealots who cannot discern the truth because they do not love the truth. They are encouraging spiritualism, rather than obedience to the Word of God. They are replacing transformation with outward conformity to religious codes and agendas.

The environment of much of the Church encourages religion, but how much of it invites the presence of God? In fact, how many Christians

---

[10] Psalm 22:3

[11] John 13:35-36; 16:13-14

are prepared to meet a holy God? Where is the virtue in all that Christians do in the name of Christ? In what way do our religious activities result in the sacrifice of praise that truly reaches the throne of God? I cannot answer these questions for others, but I must examine them in light of my own personal life before God.

All that comes from God is virtuous and worthy of praise. As a result, all that I do in regard to my life in God must be virtuous and bring Him honor and praise. Clearly, the Christian life is a life of devotion, consecration, discipline, and sacrifice.

What about your life and practices? Is your life distinguished by excellence in your way of thinking, attitude, conduct, and walk? Does your life result in the sacrifice of praise because the Lord is being lifted up in all that you do?

9

FRUITS OF THE SPIRITUAL LIFE

The mind is an incredible instrument. I am not just talking about the brain. As previously stated, our brain may orchestrate the functions of our body, but our thinking takes place in the soul. The soul contains the will, intellect, and sensibility. Our sensibility entails our emotional arena. Within these three arenas, one considers the matters of life. From the platform of the soul, people logic, interpret, judge, calculate, speculate, draw conclusions, and make decisions about life.

This brings us to the real purpose of the soul. Its main function is to connect the happenings of our world to the spiritual realm of God. Since man's fall in the Garden of Eden, he has become carnal or soulish. Such a state points to selfishness. Selfishness simply means man is considering all matters in light of self and not in light of God. In fact, he draws his influence from that which appeals to the base part of his selfish disposition, such as the world. However, all that is attached to soulish aspects of life are temporary.[1]

A self-centered perspective makes people fleshly and worldly in their conclusions. Perspective of this nature is devoid of any spiritual insight. It walks in great darkness of ignorance, deception, and death. Such a perspective is blinded by a false light (understanding), a false way (broad way of destruction), and a false confidence (personal strength).[2]

As you consider the fleshly perception, one can begin to see why Jesus' emphasis was clear in Luke 8:18a, "Take heed therefore how ye hear..." The influences of the soul will determine the spirit in which people perceive something. If individuals are fleshly, they will perceive according to the spirit of the world. The Apostle Paul tells us that the only thing this spirit will work in us is rebellion towards God.[3]

Those who are rebellious towards God will be obstinate towards His truths, contrary to His ways, and mocking towards that which is godly. There will be no attraction or desire towards His kingdom. Such people want life on their terms. Therefore, they will perceive life according to

---

[1] 1 John 2:15-17

[2] Jeremiah 17:5; Matthew 6:22-23; 7:13-14; 1 Corinthians 2:13-14;
2 Corinthians 3:5

[3] Ephesians 2:2-3

their fleshly desires and agendas. They will speculate about reality rather than face it. At times their conclusions will appear as if they are living on the edge of insanity.

As you consider these individuals, their souls fail to make the connection with God. As a result, they are clueless, harsh, angry, and unrealistic about the reality around them. They are clueless about reality because it does not serve their purpose. They are harsh to those who will not adjust to their personal reality. They are angry at life and at those who would dare challenge their reality. This includes God. They are clearly unrealistic about life. They either live in fantasy or in denial about what is true and real.

Since the connection is never made to God, reality, truth, and hope are far from these people. Their realities become fragile, their egos remain sensitive, and their mannerisms are either placating others as they maintain a false sense of superiority, or they are arrogant as they smugly, and with cruelty, exalt themselves over everyone.

The harsh reality of man in his fallen state speaks of the great tragedy of mankind. In such a state the light of the Gospel never penetrates the spiritual blindness of man.[4] He remains lost in his environment, as he is clueless about his spiritual condition, resentful towards truth, angry at the prospect of being wrong, and unrealistic about his fruit.

The real battle over the mind has to do with the reality that clearly surrounds man. This reality reveals that something is terribly amiss in this world. What is out of order is man. He refuses to come back to the center of his world—God. As a result, man is lost. And, when one has become lost and out of order, the environment is chaotic and confusing.

Man becomes indifferent to his reality as he shifts the blame and the responsibility for his chaotic world elsewhere. For example, "my miserable life is the fault of my past." "My present lot in life is due to bad breaks." Peoples' ability to shift the blame makes them indifferent to reality. Although there are success stories that would strip such logic away to prove its vanity, self-pity, and arrogance, each person in this state of mind remains indifferent to reality by becoming an "exception to the rule." After all, the person's situation is worse than other people's situation. Such logic comes from the foolishness that is bound in the heart of everyone born in the Adamic race.[5] It is not only foolish, but it is a path of self-destruction.

When a person is born again by the Spirit and the Water of the Word of God, he or she is connected to God.[6] The spirit that was once dead to God is now revived to live according to His life. The conscience that was once indifferent to the inward matters of the disposition is now sensitive

---

[4] 2 Corinthians 4:2-6
[5] Proverbs 22:15
[6] John 3:3, 5; 1 Peter 1:23-25

to His light. The will that was incapable of responding in true repentance, is now empowered to ensure the work of transformation of the mind.

The people that are truly born again will manifest this new life by producing new fruits. Jesus stated that we will know people by their fruit.[7] In other words, we will not have to judge such people because their fruits will tell on them. However, most Christians are not fruit inspectors. They are judges. Obviously, such individuals do not discern a person's fruit; rather they judge how people make them feel about life. Such people encourage flatteries and idolatry, but they do not desire reality.

The reality I am talking about is the reality that leads a person to truth about his or her own spiritual condition. God is the great "I AM." In other words, He must be a person's present reality.[8] As believers, our understanding must come from a point of truth. It must be honest to encourage His presence. It must be just to be counted as righteous. It must be pure to properly see Him, lovely to manifest His glory, and of good report to serve as a living testimony to those around us.

Most people think of fruits in terms of actions. However, the type of spiritual fruit we are talking about has to do with disposition. As stated, our thought process will determine our disposition. Obviously, the thought process is going to decide the condition of the soul. The soul is the ground, but the spirit will determine the fruit that comes forth. Many people can tell you about the nine qualities that make up the fruit of the Spirit.[9] But, how many of those people can tell you how the fruit will look, taste, smell, feel, and how it will sound when it is inspected?

The first aspect of the fruit we must consider is its source. Keep in mind that being born again spiritually connects a person to God. However, this connection begins at the point of Jesus' redemption. People who stand in Jesus' redemption will reach into His Person, character, and work to reap the full benefits of redemption. Not only does redemption connect each believer to the source of eternal life, but it also ensures an abundant or fruitful life.[10] John 15:1-8 tells us the source of this life is Jesus Christ.

People perceive eternal life to be an extension of Jesus' salvation. However, Jesus is the essence of eternal life. If you have Jesus, you possess eternal life. As His life is developed in you, it will produce the fruit of the Spirit. The fruit of the Spirit is a manifestation of Jesus in us. For example, the motivating spirit behind us comes from the base of God's love or benevolence. This love is expressed in our attitudes towards others.[11] Such benevolence cannot remain indifferent, unforgiving, or bitter, *in spite* of the unpleasant circumstances created by

---

[7] Matthew 7:16

[8] Exodus 3:14

[9] Galatians 5:22-23

[10] 1 Corinthians 1:30; John 5:21-26; 10:10; 11:25-26; 14:6

[11] 1 John 4:19-21

269

life and others. However, most people consider love in light of how others treat them, rather than their personal responsibility to others in light of what God did for them on the cross.

The person who has the love of God will also possess the joy of the Spirit. Joy is an abiding anchor that cannot be *moved* by circumstances. This is why Nehemiah stated that the joy of the Lord was his strength.[12] As you consider joy, you will realize that it is an abiding confidence before God. You cannot have this confidence unless you are abiding and walking by faith in His love.

Since the anchor of joy is in place, peace will be present. Peace is an abiding quietness that can find rest in the Lord *regardless* of the circumstances.[13] The quietness of the soul is a product of being confident before God. In other words, one is at peace with God, and such peace produces joy.

Obviously, the place of peace is not an environment devoid of conflict; rather it is coming to rest in the Person of Christ.[14] People are in constant turmoil because there is no place of rest from the conflict that bombards them in this world and in their relationships. In many cases, these people create their own conflict due to the fact that they are miserable and unstable in all of their ways. They are void of any capabilities of living at peace with others. They want life on their terms, and demand their way with people who will not submit to their self-serving, idolatrous, tyrannical demands. And what is worse, these very same people refuse to make peace with God.

Peace creates an environment in which believers will have hope. Hope comes from patience.[15] The greatest challenge for most people is to wait on God. Hope allows people to have patience or long-suffering in light of expectation. People who lack hope live in depression. Depression or despair sucks the life out of them. However, believers who keep their focus heavenward, live in hope. Such an expectation gives them the strength and liberty to be long-suffering *in* circumstances.

Some people must cling to this hope at times when circumstances are closing in on them. Heavenly hope causes one to *consider* matters in light of eternity. Eternity reveals that circumstances are as temporary and fleeting as a vapor.

An environment that is established by love, stands in joy, abides in peace, and withstands in longsuffering, will produce gentleness. Gentleness implies character, which will result in goodness. Such character will show its excellent quality by being beneficial to God's kingdom. Clearly, the manifestation of having a right base of love, the anchor of joy and the environment of peace will come forth through godly

---

[12] Nehemiah 8:10
[13] Isaiah 30:15
[14] Isaiah 26:3; Matthew 11:28-29; John 14:27
[15] Romans 5:3-5

character. This character will manifest strength that is immovable. 2 Samuel 22:36 brings out this strength, "Thou hast also given me the shield of thy salvation: and thy gentleness hath made me great."

Psalm 21:3 gives us this insight about God's goodness, "For thou preventest him with the blessings of goodness; thou settest a crown of pure gold on his head." The goodness of God on our behalf is made apparent by His incredible blessings. His blessings indeed benefit and add to our lives and relationship with Him.

The goodness of God not only reveals His intention and commitment to us, but it will inspire faithfulness. Faithfulness is an act of good faith in a matter. God's faithfulness is evident in His words, actions, and examples. We can trust Him, and due to His trustworthy character, we can and must be trustworthy towards Him.

Trustworthy character will make us more receptive to the ways of God. As we come into submission to His ways, we will become meek in attitude. "Meekness" simply means all of our strength is under the control of the Holy Spirit. Meekness also implies our disposition or spirit is in line with the character of God.

A soul that is under control is one that is tempered by Spirit and truth. There can be no self-control unless one is under control. Self-control follows knowledge in 2 Peter 1:6. Self-control takes knowledge and applies it as a personal discipline. Knowledge put into practical practice produces wisdom.

As you consider the nine ingredients of the fruit of the Spirit, you cannot help but notice that Christianity is a life under the control of the Holy Spirit. A life under the control of the Spirit means a disciplined walk that is in submission to the Holy Spirit and aligned to the truth.

The key to this life is abiding in Christ.[16] By abiding in Christ, not only will godly fruit be evident, but it will also be fruit that can be examined (looked at), tasted (tested), smelled (considered), felt (proven), and set apart by passing the test as to how it will sound when tried in the times of temptation and adversity.

It is vital that as Christians we discern the fruit of others. Fruit will identify a person's source, influence, and purpose. If Christ is not the source influencing spiritual growth and determining the purpose behind a person's life, his or her fruit will reveal such a matter.

What will people see if a person's source is truly Jesus? We get insight to this in Acts 4:13, "Now when they saw the boldness of Peter and John, and perceived that they were unlearned and ignorant men, they marveled; and they took knowledge of them, that they had been with Jesus." Clearly, people must be able to see or take notice of believers by the distinction that Jesus is present in their lives.

---

[16] John 15:1-8; 1 John 2:6

What will people taste when partaking of godly fruit? Depending on what spirit they are partaking of will determine how the fruit will taste. For example, if a person is partaking of truth, it can prove to be salty to the taste. This can offend, challenge, or heal. If a person is partaking of the Word of God, it can start out as sweet to the taste, but become bitter to the soul as it exposes and reveals the intents of the heart. If a person is actually partaking of the divine nature of Christ in communion, it will always prove to be good or beneficial to the spirit.[17] King David confirmed this in Psalm 34:8, "Oh taste and see that the LORD is good: blessed is the man that trusteth in him."

What will people smell? We know that Jesus' life will produce a fragrance that will be obvious to each person who encounters it. To God it is a fragrance that is sweet and well-pleasing. To Christians the fragrance will edify their spirit, but to the unbelieving, it will speak of death.[18]

What will the person touch when encountering the fruit of the Spirit? Those who touched Jesus were healed, and by their faith they were made whole. When you touch peoples' lives with the reality of Christ, they will experience mercy, encounter grace, and know compassion. The reality of Jesus' life is that it is meant to be offered to, spilled over, and poured into people. As Christians, we must be open-ended vessels where the life of Christ comes in, but is poured out with the intent to produce His life in others. What some Christians fail to realize is that the fruit that is being reproduced in others is the very life of Christ. [19]

Finally, what will this fruit sound like when it is tried? Once again, the sound might vary according to the disposition of the person. To God's sheep the voice will be distinct. To those who are being led by the Spirit, it may be a small-still voice. To those who are hiding, it may come in a form of a pleading question, *"Adam where are you?"* To those standing afar off, it may sound frightening. To those who are standing in iniquity, they will hear the voice of judgment. To those seeking His will it might come in the form of the written Word. Those who hear the sound of God can be assured that it will penetrate the natural ears, awaken the spirit, stir up the conscience, and bring sobriety to the soul. An upright response will ensure that a person will hear what the Spirit is saying.[20]

As you can see, the fruit for the Spirit will stand distinct from the fruit of the world, religion, and man. The world may compete with this fruit with all of its social reforms, religion may try to counterfeit it with its various rituals and activities, and man may try to imitate it with his good deeds, but it will lack the life, the disposition, and the ways of Jesus. Fruit may look according to, taste similar to, smell like, feel akin to, and sound

---

[17] Matthew 5:13, Hebrew 4:12; 2 Peter 1:4; Revelations 10:8-11

[18] 2 Corinthians 2:15-16

[19] Mark 3:10; 5:28; 6:56; 1 Corinthians 15:23

[20] Genesis 3:8-9; Exodus 20:18-20; 1 Kings 19:11-12; Matthew 7:21-23; John 10:3-10

similar to the real fruit of the Spirit, but if it lacks the right spirit and perverts the truths of Jesus, it is false fruit. False fruit will cause disillusionment, an empty taste, a stagnant smell, insecure feelings, and a brassy sound that is empty of rhythm and meaning.[21]

The question is what kind of fruit is your life manifesting? What kind of taste are you leaving with those who are partaking of your life? Remember, Jesus declared that you would be known by the fruit of your life. This means that you will not be identified by your religious affiliation, good deeds, or how well you can quote biblical truths. You will be known by your fruits, which are a true manifestation of your inward environment.

---

[21] 1 Corinthians 13:1

10

APPLICATION

We have been considering what we must think on to have the mind of Christ. Clearly it is a process that brings us under the Spirit of God. The Spirit will then lift us above the fleshly and worldly influences to consider the eternal. It is only as we are lifted up that we can be exposed to the incredible ways and thoughts of God. It is from the perspective of His Spirit, and that which is eternal that we can ensure proper thinking. Proper thinking is necessary to rightly discern our environment.

Sadly, too many people are trying to bring God down to their way of thinking. In doing so, they create their own god and speculate about the meaning of life. To uphold their personal god and their conclusions about life, they must adjust truth, become indifferent to reality, and walk in denial or delusion as to the fruits that are being manifested in their lives.

We are told what to think on to ensure integrity and righteousness. Such virtues will express themselves in godliness. Such a mind shows us the thought process will involve discipline. Instead of assumptions that turn into speculations and vain imaginations, thoughts are clearly being discerned in light of spirit and *truth*. They are being regarded in light of motivation, intention, and focus. Such examination allows for *honest* evaluation. If the thought comes from mere opinions, it is lightly esteemed. If it comes from experience, it is brought forth as a mere contrast. If it is grounded in the Word of God, it must be properly regarded in light of the whole Word of God to ensure that *just* counsel is being upheld at all times. It is from the throne of God that thoughts must originate. Such thoughts must be adhered to in humility and meekness to ensure *purity.*

Once the thought process is ensured of purity, then it can consider the *loveliness* that is being exposed in its conclusions. There is loveliness when Jesus can be distinguished in the matter. Oh, to see Jesus, to know Jesus, and to have this bit of heaven unveiled to our spirits is not only lovely, but also glorious. It is at the point of this loveliness, that a person can be ensured of his or her mind being transformed.

A transformed mind will be able to make the proper connection with reality. It is the Spirit of God that makes such connections once all of our thoughts have been brought into captivity to Christ, and our senses are under the Holy Spirit's influence.[1] It will be in this arena that all thought processes will come into line, and the soul will be able to make the connection between the spiritual and the reality around us.

Minds are not transformed when they are swayed towards an opinion. Minds are not going to think differently because a matter is proven. Rather, minds are going to be changed when their focus is made clear by a consuming reality that will not fade. In the world, such a mind can become obsessive and insane. However, in God's kingdom such a mind is so awakened by, so impressed with, so aware of, and totally caught up with Jesus that nothing else matters or makes sense. It is not like the obsession of the world that is dark from consuming lust; rather it is an obsession that finds unending glory, infinite expectation, and the wondrous revelation of God's heart. Clearly, such a mind is void of all residues of self and the world that would prey upon it.

This type of mind possesses a *good report* of God's kingdom. It walks in confidence towards God, and in righteousness towards others, as well as in godliness in this present world. Clearly, such a mind is not only beautiful, but it stands distinct in a world that is void of such beauty. Remember, this is the mind of Christ.

The Apostle Paul understood this mind. No doubt, he strove to ensure this mind was developed in him. We read these instructions, "Those things, which ye have both learned, and receive, and heard, and seen in me, do: and the God of peace shall be with you" (Philippians 4:9).

As you study the thought process, you will realize that a mind is being developed that will be disciplined enough to learn, open enough to receive, sensitive enough to hear, and enlightened enough to see. It is a mind that is ready to apply what is *true,* maintain what is *honest,* uphold what is *just,* insist on what is *pure,* pursue what is *lovely,* and demand that which is of *good report.* It is a mind that will not settle for anything less than what has been clearly established by God.

It is a mind that wants to learn the lessons of life, and a mind that desires to receive by faith the things of God. It is a mind that will not settle for anything that does not come from God; therefore, it is inclined towards hearing God, while avoiding the tendency to consider anything that possesses the world or self. Such a mind will have one desire, it will want to see and possess the revelation of heaven, so it can know the reality of God. Let us now consider the mind from the perspective of Philippians 4:9 in light of what it must learn, receive, hear, and see.

One of the things we must realize is that the mind of Christ in us means that we will display His life. What will this life look like? When you consider the life of Christ it is expressed in four ways. The Apostle Paul summarizes this expression of Christ in us in 1 Corinthians 1:30, "But of him are ye in Christ Jesus, who of God is made unto us wisdom, and

---

[1] 2 Corinthians 10:4-5

righteousness, and sanctification, and redemption." Clearly, the mind of Jesus will express wisdom, righteousness, sanctification, and redemption.

Since the mind will influence our disposition, and how we process a matter, we must begin with the main purpose for thinking. To think upon a matter has a couple of goals: 1) to get down to the basis of a matter; and 2) to gain wisdom to resolve a situation. Sadly, most people either skip or ignore the first goal. They do not want to get down to the basis of a matter, unless they can adjust it to their personal reality. Therefore, wisdom to them is reduced to becoming clever, subtle, or smart enough to get around reality. Such an attempt is to ensure and maintain their personal reality. This is the essence of foolishness. However, reality is reality. It can only be faced head on in light of *truth*, because such truth is the only means to get down to the basis of an issue.

This brings us to preference. Jesus dealt with the two main preferences in John 3:17-21 that people will naturally go the way of. These preferences are the darkness of sin or the light of truth. The reality is that we all start with a preference for that which is selfish. The selfish preference brings us into the ways of darkness and death.

For example, our initial preference is for the right to the self-life, to live life on our terms. Such rights are established by the pride of life. The pride of life sees itself as having the right to pursue, maintain, and exalt the life it thinks it deserves. However, such preference leads to condemnation because its confidence is in the arm of the flesh. It loves darkness for it can hide the evilness behind its selfish motives and ways. It will hate the light for the light will reprove and expose its evil workings.

Those who prefer the light, do so because of the awareness to discipline their ways. Such discipline starts with humility and taking responsibility. Attitude will determine approach and practice. Therefore, the disposition of humility will put pride in its place, as well as take authority over personal rights. Ultimately, such a disposition will insist on doing right.

Doing right is a manifestation of true faith. A person of the light has simply believed in the Son of God. Such people discipline their ways according to the light, knowing full well that all sins will be exposed. These individuals welcome the penetrating light, knowing that there will be reconciliation with God.

This brings us to our thought patterns. These patterns are set as to personal preferences. These patterns establish the environment in which all thinking will be done. If these patterns are wrong, we must rethink them. Rethinking thought patterns entails retraining ourselves as a means to establish different patterns.

It is from the basis of truth that we can *honestly* rethink our patterns and set up an environment that encourages wisdom from above. It is important to realize wisdom is not just a matter of having God's perspective. It involves applying God's truth to a situation. Therefore, wisdom implies truth that has been walked out, experienced, and deemed as being true. After all, truth never changes.[2] It becomes part of the basis in which we will naturally discern all matters. It is godly wisdom that ensures the integrity of an environment.

It is in godly wisdom that we *learn* the valuable lessons of life. The world serves as a great classroom. There is so much to explore about life. The lessons of life will bring us back to the same conclusion; that God is the only source and means that will make sense out of life.

The lessons of life are meant to change and enlarge our perception of God. However, these lessons cannot be learned unless we change our attitudes about a matter. Attitudes will change when our behavior adjusts to the lessons. It is as our behavior adjusts that our attitude will see the light of an issue. Changed behavior means a change in focus and preference.

As you consider God, you will see that behavior is learned. By addressing behavior, God exposes attitudes. He instructed His people upon entering the Promised Land to not learn the works and abominations of the people of the land. Clearly, behavior is learned by the perception we adopt towards life. The people of Canaan not only practiced that which God hated and would not tolerate, but they learned to war. They knew nothing of peace. No wonder the Apostle Paul instructed believers to not be conformed to this world, but to be transformed by the renewing of their minds.[3]

Obviously, the state of our mind will determine what we learn. We must learn of Jesus, His ways, and His works. We must walk according to His examples and teachings. This will ensure that we will learn not to blaspheme that which is of God. To learn of God, we must also diligently learn the ways of those who belong to Him. This will keep us from idolatry.[4]

We must learn His righteous judgments. His judgments will teach us to fear Him. Fear of the Lord is the beginning of wisdom. Those who learn to walk in His wisdom will do well in their relationship with Him and in their lives before Him.[5]

Learning implies understanding. Those who learn of God will learn of His righteousness.[6] Proverbs 9:9 summarizes the type of character that will come forth, "Give instruction to a wise man, and he will be yet wiser: teach a just man, and he will increase in learning." Godly wisdom produces a *just* man. A just man reminds us of the righteousness of Christ. There is nothing right in our life apart from Jesus.

---

[2] 2 Corinthians 13:8; James 3:17

[3] Deuteronomy 18:9; Psalm 106:35-37; Isaiah 2:4; Jeremiah 10:2; Romans 12:2

[4] Jeremiah 12:16-17; Matthew 11:29; 1 Timothy 1:20

[5] Deuteronomy 4:10; 14:23; 31:13; Psalm 110:11; 119:7

[6] Isaiah 26:8-9

The righteousness of Christ is realized at the point of faith, applied in obedience, and manifested in just character. God's eyes are upon the righteous. He knows their ways, tries their hearts, hears their cries in their afflictions, and upholds them. In the end, they shall inherit the land as they flourish like palm trees.[7]

Acceptable righteousness can only be found, established, and realized in Christ. He is the immovable Rock in which all faith is established in and confirmed by. This is why righteousness is found to be just in all of its ways. It walks in godly wisdom. As the Rock, Jesus is immovable; therefore, He can never be moved from that which is true, honest, and just.

Righteousness is imputed to us at the point of faith. In fact, all matters of God are *received* by unfeigned faith. Unfeigned faith possesses childlike qualities such as sincerity and purity; therefore, it responds in good will and trust as it walks out this new life in Christ. It asks with the confidence, trusting that it will receive.[8] It is from an upright disposition that we can truly receive from God by faith.

To "receive" means to bring near, associate with in intimacy or relationship, and to take unto.[9] To bring near implies embracing something as truth. To associate with means to identify. When it comes to intimacy, it implies familiarity, and relationship involves interaction. Therefore, to receive means to take unto something or someone, and make it or the person a matter of the heart.

The Word of God clearly shows us that we must receive the truth about the message concerning the Person of Jesus Christ in order to be saved.[10] Yet, the general invitation for today is not to receive Jesus as Lord and Savior, but to accept Him as Savior. Accept has to do with a mental assent. However, receive will bypass the mental conclusion of the matter, and reach into the very soul and heart of a person. The soul becomes stirred up to embrace a matter as life, and the heart becomes open to receive it as truth. A matter that does not get past the mind will simply remain on an intellectual plane. It will be a notion, but it will lack life. It will be a belief, but it will lack spirit. However, a matter that gets into the heart will become reality. The mind of Christ is always open to receive that which is of God. Not only will it receive it, but it will also maintain the integrity of it so that it can have its way in the person's life.

Many people walk in unbelief towards God. Such individuals want life on their terms. However, unfeigned faith wants to know life according to the life, heart, and will of God. Faith is active and will walk out what is

---

[7] Deuteronomy 25:1; Psalm 1:6; 34:15, 17, 19; 37:9, 17; 92:12;

[8] Matthew 7:7-8; 18:1-5

[9] Strong's Exhaustive Concordance, #3880

[10] John 1:12; 20:22; Romans 10:9-10; Acts 10:43; 1 Corinthians 15:1-3;
    Colossians 2:6

right in order to be established in righteousness. If such faith is missing from the equation, it will be considered sin.[11]

Proverbs 20:11 states, "Even a child is known by his doings, whether his work be pure, and whether it be right." Righteousness ensures *purity*. It is from purity that a person can hear what the Spirit is saying without perverting it, while seeing the reality of God.

Obviously, purity is a manifestation of righteousness, but it also serves as the evidence of godly wisdom. After all, wisdom from above is first of all pure.[12] Proverbs 1:5 tells us a wise man will hear and increase in learning. He will handle all matters in purity to ensure integrity. Such purity points to sanctification. Due to Jesus' state of purity in His humanity, He was clearly separated from the unholy and separated unto the holy.

Wisdom gives direction in seeking out deeper revelation in light of Jesus, righteousness opens up the means of understanding the ways of Jesus, but sanctification prepares the way for us to perceive the things of God. Positionally in Christ we are in a place of sanctification. In other words, we are set apart by the reality of being in Christ, and His life being in us, to be separated unto God. It is up to us to consecrate ourselves. "Consecration" means we separate ourselves from the unholy and come into subjection to the work of sanctification in our lives. The work of sanctification belongs to the Holy Spirit. He must cleanse, purify, and make us pure before God so that He can use us for His glory and work.[13]

It is in the arena of sanctification that the life of Christ can be unveiled in us. Obviously, sanctification will produce the *loveliness* of Christ in us, as we give way to His work. The Apostle Paul said it best when he declared, "...I live; yet not I, but Christ liveth in me:..." (Galatians 2:20b)

It is in purity and the state of holiness (sanctification) that we can begin to hear what the Spirit is saying. However, a person's state is determined by what he or she exposes self to. Although we can convince ourselves that we can handle that which is profane, few understand that there is also a spirit that is in operation. The more we expose ourselves to the unholy, the more desensitized we become to the wrong spirit, and the more lukewarm we become towards the Spirit of God. The fruit of ungodly influences is that many ears have become dull of hearing. Dull hearing implies a heart that has become gross or indifferent to the things of God. Therefore, if we are to properly hear, we must be in the right state.

Spiritual hearing prepares us to actually see God. Hearing brings us to a state of knowing. However, seeing brings us to a place where we will experience the fullness of what we know. This was brought out in the life

---

[11] Romans 14:23; James 2:14-26

[12] James 3:17; 1 Peter 2:22-24

[13] 2 Timothy 2:19-22; Titus 3:5; 1 Peter 1:2

of Job. Job had been greatly tested. Through the fiery process, he held on to what he knew about Jehovah God. At the end of his ordeal, he experienced the reality of his God. Consider his words, "I have heard of thee by the hearing of the ear: but now mine eye seeth thee" (Job 42:6).

Hearing something may make you aware of a matter, but seeing it makes you a witness to it. Many believers are aware of spiritual truths, but how many of them are living witnesses of these truths because they have experienced them in a living relationship with God through Jesus Christ? This is what makes Jesus a reality to our spirit and nourishment to our soul. It is by being a witness that one is able to give a *good report*.

What will this good report entail? Job summarized it by faith, "For I know that my redeemer liveth…(Job 19:25).

The angels gave this incredible report to the two Marys one Sunday morning centuries ago, *"…Why seek ye (Jesus) the living among the dead? He is not here, but is risen: remember how he spoke unto you when he was yet in Galilee, Saying, The Son of man must be delivered into the hands of sinful men, and be crucified, and the third day rise again"* (Luke 24:5c-7). (Parenthesis added.)

Jesus made this beneficial and insightful statement about the report that would surround His life and ministry in John 11:25-26, "…I am the resurrection, and the life: he that believeth in me, though he were dead, yet shall he live: And whosoever liveth and believeth in me shall never die. Believest thou this?"

The good report that must be a reality to every saint is Jesus' redemption. The price for our sins was paid in full. Clearly, Jesus died to ransom us, and was raised again in a new glorious body to confirm it. He indeed lives to ensure this incredible redemption. In fact, the Holy Spirit has sealed us unto the day of redemption. Everything that is made available to me as a believer is the result of Jesus' redemption. I have been bought back from the slavery of sin and the judgment of death.[14] I have received the surety of His payment by faith. As a result, I am an actual witness of this good report that is being offered to all who will by faith recognize its wisdom, receive it as true, walk it out in honesty, know it is just, hear it in purity, and see the loveliness and reality of it.

His redemption is the ladder that connects earth-bound man to heaven. Nothing can come from God to me except through Jesus' redemption. Nothing can ascend from me to the heights of heaven, unless it goes by way of this ladder. Wisdom will always direct me to His redemption to keep my perspective in check. Righteousness will open up the way for me to be receptive in gaining a greater understanding of His redemption, while sanctification prepares me to walk in humility in light of His redemption.

Do you have such a report about Jesus' redemption? Does your attitude speak of His redemption? Is your mind lifted above this world to

---

[14] Ephesians 1:13-14

consider the depth of His redemption? Are you walking out your life in Christ in light of redemption?

In Conclusion

We have been considering the mind of Christ. The mind of Christ is a disciplined mind in how it thinks. First of all, it is disciplined in the premise in which it begins. It disciplines the type of environment that is developed, and it is disciplined by the approach it must take. The mind of Christ reveals its level of discipline by its attitude, thereby, becoming a point of discipline in how a person conducts his or her life.

In studying this mind, we must note that it begins from the premise of truth. In examining this mind, we see how it will process information to ensure an honest environment. As we examine this process, we can begin to see how we can actually count a matter as being just. This is all possible due to the fact that we will be able to trust the character behind our reasoning. Given that integrity will be upheld in our reasoning, we can be assured that our conclusions will be pure in their approach. Since the approach is pure, we can reckon that a matter will express the loveliness of heaven. This loveliness will bring forth a good report in regards to our conclusions, revealing the fruit of the mind.

The fruit of this type of mind will confirm that we can determine that the matter at hand is a reality. Once we determine that a matter is so, we need to take the lessons and responsibilities that have been illuminated and practice them in our daily life. The Apostle Paul stated that if we allow the mind of Christ to grasp and learn from what is true and honest, receive what is just, hear what is pure, and see what is lovely, we would be able to report that the God of peace has been found in the midst of the situation.

Jesus is our place of rest, but we must come to this place by way of our mind. Most of us faint in our mind before we can seek out this place. The reason fear takes over such a mind is because it lacks the necessary discipline to step over the tormenting feeling by placing faith in the one true God. It is faith in God that allows His peace to reign and guide us through trying times.[15]

As we come to the end of this book, I want to challenge you to examine yourself to see if you have the mind of Christ. This mind is not developed within us overnight. It is a process that involves faith and discipline. Take up the challenge, and let the mind of Christ Jesus be developed in you. Be assured that if you possess the mind of Jesus and keep it disciplined through Him, you will also possess the peace of God that passes all understanding.[16]

---

[15] Matthew 11:28-29; Hebrews 11:1, 6: 12:3
[16] Philippians 4:7

Book Five

FOLLOW
THE
PATTERN

INTRODUCTION

One of the most rewarding studies to me in the Word of God has to do with patterns. As people soberly meditate on the world around them, they cannot help but recognize that everything that is visible and functioning operates according to some kind of pattern.

Patterns involve designs, shapes, features, and configurations. They characterize the base, purpose, or function of something, as well as reveal the attributes or qualities of those who are behind the design. Without such patterns, there would be chaos and destruction.

The Word of God is full of priceless patterns that reveal the character of its designer, God. Hebrews 8:5 gives us this insight about patterns, "Who serve unto the example and shadow of heavenly things, as Moses was admonished of God when he was about to make the tabernacle: for, See, saith he, that thou make all things according to the pattern shewed to thee in the mount."

As we can see, God entrusted Moses with one of the most incredible patterns that was to serve as shadows of heavenly things. If was as if God was trying to bring a bit of heaven to earth to reveal to man His beauty, holiness, and glory. It was His way of allowing man to witness His character and experience a bit of His greatness.

We know that these heavenly patterns pointed to Jesus Christ, the Son of God. They simply cast the shadow of the real image of the Person of Jesus. These various patterns emerge out of the shadows as you follow Jesus through His ministry to Gethsemane and finally to Calvary, where all the promise and reality of redemption was culminated at a cross, and would later be fully realized by an empty tomb. Admittedly, I will not exhaust or reveal every pattern, but hopefully those that are outlined will give the reader valuable insight into that which has been veiled.

My goal in writing this book is to reveal some of the patterns in the Bible veiling the mystery of godliness and bring them to the light. The intent behind such revelations is to make the patterns alive and real to the hearts of those who desire to see Jesus in Scripture. I pray you will enjoy discovering the heavenly treasure that is hidden in these patterns. I can assure you that once you possess the heavenly treasures, they will become more priceless to you than the world's gold and silver.

Are you ready to go on this treasure hunt? Ask the Holy Spirit to prepare you and to guide you to each nugget, so that you can become rich in God's kingdom. And, do not forget to enjoy the treasure hunt, for in it you will come out possessing the real pleasures and rewards of heaven.

1

THE GARDEN

All treasure hunts must begin where treasure has been discovered in the past. Here in Idaho, many people seek gold in some of the rivers. However, in other areas, such a search can take individuals to caves, deserts, and mountains. For the Christian, the treasure hunt must begin in a garden.

There are five types of gardens in Scripture. These gardens together represent a complete picture of man's plight and God's pattern to bring man to a desired place of deliverance and rest. Each of these gardens represent different stages of growth in the Christian's life. Some of these gardens can be pleasant to the eye, but dangerous to the soul. They can present destruction, only to produce life. Some are plush with the abundance of blessings, while with other gardens, a person must travel far, dig deep, and endure great hardships before any treasure can be discovered.

The reason a Christian starts in a garden is because that is where man first came into close contact with God, his Creator. Genesis 2:15 states, "And the LORD God took the man, and put him into the garden of Eden to dress it and to keep it."

"Eden" means paradise. God's plan for man was to enjoy his Creator; therefore, He created a perfect place of peace to encourage joy and communion. It was a place of beauty and full of life. Since man could freely walk with his God, this life operated in harmony.

God made everything in this garden good. Everything about Eden was beautiful and bountiful; that is, until man chose to disregard his Creator's warning and eat of the tree of knowledge of good and evil.[1] It was at the point of man's blatant rebellion that evil took root in the garden and rendered Paradise into a place of tragedy and failure.

Adam had been given the dominion over this paradise, but in his independent act of disobedience, he turned his dominion over to the enemy of God, Satan. As a result, man was banished from Paradise,

---

[1] God called Adam and Eve, "Adam" or "man." Therefore, where the term "man" is often used in reference to both male and female. See Genesis 5:1-2.

ushering him into a new garden that would be ruled by Satan. This garden would be known as the world.[2]

God described the essence of this new garden in Genesis 3:17-19:

...cursed is the ground for thy sake; in sorrow shalt thou eat of it all the days of thy life; Thorns also and thistles shall it bring forth of thee; and thou shalt eat the herb of the field; In the sweat of thy face shalt thou eat bread, till thou return unto the ground...

The world has many attractions, but its fruits are temporary and stand cursed. This world will yield fruit that will nourish the physical body of man, but because it cannot satisfy the soul, he will eat it in sorrow instead of joy. Rather than being a keeper of this garden, man will toil in the garden of the world in order to survive. In fact, man will be nothing more than a land serf who is being used up by the lord of this garden. Every accomplishment will be done by the sweat of man, as he watches much of the fruit of his labor being robbed, killed, or destroyed in some way.

Man will find life to be a burden in the garden of the world, as he struggles against the curse that plagues him, the sorrow that mocks him, and the bread that will eventually leave him empty and hungry. He will often find himself in utter despair, as he hopes for a better day, a brighter future, and a new life that continually eludes him, as more of his life is poured out into the endless vanity of this garden. All seems lost, as each day, he is faced with the fact that he was formed from dust, and one day, he will return to it without ever discovering the life that still haunts him in the recesses of his mind.

The life that haunts him is that of Paradise. Somehow, the thought of Paradise is etched in the heart of man. It is as though he knows it existed, and now he must discover it in the midst of the toil and hopelessness of this new garden. He will search for it in the things that comprise his present existence. However, as many will testify, the things that comprise the garden of the world leave a person with a greater vacuum, for there is no real substance to its fruits. Yet, how many people continue to search for Paradise in the garden of the world, only to come out disillusioned?

This disillusionment has caused many to curse God, as they realize that nothing makes sense in the garden of the world. They blame Him for the sorrow, mock Him for the vanity that emerges from their sweat, and falsely accuse Him for their gnawing emptiness and hunger.

The reality of the garden of the world that haunts many is that Paradise is reduced to a fable, rather than a real place, and that the core of life is tragic. To survive the tragedy of life man unwisely prides himself in his ability to control his world as he resorts to standing in a delicate delusion that is setting him up for a fall.

---

[2] Genesis 1:26; 3:22-24; 2 Corinthians 4:4

The higher the individual climbs in his or her delusion, the greater the fall. Like all who climb higher in this personal delusion, such an individual will eventually reach a pinnacle that will cause him or her to fall into the abyss. This fall is like a free fall where a person's world spins out of control. Losing such control causes fear that often graduates into hopelessness, skepticism, and unbelief, causing the person's unbelieving heart to become harder towards God.

Life eventually breaks a person when he or she realizes that the depravity of one's world originates in personal depravity. This harsh reality will cause utter despair or drive the person into the next garden: the spiritual wilderness.

The Wilderness

Man is in search of Paradise, but the reality of life in the garden of the world brings him face-to-face with a life devoid of God. After all, the Garden of Eden did not find its source or beauty in the presence of man, but in the ruling sovereignty of God. God is the one who created Paradise for man, and as long as God remained the center of man's life, he could enjoy the fullness of it.

Adam had it all in the Garden of Eden, but somewhere along the way, he lost sight of God. As a result, transgression took root in his heart.[3] This transgression caused Adam to toy with a world that allowed him to be independent from God's reign. Although it appears as if Adam had no qualms with God being in his world, he was vying for the right to rule his world outside of God. This is the essence of sin that results in rebellion and transgression.

Adam found the means to put God to a foolish test when Satan beguiled his wife to partake of the one tree that God had forbidden them to eat. In the moment Adam ate of the tree the eyes of the couple were opened, to reveal not only physical nakedness, but also spiritual vulnerability.[4]

Paradise represented the life that God intended for man, but due to sin, the wilderness is symbolic of the present condition of man. The world stands in-between Paradise and the wilderness. The garden of the world shifts man's attention from his spiritual nakedness, by making his life a matter of the flesh, rather than the heart. As long as he can attempt to fill up his soul with the things of the world, he can ignore the torments and emptiness of his life. Although this garden can temporarily cover up his spiritual vacuum, it always leaves man feeling insecure or indifferent to God, by either causing him to feel far from God because of sin, or self-sufficient in his own abilities. As people give way to the world, they fall

---

[3] Job 31:33
[4] Genesis 3:1-10

under its spirit, which encourages them to mock God and walk in unbelief, as they strive to rule their own worlds.[5]

The garden of the world causes people to ultimately blame God for their substandard life, while ignoring or deceiving themselves about their part in this life. However, once they come to the end of the vanity of their personal worlds, they will be face-to-face with the spiritual wilderness of their lives.

When you follow the lives of the great men of the Bible, many ended up in the wilderness, including Moses, John the Baptist, Elijah, and Jesus. All of God's people will come by way of this wilderness. Their attitude towards it will determine their level of spiritual growth and well-being. People can react one of three ways when they encounter this spiritual barrenness in their lives: 1) They can ignore it and continue on as always; 2) they can become angry and bitter about it, or 3) they can face it and begin to come to terms with it in light of God.

It is important to point out that the wilderness has the potential of being a beautiful garden. The only things that separate a beautiful garden from the wilderness are the elements. The wilderness is harsh because of the extremeness of elements, such as heat and wind. These elements are not balanced out by rain and the proper mineral content in the soil.

This is true for man. He operates in extremes. He is full of self, sin, and the world; therefore, minus the reality of God, righteousness, and distinction. As a result, his soul is barren, wasting away in the relentless heat of judgment, condemnation, and hopelessness.

The spiritual wilderness is an unattractive place in light of the world, but it is the only place where man's soul can begin to come into balance with God. This is why many saints embrace the wilderness in their spiritual journey. They realize it is in the garden of the wilderness that man can regain what Adam gave up in Paradise, dependency on God.

In the garden of the world, man can convince himself that he is self-sufficient; therefore, he has need of no one. The wilderness separates man from the influence of the world and strips away his false sufficiency. The process not only reveals his spiritual depravity, but his vulnerability. This brings us down to the biggest casualty of the wilderness: man's pride.

The spiritual wilderness proves that man needs God or he will not survive the relentless harshness of this wilderness garden. He has to depend on the unseen, and humble himself to partake of the unacceptable. He has to allow the severity of the wilderness to break him, the heat of it to purge him, and the wind to separate him from the vanity of his selfish, worldly life.

It is in the wilderness that man discovers hidden treasure, as bits and pieces of self are left along the way. After all, man cannot carry a heavy

---

[5] Ephesians 2:1-2

load through the wilderness if he is going to survive. He must be willing to put aside that which hinders him, in order to embrace that which will prove to be sustaining.

I have found myself in the wilderness garden many times. I have not only found abundant life in this garden, but I have discovered treasures that have enriched my life beyond words. One of the most valuable nuggets I have obtained in the wilderness is the revelation of God's faithfulness.

God has faithfully brought me through each wilderness experience that has always proved to be trying, as well as a place of intense preparation. After each wilderness experience, I have discovered areas of my life where He went deep to rid me of defeating traits and habits in order to refresh my life with the rivers of Living Water. As I look back on His work in my life, I can see His abiding faithfulness to bring me forth through each period of testing and point of preparation. The world has become less important, as the reality of God became my source of water and bread. Through it all, I realize He was establishing a greater testimony of Himself in my life.

The garden of the wilderness never failed to prepare me for the next garden. This garden always proved to be more trying than the harsh wilderness.

The Garden of Gethsemane

In the wilderness, various aspects of self were being broken down, so that I could endure the next garden that would require me to totally deny self, and pour it out on the ground as a necessary offering. We see this same pattern in Jesus' life. According to Luke 4, Jesus was led in the wilderness where Satan tempted Him to give in to the three avenues of the world: the lust of the flesh, the pride of life, and the lust of the eyes. Even though the temptation was extreme, He triumphantly overcame the world.[6]

In the next garden, we see a greater struggle emerge. This struggle was so great that an angel had to minister to Jesus in the midst of the battle.[7] His sweat was as great drops of blood, falling to the ground. It was as if another type of offering was being made in this garden.

In the garden of the wilderness, man learns dependency on God, but in the Garden of Gethsemane he must abandon all in order to give way to the will of God. In the wilderness, one discovers how far-reaching the world's tentacles are, as they cling to the person. However, in the Garden of Gethsemane, flesh raises its ugly head to retain its right to rule. In the garden of the wilderness, the influence of the world must be

---

[6] 1 John 2:15-16; John 16:33
[7] Luke 22:41-46

purged out of man, while in the Garden of Gethsemane, the flesh will lose in order to give way to acceptable obedience.

The wilderness is a preparation for the Garden of Gethsemane. As self is left behind in the barren landscape, the attractions of the world become less important. The more that self is left out of the wilderness, the more the power of the flesh is being broken. If a person is still dependent on the world and full of self, he or she will automatically give in to the flesh in the Garden of Gethsemane.

In the wilderness, bits of self are left behind, but in the Garden of Gethsemane, all that remains must go through a refining process like the olive. "Gethsemane" means olive press, and to retain pure olive oil, the olive must be completely crushed. Likewise, man must be crushed for his life to be purified and poured out for the glory of God. It is in the crushing process that the anointing comes forth which breaks the yoke of bondage. The breaking is necessary because such bondage prevents a person from being all that he or she can be.[8]

Jesus was prepared for His next step in the Garden of Gethsemane: The cross. 1 John 2:6 instructs believers, "He that saith he abideth in him ought himself also so to walk, even as he walked." In the Garden of Gethsemane, Jesus was being crushed, but on the cross, He would be completely broken and spilled out. This is true for the Christian. We must be crushed first, before we can be broken as a vessel, and the contents spilled out for God's use and glory. In order to have our life count for eternity, we must walk as Jesus did. This means that we must go to the cross by way of the Garden of Gethsemane.

The cross will bring a person to the next garden: that of the empty tomb.

The Empty Tomb

We have been studying the pattern found in the major gardens of the Bible. These gardens give us an important contrast. For example, we see the difference between what God intended for man and what the world can offer. We can observe how the wilderness and Gethsemane addressed man in different ways to prepare him to embrace the ultimate place of victory—the cross. Each garden prepares the person to confront the lessons of the next garden.

These gardens bring us to the final garden where we will find an empty tomb. E. W. Bullinger summarized this garden in *The Companion Bible* by relating how the Garden of Eden represented death *in* sin, while the Garden of Gethsemane reminds us of death *for* sin, but the sepulcher or the tomb speaks of death *to* sin.

The concept of the empty tomb reminds every Christian of the victory that was wrought on the cross by Christ, and verified by His empty tomb.

---

[8] Isaiah 10:27

It is true that every Christian must come to this tomb. However, it is important to keep in mind that these gardens represent the spiritual pattern for the Christian to follow to ensure spiritual maturity.

To the Christian who is following this pattern, the empty tomb represents the heart. Jesus talked about the heart and how it is the source of sin. In Matthew 15:19-20, He stated, "For out of the heart proceed evil thoughts, murders, adulteries, fornications, thefts, false witness, blasphemies: These are the things which defile a man..."

In Matthew 23:27-28, Jesus described what was in the heart of the religious people of His day, "...for ye are like unto whited sepulchres, which indeed appear beautiful outward, but are within full of dead men's bones, and of all uncleanness. Even so ye also outwardly appear righteous unto men, but within ye are full of hypocrisy and iniquity."

Each garden will reveal different types of heart conditions. Those who cling to the world will develop a hard heart of unbelief towards God. The wilderness will expose a stony heart, as self is unveiled, while the Garden of Gethsemane will reveal where the flesh has given in to the enticements of the world, choking out the life of God, producing a divided heart.[9]

The challenge in the last two gardens is to give way to the process of God changing a person's heart. For example, in the wilderness, testings can plow up the stony heart. In Gethsemane, such temptations will crush the worldly influences, while the cross will break the hard heart. Therefore, the heart must be plowed up, crushed, and broken for it to become an open tomb towards the work and purpose of God.

Mary Magdalene came to the sepulcher of Jesus with a heavy heart. Her heart had been plowed up by the work of deliverance, crushed by sorrow, and broken by a cross. She had witnessed her precious Lord and Savior suffering, dying, and placed in a tomb. He had, after all, delivered her from seven devils, and she had shown her appreciation and devotion by following Him, as well as ministering to Him along the way. It had been such a glorious time as she watched Him touch the lives of societies' outcast.[10]

She came at the dawn of the day, after the darkest period of her life. She came seeking a dead Lord, only to discover an empty tomb. When she first encountered the empty tomb, it must have reminded her of the part of her heart that was left empty. She did not realize that the empty tomb represented a new life that possessed resurrection power, until she met whom she thought was just an ordinary gardener. This ordinary gardener turned out to be her Lord and Savior. It was at the place of the empty tomb that she rediscovered her greatest treasure, Jesus. Her

---

[9] Matthew 13:1-23

[10] Luke 8:2; Mark 15:40-41; John 19:25

heavy heart was replaced with a joyful heart that rejoiced in the reality of the living, resurrected Christ.[11]

An open heart is receptive to the life of Jesus. It is a heart that is ready to be filled by the presence of the Spirit, manifesting His abounding fruit.[12] It is with an open heart that a person will enter into an intimate relationship with God, and learn to walk with Him in the bountiful garden of the heart. The Song of Solomon makes reference to the heart being the garden. In Song of Solomon 6:1-2, it talks about the young Shulamite woman seeking her beloved, and she finds Him in the garden. Obviously, the garden represented her heart, where his reality abides.

As I mentioned, there are five different gardens. The number "five" represents grace. This shows that all that is done in an open heart is the work of grace. Such a heart has been cleansed by the blood of Jesus, established on the Rock by the love of the Father, and sanctified for the work and glory of God by the Holy Spirit.

When Jesus freely reigns in the heart, Paradise is once again restored. However, this paradise cannot be found within this world, but only within the hearts of people. It is the presence of God that ensures Paradise and brings forth joy to those who learn to walk with Him in the bountiful gardens of their own hearts.

God's heart is to restore Paradise, in order to bring restoration and joy to hard, stony, crushed, and broken hearts. However, the person must first go the way of the wilderness, Gethsemane, and the cross. This is the pattern that the heart must take in order to empty itself of those things which constitute death as a means to become open to the resurrected life of Jesus. It is His life that produces a garden that is bountiful in fruits and beautiful with His fragrance.

Have you traveled the pattern of these gardens to rediscover Paradise? If not, will you not come to the wilderness, and then go by way of Gethsemane to embrace the cross? Keep in mind that, on the other side of the cross is the open tomb where you can experience the reality of Christ in your midst, and once again rediscover the Paradise that was lost in the Garden of Eden.

---

[11] John 20:1-18
[12] 1 Corinthians 3:16; Galatians 5:22-23

2

ALTARS

To me, one of the most fascinating subjects in the Bible concerns altars. As I have meditated on altars, I have found there are four different types of altars. Through my study of this subject, the Lord has graciously revealed a pattern in them.

The first altars were made of earthly rudiments, such as mud or stone.[1] God gave instruction about the stone altars in Exodus 20:24a-25 that gives us some insight, "An altar of earth thou shalt make unto me...And if thou wilt make me an altar of stone, thou shalt not build it of hewn stone: for if thou lift up thy tool upon it, thou hast polluted it."

Obviously, if man had any real part in the makeup or design of the altar, it would be considered polluted. This brings us to the first part of the pattern found in altars. The ingredients of these altars must come from the earth, and they must be constructed according to God and not man.

The fact that God designed the altar pointed to His divine touch and approval. This approval was vital because the altar served four purposes. It was to serve as a place of sacrifice, remembrance (memorial), worship, and communion.

Surprisingly, the first altars were ambiguous. There were sacrifices being made, but no description of the altar can be found. Most likely, they were made of earth or stone.

The fact that the earliest altars were present, but not defined, brings us to another part of the pattern found in altars. They have no meaning unless a person comes to terms with God. Without understanding the character of God and man's hopeless, spiritual plight, there would be no need to worship, offer sacrifices, or establish memorials and a relationship with God.

With the introduction to altars out of the way, let us consider how the altars that were made from the rudiments of the earth showed a pattern as to how to **approach** God. The first recorded sacrifice was that of Abel. His example shows us that our first goal in approaching God is for the sole purpose of pleasing Him. Any time a person comes to God with this motivation, it will be accounted as righteousness to him or her.

---

[1] Exodus 20:24

God confirms the example of Abel in Hebrews 11:4, "By faith Abel offered unto God a more excellent sacrifice than Cain, by which he obtained witness that he was righteous, God testifying of his gifts: and by it he being dead yet speaketh."

Noah erected the first altar that was mentioned in the Bible. He made it after he exited the ark.[2] His actions tell us that his first order of business was not to secure a place for his family, but to ensure God's presence in his midst. His actions also showed that he recognized the need for God's preeminence in his life. This is a valuable part of spiritual growth and leadership in any spiritual pattern.

This is one lesson that the Israelites failed to put into action when they reestablished the presence of Israel in the Promised Land. They had been in captivity in Babylon for 70 years. Understandably, their first order of business was to build their homes. But, in preparing for their physical lives, they failed to erect the temple to ensure the presence of God. Their misguided priorities brought leanness to their quality of life, as well as a drought.[3] Haggai 1:7-8 gives us this insight, "…Consider your ways. Go up to the mountain, and bring wood, and build the house; and I will take pleasure in it, and I will be glorified, saith the LORD."

Noah offered a burnt offering on his altar. According to Leviticus 1:9 and 13, this offering was made by fire. In other words, the sacrifice was consumed by fire. The smoke that ascended to the heavens from this sacrifice served as a sweet savor unto the Lord.

The burnt offering proved that the altars had to stand and withstand in the purifying fires that would consume the sacrifice. The only thing that can stand the purifying fires of God in the Christian's life is genuine faith. In fact, faith is established within the fiery ovens of adversity.[3]

When you combine the purifying fires and faith, you have the combination that will produce an acceptable sacrifice before God. As a result, it will bring Him glory, allowing Him the opportunity to respond.

The sweet savor from Noah's sacrifice allowed God to respond to him with a blessing and the covenant of the rainbow. This brings us to another important aspect of altars. Altars that truly represent God's interest will serve as a point of blessing and covenant for His people to remember, hold onto, and stand according to the light of His unwavering faithfulness.

The next altar was a response to God's promise. Genesis 12:7 says, "And the LORD appeared unto Abram, and said, Unto thy seed will I give this land: and there builded he an altar unto the LORD, who appeared unto him." Abraham built this altar between Bethel and Ai (Haion). "Bethel" means the place of God, and "Ai" means a heap of ruins.[4] Bethel

---

[2] Genesis 8:20

[3] Haggai 1:2-11

[3] 1 Peter 1:6-8

[4] Smith's Bible Dictionary; Thomas Nelson Publishers

represents the religious life, while Ai represents the temporary glory of the world and man's strength.

This particular altar reveals that a person's spiritual life in God must be established between religious activities and worldly demands. In fact, if Bethel reigns without the proper balance, a person can develop a religious indifference to God. And, if the person comes from the perspective of Ai, he or she will be operating according to the fleshly motivation of pride. The Christian life is always established outside of the religious environment and apart from man's personal attempts.

Like Abraham, a believer must find a balance between his service to God and his worldly demands. Balance can only be understood and maintained in a relationship with God. Equally important is the reality that God must be involved in every area of the individual's life. This means that the various demands of religion and the world can only come together and be kept in proper perspective in a relationship with God. Such a relationship implies personal separation and intimacy.

We see that Abraham came back to this altar a second time in Genesis 13:4. Abraham had been in Egypt due to a famine. During his years in Egypt, God remained silent. It was only after he left Egypt and came back to the altar that God once again reestablished His covenant with him.[5]

Interestingly, there is no record that Abraham offered a sacrifice upon this altar either time, but he called upon the name of the Lord both times. The reason that sacrifice was not emphasized is because this altar served as a memorial in regards to the promise of God. This promise served as a stake to Abraham of God's ongoing faithfulness.

We see other altars that served as memorials or a point of remembrance. In the case of Moses, he built an altar in Exodus 17:15-16 as a remembrance that war would rage with Amalek from generation to generation. The children of Reuben, Gad, and the half tribe of Manasseh built an altar to serve as a reminder that they were part of Israel and that the LORD is God.[6]

God encouraged His people to remember always what constituted the essence of their life by not forgetting His works or promises. If they forgot about Him, they would also cease approaching His altars to confirm or reestablish their relationship with Him. If they failed to seek Him, they would forget that they had been purged of their sin, causing them to leave their first love and chase after other gods.[7]

Unused altars eventually become broken down from neglect. We see this in the case of Israel in 1 Kings 18. Israel was in idolatry. The people of Israel had erected altars to their idols, while allowing the altar of God

---

[5] Genesis 13:15-17

[6] Joshua 22

[7] Deuteronomy 5:15-22; 7:18; 8:2, 18-20; 2 Peter 1:8-15; Revelation 2:1-5

to erode away. Elijah confronted them about their idolatrous mixture and he repaired the altar of God.

After repairing the altar, Elijah built another altar by taking twelve stones that represented each of the tribes of Israel. There, he made a trench, filled it with water, and poured water on the sacrifice, and then cried out to Jehovah God. God accepted his sacrifice in a miraculous way, causing the people to fall on their faces, declaring that He was indeed God.

It is easy for Christians to neglect their lives in God. They allow their commitment to God to be eroded away by activities. This erosion causes them to become indifferent to their relationship with Him. Hebrews 2:3 gives this warning about neglecting our salvation, "How shall we escape, if we neglect so great salvation; which at the first began to be spoken by the Lord, and was confirmed unto us by them that heard him."

Calling upon the name of the Lord is associated with salvation in the New Testament.[8] It is important to point out that calling upon the name of the Lord implies appealing to God according to His immutable character and unchanging promises. This shows real reliance and faith in the Person of God.

We see Isaac, erecting an altar in Beersheba in Genesis 26:25, "And he builded an altar there, and called upon the name of the LORD, and pitched his tent there: and there Isaac's servants digged a well." (Emphasis added.) Like his father, Isaac called upon the name of the LORD after he erected his altar. God had reiterated twice to Isaac that he was a recipient of His promise and blessings because of his father Abraham.[9] This shows us that Isaac had not yet established his own relationship with God.

Isaac's example reminds us that an altar of God is a place to call upon the name of the Lord to appeal to God. As Christians, we can be recipients of the treasures of heaven because of what Jesus did on the cross. Keep in mind that God blesses each of us as believers for the sake of Christ, and not because of who we are.

Salvation is a work of God, but one must embrace it. Genesis 26:25 tells us that Isaac pitched a tent. This implies that he was willing to abide at this place until God met with him in a personal way. This altar and tent were Isaac's way of establishing his personal life in God.

A person must be willing to abide at the altar until God meets with him or her. The problem is many do not feel they have the time to wait at any altar. However, the truth is, God's people cannot afford not to wait. We need to wait before our altars until we meet God, and our lives have been firmly established on Him.

---

[8] Romans 10:13
[9] Genesis 26:2-5, 24

The next altar points to an important location. This location has a pattern of events that reveal how one's spiritual life is **established** at the altars of God.

Chosen by Jehovah

The next altar that Abraham built is where he offered the promises of God back to Him as an act of faith. It is found in Genesis 22, and it is the altar that Isaac was placed upon. Isaac represented God's promise and Abraham's blessing.

God instructed Abraham to take Isaac to Moriah and offer him up as a burnt offering. "Moriah" means "chosen by Jehovah."[10] Although no one is sure of the exact location where Abraham offered Isaac, this vicinity would later serve as a place where David sacrificed an offering to stay judgment on Israel, and where Solomon erected the temple.[11]

The importance of Moriah is that it does give us a location for an altar to be established. We see that, for Abraham, God definitely chose this area in which Abraham would offer up Isaac.

There are three important representations here. First, God chose the place. God will only put His mark on what He chooses or designates for Himself. Secondly, a special sacrifice had to be offered to God on this altar. This sacrifice was not just any sacrifice. Isaac represented the promise of God, the hope of Abraham, and the lineage of the Messiah. Finally, this area would mark the spot where God would establish His name in the future when the temple was erected.

You might wonder what kind of pattern could be revealed here in the situation with Abraham. God always begins with an altar. For the Christian, the altar is the cross of Calvary. Calvary stands distinct from all other places because one major event took place that forever changed the course of man.

Next, God chose the sacrifice, Abraham's son. It appeared that all of the promises of God were being offered up in Isaac; yet Abraham willingly obeyed. This obedience was a product of faith. Hebrews 11:17-19 confirms this:

> By faith Abraham, when he was tried, offered up Isaac: and he that had received the promises offered up his only begotten son, Of whom it was said, That in Isaac shall thy seed be called: Accounting that God was able to raise him up, even from the dead; from whence also he received him in a figure.

We know that a sacrifice was chosen for the altar on Calvary: the only begotten Son of God. Like the sacrifice that David made to stay judgment on Israel, Jesus would stand between life and death, grace and

---

[10] Smith's Bible Dictionary
[11] 2 Samuel 24; 2 Chronicles 3:1

judgment, and hope and despair. Just as Abraham believed that God would raise his son from death, God the Father knew that His Son would rise from the dead, to prove victorious over the grave and death.[12]

Abraham took Isaac to Moriah to sacrifice him, knowing that he would receive the promise back from God. He had this confidence because he knew Isaac was a promise from God who would usher in a nation. Likewise, it was the Father's will that Jesus die on the cross, knowing the full ramifications of His death. He knew that Jesus' sacrifice would redeem hopeless man and usher in eternal life.

Abraham never withheld anything from God, and as a result, God was able to give Isaac back to him and provide another sacrifice. Therefore, on Moriah, there were two sacrifices present, one was offered up and the other released.

The cross of Jesus represents two sacrifices. You might be wondering who or what serves as the second sacrifice. Romans 6:5 and 12:1 tells us who the second sacrifice is, "For if we have been planted together in the likeness of his death, we shall be also in the likeness of his resurrection...I beseech you therefore, brethren, by the mercies of God, that ye present your bodies a living sacrifice, holy, acceptable unto God, which is your reasonable service."

Positionally, every Christian is put into the death of Jesus. The beauty of this picture is that Jesus was offered up, while the believer is always being released. This release does not give followers of Jesus the right to live their lives according to personal dictates. Rather, it gives them the freedom to live their lives unto God. This is why every believer is instructed to present his or her body as a living sacrifice. Like Abraham, Christians must not withhold anything from God, but must be willing to offer it all up, knowing that God is able to give it back in greater measure if He so wills.[13]

It was on Moriah that God built the temple. John 15:16 tells believers that they have been chosen. 1 Corinthians 6:19 states, "What? know ye not that your body is the temple of the Holy Ghost which is in you, which ye have of God, and ye are not your own?"

God has chosen a modern-day temple where He can reside in the midst of men through the Holy Spirit. This place consists of people who have received His provision of salvation. Christians are the place or the temple of God. His name is not only declared by their lips, manifested in their lives, but written on their hearts.

For the Christian, the heart serves as his or her personal altar. All devotion towards God must come from the heart. The reality of all that He has done must be an ever-present reality in the heart. The heart must be broken by sin, purified by His Word, established by consecration, and set apart by the life and glory of the Son of God.

---

[12] Hebrews 2:14-15; 11:17
[13] Matthew 10:39; Luke 6:38

This brings us to the third group of altars. These altars revealed the pattern behind the **life** of a believer. This life is comprised of death, service, and communion. These altars are found in the tabernacle.

The Pattern of Life

There were three altars in the tabernacle. They were the Altar of Burnt Offering, the Altar of Incense, and the Ark of the Covenant. These altars were located in the different areas of the tabernacle.

The altars of the tabernacle were made of unique or priceless materials that came from the earth. They were made of wood, gold, and/or brass. Each of these materials found in the altars represented different aspects of Christ's character or work on behalf of man. However, the actual altars were to represent man's responsibility and privilege as a child of God.

For example, both the Altar of Incense and the Ark of the Covenant were made of shittim wood that was overlaid with gold. Shittim wood was found in the wilderness and symbolized the humanity of Jesus. Gold represented Jesus' divinity, while brass pointed to God's judgment upon sin.[14]

In the Old Testament man's life began with the Altar of Burnt Offering. It was located in the outer court. It was on this altar that all sacrifices were offered on behalf of the individual. This altar was made of shittim wood and brass.[15]

The makeup of this altar pointed to the work of the cross. The shittim wood was symbolic of Jesus, as man, becoming the sacrifice on the cross. The brass represented Jesus becoming sin for mankind, by taking the judgment of it upon His body. This reminds Christians that their lives begin with the sacrifice and death of Jesus and end with resurrection of His life being established in them. Therefore, the Altar of Burnt Offering for the follower of God serves as a place of sacrifice and memorial as to how sin cost God His best.

The next altar is located in the Holy Place. The Altar of Incense stood before the veil that separated the Holy Place from the Most Holy Place. It was made of shittim wood and overlaid with gold.[16] Again, the shittim wood represented the humanity of Christ. The wood on this altar actually pointed to the man, Jesus as the Great High Priest who stands as a mediator between man and God. The gold of this altar was symbolic of Christ's divinity. Between these two altars we have the representation of God Incarnate.

---

[14] Most Bible Scholars agree upon what these different materials represented, but my favorite source of information is A Dwelling Place For God by Ruth Specter Lascelle.

[15] Exodus 27:1-8

[16] Exodus 30:1-10; 1 Timothy 2:5

John 15:7 says, "If ye abide in me, and my words abide in you, ye shall ask what ye will, and it shall be done unto you."

John 16:24 states, "Hitherto have ye asked nothing in my name: ask, and ye shall receive, that your joy may be full."

Jesus is the one who stands between a place of service and communion. The veil separating the Holy Place from the Most Holy Place pointed to Jesus' body. Hebrews 10:19-22 tells us,

> Having therefore, brethren, boldness to enter into the holiest by the blood of Jesus, By a new and living way, which he hath consecrated for us, through the veil, that is to say, his flesh; And having an high priest over the house of God; Let us draw near with a true heart in full assurance of faith, having our hearts sprinkled from an evil conscience, and our bodies washed with pure water.

The Altar of Incense pointed to a believer's prayer life as he or she stands in the gap for others. 1 Peter 2:9 says, "But ye are a chosen generation, a royal priesthood, an holy nation, a peculiar people; that ye should shew forth the praises of him who hath called you out of darkness into his marvellous light."

Christians are priests who have the responsibility to stand in the gap in prayers and supplication. Ephesians 6:18 gives this instruction, "Praying always with all prayer and supplication in the Spirit, and watching thereunto with all perseverance and supplication for all saints."

Effective prayer is a privilege that belongs to those who understand the covenant and inheritance available to them as children of God. Hebrews 4:15-16 states, "For we have not an high priest which cannot be touched with the feeling of our infirmities; but was in all points tempted like as we are, yet without sin. Let us therefore come boldly unto the throne of grace that we may obtain mercy, and find grace to help in time of need."

James 5:16c says, "...The effectual fervent prayer of a righteous man availeth much."

Jesus Christ gives His followers authority and power to minister at the Altar of Incense. This allows them the means to make a difference in the kingdom of heaven.

Finally, Jesus is the way and truth into life with the Father. John 14:6 says, "...I am the way, the truth, and the life: no man <u>cometh</u> <u>unto</u> <u>the</u> <u>Father</u>, but by me." (Emphasis added.) Saints must get beyond the veil to experience life with the Father. Experience with the Father brings us to the final altar, the Ark of the Covenant. This altar represented God's abiding presence and glory among His people.[17] It was made of shittim wood, overlaid with gold. Within the ark were three objects: the Law, the manna from above, and Aaron's rod. These objects pointed to Jesus' ministry as the way in relationship to righteousness (Law), the truth about

---

[17] Exodus 25:10-22

our need to be sustained from above by God (manna), and the life (that was raised out of the grave with resurrection power).

There was a mercy seat made of pure gold that rested upon the ark. This represented Jesus as the place of mercy and rest for every believer. It was at the mercy seat that Moses was told to commune with God in Exodus 25:22. The quality of a person's life in God hinges on the type of relationship or communion he or she has with God. It is in communion that a person's life in God is fully realized.

This brings us to the purpose and pattern of altars. If they were not reminding God's people of His faithfulness, they were serving as a shadow of His commitment to save mankind. These altars not only served as a place of adoration and worship that resulted in the abiding presence of God, but became a door by which to enter into sweet communion with Him.

The altars of God ultimately pointed man heavenward to his only source of life, hope, and purpose. In the end, they were meant to establish a growing, vital relationship with God.

Have you neglected the altar in your life? When was the last time you approached God to establish a greater life in Him? Make sure your altar is not eroding away from neglect that comes out of a lack of devotion and love towards your Lord.

3

THE PLACE OF GOD

One of my favorite patterns to follow in the Bible that casts an incredible shadow is that of Bethel. As already pointed out, "Bethel" means the place of God. Every Christian should be searching for his or her place in God. However, there are many hindrances and pitfalls in coming to this place. Not only are there challenges that discourage believers from pursuing their own Bethel, but it can also serve as a place of testing, preparation, and failure.

Bethel was 12 miles north of Jerusalem. It was formerly known as Luz, until Jacob changed its name to Bethel.[1] Although Jerusalem is the place where God chose to put His name, Bethel played an important part in the history of the children of Israel. It served as a significant place for the early patriarchs. Abraham came by way of Bethel after his detour to Egypt. He had previously built an altar between Ai and Bethel. "Ai" meant the heap of ruin.[2]

Here Abraham stood between the ruin brought on by sin upon mankind and the place of God. He stood between man's attempts and God's purpose. It was here he dwelt, built an altar, and called upon the name of God.[3] "Dwelling" implies that he was waiting on the Lord. To call upon the name of God meant that Abraham was recognizing the character of his God and seeking Him.

From this place, Abraham went to Egypt where he lied to protect himself. His lie brought distress on others until it was uncovered.[4] Egypt represented the world. Obviously, by turning to Egypt without regards to God, in a time of famine, was a noticeable detour. In spite of the detour, God maintained Abraham's life and purpose. During that time, God remained a silent partner. It was only after Abraham came back to this place of the altar, by way of Bethel, that communion was once again restored with God.

Abraham's encounter with Bethel reminds us of our initial encounter with God. As Christians, this usually takes place at salvation. We have

---

[1] Genesis 28:19
[2] Smith's Bible Dictionary
[3] Genesis 12:8
[4] Genesis 12:11-20

sought out God because of the ruin in our lives due to sin. We come to the altar of the cross of Jesus that stands outside of the religious activities of man, and call upon His name to be delivered from the hopeless bondage of sin. There, we find hope, as mercy is revealed in forgiveness and grace is given by way of salvation.[5]

Our first encounter with God is precious, but then, we must go back out into the world. The world begins to drown out God's work with demands.[6] Eventually, many take detours at this place where they are led away from their life in God. Although God keeps His hand on these wayward individuals, leanness comes into their soul. Sooner or later, these individuals are compelled to come back to the last place where they met with God. Once again, they establish their relationship with Him.

Jacob's experience at Bethel serves as a pivotal point in his life. There, he did meet with God. It was during a time of transition. Isaac and Rebekah had sent him to his uncle's place to protect him from the revengeful plans of his brother, Esau, as well as search for a bride. His brother Esau wanted to kill him because Jacob, along with his mother, had deceived his father in giving Jacob the blessing. Both Isaac and Rebekah were weary of the Canaanite women, and wanted Jacob to seek a bride within the confines of relatives.[7]

Jacob came by way of Bethel. He stopped at this place to simply rest. I am sure that Jacob had no idea that on this particular night, he was about to encounter the God of his grandfather and his father. In fact, Jehovah God would introduce Himself to Jacob. This night would not only prove to be a pivotal point in Jacob's life, but life as he knew it would never be the same.[8]

God often has to intrude into man's normal activities or journeys. Otherwise, man would most likely never give Him a thought. You never know when and how He will intrude, but when He does you will never forget it. God intruded into Jacob's dreams. No doubt Bethel had seemed like any other place to Jacob, except for some reason God made His presence known at this place. And, whenever God intrudes into man's life, a typical place ceases to be normal or insignificant, and becomes a foundation upon which a memorial is erected and a life is redefined and established.

Jacob had settled in for the night. As he was sleeping, he had a dream. He saw a ladder extending from the earth to heaven. He beheld as the angels ascended and descended. At the top of that ladder was the Lord. He introduced Himself to Jacob, "...I am the LORD God of

---

[5] Matthew 9:13; Ephesians 2:8-9
[6] Matthew 13:22
[7] Genesis 26:34-35; 27
[8] Genesis 28

Abraham thy father, and the God of Isaac: the land whereon thou liest, to thee will I give it, and to thy seed" (Genesis 28:13).

God intruded into Jacob's dream to introduce Himself, and to reaffirm His covenant with Abraham. He used the ladder that extended from heaven to earth. Jesus also used this ladder to verify His identity in John 1:51, "Verily, verily, I say unto you, Hereafter ye shall see heaven open, and the angels of God ascending and descending upon the Son of man."

Jacob saw the Lord at the top of the ladder. Twenty centuries ago, Jesus stood at the bottom of the ladder between heaven and earth. God had once again intruded into history, only it was in the form of a man, Christ Jesus. Jesus actually embraced the ladder of the cross and became a bridge of reconciliation between man and God.

God's intrusion can cause various reactions. For Jacob, he became frightened. Instead of being able to bow before God at this place, he declared it to be a dreadful place.[9] Encountering God will produce humility and worship, or it will cause fear and anger.

For some of the Jews of Jesus' day, it caused anger. In one of His discourses with the Jewish people, Jesus made this statement, "...Verily, verily, I say unto you, Before Abraham was, I am" (John 8:58). The people understood what Jesus was saying. He was claiming that He was the "I Am" that intruded into the normalcy of Abraham's life, the struggles of Isaac, and the dreams of Jacob. He is the God who not only introduced Himself to these three patriarchs, but to Moses in the wilderness. These people understood what He was saying. He was claiming to be the manifestation of God that intruded into these ordinary men's lives to forever change their course. This made the people pick up stones to cast at Jesus, but He simply passed through their midst.[10]

Obviously, Jacob must have considered his encounter with God through the night. The next morning, he rose up early. He took the stone he had used as a pillow the night before, and he set it up for a pillar. There, he poured oil on top of it and made a vow: "...If God will be with me, and will keep me in this way that I go, and will give me bread to eat, and raiment to put on, So that I come again to my father's house in peace; then shall the LORD be my God" (Genesis 28:20-21).

Jacob's vow was a turning point for him. Many religious people know his story. He does make it to his uncle's place. He marries both of his cousins, Leah and Rachel. He spends 20 years serving his uncle for his two wives, and some earthly possessions. He does right by his uncle in spite of his uncle's deceitfulness. God exceedingly blesses Jacob. Twenty years after he left home, the Lord leads him back to his homeland.[11]

---

[9] Genesis 28:17
[10] Genesis 12:1-3, 7; 13:14-18; 26; 28:13-15; Exodus 3:14; John 8:59
[11] Genesis 29-31

Keep in mind his vow he made at Bethel. Jacob just asked for his needs to be met, and to be brought back to his father's house in peace. God not only maintained his life, but he greatly blessed him. The last part of the vow that Jacob would come again to his father's house in peace was not yet fulfilled. This was a touchy situation since Jacob's last recollection of his brother was that Esau wanted to kill him. However, the complete fulfillment of God's part in the vow was about to be realized. Jacob was coming home, and he would have to face his brother.

Jacob wrestled all night with a heavenly being about his encounter with Esau. He literally emptied himself of his strength as he contended with the being. When he left the encounter, he no longer was known as Jacob, but Israel. He would meet his brother in this new capacity. As we know, Esau embraced Jacob. God fulfilled His end of the vow. Now, Jacob needed to make Him his personal God. [12]

How many people make bargains with God? Once God honors their requests, many continue on as before, without any regard to keeping their end of the bargain. Would Jacob keep his part of the vow with God?

Jacob ended up in the Succoth, at the city of Shalem where he purchased some land. Disaster eventually enveloped him, as the son of the leader of the area defiled his daughter. Two of his sons sought revenge by destroying the city. Their vengeful actions brought trouble upon Jacob.[13]

Once again, God intrudes into Jacob's world. He instructs him to go to Bethel to dwell there and build Him an altar.[14] Jacob's vow may have become a fading memory to him, but God never forgot. It was time for Jacob to keep his end of the vow. He needed to make the Lord his God.

Before traveling to Bethel, Jacob makes the first initial step of keeping his vow. He instructed those of his household to get rid of all their strange gods. This step was vital. There must not be any division or hindrance in ensuring God takes His rightful place. He will not accept any competition, for He is rightfully jealous and deserves, as well as demands total devotion and worship.[15]

As Christians, we need to take heed of this example. There can be many hidden idols in our lives. We need to be vigilant in ridding ourselves of such hindrances. God alone must stand in our hearts. After all, idols always represent man's best attempts of erecting his own gods, in order to subdue his religious conscience.

The second step of making the Lord his God was to obey Him. Jacob took his family to Bethel, where they would dwell until God said differently. It is not enough to get rid of idols; God's people must strive to

---

[12] Genesis 32:7-28; 33:4
[13] Genesis 34:2-3; 25-31
[14] Genesis 35:1
[15] Genesis 35:4; Exodus 20:2-5

know the real God. Again, "dwell" means taking the time to wait before Him, until He meets with the individual.[16]

As Jacob traveled to Bethel, the protection of the Lord was with Him. Fear fell upon the occupants of the land. God not only calls us forth to make Him God, but He is with us in the way, as we journey to the place where we will discover Him. It is at the place of God that we must give way to His preeminence in our lives.[17]

When Jacob arrived at Bethel, the first thing he did was build an altar. Remember, Jacob had simply erected a pillar and poured oil over it to signify that a vow was made at this place of God. Now, he builds an altar, a place of communion.

Death invades this place of communion when his mother's nurse, Deborah, dies. This signifies the cessation of the old, so the new can come forth. It was after Deborah's death that God once again appears to Jacob and reestablishes his new identity as Israel. God introduces Himself as God Almighty who is able to bring forth the promises that he gave Abraham. Upon God's departure, Jacob once again erects a pillar and pours a drink offering and oil on it. After his encounter with God, he moves on.[18]

The place of God is where we encounter God. For the saint, there are many such Bethels in his or her journey. Each Bethel signifies the same thing. It is a place where God intrudes into one's life and reality. It is a place to reestablish one's relationship with God. To establish this relationship, a person must dwell in this place, until he or she meets with God at the altar of the heart. At Bethel, the person's call and identity, as well as God's promises are verified.

For the new life to come forth, death must occur. For the saint, it is death to the present life he or she knows to embrace a new life. This dying out process is not fun, but necessary. The new must be in place to ensure that the calling and identity come forth for the glory of God.

Bethel is a time of preparation for the next part of the spiritual journey. In fact, we usually come by way of Bethel, before there is great testing. We can declare that God is God, but does He truly sit on the throne of our hearts? It was after his Bethel experiences that Jacob lost Rachel in childbirth.[19] This had to be a dark night of testing for Jacob. The sorrow must have been overwhelming, even though he had a son who could bring some comfort. Again, we see where the old must give way to the new.

One must remember that Rachel is the one who stole and hid her father's idols. Jacob declared death upon the person who possessed the

---

[16] Genesis 35:1-7
[17] Ibid
[18] Genesis 35:9-15
[19] Genesis 35:16-20

idols.[20] Although the idols were not discovered by Rachel's father, and were probably given up when Jacob called for the purging of all strange gods, you wonder if this had any impact on her early demise. One never knows what circumstances or separation might take place on the spiritual journey.

This brings us to the sin that often plagues the place of God: that of idolatry. Bethel played a significant part in the history of Israel. It was part of Samuel's circuit as judge. Elijah was instructed to go to Bethel where the sons of the prophet were located.[21] Sadly, this place of God also became a place of idolatry.

In spite of its rich history as a "place of God," it became an idolatrous substitute for God as well. This was during Jeroboam's reign. Due to the harsh reign of Solomon, ten tribes broke off from the other two tribes, Judah and Benjamin. This separation happened at the time Solomon's son started his reign as king. Jeroboam was appointed as the new king of this new northern kingdom of Israel. He was afraid of losing his throne as long as his subjects traveled to Jerusalem for all the religious activities.[22]

It was at Bethel where Jeroboam replaced Jehovah God with idols in order to maintain control over the people. From this point on, the Northern Kingdom of Israel slid into blatant idolatry that resulted in its demise two hundred years before Judah fell to Babylon.[23]

Bethel also represents man's false religion. Idolatrous, occultist religion may run parallel or close to the real thing, but the true God is missing. When God is missing, it may give people a false sense of their spiritual condition, while blinding them to their real condition.

Sadly, Bethel is an attraction for the counterfeits. These counterfeits like to take up residence in this place. However, for the saints, it takes integrity and purging to ensure that Bethel always remains a place of God, where communion is encouraged and spiritual preparation takes place for God's purpose and glory.

When was the last time you have been to Bethel? Does it serve as a place of commitment and rededication to God, or is it a place where the altar of God is cold and the idols have prospered? Perhaps, you have never established a place of God. Let me encourage you to do so. At Bethel, you will receive greater revelations of God as He meets you there to introduce Himself, and to confirm your calling and identity in the midst of a busy and uncertain world.

---

[20] Genesis 31:19, 32

[21] 1 Samuel 7:16; 2 Kings 2:2-3

[22] 1 Kings 13-14:18

[23] 2 Kings 17

4

THE WILDERNESSES

In chapter 2 of this book, we considered the wilderness in light of the heart. However, as you study the wilderness in the Word of God, you will see that there are many priceless patterns for the Christian to consider in regard to the wilderness experience. Each pattern shows the path of spiritual growth, but also reveals how the spiritual life is to be established.

Deuteronomy 1:19 talks about the Israelites going through the great, terrible wilderness, but the children of Israel's wilderness experience encompassed five different wildernesses. Spiritually speaking, each wilderness deals with a different aspect of a person's spiritual life. They are located at significant points of the spiritual journey, and have the ability to expose, reveal, and prepare a person towards the next step of perfection or maturity. The work of these wildernesses was the means by which God prepared His people to enter into the Promised Land. The number "five" symbolizes grace, and as you will see, the work of perfection is an act of grace on God's part. We do not deserve His attention or commitment. However, as you study these different wildernesses, you can see how God was thorough in bringing forth perfection.

The first wilderness was marked by the wilderness of Etham. According to *Smith's Bible Dictionary,* it was also known as the wilderness of Shur. It was in this wilderness that the children of Israel traveled for three days. Remember, Moses asked Pharaoh to let the people go three days into the wilderness to serve or worship God. The purpose of the spiritual journey is to learn how to worship God in a proper manner. In this wilderness, the children of Israel encountered both bitter and sweet waters of Marah and Elim. Our journey to learn how to worship God is both bitter and sweet, but through it all, we can come out possessing the One who gives us Living Water.[1]

The bitter waters of Marah bring a reality check about the drought of personal wretchedness. However, the reality of the intervention of God allows His people to experience the abundance of Elim, an oasis that was marked by 70 palm trees, where the waters ran freely in 12 fountains.[2]

---

[1] Numbers 33:7-9
[2] Numbers 33:9-10

However, the children of Israel could not remain at this blessed oasis. They had to endure the next wilderness. This shows that God does not allow His people to stay in an oasis when He has a complete life for them elsewhere. The waters of Elim were meant to refresh and prepare Israel to go on just as the Living Waters of the Holy Spirit serve in the same capacity for the Christian who must discover his or her life in God.[3]

The second wilderness occurred right after the Red Sea. The Red Sea was representative of baptism. Baptism is symbolic of separation from the world, as well as the old life and practices in order to embrace the new. Baptism represents total abandonment to the old and identification with the new. The New Testament makes reference to this baptism.[4]

It was right after this baptism that the Israelites began their trek through the next wilderness. It is hard to accept that total identification with God does not bring you into a place of abundance, but a place of leanness.

Realistically, the journey through the wilderness should never surprise followers of Jesus. Jesus took this same journey after He was baptized in the river of Jordan. Luke 4:1-2 gives us this insight into the next steps of Jesus, "And Jesus being full of the Holy Ghost returned from Jordan, and was led by the Spirit into the wilderness. Being forty days tempted of the devil..."[5]

Surprisingly, the name of the second wilderness the Israelites encountered was the wilderness of Sin. This wilderness served as a place of testing for the Hebrews. It was here that God gave them manna from heaven and water from the eternal Rock of ages.[6] Times of testing bring people to a spiritual drought where their heart condition is revealed. They discover they have no inward substance that can nourish them, nor do they have the ability to change circumstance or the terrain of their lives. They have no means to provide for their well-being, and that such things come from God.

Sadly, many people arrogantly believe they control the direction of their lives until they find themselves in a wilderness. Up until then, they convince themselves that they are not vulnerable, reliant, or subject to anything. They are blinded to their depravity, indifferent to their sin, and often prove to be inhumane to the plight of others.

The wilderness of Sin is where the ingratitude of humanity is revealed. It exposes humanity to be nothing but an empty shell. This humanity can only reflect that which brings purpose or meaning to its existence, whether it be that of the world, self-serving pursuits, or God.

---

[3] John 7:36-37
[4] Numbers 33:11; 1 Corinthians 10:1-2
[5] Matthew 3:13-17
[6] Numbers 33:11-12; 1 Corinthians 10:3-4

This wilderness often brings a person to face the vanity of self. It uncovers the spiritual drought and death that plague all who have not found their life in God. This was brought out at the place called Rephidim. "Rephidim" means *rests or stays*. Israel rested at this place, but the people could not stay for long because there was no water to drink. Without water there is no life.[7]

For believers, there is no life without the Living Waters of the Holy Spirit. As Christians, we can do many religious things in our strength, while coming into rest in the shadow of religion. But, without the spiritual water from above there is no inner life or heavenly connection to sustain us.

People are quick to stay in comfort zones no matter how the situations in such places may lack life, but God will not allow His sojourners to stay long in such a dead-end place. He will cause or bring about a drought to urge the traveler on to greater places with Him.

The wilderness of Sin is a place where one will not only come to the end of self, but also come face to face with his or her personal wretchedness. It is in this type of place that individuals learn that they have no power, except what is given to them. They have no means, except what is provided outside of themselves. They have no substance that comes from within. God will also not allow His people to stay in the shadow of memories of the miraculous, for He wants them to discover the greatest miracle of all: The life He has prepared for them in the Promised Land.

The greatest miracle for the Christian is the resurrection of Jesus, but this miracle means nothing unless His life is truly realized within the believer. Have you come to the wilderness of Sin or are you holding back because you feel you have just what you need? The problem with this attitude is that you will never embrace the life God has for you.

The next wilderness is Sinai, which means "*thorny*." It is nearly in the center of a peninsula that stretches between the horns of the Red Sea. There lies a wedge of granite, grunstein, and porphyry rock that stands between 8,000 and 9,000 feet above sea level.[8] It was in this setting that God's awesome holiness and power were revealed to the people of Israel. Exodus 20:18 gives us insight into this display, "And all the people saw the thunderings, and the lightenings, and the noise of the trumpet, and the mountain smoking: and when the people saw it, they removed, and stood afar off." It was on Mount Sinai that God gave Moses the Law. The Law was to show men that they were sinners, far from God, and incapable of saving themselves.[9]

What a scene it must have been when the Israelites witnessed the awesome reality of God's holiness, and watched Moses meet God in the

---

[7] Numbers 33:14

[8] Smith's Bible Dictionary

[9] Exodus 19; Romans 3:19-20, 23; 5:13; 6:23

midst of thick darkness. It is humbling to think that God must always clothe Himself in some way because of His holiness and majesty to keep man from experiencing judgment and death.[10]

For example, He clothed His holiness in darkness on Mount Sinai, His glory in a tabernacle in the wilderness, and His majesty in the form of a man.[11] Each time He encountered man, He reached out to him, and declared His desire to walk and reside in his midst. In spite of God revealing Himself in power, in a cloud or fire, or in bodily form, man usually still insists on going his own way. When man steps outside of God's protection, he ends up in idolatry, rebellion, and delusion.

Mount Sinai was also a place where the Hebrews had to wait on God. Waiting is very hard on the soul and causes restlessness. The problem with a restless soul is that it reveals various factors about the extent of our character, such as fear, discontentment, and dissatisfaction.

People do not know how to wait on God. In other words, they do not know how to get ahold of Him for themselves. As a result, they fail to learn the lesson and benefits of waiting on God in quietness and confidence. Isaiah 30:15 states, "For thus saith the Lord GOD, the Holy One of Israel; In returning and rest shall ye be saved; in quietness and in confidence shall be your strength: and ye would not."

It is in the times of waiting for God that people often fall into idolatry. Waiting tests one's faith or confidence. What the wilderness of Sinai showed is that not only do people stand afar off from God's righteousness, but they also do not intend to put their reliance and confidence in God. Their reliance is still on what they personally perceive, do, or can observe.[12] As a result, they fail to wait on or for God.

The fourth wilderness was Paran. This was the wilderness that brought the children of Israel to the borders of the Promised Land. However, it was also in this wilderness that they allowed the obstacles of the Promised Land to keep them from entering into the promises of God. This wilderness served as a grave for a whole generation of Israelites.

In the wilderness of Paran, the children of Israel wandered for at least 38 years. It was referred to as the wilderness of wandering.[13] Moses describes the different places of this wilderness or region in Numbers 33:17-33. Deuteronomy 8:2 states this about this wilderness, "And thou shalt remember all the way which the LORD thy God led thee forty years in the wilderness to humble thee, and to prove thee, to know what was in thine heart, whether thou wouldest keep his commandments, or no."

---

[10] Exodus 20:21; 33:20
[11] Exodus 40:38; Colossians 2:9
[12] Exodus 32
[13] Smith's Bible Dictionary

The next wilderness the children of Israel had to confront was Zin. "Zin" means *flat*, and one of its boundaries is the Dead Sea.[14] Zin represents the fifth and final wilderness before possessing the life God has for a person. Once again, we are reminded of God's grace. His grace is what keeps us, even in the times of great testing.

It is important that Christians keep in mind the purpose of the wilderness. It is a place of preparation, proving hearts, testing faith, exposing depravity, and revealing God. It causes separation from the world and self.

The wilderness of Zin is a place of preparation and separation. Much of preparation involves separation or consecration. It was this wilderness that led up to a significant event for Israel. This wilderness leads right up to Mount Hor. Numbers 33:38 speaks of this event, "And Aaron the priest went up into mount Hor at the commandment of the LORD, and died there, in the fortieth year after the children of Israel were to come out of the land of Egypt, in the first day of the fifth month."

The wilderness of Zin represents a place of death, where one puts off the old, in order to enter into a new life. Aaron represented the old way of doing things. He is traced back to Egypt, which represents the world. Aaron was also at the center of idolatry when he formed the golden calf at the request of the Israelites. The Apostle Paul gives this instruction to all believers, "Wherefore, my dearly beloved, flee from idolatry" (1Corinthians 10:14).

Aaron also represented rebellion that is a product of religious arrogance. We see this religious arrogance in Numbers 12. Aaron and his sister Miriam rebelled against the leadership of Moses. The only accusation they could bring against this righteous man was the fact that his wife was Ethiopian. The truth is that their accusation had nothing to do with Moses' wife, but with their high opinion of themselves. They felt that they had as much right as Moses to be in the leadership position that he held. They failed to realize that God had put Moses in that position, and not any other individual. Miriam ended up with leprosy, and Aaron would have had this wretched disease if he had not been a priest.

The Apostle Paul gives this warning in Romans 12:3, "For I say, through the grace given unto me, to every man that is among you, not to think of himself more highly than he ought to think; but to think soberly, according as God hath dealt to every man the measure of faith."

Aaron is also identified with self-sufficiency. This sin was exposed when Moses and Aaron were to speak to the rock to bring forth water. Instead of giving God the credit, they took the glory for themselves. Numbers 20:12 tells us the consequences for this act, "And the LORD spake unto Moses and Aaron, Because ye believed me not, to sanctify me in the eyes of the children of Israel, therefore ye shall not being this congregation into the land which I have given them."

---

[14] Ibid

The Apostle Paul makes this statement in 2 Corinthians 3:5, "Not that we are sufficient of ourselves to think any thing as of ourselves; but our sufficiency is of God."

The wilderness of Zin showed God's people that they cannot effectively enter into all that God has for them if they have any residue of self-importance or worth left. People can hide behind all kinds of religious cloaks and activities to cover up different aspects of their lives, but until the old man is put off, they remain ill equipped to enter into the deeper life with God.

It was on Mount Hor that Aaron put off his priestly garments and placed them on his son, Eleazar. After that, he died on Mount Hor. His death represented the mortification of the old man, while Eleazar represented putting on the new man or life that establishes a person as a priest and king of God.[15]

The word "Hor" means mountain. The idea of Hor also pointed to a mount where the cloak of humanity was put aside to reveal the majesty of God. This mount in the New Testament was the Mount of Transfiguration where Jesus' cloak of humanity was put aside to reveal His heavenly glory.

Ezekiel 36:26 talks about God giving His people a new heart and spirit. Every blood-bought saint has this new heart and spirit within him or her. The new heart and spirit will produce a new life. Christians must put off the old and put on the very life of the Lord Jesus Christ. As a Christian puts on Jesus, he or she not only puts on a new life but the armor of God.[16]

When you study the armor of God, you realize that it points to the Person of Jesus. For example, He is our truth and righteousness. We are to walk as He walked, spreading the Gospel that speaks of His death, burial, and resurrection. He is the author and finisher of our faith, as well as the author of our salvation. It is the reality of who He is that makes our sword sharp, as revelations of His character are unveiled, the authority of His teachings come forth, and the living reality of His power and truth stands distinct.[17]

Putting on the armor is important because one cannot obtain the victorious Christian life without fighting for it. It was not long after Aaron's death on Mount Hor, that the Israelites began to do battle with the Canaanites in order to possess the Promised Land.

The pattern of these wildernesses also reminds us of Jesus' temptation in the wilderness.[18] Jesus came to do the will of the Father, and to subdue the enemies of man's soul. He had to face the inability of

---

[15] Numbers 20:24-29; Colossians 3:1-17; 1 Peter 2:5, 9; Revelation 1:6

[16] Romans 13:14; Ephesians 6:10-18

[17] John 1:1, 14; 14:6; 1 Corinthians 1:30; 15:1-4; 1 John 2:6; Mark 16:15-16; Hebrews 4:12; 5:9; 12:2

[18] Matthew 4:1-11

the flesh to change circumstances outside of God's will when He was tempted to change stones into bread. His righteousness was on the line when Satan encouraged Him to give in to pride, and man's judgment of death would have remained intact if He had taken the kingdoms of the world before the proper time.

These wildernesses also pointed to the work of the Holy Spirit. John 16:8 states this about His work, "And when he is come, he will reprove the world of sin, and of righteousness, and of judgment." The wilderness of Shur reveals that separation or consecration is necessary before the Spirit of God can move on the terrain of our lives. In the wilderness of Sin, man's depravity is exposed, but in Sinai, God's righteousness is lifted up to reveal how far away man stands from God. Paran reveals how the old must die before it can embrace the newness of the Spirit, while the wilderness of Zin pointed to judgment upon the old, in order for the new to come forth.

Now that each wilderness has been exposed, are you having a wilderness experience as you contend with an aspect of your spiritual life that is hindering your spiritual growth?[19] If so, are you learning the lessons of the specific wilderness, and allowing God to have His way so you can enter into all that our Lord has for you?

---

[19] If you want to learn more about these wildernesses, see the author's book, *The Victorious Journey* in Volume Six of her foundational series.

5

THE ROCK

One of the amazing events in the journey of the children of Israel was their encounter with the Rock. Scripture identifies this Rock to be Jesus. One of the most inspiring pictures of Jesus as the Rock can be found in Moses' life. Moses had been on the mountain for 40 days and nights, receiving instructions. In his absence, the children of Israel instructed Aaron to make a golden calf. Their idolatry brought Moses down from the mount. The Tent of Meeting was moved outside of the camp, due to the defilement of idolatry.[1] There in the temporary meeting place Moses spoke face-to-face with the LORD. He had been in the presence of God for many days, but he knew there was more. He made this request to God, "...I beseech thee, shew me thy glory" (Exodus 33:18).

Moses could not see the fullness of God's glory without actually dying. The Lord instructed Moses to stand upon a rock that stood beside a place located by Him. He then said this to Moses, "And it shall come to pass, while my glory passeth by, that I will put thee in a cleft of the rock, and will cover thee with my hand while I pass by" (Exodus 33:22). What an incredible picture of the Christian life! The place points to the place every believer has in God because of Jesus. Jesus serves as the Rock or foundation that every Christian is established upon. Once a Christian grows in the knowledge of Christ, Jesus becomes the cleft in which every believer learns to flee to in order to hide from enemies and abide in His presence.[2]

The children of Israel had a different type of encounter with the Rock. 1 Corinthians 10:4 says, "And did all drink the same spiritual drink: for they drank of that spiritual Rock that followed them: and that Rock was Christ." This Scripture verse tells us three facts about the Rock. The first insight we have about the Rock is that the children of Israel drank of it. Such an act pointed to the reality that the Rock provided nourishment to their souls.

Secondly, we must observe that this Rock followed them. Exodus 13:21-22 talked about the Lord going before Israel as a pillar by day and residing among the children of Israel as a pillar of fire by night. The concept that the Rock was behind them as well as in front of them

---

[1] Exodus 33:7; 1 Corinthians 10:2-4

[2] John 14:1-3; 15:1-8; 1 Corinthians 1:30; 3:11; Colossians 3:3

unveils a powerful picture of how God surrounds His people with His ever-abiding awareness and protection.

The way God is positioned as the Rock is a beautiful picture of a fortress of protection. God, during the day, leads His people through different types of terrain, away from traps and enemies. At night, He serves as the illuminating light, so enemies will stay away, fearing their exposure and defeat. This light reminded His people, "He will not suffer thy foot to be moved; he that keepeth thee will not slumber" (Psalm 121:3).

As the Rock that follows, the Lord also served as the wall that stood between enemies and sneak attacks. Clearly, this incredible Rock is aware of what is going on ahead, behind, and on each side. 1 Corinthians identifies this Rock to be Jesus, the second Person of the Godhead. As you follow the pattern of the Rock, you will understand how it represented Jesus.

Israel's initial encounter with the Rock took place in the wilderness. The wilderness represented the unveiling of the leanness and depravity of man. Twenty centuries ago, Jesus was placed in the midst of this wretchedness as God Incarnate. He came to bring water to parched, dying souls. His heart was to revive souls in the midst of this great barren wilderness of fallen humanity.

In order to understand the pattern of Jesus as the Rock, we must follow the trail that leads to the different places of water in the wilderness. The first place was Marah. God led the children of Israel to waters that were bitter and undrinkable. They could not partake of the wretched springs, and began to murmur against Moses.[3] Moses cried out to God and God showed Him a tree. This tree was thrown into the midst of the bitter waters, producing sweet, refreshing waters.

Jesus became man to partake of the bitter cup of death. He drank every last drop of the unbearable cup, from the Garden of Gethsemane to a tree on Calvary. As a result, the convicting power of the Holy Spirit will lead sin-laden people to the tree or cross on Calvary. There, God the Father will unveil the glory and purpose of that tree: "to reconcile all things unto himself."[4]

This reconciliation happens when the message of the cross is properly applied to the wretchedness of man. The bitterness wrought by sin on the cross will give way to the sweetness of the Son of God, manifesting His life in His followers.

The next place for water was Elim. It was an oasis in the desert. It had 12 wells and 70 palm trees. Wells always symbolize the work of God. The number "12" points to governmental perfection, while the

---

[3] Exodus 15:22-27
[4] Matthew 20:22; Colossians 1:20

number "70" (7 x 10) represents divine order that will produce spiritual perfection.[5]

The wells pointed to the complete work of salvation that was wrought by Jesus on the cross. This work was part of the divine order that would bring man to spiritual perfection and establish him in a perfect government, ruled by the King of kings and the Lord of lords. However, to receive spiritual refreshing, man would have to personally partake of these wells to experience order, as well as be brought into perfection. As Isaiah 12:2-3 declares, "Behold, God is my salvation; I will trust, and not be afraid: for the Lord Jehovah is my strength and my song; he also is become my salvation. Therefore with joy shall ye draw water out of the wells of salvation."

God led the children of Israel to the first sources of water, but in the next incident, He provided it. This incident happened after God led Israel to Rephedim. Rephedim was a valley between the wilderness of Sin and the wilderness of Sinai.[6]

Valleys represent places of humiliation. Humiliation comes out of an awareness of how vulnerable and needy a person is. Rephedim was a place where Israel could rest, but there was no water. The children of Israel began to murmur. Once again, Moses cried to God on their behalf. He was given this instruction in Exodus 17:5-6,

> And the LORD said unto Moses, Go on before the people, and take with thee of the elders of Israel; and thy rod, wherewith thou smotest the river, take in thine hand, and go. Behold, I will stand before thee there upon the rock of Horeb; and thou shalt smite the rock, and there shall come water out of it, that the people may drink. And Moses did so in the sight of the elders of Israel.

The rock at Horeb represented Jesus. When Moses smote the Rock, it pointed to Jesus being smitten on the cross. Isaiah 53:4 says this in regard to this action, "Surely he hath borne our griefs, and carried out sorrows: yet we did esteem him stricken, smitten of God, and afflicted."

God, standing in front of Moses, pointed to Jesus as God Incarnate. Jesus became man, so that He could stand in the gap between God and man as He was offered up as God's Passover Lamb. He would be despised and beaten by man, but all of this was necessary to bring forth life.

The water coming forth out of the Rock represented life. We know according to John 3:5 that believers are, "...born of water and of the Spirit." This spiritual water shall be, "...a well of water springing up into everlasting life" (John 4:14).

---

[5] You can find the meaning of numbers in E. W. Bullinger book, Numbers in Scripture.

[6] Exodus 17:1

The next significant place in regards to water was in the wilderness of Zin. Once again, the children of Israel were brought to a place where there was no water. As in the past, this new generation strove with Moses and Aaron who went before the Lord. The Lord gave them these instructions in Numbers 20:8, "Take the rod, and gather thou the assembly together, thou, and Aaron thy brother, and speak ye unto the rock before their eyes; and it shall give forth its water, and thou shalt bring forth to them water out of the rock."

The second incident with the Rock in the wilderness of Zin took place forty years after the first encounter with the Rock at Horeb. In the first incident, only the elders witnessed the miracle, but in this situation, the whole congregation was present. Keep in mind, the old generation that had witnessed some of the great miracles had died in the wilderness of Paran. Much of this new generation had encountered God's faithful provision through the years, but had not seen miracles such as the parting of the Red Sea.

In the first encounter with the Rock, Moses had to strike it once. This pointed to Jesus dying on the cross. However, in the second incident, Aaron, the High Priest, was instructed to only speak to the Rock. For the Christian, this represented that redemption was complete, and Jesus is alive and serving as the High Priest. Hebrews 7:25 says, "Wherefore he is able to save them to the uttermost that come unto God by him, seeing he ever liveth to make intercession for them."

The fact that Aaron was to speak to the rock was symbolic of communication or prayer. This is one of the greatest Christian's privileges. Hebrews 4:15-16 states, "For we have not an high priest who cannot be touched with the feeling of our infirmities; but was in all points tempted like as we are, yet without sin. Let us, therefore, come boldly unto the throne of grace, that we may obtain mercy, and find grace to help in time of need."

Jesus said in Matthew 7:7-8, "Ask, and it shall be given you; seek, and ye shall find; knock, and it shall be opened unto you: For everyone that asketh receiveth; and he that seeketh findeth; and to him that knocketh it shall be opened."

Exodus 20:10-11 tells us how Moses and Aaron handled this incident:

> And Moses and Aaron gathered the congregation together before the rock, and he said unto them, Hear now, ye rebels; must we fetch you water out of this rock? And Moses lifted up his hand, and with his rod he smote the rock twice: and the water came out abundantly, and the congregation drank, and their beasts also.

Moses and Aaron miserably failed to carry out simple instructions. Aaron was only to speak to the Rock for the water to come forth. Yet, Moses was the one who not only spoke where the rock was concerned, but he also smote the rock twice. Keep in mind, smiting the rock the first time pointed to Jesus' death. His death on the cross was sufficient to redeem mankind. This is clearly brought out in Hebrews 10:12. "But this man, after he had offered one sacrifice for sins for ever, sat down on the right hand of God."

In light of the symbolism, Moses' actions would have implied that Jesus' death was not enough to secure man's salvation. Hebrews 10:26 and 29 show us the seriousness of such an attitude towards Jesus' salvation:

> For if we sin willfully after we have received the knowledge of the truth, there remaineth no more sacrifice for sins...Of how much sorer punishment, suppose ye, shall he be thought worthy, who hath trodden under foot the Son of God, and hath counted the blood of the covenant, with which he was sanctified, an unholy thing, and hath done despite unto the Spirit of grace.

We also see where Moses and Aaron took credit for the water. To take credit for God's miraculous intervention is to touch His glory. As a result, Moses and Aaron were not only rebuked, but God pronounced judgment on them. "...Because ye believed me not, to sanctify me in the eyes of the children of Israel, therefore ye shall not bring this congregation into the land I have given them" (Numbers 20:12). Moses and Aaron never entered the Promised Land because of mishandling the Rock. These men had come so far, only to fail on the last stretch. It is a serious matter to misrepresent God's interest and touch His glory.

Scripture says much about the Rock. 1 Samuel 2:2 says, "There is none holy like the LORD; for there is none beside thee, neither is there any rock like our God." This rock is clearly identified as the one true God.

Psalm 62:2 declares, "He only is my rock and my salvation; he is my defense; I shall not be greatly moved." This rock is able to save us, as well as serve as our defense. Likewise, Jesus not only saves us, but also serves as our immovable foundation; therefore, a person will not be moved as long as he or she clings to Him.[7]

In Psalm 94:22 we are told, "But the LORD is my defense; and my God is the rock of my refuge." God is LORD and serves as a refuge. Jesus is the Lord of lords and serves as the Christian's defense. He serves as a formidable fortress in times of attack, and as a high tower to lift His people above the challenges of life. He is the wall that will stop the advancements of the enemy.[8]

In Deuteronomy 32, one gains other valuable insights about the Rock that followed Israel. Deuteronomy 32:4 declares that the works of the Rock are perfect. This means that the works God does on behalf of others never sway from His character and ways. Jesus verified this in

---

[7] 1 Corinthians 3:11
[8] Psalms 18:2; Colossians 3:3

John 5:19, "...Verily, verily, I say unto you, The Son can do nothing of himself, but what he seeth the Father do: for whatever things he doeth, these also doeth the Son likewise."

Deuteronomy 32:4 also states that, "all his ways are judgment." "Judgment" in this text implies that God's ways are just and right. Jesus brought out the reality of this just judgment in John 5:22, "For the Father judgeth no man, but hath committed all judgment unto the Son."

The Stone

Jesus is also referred to as the cornerstone.[9] My understanding of the cornerstone in a building is that all other stones or bricks are shaped according to the cornerstone. Jesus is the cornerstone of the Christian life and His Church, the Body of believers. As the builder of the spiritual building, the Holy Ghost shapes each of our lives according to our spiritual Cornerstone, Jesus Christ.

You can see Jesus as the Stone throughout Scripture. The stone that was erected by Jacob and anointed represented Him. Jacob's actions pointed to Jesus' life being erected in the midst of His believers. His exaltation would bring about anointing.

Jacob erected and anointed a stone twice, serving as a witness of his commitment. We see Joshua using a stone to serve as a witness that all the words of the Lord had been spoken. Such a witness implies that there will be no excuse upon judgment day.[10] Jesus is a witness of God's commitment to save mankind. If man refuses to adhere to the witness, there will be no way to escape God's wrath upon those who have rejected His salvation.

Jesus was the stone upon which Moses rested during the battle with the Amalekites, to ensure victory. He is the stone that David flung in the name of the LORD, hitting his mark and defeating Goliath [11] Jesus, as the Stone, often pointed to judgment, but each man of God revealed why the Stone gave him the edge on victory. Moses showed endurance, and David displayed confidence in God. Both virtues are fruits of faith.

Jesus is a Stone of witness that will bring judgment to those who refuse to adhere to Him. There is also the stone in Daniel that destroys all the governments of the world. Daniel 2:35 says this about the stone,

> Then was the iron, the clay, the brass, the silver, and the gold, broken to pieces together, and became like the chaff of the summer threshingfloors; and the wind carried them away, that no place was found for them: and the stone that smote the image became a great mountain, and filled the whole earth.

---

[9] 1 Corinthians 12:11-13; 1 Peter 2:5-9
[10] Genesis 28:18; 35:14; Joshua 24:27
[11] Exodus 17:12; 1 Samuel 17:49-51

This stone will break in pieces and consume all the worldly kingdoms, giving way to an everlasting kingdom. The Rock will not only judge people, but also nations and kingdoms.

Jesus also talked about the type of judgment He would bring to man as the Stone. Matthew 21:44 says, "And whosoever shall fall on this stone shall be broken: but on whomsoever it shall fall, it will grind him to powder." People will not be able to get around this Rock. It will either break people to bring them to a state of humility, a place of repentance, and the work of salvation or it will grind the unrepentant in judgment.

The Lord of lords is the spiritual Cornerstone that was rejected by the builders who were the religious people of Jesus' day. Jesus said of this matter, "...The stone which the builders rejected, the same is become the head of the corner: this is the Lord's doing and it is marvelous in our eyes" (Matthew 21:42). Both verses in Matthew show believers that they must not only establish their spiritual lives on Christ, but they must also line them up to His character and ways.

Obviously, we cannot afford to regard the Stone or Rock of God lightly. Deuteronomy 32:15 talks about lightly esteeming the Rock of salvation. To lightly esteem the Rock means to disgrace and dishonor God.[12] Hebrews 2:3 gives us insight into how this may occur with Christians. "How shall we escape, if we neglect so great salvation; which at the first began to be spoken by the Lord, and was confirmed unto us by them that heard him."

Jesus' death on the cross was God reaching out to man in a loving, sacrificial way. He provided this sacrifice, so that man could be spared judgment and eternal consequences. When man abuses this gift, ignores or rejects the salvation freely offered, he is neglecting it. Such a person will not escape the consequences or judgment to come.

Deuteronomy 32:18 goes on to say that the children of Israel were unmindful and had forgotten the Rock. It is easy to forget who God is. For the Christian, we can forget that we were cleansed from sin. In the case of unbelievers, they choose to ignore or deny creation, declaring that there is no Creator. Their rejection of God makes them fools.[13]

Colossians 1:16-17 says this about Jesus, "For by him were all things created, that are in heaven, and that are in earth, visible and invisible, whether they be thrones, or dominions, or principalities, or powers: all things were created by him and for him. And he is before all things, and by him all things consist."

As the Rock, Jesus holds the world and our lives together. There is no life outside of Him. There is no meaning, purpose, or order outside of the Rock of Ages. When all else fails, He will be standing in power and glory. And, those who are standing on Him will be left standing as well. He said this to Peter, "...That thou art Peter, and upon this rock I will

---

[12] Strong's Exhaustive Concordance; #5034
[13] Romans 1:20; Psalm 53:1; 2 Peter 1:8-9

build my church; and the gates of hell shall not prevail against it" (Matthew 16:18).

What have you done with the Rock? Have you followed the pattern of the Rock from Marah to Sinai, or from the cross to salvation? Have you followed the pattern of the Rock from its resurrection as the rejected Cornerstone to the establishment of the immovable foundation? Do not be as the children of Israel. They forgot the Rock, and as a result, lightly esteemed Him as the only sure immovable foundation to their hope, protection, and life. Their action caused them to be separated from God, who became a Rock of judgment that would end up crushing them.

6

THE TABERNACLE

God is a God of order.[1] Order is the opposite of confusion and chaos. It points to discipline. This is why the Word of God is full of orderly patterns to observe and follow. A good example of this order can be found in the construction of the tabernacle.

God gave the design of the tabernacle to Moses when Israel was in Sinai. The design of this tabernacle was taken from the pattern of the heavenly tabernacle.[2] Moses had the responsibility to make sure that there were no variations in the design or procedure surrounding the tabernacle.

We know it took almost two years to do the complete construction of the tabernacle. God was establishing the spiritual life of Israel from the ground up as the tabernacle was being constructed. This was necessary before He would take the children of Israel into the Promised Land. This complete spiritual design affected every facet of their lives from worship and sacrifice to celebration.

This shows that a spiritual life is not resurrected overnight. There must be preparation of the heart and mind before the actual work can take place. America's instant society has created disillusionment for Christains, because many believe that after their initial encounter with Jesus, they have arrived. The opposite is true. The work is just beginning.

The purpose of the tabernacle was to serve as a place where God could reside and walk in the midst of His people. It was a way of revealing a bit of heaven on earth. The tabernacle was not only a shadow of a place, but of a person: Jesus Christ. One of the names of Jesus is Emmanuel, God with us.[3]

Twenty centuries ago, Jesus came from heaven in human form. He referred to His earthly body as a temple.[4] Therefore, this tabernacle in Sinai cast a shadow of God Incarnate walking among man. It revealed that He would reside with us, and touch the lives of many. It would

---

[1] 1 Corinthians 14:33
[2] Hebrews 8:5
[3] Isaiah 7:14
[4] John 2:19-21

foreshadow His nature, ministry, and redemption, as well as the saints' position and responsibility in His kingdom.

Acts 17:24-25 states, "God that made the world and all things therein, seeing that he is Lord of heaven and earth, dwelleth not in temples made with hands; Neither is worshipped with men's hands, as though he needed any thing, seeing he giveth to all life, and breath, and all things."

The Apostle Paul identified the temple where God personally would reside in the New Testament. "Know ye not that you are the temple of God, and that the Spirit of God dwelleth in you" (1 Corinthians 3:16)? The believer serves as the New Testament temple. Everywhere the believer goes, the presence of God is there. Wherever the saint walks, the presence of God is residing and walking in the midst of humanity and the world. Any time a Christian touches a person in the power and anointing of God, he or she is serving as an extension of the Son of God's hands, feet, mouth, and heart.

God gave Moses detailed instructions as to how the tabernacle was to be designed. The design surrounding the New Testament temple is clear as well. It will be based on the heavenly design of Jesus. Its construction will not be done by man's hands or attempts, but rather by the Holy Spirit.

One of the important factors of the design of the tabernacle was the order in which the furnishings were constructed. This order shows us how God works within the lives of men to construct a holy temple that will bring honor and glory to Him.

This order can be studied in Exodus 37-38. To accomplish the proper construction of the tabernacle, God had to give wisdom and ability to the people who would oversee this project. This responsibility was given to Bezalel and Aholiab. He then had to supply the material for the tabernacle. Exodus 36:2 tells us that God stirred up the people to participate in the construction of this tabernacle. The people's conviction to give the necessary materials caused such a response that they had to be "restrained from bringing" more supplies.[5]

If only Christians would allow the love of God to compel them to give the best, and give it all for the work of God. Unresponsiveness towards that which is righteous and benevolent causes hearts to become hardened. How many hearts are becoming hard? How many visions are being lost because Christians are heaping so much of the world upon themselves that they have lost sight of heaven? How many ears have become dull to the cries of the lost, due to a lack of compassion? How many eyes have become blind to the plight of others in order to avoid responsibility? The Apostle Paul tried to stir up the Church with these words, "Wherefore he saith, Awake thou that sleepest, and arise from the dead, and Christ shall give thee light" (Ephesians 5:14).

---

[5] Exodus 36:6

In 1 Thessalonians 5:5-6, the Apostle Paul said, "Ye are all the children of the light, and the children of the day: we are not of the night, nor of darkness. Therefore, let us not sleep, as do others; but let us watch and be sober." Christians must soberly respond to God's heart and work, as well as be vigilant about seeing a challenge or responsibility through to the end.

The first part of the tabernacle that was constructed was the four coverings and boards. This would represent the skeletal structure of the tabernacle. The building of the Christian life begins with man. Like the tabernacle, his outward structure consists of four coverings over the skeleton—three layers of skin and the muscles.

Each of the tabernacle coverings pointed to the complete work of redemption that was secured by Jesus. For example, the inner multi covering of blue, purple, and scarlet pointed to the spotless Savior who came from heaven (blue), as King (purple), and as the Man who served as the Lamb that took away the sins of the world (scarlet).[6]

The second covering was black. This pointed to the suffering Savior who learned obedience by the things He suffered. He became sin, so man could be made in the righteousness of God.[7] Suffering pointed to Jesus' ordeal before the cross.

The third covering was red. It represented Christ becoming our substitute sacrifice on the cross. He became an exchange for us, to pay the price for our sins. He took upon Himself the judgment we rightfully deserved.

The final covering was the one that was visible to the world. It was brown and unattractive. This covering represented Jesus as the unattractive Savior whose life of service was developed outside of the public view. He spent 30 years in obscurity, forty days in the wilderness, over three years in ministry, six hours on a cross, and three days in the belly of the earth. When He became the sacrifice, "...his visage was so marred more than any man, and his form more than the sons of men" (Isaiah 52:14).

Much of the Christian life is formed in obscurity, away from public observation. This proves that the life must come and be developed from within. God begins with who man is, but His goal is to end with the manifestation of Jesus being unveiled through each believer as a heavenly reflection for the world to consider.

Sadly, most people invest in the vanity of the outward man, rather than in the eternal status of the inward man. This regrettable priority has caused many to miss that which is beautiful and eternal.

Once the outer structure was established, the next project was the *Ark of the Covenant*.[8] God always begins with a covenant with man.

---

[6] John 1:29

[7] 2 Corinthians 5:21; Hebrews 5:8

[8] Exodus 36:1-9

Covenants show God's intention and commitment. They also serve as valuable boundaries for God and man to operate within, as they clearly lay out the responsibilities.[9]

The Ark of the Covenant represented God's presence in the midst of Israel. Compliance to a covenant with God was a way to ensure His presence. For the Christian, the New Testament covenant started with a new birth experience. [10]

The Ark of the Covenant was located in the Most Holy Place. This represented that God must reside in the innermost part of man. The innermost part of man is his spirit. The presence of God in the spirit of man will only be a reality that man has truly been born from above of water (the Word of God) and of His Spirit.[11]

The Ark of the Covenant was made of shittim wood and overlaid with pure gold. Shittim wood was readily available in the wilderness. It is a species of acacia wood and is a hard, grained wood. It was orange-brown in color and appeared to be thorny in appearance, but it could admirably be adapted to cabinetwork.[12]

The shittim wood pointed to Jesus' humanity. Isaiah 11:1 states, "And there shall come forth a rod out of the stem of Jesse, and a Branch shall grow out of his roots." Jesus came out of the lineage of Jesse, King David's father. He came out of the midst of fallen, depraved humanity, and became an ensign of hope and rest to the people. [13]

Jesus came as the Lamb of God to take away the sins of the world. His heart was to bring reconciliation between God and man through redemption. Once man receives Jesus' redemption by faith, he will cease to be an empty shell, and will become a temple of the Living God.[14]

"Arks" in the Bible always pointed to Jesus. The ark of Noah reminds us that we are hid in Christ, and will be spared from God's wrath. The baby Moses' ark in the Nile River pointed to both the protection that is found in Christ, as well as the Living Water that will abound in and around us when we come to Christ seeking His eternal, satisfying life.[15]

The Ark of the Covenant not only represented the Christian's covenant that was wrought by Jesus' death, but His complete ministry. Inside the belly of the ark were three objects: The Law, manna from heaven, and Aaron's rod that budded. The Law pointed to Jesus as the only way of righteousness, and the manna to Jesus as the Bread of Life

---

[9] If you would like to know more about covenants, see the author's book, *The Place of Covenant*, in Volume 1 of her foundation series.

[10] John 3:5

[11] Ibid

[12] Smith's Bible Dictionary

[13] Isaiah 11:10

[14] John 1:29; 2 Corinthians 5:18-19; Colossians 1:14, 20-21

[15] Colossians 3:3; 1 Thessalonians 5:9; John 7:27-29; 10:10

from above, as well as the truth concerning the heavenly, eternal character of God, while Aaron's budded rod symbolized Jesus as the life. Out of Jesus' lifeless body came resurrection power that brought forth new life. It is His life in us that brings authority and power to us.

This brings us to an important point. God may begin with the inner man and work outward, but man must begin with God and work inward. This shows us that man must ultimately meet God at the mercy seat.

The mercy seat was made of pure gold. "Gold" represents Jesus' divinity. Jesus was fully man and fully God. The ark's inward structure was made of shittim wood, while the outward structure was overlaid with gold. This combination represented the revelation of God becoming Man to walk among us.

The mercy seat was located on top of the Ark of the Covenant. The wings of two seraphim overshadowed it. These wings touched in the middle. The pure gold of the mercy seat revealed that mercy only comes from God. Without it, there is no forgiveness of sin.

This is why mercy must follow the revelation of Jesus. Without mercy there is no hope and no communion with God. The Lord said this to Moses in Exodus 25:22, "And there I will meet with thee, and I will commune with thee from above the mercy seat, from between the two cherubim which are upon the ark of the testimony." This proves that true communion can only occur at the point of mercy. Such communion points to agreement in Spirit and truth.

The angels' wings were extended towards one another. This represented mercy and judgment coming together on the cross of Christ to produce grace. "For by grace ye are saved through faith; and that not of yourselves: it is the gift of God" (Ephesians 2:8).

The wings extended above the mercy seat, pointing to Jesus being lifted up on the altar of the cross. John 12:32 states, "And I, if I be lifted up from the earth, will draw all men unto me." It was when Jesus, the sacrifice, touched the altar of the cross that grace began to flow downward upon every repentant sinner who would humbly seek and find Him at the foot of the cross.

These angels faced each other, but from my understanding, they were looking downward in humility as if they were trying to study the mercy seat. This reminds me of what 1 Peter 1:12 says, "Unto whom it was revealed, that not unto themselves, but unto us they did minister the things, which are now reported unto you by them that have preached the Gospel unto you with the Holy Ghost sent down from heaven; which things the angels desire to look unto." Angels can look into salvation, but they can never experience it. They will never know God's mercy or grace because they have no need for it.

The next article to be constructed was the *Table of Shewbread*.[16] This furnishing was located on the right in the second compartment of

---

[16] Exodus 37:10-16

the tabernacle that was known as the Holy Place. It was also made of shittim wood (Christ's humanity) and overlaid with gold (Christ's deity). Here again, we see Jesus' humanity and deity coming together.

The Table of Shewbread revealed God as our provider, and pointed to the Bread that came from heaven.[17] Jesus, as the living Manna from heaven, is the only one who can add substance to our lives. His heart is not only to nourish us, but to make us whole. Before He could make us whole, He had to become broken bread on the cross, so that we could partake of His life.

The Table of Shewbread represented one other point of significance: communion. There are two types of communion. The Ark of the Covenant pointed to communion that brings agreement. However, the Table of Shewbread represented communion that comes from partaking of the life of Jesus. God's whole desire is to commune with us at His table. This is why Jesus came—to bring reconciliation between man and God. He said in John 14:6, "I am the way, the truth, and the life: no man cometh unto the Father, but by me." (Emphasis added.)

Before Jesus could bring reconciliation, He had to do the work of redemption. Because of His redemption, He is the only access to the Father. His desire remains consistent, "Behold, I stand at the door, and knock: if any man hear my voice, and open the door, I will come in to him, and will sup with him, and he with me" (Revelation 3:20).

The next article that was constructed was the *candlestick*.[18] The Ark of the Covenant represented the presence of God, and the Table of Shewbread, communion, but the candlestick pointed to the Christian walk.

The candlestick was located on the left side of the tabernacle, facing the Table of Shewbread. It was made of pure gold. The gold pointed to the deity of Christ. He is the light of the world and there is no darkness, deviance, weakness, or discrepancy in His character, life, or conduct.[19] The gold was beaten into the form of the candlestick. This represented Jesus being prepared and beaten to fit the cross, and serve as a perfect sacrifice on man's behalf.

Within the tabernacle, there was total darkness. The candlestick was the only light in the Holy Place; therefore, the priests were depending on this light to properly carry out their duties and minister to God. This brings us to the secret of a victorious life. A Christian must walk in the light of Jesus. 1 John 1:6-7 says, "If we say that we have fellowship with him, and walk in darkness, we lie, and do not the truth: But if we walk in the light, as he is in the light, we have fellowship one with another, and the blood of Jesus Christ, his Son cleanseth us from all sin." Jesus' light

---

[17] John 6:32-35
[18] Exodus 37:17-24
[19] John 1:3-10

is the only light in the world that will guide the believer in the ways of righteousness.

As one compares the different areas of the tabernacle, you can observe three different lights. The outer court was in the natural light, while the Holy Place had an artificial light. This means that man had a part in the lighting. For example, the priests had to trim the candlestick to keep the light going. The third light was the Shekinah glory of God. When His presence was evident in the Most Holy Place, the light from His glory was present in this compartment.

All men experience the natural light of the world, while only some make it into the Holy Place to stand in the light of the candlestick. However, few ever make it into the Most Holy Place where they experience His Shekinah glory.

The light of the candlestick represented two types of Christians. You have those who settle for walking in the artificial light of religion. They may invest in religious activities, but they do not make an ongoing investment in their relationship with God. As a result, they spend much time in the shadows, hiding compromise, sin, and defeat.

The others belong to a group that stand in the light of Christ and walk according to His character, life, and teachings. There is no deviance in their commitment. They stand upright, walk in confidence, and pursue after communion with God. This walk also means that they are adhering to 1 John 2:6, "He that saith he abideth in him ought himself also so to walk, even as he walked."

Since the candlestick had to be trimmed, this shows that man does have a responsibility to keep his life upright before God. Obviously, the priest had to keep the candlestick trimmed with oil to effectively take care of the Table of Shewbread. People cannot have communion with God unless they are walking in the light. Without communion, they will not know God and be ready for the time He might intervene, intrude into their reality, or return. Christians only have to read the parable of the ten virgins in Matthew 25:1-13 to realize that the oil of the Holy Spirit must be present, to ensure that they will be ready for the Bridegroom.

The next article in the Holy Place is the *Altar of Incense*. This altar points to prayer and intercession. Both of these elements must be prevalent in the saint's life.[20]

The Altar of Incense stood before the veil that separated the Holy Place from the Most Holy Place. As you consider the pattern from the Ark of the Covenant to the Altar of Incense, you will see a complete life in God. For example, you must begin with the presence of God (Ark of the Covenant), which will lead you into communion (Table of Shewbread). Communion allows you to walk in the light (candlestick). This light will bring you to the Altar of Incense (prayer and intercession), where you will discover the essence of real ministry.

---

[20] Exodus 37:25-28; Ephesians 6:18; 1 Thessalonians 5:17

A person who has an effective prayer life will display both authority and power. This authority and power can only be realized in an intimate relationship with God.

Once this relationship is right, then a person has the authority to stand in the gap and the power to get things done. This is why James 5:16 states, "Confess your faults one to another, and pray one for another, that ye may be healed. The effectual fervent prayer of a righteous man availeth much."

Ezekiel 22:30 says, "And I sought for a man among them, that should make up the hedge, and stand in the gap before me for the land, that I should not destroy it: but I found none." God is searching for those who are righteous enough to stand in the gap. Twenty centuries ago, He established such a man who not only stood in the gap, but also closed it by presenting Himself as a sacrifice on our behalf. Today, He lives as our High Priest, making intercession for us. His name is Jesus Christ.

Hebrews 7:24-25 says this about Jesus Christ in regards to His intercession, "But this man, because he continueth ever, hath an unchangeable priesthood. Wherefore he is able also to save them to the uttermost that come unto God by him, seeing he ever liveth to make intercession for them."

The Altar of Incense was made of shittim wood that was overlaid with gold. As man in the courts of heaven, Jesus serves as man's only mediator. The Apostle Paul confirms this, "For there is one God, and one mediator between God and men, the man Christ Jesus" (1 Timothy 2:5).

In His deity, Jesus serves as a representative of God's heart and character. Because He understands the plight of man and knows the heart of God, He serves as an effective mediator between struggling man and a holy God.

According to Exodus 37:29, the anointing oil was part of the incense that floated from the Altar of Incense upward to God in heaven. There is a pattern to this oil that we will consider in a later chapter. This oil had certain ingredients and represented the work of the Holy Spirit in the believer. He mixes the right ingredients to bring forth both an anointing and fragrance that will be pleasing to God and effective in the world.

This brings us to the outer court. God works from the inside out, going to the left to establish the light, then to the right to reveal His provision of the bread and desire to commune, back to the veil. Man works from the outside in, starting on the left with the light of the world (Jesus), moving to the right to the Table of Shewbread to partake of the Bread of Life, then on to the Altar of Incense (prayer), and finally into the Most Holy Place to fellowship with God between the cherubim at the mercy seat. However, before a person can come into the inner courts with God, he or she must face his or her depravity.

331

The first furnishings that people encountered in the outer court addressed their depravity. It was known as the *Altar of Burnt Offering.*[21] It was made with shittim wood and overlaid with brass. The wood pointed to humanity, while the brass represented judgment on sin. Jesus took on the form of man to become the Lamb of God, so that God could bring judgment on sin. Therefore, the Altar of Burnt Offering was a shadow of the cross of Christ.

Like the Altar of Burnt Offering, the cross displayed the consequences of sin. Every day, sacrifices were being offered up on the Altar of Burnt Offering. People were being constantly reminded that their actions cost the life of an innocent animal who served as their substitute. This shows us that even though many try to hide their sin, it was visible to God, and will be uncovered for the world to see.[22]

Proverbs 28:13 says, "He that covereth his sins shall not prosper, but whoso confesseth and forsaketh them shall have mercy." Sin must be faced and properly dealt with at the Altar of Burnt Offering to ensure a relationship with God.

Blood was sprinkled on this altar from the sacrifice, and then poured out at its base. Jesus' blood was sprinkled on the cross and ran down to those below. It would cleanse those who bowed at the foot of the cross from all unrighteousness, ensuring fellowship.[23]

The Altar of Burnt Offering had four horns at each corner. These horns pointed in four directions, representing that judgment on sin was universal and would be satisfied. This reminds us how Jesus' redemption was complete, and as Psalms 103:12 declares, As far as the east is from the west, so far hath he removed our transgressions from us."

There were vessels made for this altar. They had to be formed and shaped out of brass. This reminds us of the power of sin to influence and shape people's lives. However, for saints, they have the great Potter who will take their marred lives and reshape them for His glory.[24]

The Altar of Burnt Offering was hollow inside. Sin leaves a person hallow until God fills his or her life with His Spirit. Are you hollow today because much is lacking in your relationship with God?

The next and final object was the laver.[25] It was made of brass, and served as the place where the priest would wash. This laver represented the Word of God that can both cleanse and bring judgment. Ephesians 5:26 says, "That he might sanctify and cleanse it with the washing of water by the word."

---

[21] Exodus 38:1-7
[22] Matthew 10:26-27
[23] 1 John 1:7
[24] Jeremiah 18:1-6
[25] Exodus 38:8

Jeremiah 23:29 said this of the Word of God, "Is not my word like as a fire? saith the LORD; and like a hammer that breaketh the rock in pieces?".

God's Word will either bring life or judgment, for it will not return void. "So shall my word be that goeth forth out of my mouth: it shall not return unto me void, but it shall accomplish that which I please, and it shall prosper in the thing whereto I sent it" (Isaiah 55:11).

The laver was made from the looking glasses of the women. These looking glasses point to God's Word serving as a mirror to a person's spiritual life. Such a mirror will give a person a realistic evaluation about his or her spiritual status as it cuts through the images of delusion to reveal sin and compromise. James 1:22-25 gives us this warning and promise in regards to this matter,

> But be ye doers of the word, and not hearers only, deceiving your own selves. For if any be a hearer of the word, and not a doer, he is like unto a man beholding his natural face in a glass: For he beholdeth himself, and goeth his way, and straighway forgetteth what manner of man he was. But whosoever looketh into the perfect law of liberty, and continueth therein, he being not a forgetful hearer, but a doer of the work, this man shall be blessed in his deed.

God's Word cleanses, changes. and sanctifies.[26] This means that the Word and the Spirit are God's avenues of doing the work of sanctification. After the cleansing, an individual can enter into the Holy Place and begin to walk in Jesus' light, partake at His table, and enjoy authority and power in his or her prayer life. Eventually, he or she will be able to enter into the Most Holy place in sweet communion and rest in God.

This is God's pattern to ensure a powerful relationship with Him. It is on His terms and not on ours. It will be His reality and life, not ours. Clearly, His life is not about you or me, but about the manifestation of Jesus' powerful, eternal life being manifested in and through us.

You are following some pattern in your spiritual life. You could be in the outer court because you are still too close to the world. Perhaps you are in the Holy Place, but functioning in the shadows of religion, rather than walking in Jesus' light. My hope is that you have come into the Most Holy Place where you experience God's Shekinah glory, sweet communion, and spiritual rest.

What pattern are you following? Is it the pattern of self where all lust is appeased, or is it the pattern of the world where self is exalted and Satan is worshipped? I pray you are following the pattern that God has put before you, where you will experience abundant life along with victory, authority, and power in the Holy Ghost.

---

[26] John 17:17; Romans 15:16

7

FOLLOW THE ARK

In the last chapter, we discovered that the Ark of the Covenant represented the presence of God. In many incidents, we see where the priests carried the Ark of the Covenant before the children of Israel, in order to lead them through the wilderness, into battles, and finally into and through the Promised Land.

The leadership and journey of the Ark of the Covenant not only give us insight into God, but also reveals a pattern as to how God moves. This pattern shows us the atmosphere in which God will move, as well as the consequences for those who do not properly recognize His presence in their midst.

A person cannot properly study the tabernacle without considering the movements and happenings around the Ark of the Covenant. The reason for this is because wherever the Ark came to rest, the tabernacle or God's abiding place was erected. When the Ark was lifted up, it was for the sole purpose of leading the Israelites into the glorious and victorious ways of God. Let us now take this journey with the Ark of the Covenant to establish the pattern.

The first place we are introduced to the Ark of the Covenant is in the wilderness of Sinai. This is where it was constructed. It was clear that the spiritual life of God's people had to first be established to maintain the presence of God. Interestingly, God had this constructed out in the barren wilderness in the middle of the prickly terrain of Sinai. (As a reminder, "Sinai" means thorny.)[1] This shows us that God can only come into the midst of spiritual barrenness. It is in this barrenness that He can establish His presence.

As Jesus stated in Matthew 5:3, "Blessed are the poor in spirit: for theirs is the kingdom of heaven." The word "poor" points to a cringing beggar.[2] This concept implies the barrenness of the soul. Such a soul is a candidate for the kingdom of heaven.

The next incident we see is where the Ark led the children of Israel out of Sinai into the wilderness of Paran. Numbers 10:33 says, "And they departed from the mount of the LORD three days' journey: and the ark of

---

[1] Smith's Bible Dictionary
[2] Strong's Exhaustive Concordance, #4484

334

the covenant of the LORD went before them in the three days' journey, to search out a resting place."

The goal of the Ark was to lead Israel to a place of rest. Rest points to preparation. It is in the presence of God that saints find rest or communion for their souls. This rest allows God to prepare them for the next part of the Christian walk. Jesus made reference to this precious rest in Matthew 11:28, "Come unto me, all ye that labour and are heavy laden, and I will give you rest."

Rest also allows a person to gain proper perspective. It is natural for people to accumulate things that weigh them down with cares and anxieties. The cares of this world subtly crowd out priorities that maintain the quality of life. A journey that leads to spiritual rest allows a person to examine self, and rid his or her life of any hindrances. This rest allows a person to recognize these hindrances and cast them before the feet of Jesus, bringing about revival.[3] Isaiah 40:31 confirms this, "But they that wait upon the LORD shall renew their strength; they shall mount up with wings as eagles; they shall run, and not be weary; and they shall walk, and not faint."

The presence of God will lead people to places of rest, to separate them from excess personal baggage. At the point of rest is communion where the Lord can prepare each individual for future challenges that he or she will encounter along the way.

The next significant place the Ark of the Covenant led Israel was into the Promised Land.[4] Jesus commanded His disciples to follow Him. A person can only obtain the life God has for him or her by following the Ark (Jesus). Only the Ark can lead individuals through dangerous and uncertain terrain. Therefore, Jesus' command is simple, "Follow me."

The Jordan River parted at the presence of the Ark. Israel passed over to the Promised Land on dry ground.[5] Isaiah 43:2-3 gives this promise, "When thou passeth through the waters, I will be with thee; and through the rivers, they shall not overflow thee: when thou walkest through the fire, thou shalt not be burned; neither shall the flame kindle upon thee."

Likewise, Jesus Christ went through the fires of persecution, the waters of death, and the river of the grave for us. In spite of it all, He was raised in resurrection power. Today, every believer is baptized into His death as a means to be raised up in resurrection power unto new life.[6] They will spiritually pass through impassable waters of challenges, the swift rivers of judgments, and the fires of affliction, but will spiritually remain unharmed.

---

[3] 1 Peter 5:7
[4] Joshua 3
[5] Joshua 4:11-16
[6] Romans 6:3-6

The next point of leadership for the Ark of the Covenant was the battle of Jericho. The Ark led the way of victory for Israel. The great army of Israel had marched around the city as the priests carried the trumpets. The Ark was behind this host, but on the seventh day, the walls of Jericho came down before the Ark of the Covenant.[7]

God won the battle for Israel. Nothing can remain standing before His presence. All opposition must bow before Him, no matter how strong and mighty it may stand. This is clearly brought out in Philippians 2:10-11, "That at the name of Jesus every knee should bow, of things in heaven, and things in earth, and things under the earth; And that every tongue should confess that Jesus Christ is Lord, to the glory of God the Father." This is the secret of victory in the kingdom of God. Nothing can stand in opposition to God when He steps on the scene. Such opposition will come down before the feet of Jesus.

Christians must keep this secret in mind about their personal lives. Those things that represent opposition against the work of God in their lives will be brought down before the King of kings and Lord of lords in utter defeat. They will lay in ruin at the feet of Jesus to ensure victory. If such personal opposition is not voluntarily taken care of through repentance, it will result in judgment that leaves devastation in its wake.

Jericho reminds Jesus' followers that God wrought the victory with His presence, authority, and power. As soldiers of the cross, believers simply take the sword of truth to what is left, and claim His victory before heaven and earth.

The next incident in which the Ark is mentioned is Joshua 7:6, "And Joshua rent his clothes, and fell to the earth upon his face before the ark of the LORD until the eventide, he and the elders of Israel, and put dust upon their heads." The Ark is a place of seeking God in humility and repentance. There was sin in the camp, and it resulted in defeat for the army of Israel. Joshua's response was not to run to the other leaders or withdraw in his own understanding. His response was to fall before the Ark to intercede and seek God's perspective.

This shows us that when God's presence is missing, there is defeat. To gain God's perspective in such times, His presence must be sought and reestablished. This means that a person must become transparent and humble before God in order to inquire of Him.[8]

1 Samuel 4:3 shows us that once in the Promised Land, the Ark came to rest at Shiloh. "Shiloh" means place of rest. It was located within the inheritance of Ephraim on the north side of Bethel. We have already established that "Bethel" means house of God.[9] However, the Ark was not taken to the house of God, but to the place of rest. Sadly, Shiloh did not prove to be a place of rest for the Ark. Sin was rampant in the

---

[7] Joshua 6
[8] Judges 20:27
[9] Smith Bible Dictionary

priesthood, bringing disgrace to Israel. Due to this sin, Israel began to suffer defeat in battles at the hands of the Philistines. In one such battle, the Israelites began to call for the Ark of the Covenant to change the course of the battle.

Surprisingly, God did not protect His Ark. He had withdrawn His presence due to the sin in the priesthood that was being practiced by Eli and his wicked sons. The Israelites were not only defeated, but the uncircumcised Philistines also did the unthinkable and captured the Ark.

At this point, we see the Ark placed in the temple of an idol name Dagon. "Dagon" means a fish.[10] What an insult this was to the God of Israel, the Creator of heaven and earth. The Philistines fit the Apostle Paul's scenario in Romans 1:23, "And changed the glory of the uncorruptible God into an image made like to corruptible man, and to birds, and fourfooted beasts, and creeping things."

The result of the idolatrous excursion for the Ark was that God humbled Dagon and brought judgment upon the Philistines. 1 Samuel 5:3 tells us what happened to Dagon the first night the Ark was in his temple, "And when they of Ashdod arose early on the morrow, behold, Dagon was fallen upon his face to the earth before the ark of the LORD. And they took Dagon and set him in his place again."

All idols will be brought down before God. I know this has been true for my life. In light of Jesus' presence, glory, and power, my idols could not remain standing. They were exposed for their foolishness and brought low before Him.

The Philistines did not get the message the first time that their idol, Dagon, could not stand before the holy God of Israel. They set Dagon in his place again. 1 Samuel 5:4 tells us the scene that the Philistines were faced with when they entered Dagon's temple the next morning. "And when they arose early on the morrow morning, behold Dagon was fallen upon his face to the ground before the ark of the LORD; and the head of Dagon and both palms of his hands were cut off upon the threshold; only the stump of Dagon was left him."

God made sure that the Philistines would not set Dagon up again. He basically took the idol's identity away by cutting off his head and destroying his hands. The destruction of his hands pointed to the fact that Dagon was incapable of helping them.

God's hand was also heavy upon the priests of Dagon.[11] Even if they could resurrect Dagon, the priests were unfit to minister before this silent god because the Lord had struck them with hemorrhoids.

The Ark had started out being a sign of victory for the Philistines. Now, it was becoming a source of grave judgment. Fear fell on the Philistines as Jehovah God struck each Philistine town that dared to

---

[10] Smith's Bible Dictionary
[11] Joshua 5:6

house what was becoming "the unpopular Ark." The Ark had become a hot potato among the uncircumcised Philistines.

The Philistines devised a plan to return the Ark. They supplied a new cart, two milch kine, and jewels of gold. They put the Ark on the cart and sent it away. They knew if the kine went towards Israel with the Ark that the God of Israel was the one who was bringing judgment upon them.

The kine went straight towards Israel. As the cart approached Bethshemesh, those in the field rejoiced. Bethshemesh marked the northern boundary of Judah. The Ark came to rest in the field of Joshua.[12] "Joshua" means Jehovah is our salvation, and pointed to Jesus Christ. All hope and reality for the Christian must come to rest in Jesus, the Lion of Judah.

The Israelites rejoiced over the return of the Ark. However, that rejoicing quickly turned into mourning. Like the Philistines, they failed to recognize the holiness of God, and improperly responded and mishandled the Ark. 1 Samuel 6:19 summarizes the incident, "And he smote the men of Bethshemesh, because they had looked into the ark of the LORD, even he smote of the people fifty thousand and three score and ten men: and the people lamented, because the LORD had smitten many of the people with a great slaughter."

It is dangerous to take the presence of the Lord lightly. When you do not regard God, you can improperly respond and mishandle the things of God. The Israelites had been flippant with the Ark, bringing judgment on them.

God had strict rules for handling the Ark. Deuteronomy 10:8 stated, "At the time the LORD separated the tribe of Levi, to bear the ark of the covenant of the LORD, to stand before the LORD to minister unto him, and to bless in his name, unto this day." Only the priests could bear the Ark without judgment. King David learned this the hard way when he improperly moved the Ark, costing Uzzah his life.[13]

God is holy, and people must honor His presence with the right attitude. They must not be flippant or casual about His requirements. Christians need to keep in mind that they are all priests, but their authority to stand before God rests with their level of holiness before Him.[14]

Like the Philistines, fear fell on the men of Bethshemesh. They said, "...Who is able to stand before this holy LORD God? and to whom shall he go up from us" (1 Samuel 6:20)?

The next journey of the Ark can be found in 1 Samuel 7. The men of Kirjathjearim came and fetched the Ark. They brought it into the house of Abinadab. He was a Levite, and his son Eleazar was sanctified to keep

---

[12] 2 Samuel 6:12-15
[13] 2 Samuel 6:6-7
[14] 1 Peter 2:5, 9

the Ark of the Covenant. It remained at Kirjathjearin for 20 years until King David came for it.

It was King David's mishandling of the Ark that not only cost Uzzah his life, but also brought fear to King David. He left it at the house of Obededom, the Gittite for three months. In those three months, Obededom was greatly blessed because of it. The presence of God does bless people. For King David, this reality stirred him up to go and bring the Ark to Jerusalem, the place of peace. This time, David showed proper regard for the Ark.

When God's presence is with and in His people, it can stir up others to become attracted towards Him. They realize that His presence is something worth possessing, and will not accept any hindrance that keeps them from realizing Him in a personal way.

The Ark was finally brought to Jerusalem, its resting place for many years. It had traveled from the wilderness into the Promised Land to Jerusalem, the city of peace. It had led Israel to places of rest and into battles. It caused idols and cities to fall before God, as well as bring judgment on the uncircumcised. It brought fear upon many, along with blessings to those who gave it a proper place in their midst. It was finally placed in a beautiful temple after it had resided in a tent for many years.

The Ark of the Covenant has long since disappeared, but the presence of God can be found in a pure heart, in the praises of His people, and in the midst of brokenness and humility.

Today, there is a big move to locate the original Ark of the Covenant. There are some interesting stories about this mysterious furnishing. Some believe that before Babylon totally destroyed the temple and Jerusalem, Jeremiah hid the Ark under the city of Jerusalem. One archeologist claimed that he had actually located it.

Recently, I watched a television documentary on the Ark of the Covenant on the Discovery Channel. There is a belief that under the reign of the wicked King Mannasseh, the priest took the Ark and went to Africa.[15] Today, there is a claim that the Ark rests in a temple in Africa. The overseers of it will not allow anyone to see this object, so their claim cannot be confirmed. However, according to the keeper, there is such a bright light surrounding it, that it brings fear to him.

Where is the Ark? For the curious seeker, the archeologist, and the Orthodox Jew, it might be the million-dollar question. However, for Christians, their Ark is more than an object that casts an incredible shadow throughout the history of Israel. The Christian knows that that shadow became real and cast reality into the hearts of those who believe. That reality is God in the flesh, Jesus Christ, who now sits on the right hand of the Father, and resides within each believer through the presence of the Holy Spirit. Like the Ark, Jesus leads every follower through the wilderness into the Promised Land. He brings each of them

---

[15] 2 Chronicles 33

into His place of peace, as well as goes before them to prepare the way and subdue the enemy.

Is the living revelation of the Ark of the Covenant with you or are you missing the reality of God in your life? If you are missing the reality of God, you are open to defeat, and will eventually be brought down in judgment and destruction.

8

HIS GLORIOUS NAME

One of the subjects that fascinate me surrounds the name of God. I am often reminded of when God first introduced Himself to Moses in Exodus 3:14, "And God said unto Moses, I AM THAT I AM: and he said, Thus shalt thou say unto the children of Israel, I AM hath sent me unto you." His name speaks volumes. There is no way to describe Him. He is the ever-present reality that never changes. In a sense, He was making a declaration that finite man could never fully grasp.

Jesus, God Incarnate, often capitalized on this incredible reality. "Before Abraham was, I am...I am the Alpha and Omega, the beginning and the ending...I am...the first and the last" (John 8:58; Revelation 1:8, 11).

Daniel 7:9-10 describes Jesus in this way:

I beheld till the thrones were cast down, and the Ancient of days did sit, whose garment was white as snow, and the hair of his head like the pure wool: his throne was like the fiery flame, and his wheels as burning fire. A fiery stream issued and came forth from before him: thousand thousands ministered unto him, and ten thousand times ten thousand stood before him: the judgment was set, and the books were opened.

What is in a name? Names are valuable because they identify a person as to position, family, and heritage. In some cases, people must live up to a name, while others hide behind generic names that will cause them to fade into the crowd due to bad associations, shame, and disgrace. Some avoid, or change, their name because it can invoke terror in others.

As one studies the names of God in light of this understanding, he or she will realize the significance of coming to terms with the importance of His name. The meaning of the word "name" in relationship to God not only reveals His identity, but also His position in the scheme of things. It implies honor, authority, and character. His name is a mark or memorial of a Living Being with a personality that can interact with us, as well as develop an intimate relationship with us in a personal way. As you study the reality of God, you realize that He does not have to live up to His excellent name; rather His name describes who He is.

As you follow the pattern of God's name, you will see in the very beginning of Genesis that He is introduced as a being with a distinct personality. This personality means that He is capable of being touched, but due to His deity, He will not be fully comprehended in our present finite state. The initial introduction to God clearly sets precedence. He was in the beginning and must be first in every aspect. He created the universe; therefore He has intelligence, imagination, and the power to make it all work. Within creation, we see majesty that is indescribable, as well as incredible unseen laws and principles that ensure order. There is also simplicity that makes His entire work appear easy, and yet the profoundness that reveals His work cannot be completely explored or exhausted by finite man.

In fact, "Elohim" is the name of God in Genesis 1:1. The "el" in Elohim is essentially the Almighty, which points to His strength and power. Elohim occurs 2,700 times, and it is always in relationship to God being our creator.[1]

Creation gives us a small glimpse into the God that was introduced in Genesis 1:1. His vastness is beyond exploration. This fact gives us an insight into the reality that there is no beginning or end to God. The word "in" means all-inclusive. In other words, there is no beginning, just the understanding that everything begins and fits within the inexhaustible reality of God's character, working, power, ways, and will.

From Genesis 1:1 to the last verse in Revelation, we are given various revelations of this God, only to realize Him in the person of Jesus Christ. The Apostle Paul confirmed this in Colossians 2:9, "For in him (Jesus) dwelleth all the fulness of the Godhead bodily." (Parenthesis added.)

The journey through the Bible to discover this God is one of the most incredible journeys. His depths are immeasurable, and the heights one can reach in Him are never ending. His love is unfathomable, His mercy expressed in compassion that is new everyday, and His grace capable of abounding where sin once supremely reigned.[2] The Apostle Paul summarized it in this manner, "O the depth of the riches both of the wisdom and knowledge of God! how unsearchable are his judgments, and his ways past finding out! For who hath known the mind of the Lord? or who hath been his counsellor?" (Romans 11:33-34).

True to His character, this God of heaven introduces Himself to mere man. To Abraham, He introduced Himself as his shield (protection) and exceeding great reward (His inheritance or possession).[3] This showed Abraham that the Lord not only preserved his life, but He also served as his real inheritance. Abraham understood the real essence and hope of life. Hebrews 11:10 gives us insight into his confidence, "For he looked for a city which hath foundations, whose builder and maker is God."

---

[1] The Companion Bible, Kregel Publications, Appendix #4
[2] John 3:16-18; Romans 5:20-6:2; 8:35-39; 11:33; Lamentations 3:21-22
[3] Genesis 15:1

When God introduced Himself to Isaac, He declared Himself to be the God of Abraham.[4] He was reminding Isaac of his father's rich spiritual roots that led back to Him. This confirmed that He was the desired treasure and possession of Abraham's heavenly inheritance.

God introduced Himself to Jacob in Bethel in a similar way. "And, behold, the LORD stood above it, and said, I am the LORD God of Abraham thy father, and the God of Isaac: the land whereon thou liest, to thee will I give it, and to thy seed" (Genesis 28:13).

When Jacob encountered God over two decades later in Genesis 31:13, God introduced Himself as "the God of Bethel." It was His way of reminding Jacob of their previous encounter, and the vow Jacob made when God had finally brought him back to his father's land in peace. Jacob's vow had been simple, "…If God will be with me, and will keep me in this way that I go, and will give me bread to eat, and raiment to put on, So that I come again to my father's house in peace; then shall the LORD be my God" (Genesis 28:20-21). When God introduced Himself the second time, it was an indication that it was time for Jacob to keep his vow with Him.

God introduced Himself to Moses as I AM. He is the one who is always abiding in the present. In fact there is no time in the realm of eternity. Therefore, God works to bring the lessons of the past into practical terms for the present to prepare His people. Application of these lessons will help a person to be in step with God in the present and future.

To the children of Israel, He was a dreadful God to fear. They not only heard His voice, but they witnessed His holiness and power on Mount Sinai.[5] In spite of their encounter with Him, they stood afar off from Him. Therefore, His main way of introducing Himself to the children of Israel was through His Law. The first two commandments confirmed His dreadful reality. He alone was God and would not tolerate any other god before Him. In His third commandment, He demanded that they made sure they properly responded even to His name, "Thou shalt not take the name of the LORD thy God in vain; for the LORD will not hold him guiltless that taketh his name in vain" (Exodus 20:7).

God's name was to invoke humility, awe, and worship. It was to produce an attitude of fear towards Him. It was not to be used lightly or without regard to His existence, character, and ways. After all, He was not a fantasy. He was and is a holy God; therefore, flippancy and casualness towards His name were unacceptable because it implied defiance against His character and authority. Hebrews 12:28-29 gives this insight, "Wherefore we receiving a kingdom which cannot be moved, let us have grace, whereby we may serve God acceptably with reverence and godly fear: For our God is a consuming fire."

---

[4] Genesis 26:24
[5] Exodus 20:18-21

Throughout Scriptures, God introduces Himself with a variety of names that describe His character. His introduction came to fruition when Jesus came to earth. Jesus introduced the character of God in a personal way as He met each person in his or her plight.

To the woman at the well, He was the giver of Living Water. For the woman with the issue of blood, He was the great physician. Zacchaeus encountered Him as an unprejudiced Savior. The disciples were told that He was the visible image of God, the Father, and to Peter He was unveiled as the Christ, the Son of the Living God.[6]

As you follow the pattern revealed by His name, you begin to see a God who is personal and up front, as He introduces Himself to the Abrahams of the world. For those like Moses, He is ever-present, ready to meet with those who are willing to risk the reality of facing His holiness, in order to come into the beauty of His presence.

To those like the children of Israel He seems far from them because their desires, commitment, and worship remain far from Him. He is as close as a person's faith allows Him to be, but because of unbelief, He often remains shrouded by speculation and ignorance.

God's heart is to come near to man and touch His life with His love, grace, and glory. He revealed this heart desire through Jesus Christ. Jesus Christ came near to man and His invitation was clear: "Come unto me." God came as close as He could, but man had to accept His invitation by coming to Him.

This proved that God wants a relationship with man. He did all He could to make this relationship a living reality. It is up to man to come and embrace this reality as he grows in the knowledge of the Lord Jesus Christ.

The Lord used His name many times in Scripture as a means to introduce or acquaint man with His character and ways. He made this statement about His name in Deuteronomy 16:11,

> And thou shalt rejoice before the LORD thy God, thou, and thy son, and thy daughter, and thy manservant, and thy maid servant, and the Levite that is within thy gates, and the stranger, and the fatherless, and the widow, that are among you, in the place which the LORD thy God hath chosen to place his name there.

God wanted to place His name on a particular location. How was this possible? King Solomon posed this thought in 2 Chronicles 2:6, "But who is able to build him an house, seeing the heaven and heaven of heavens cannot contain him? who am I then, that I should build him an house, save only to burn sacrifice before him?"

God has a glorious throne in heaven. However, His desire to have a place in which He could place His name on earth had nothing to do with

---

[6] Matthew 9:20-22; 16:16; Luke 19:1-10; John 4:13-14; 14:9

need, beauty, importance, or significance. The reason for this desire is because He wanted to dwell among and with man.

This place would be designed to ensure proper worship and discipline for God's people. It would be specific to avoid confusion about acceptable worship. It would be a place where all religious activities and obligations would be fulfilled to rid of religious ignorance. At this one place, a permanent dwelling place would be established. There, God's priests could offer sacrifices and eat of them.[7] It would be here that God's people could rejoice together and celebrate His many blessings.

What kind of place would God choose? It had to be in the Promised Land, but in whose inheritance? Would He choose a beautiful city? What kind of terrain would surround this extraordinary place? Would it be a place of incredible beauty and abundance?

For the Christian, the Person of Jesus Christ fits all of the criteria. He not only wore the name of God, He is God.[8] He is the one point in which all people must meet God to experience salvation, obtain their inheritance, and properly worship. Although He came as man, His humanity veiled the magnificence of His divine nature.

Jesus is also the High Priest who oversees a lively priesthood of believers.[9] On the cross, He was surrounded by humanity with their various rebellious attitudes towards Him, while in heaven, on the right hand of the Father, He is surrounded by those who love and worship Him. Therefore, He was initially discovered by man in the midst of the lost, but now, He can be found in the midst of the glorious beauty of heaven.

For Israel, the idea of stamping God's name on one particular place had to be challenging, even though God had made reference to it. His presence had manifested itself in a tent for years. It was King David who brought up the idea of a permanent location. When he was considering that the Ark of the Covenant dwelt in a tent, he made this statement to the prophet Nathan in 1 Chronicles 17:1, "...I dwell in an house of cedars, but the Ark of the Covenant of the LORD remaineth under curtains."

King David wanted to establish a permanent house for God. The prophet gave him the go ahead, but how could mere man do God's permanent residence justice? It would have been an incredible task. However, this was a task that was clearly in David's heart. There is one thing he understood about this place that he expressed to his son, Solomon, in 1 Chronicles 22:5, "...the house that is to be builded for the LORD must be exceeding magnifical, of fame and of glory throughout all countries..."

---

[7] Deuteronomy 14:23-24; 16:2, 6, 11
[8] John 1:1
[9] Hebrews 8:1-2; 1 Peter 2:5, 9

God had resided in a tent that seemed simple and unattractive to the outside world. David wanted to change that appearance. The dwelling place of God had to be magnificent or great, beyond the existing religious places of David's day. Solomon confirmed this in 2 Chronicles 2:5, "And the house which I build is great: for great is our God above all gods." If this temple existed today, I have no doubt that it would exceed the magnitude of all religious buildings.

It had to be wonderfully made to ensure separation and holiness. 1 Kings 6:7 shows us the great measures that were taken to keep it holy, "And the house, when it was in building, was built of stone made ready before it was brought thither: so that there was neither hammer nor axe nor any tool of iron heard in the house, while it was in building."

Everything was brought from the outside to make sure that man did not defile the temple with his personal touches. This reminds us that the life God has for us comes from the outside of personal attempts. Ephesians 2:8 confirms this truth, "For by grace are ye saved through faith; and that not of yourselves: it is the gift of God."

This temple would be made in a wonderful way. The word "wonderful" implies beyond description.[10] Acts 17:24-25 gives us this criterion about the New Testament temple, "God that made the world and all things therein, seeing that he is Lord of heaven and earth, dwelleth not in temples made with <u>hands</u>; Neither is worshipped with men's <u>hands</u>, as though he needed anything, seeing he giveth to all life, and breath, and all things." (Emphasis added.)

The New Testament temple is absent of man's involvement. It is a temple designed and formed by God. It has already been purchased, established and is in the process of being completed.[11] 1 Corinthians 3:16 and 6:19 reveal the location and identity of this temple: the saints of God.

God has found a permanent residence in the heart of man. This New Testament temple fits the qualification of being wonderfully made by God. Psalm 139:14 confirms this, "I will praise thee; for I am fearfully and wonderfully made: marvellous are thy works; and my soul knoweth right well."

The God of heaven has wonderfully constructed man. This unique work was done outside of man's personal attempts. As previously discussed, it is not enough for the temple to be constructed. God must put His name on it for it to receive its proper fame, honor, or authority. He has chosen man to place the name of Jesus in their hearts and on their lips. However, Jesus must be present in their lives. John 1:12 says, "But as many as received him, to them gave he power to become the sons of God, even to them that believe on his name."

---

[10] Strong's *Exhaustive Concordance,* #6381
[11] Ephesians 1:6

Acts 4:12 states this about Jesus' name, "Neither is there salvation in any other: for there is none other name under heaven given among men, whereby we must be saved."

It is only as Jesus' life is built by God and established in His people that they can know His power and their inheritance. God puts His name on the New Testament temple by giving a believer Jesus Christ.

It is the presence, power, and life of Jesus that set the New Testament temple apart. The temple not only possesses the character of God, but it declares and maintains His very name. It is His presence, rather than the design, that makes the temple magnificent. Is it not appropriate that one of Jesus' names is "Wonderful"?[12]

This temple also had to reflect God's glory. As we study the concept of glory, we must realize that only man has the true capacity to reflect God's real glory. Genesis 1:26 speaks of man being created in the image of God. This simply means that Adam had the ability to reflect his Creator, but sin marred that potential. Romans 3:23 confirms this, "For all have sinned, and come short of the glory of God."

The whole purpose of both testament temples was to reflect the reality of God in the midst of man. For the Christian, this reality is only realized when the life of Jesus is being manifested in and through his or her life. 2 Corinthians 3:18 confirms this, "But we all, with open face beholding as in a glass the glory of the Lord, are changed into the same image form glory to glory, even as by the Spirit of the Lord."

Now that we understand the design of the temple and the purpose for it, the builder must be unveiled. It was King David's desire to build a permanent place for God. He shared this with Nathan, the prophet. His reply was, "...Do all that is in thine heart; for God is with thee" (1 Chronicles 17:2).

That very night, God came to Nathan, informing him that King David was not to build Him a house. The reason why David could not build the house for God was because he was a man of war.[13] God did not leave David with this harsh reality, but promised him that He would ordain a place for His people, and plant them there. He would also build a house, but it would be after his death. This promise followed, "...I will raise up thy seed after thee, which shall be of thy sons; and I will establish his kingdom. He shall build me an house, and I will stablish his throne forever" (1 Chronicles 17:11-12).

David's son Solomon would build God's house. As you study the establishment of the temple, you can begin to distinguish important patterns. The first one surrounds the concept of peace.

The temple is symbolic of the Christian life. Such a life cannot be established if there is conflict. It can only be developed when one is at peace. This life points to peace with God. There is no peace when God

---

[12] Isaiah 7:6
[13] 1 Chronicles 17:6-14; 22:8; 28:3

347

is absent. David had been a man of war, but his son, Solomon, would be a man of peace.

Scripture tells us that man is at enmity with God.[14] As a result, God sent His Son to close this gap. Jesus said of Himself in John 14:27, "Peace I leave with you, my peace I give unto you: not as the world giveth, give I unto you. Let not your heart be troubled, neither let it be afraid."

Like Solomon, the Son of God was a man of peace. But, unlike Solomon, Jesus is the one who truly establishes the reality of peace in every New Testament temple.

Even though King David did not build the house for God, it did not stop him from preparing for it.[15] In fact, David practically supplied all the means Solomon needed to build the temple. As a result, David said this to Solomon, "Take heed now; for the LORD hath chosen thee to build an house for the sanctuary: be strong and do it" (1 Chronicles 28:10). (Emphasis added.)

Solomon oversaw the project. He used talented people to build God's house.[16] This joint effort represented the Godhead. David represented God, the Father, who gave the responsibility for establishing the temple to His Son. Solomon is symbolic of Jesus who was given the responsibility to establish the temple. The many talented workers and strangers who built the temple represent the work of the Holy Spirit in the midst of the many-member Body or the Church of Jesus.

This brings us to Christians. Christians serve as the material or building blocks of the temple. Romans 12:1 shows believers what they must supply, "I beseech you therefore, brethren by the mercies of God, that you present your bodies a living sacrifice, holy acceptable unto God, which is your reasonable service."

Christians must supply their bodies for this work to be done. This is a form of consecration. Consecration involves submitting to the will of the Father. It means giving way to the work of the Holy Spirit. To become manageable under the Holy Spirit, the Christian must become pliable (humble), responsive (submissive), and controllable (meek). Such a disposition will allow the Holy Spirit to conform the believer to the image of Jesus.

The process of bringing forth the life of Christ in His New Testament Church will involve the hammer of the Word and the sanctifying fire of the Holy Spirit. It will mean that the hammer will separate, while the fire will purify and establish the person on the foundation of Jesus Christ. In the midst of such construction, the life of Christ will come forth. As His

---

[14] Ephesians 2:12-19
[15] 1 Chronicles 22-29
[16] 2 Chronicles 2:17-18

glory is unveiled in His temples, His name will be established and honored. This will bring glory to the Father.[17] What a glorious picture!

It would serve Christians well to follow the pattern of the temple. It means that they will truly be established upon the immovable Rock of Ages. They will come to understand the plans, purpose, construction, and builders of their spiritual lives.

However, there is one more detail that must be resolved. What place would God choose? Like its builder, it must represent a place of sanctuary, rest, and peace for the spiritually weary sojourner. 2 Chronicles 6:6 gives us the identity of this place, "But I have chosen Jerusalem, that my name might be there."

"Jerusalem" means habitation of peace. This well-known city is located in the region of Moriah. As we are about to see, Moriah has its own pattern where hidden treasures can also be discovered by the spiritual sojourner.

---

[17] Matthew 5:13-16

9

THE PLACE OF DEDICATION

We have talked about the heart, the Rock, the tabernacle, and the significance of God's name. Now, we must consider the permanent location He chose for His residence and work. When one studies the Christian life, he or she must realize it is designed according to God's plan and terms.

God's timing is also another important factor in His plan. Man sees time in light of his finite, limited appearance on earth, while God sees it according to eternity. The eternal perspective changes the reality of man's time to embrace the unusual, the miraculous, and the eternal. This eternal reality changes man's length, type, and quality of work.

This brings us to the fact that God must choose all things, including the place He will work within and from to ensure sanctification. There are various places in the travels of the patriarchs that stand out, but there is only one place where God put His definite mark in the world, Moriah.

"Moriah" means chosen of Jehovah. It encompasses a region as well as a mount. It is located in the eastern eminence of Jerusalem, and is separated from Mount Zion by the Tycopoeon Valley. It actually faces the upper city of Jerusalem. In King David's day, Jerusalem was a small, isolated hill fortress that was valued more for its location than size or splendor.[1] As you study Moriah's location, you can begin to see why God might have valued its location and set it apart for His work and purpose.

The first pattern surrounding Mount Moriah begins with the fact that a valley separates it from Mount Zion. "Moriah" represents the work of God, while "Zion" points to the fulfillment of God's promises. The valley between these mounts is symbolic of humiliation. This points to how God works to bring man to a place of humiliation. Humiliation is a prerequisite for people to partake of God's many promises that will keep them from the corruption of the world.[2]

"Mounts" represent pinnacles of growth and revelation to the Christian. God's work is to bring forth growth, while His promises can only be realized in light of revelation. And, always in between the growth and revelation is the point of balance for the Christian life—that of humiliation.

---

[1] Smith's Bible Dictionary
[2] 2 Peter 1:4

There can be no revelation without humiliation. Spiritual growth means that God is going deeper, while bringing the individual higher in his or her spiritual life. Revelation implies that God has started from a base place of spiritual struggle, and is now exalting the individual in a greater knowledge of Jesus. Spiritual growth changes the disposition of a person, while revelation changes one's perspective of God.

Moriah plays a significant part in the establishment of the spiritual life. To understand its representation, we must follow its pattern in Scripture. This pattern begins with Abraham in Genesis 22:2, "And he said, Take now thy son, thine only son Isaac, whom thou lovest, and get thee into the land of Moriah; and offer him there for a burnt offering upon one of the mountains which I will tell you." The first part of the pattern begins with a call. God calls us to a life set apart from the world, and what we perceive to be the essence or meaning of life.

The next part of this pattern is obedience. Abraham had to obey God's instruction. When you consider what God was requiring from Abraham, it would have caused confusion for the most spiritual person. Nevertheless, Abraham seemed to comply without any real qualms.

This brings us to the next part of this pattern: that of faith. Obedience is the manifestation of genuine faith. Abraham believed God, and even though God was requiring the sacrifice of his promised son, his confidence remained firm. Hebrews 11:17-19 states,

> By faith Abraham, when he was tried, offered up Isaac: and he that had received the promises offered up his only begotten son, Of whom it was said, That in Isaac shall thy seed be called: Accounting that God was able to raise him up, even from the dead; from when also he received him in a figure.

Notice how Abraham accounted or reckoned that God would raise up Isaac from death to life. To reckon something means that it is a present truth or reality, even though it has not happened. This showed Abraham's faith in God's character and promises.

The final part of this pattern is sacrifice. Abraham went up to Moriah out of faith and obedience to offer a sacrifice. Isaac gives us special insight into what was and is constituted acceptable sacrifices to God. He represented the best Abraham had to offer. He pointed to the miraculous, for his conception and birth was a miracle. He also represented the blessing of God, for out of him God would fulfill His promises to Abraham.

Abraham had another son, Ishmael, but he represented the activities of the flesh. He was the product of man's attempts to bring about God's promises. He was born of the will of man.[3]

Isaac also pointed to God's intervention. He is a type of the Son of God, Jesus Christ. Like Isaac, Jesus was conceived in a miraculous way.

---

[3] Galatians 4:28-31

He was the fulfillment of many promises given to Israel. He was not conceived by the will of man, but by the will of God. John 1:11-13 gives us this insight about Jesus, "He came unto his own, and his own received him not. But as many as received him, to them gave he power to become the sons of God, even to them that believe on his name: Which were born, not of blood, nor of the will of the flesh, nor of the will of man, but of God."

The key to this particular pattern, for those who are searching for God, is that they must begin with the sacrifice of Jesus Christ. By embracing this sacrifice by faith, in light of their depravity, they can receive everlasting life.

For the new Christian, he or she must choose to walk by faith. The faith walk means making the decision to obey the Word of God because of who He is. Such obedience will lead the individual through deep valleys of temptation, up foreboding mountains of challenges, and into wildernesses of uncertainty. In fact, everything about the Christian walk will make the Christian life seem full of drudgery at times, while proving to be unpredictable at others. The Christian life is not dependent on the terrain or the surroundings, but on the immovable Rock that never sways from its eternal character and foundation.[4]

Abraham's confidence rested in the Rock and not in the circumstances. He believed what God promised and responded in obedience. As a result, without hesitation, he could offer his best to God, the gem of his life, his son, Isaac.

When Christians have the same type of confidence, they can offer their lives to God without reservation. Such an offer is a form of consecration. This type of sacrifice ends in pure, unadulterated worship. This brings us back to what Abraham told the young men who were with him and Isaac, "...Abide ye here with the ass; and I and the lad will go yonder and worship, and come again" (Genesis 22:5).

Moriah is about worship. Acceptable worship entails faith, obedience, and sacrifice. The right spirit inspires genuine faith, while obedience is a matter of confidence and truth expressing itself in action. Is it any wonder that Jesus said, "God is a Spirit: and they that worship him must worship him in spirit and in truth" (John 4:24).

If you have not learned to worship God in spirit and truth, you have not spiritually traveled the way of Moriah. Therefore, your life is greatly missing the reality of communion and joy with God.

The next incident that surrounded Moriah can be found in 2 Samuel 24 and 1 Chronicles 21. There appear to be contradictions between these two accounts of the same event. As I have studied them, I believe both are in agreement with each other, but are approaching the event from different angles, so that an individual can gain a complete picture.

---

[4] Deuteronomy 32:4; 1 Corinthians 10:4

352

2 Samuel 24:1 tells us that the anger of the Lord was kindled against Israel; therefore, He moved on David to number Israel. In 1 Chronicles 21:1, it states that Satan stood up against Israel and provoked David to number Israel. How do you bring these two introductions together?

James 1:13 tells us that God does not tempt people to do evil. Apparently, God was upset with Israel. There is no indication that the children of Israel were outwardly doing anything wrong. In fact, this was a time of peace with their enemies. However, such peace can make people complacent towards God. The children of Israel may have been going through all the religious motions, but their hearts may have been getting further away from God.

Complacency towards God usually points to self-sufficiency. Self-sufficiency is hidden idolatry that cannot be seen by the physical eye, but cannot be hidden from God. Such idolatry will bring forth judgment. In order for God to bring forth judgment, the inward sin must be revealed by outward actions. To accomplish this, God allowed Satan to move on King David.

"Provoke" in 1 Chronicles 21:1 means to seduce, entice, move, persuade, set on, or take away.[5] Satan basically seduced or enticed David to number the people. This means that David was swept away by a strong desire that would border on obsession. It implied that David came under an evil covering and was being moved by forces beyond his control. He became so caught up with numbering the people that he was unable to discern or be reasoned with. When you consider David in past situations, this would be totally out of character for him.

One must keep in mind that David was a pawn in this situation. Satan was not testing him: rather, he was being used to bring judgment upon Israel. This is why this particular incident was not accredited as sin to David. 1 Kings 15:5 confirms this, "Because David did that which was right in the eyes of the LORD, and turned not aside from any thing that he commanded him all the days of his life, save only in the matter of Uriah the Hitite."

What was the big deal about numbering the people? God had already redeemed Israel. To ensure that they understood His redemption, He set up strict procedures in numbering the people of Israel in Exodus 30:12-16. Every man over 20 had to pay a ransom of a half a shekel of silver before he could officially be numbered. This was a way of making atonement, as well as establishing a memorial to remind the children of Israel who really redeemed them. The consequence for failing to adhere to these strict guidelines was a plague.

After David numbered the people of Israel, he was convicted in his heart.[6] He confessed his sin and asked the Lord to take away his iniquity. David was given a choice between three different judgments: 1) seven

---

[5] Strong's Exhaustive Concordance, #5496
[6] 2 Samuel 24:10

years of famine, 2) being chased by their enemies for three months or 3) three days of pestilence.

David actually chose the consequence of pestilence that had already been pronounced in Exodus 30 for improperly numbering the people. 2 Samuel 24:15 states, "So the LORD sent a pestilence upon Israel from morning even to the time appointed: and there died of the people from Dan even to Beersheba seventy thousand men."

As I have studied this incident, I realized that God had a man in Israel who had the capacity to stand in the gap for the people. That man was King David. He was a man who understood repentance and intercession.

As the angel stretched his hand over Jerusalem, the Lord changed His mind and instructed the angel to stay his hand. The angel of the Lord was by the threshing place of Araunah, the Jebusite. David began to confess and intercede. "I have sinned greatly in that I have done: And now, I beseech thee, O LORD, take away the iniquity of thy servant; for I have done very foolishly" (2 Samuel 24:10).

King David was instructed by the prophet Gad, to go and construct an altar unto the Lord at the threshing floor of Araunah. He obeyed. When King David approached Araunah about building an altar on his threshing floor, Araunah simply agreed to give him the land. David's reply is priceless, "Nay, but I will surely buy it of thee at a price; neither will I offer burnt offerings unto the LORD my God of that which doth cost me nothing. So David bought the threshingfloor and the oxen for fifty shekels of silver" (2 Samuel 24:24).

We are given three more aspects about the Christian life in this incident that must be observed. The first one is that David realized his life in God was priceless; therefore, it would personally cost him to possess it.

Salvation is free, but to possess the life God has for each of us will personally cost an individual. This simply means it costs to know, experience, and do right by God. David was willing to personally pay the price of fifty shekels to do right.

The fifty shekels are also significant and point to the second aspect of the Christian life. "Silver" represents redemption. Redemption points to the reality that believers have been bought back from the harsh taskmasters of darkness. The number "50" points to Pentecost.

The disciples of Jesus were told to wait in the upper room. But, what were they waiting for? After all, Jesus' work was done on the cross. But, His disciples had to be endued with power from on high in order to live the victorious life, as well as be powerful witnesses in the world. This powerful life would produce a fruitful life.[7]

---

[7] Luke 24:44-49; John 15:1-8; Acts 1-2

This brings us to the third aspect of the Christian life that can be distinguished in this incident—the threshing floor. King David is a type of Jesus that stands between life and death. The threshing floor represented Jesus standing in the midst of judgment, in order to bring life.

To bring forth life, the grain (holy) must be separated from the chaff (unholy). This separation is a form of judgment. There must be a sacrifice to suffice judgment. Praise God! Jesus became that sacrifice. His sacrifice produced the firstfruits.[8] He was sifted by the cross and discarded in a grave, but rose in resurrection power to ensure other fruits.

Jesus' sacrifice shows Christians the cost—the right to self. Every Christian must come back to the threshing floor to deny self and pick up the cross. This will immediately cause separation between that which constitutes life and death. It will mean purification of that which remains. And, that which remains will be used for God's glory.

David paid the price of 50 silver shekels. He built an altar, offered the sacrifice, and stayed the judgment on Israel. Jesus paid the price for our sins on the altar of the cross. Everyone who receives Him as God's provision for salvation will be spared from the wrath to come. 1 Thessalonians 5:9 confirms this, "For God hath not appointed us to wrath, but to obtain salvation by our Lord Jesus Christ."

It was on this threshing floor that the temple was built. Obviously, the Christian life is established at a high price. It cost God His Son, and His Son His life. For Christians, it will cost them everything that is associated with self, the world, and Satan. Such a price is our reasonable service, but for many Christians, they think it is a great sacrifice that should being them honor. The truth is when Christians begin to pay the price to know God, it will be Jesus who will be exalted as the kingdom of God is realized on a personal level.

Let's consider the first two patterns of Moriah. Moriah represents the life of a Christian. The first pattern summarizes the humble beginnings of the Christian's life. For Abraham, we see where his life began with a call that required obedience. This obedience was a product of genuine faith that brings us to the final part of this pattern—sacrifice. For Christians, their pattern is the opposite of Abraham's. They begin with the sacrifice of Jesus, proceed forward by faith to discover the treasures of heaven, and respond in obedience to fulfill the call of God in their lives.

The second pattern of Moriah points to is spiritual growth. There cannot be growth without paying the price that comes through separation. This separation serves as a form of judgment and sacrifice.

This brings us to the final pattern of Moriah that can be seen in the history of Jerusalem. God put His name on Jerusalem. Solomon built the temple in the vicinity of Jerusalem. Although Jerusalem has been

---

[8] 1 Corinthians 15:20, 23

attacked and destroyed many times, it still exists. Even though Jerusalem will be at the center of one more great battle in the future, it will remain the place that God put His name upon, the place where Jesus will reign as King of kings and Lord of lords.

The history of Mount Moriah is where the temple was erected and dedicated. It is where King David reigned and the King of kings gave way to a cross. This is where protective walls were destroyed by the enemies, but where Nehemiah also reestablished them.

Jerusalem has been a city that has seen great devastation as well as victory. It has seen the rise and fall of many great men. It has watched man's best attempts and beauty succumb to vanity and ashes. It is alive with history, but it is also a city with a glorious future.

Jerusalem reminds Christians that they are also in a battle. At times, they taste the bitterness of persecution. They watch the best attempts of man fail or give way to destruction. They struggle in the midst of enemies who watch and plan for their demise. They are at war with their flesh. They struggle to establish their lives in God in the midst of that which opposes His reign. The harsh reality is that they must overcome their enemies to embrace the fullness of the glorious future that awaits those who endure. They must avoid insisting on their own way with God and others, while ensuring Jesus' place as Lord and King.[9]

What about you? Have you followed Abraham up to Moriah to sacrifice your best? Have you paid the necessary price like David to make peace with God, or allowed your life to be totally dedicated like Solomon's temple? Does your life stand out because the presence and glory of God are evident? Does the Prince of peace rule from your heart, or are you in turmoil because self is calling the shots? Make sure you have come to rest on your Moriah, thereby, allowing God to establish your life in Him.

---

[9] Hebrews 12:11, 14; James 3:8

10

FOLLOWING THE PATTERN
OF HOLINESS

What will it take to maintain His presence in my life, now that the place of God has been chosen (my body) and His dwelling place erected (the life of Jesus in me)? The answer to this question cannot be realized in light of who I am, but in light of who God is. The truth is God cannot reside in the midst of an unholy people. The tabernacle and temple represented the dwelling presence of God, but He withdrew that presence whenever His people forsook Him to chase after other gods.

In the case of Israel, He allowed His temple in Jerusalem to be utterly destroyed, His name discarded, and His people taken into captivity. This is the harsh reality behind God's presence. Without Him in our midst, we are a doomed people who live on borrowed time. His presence must be in our midst if we are going to experience the life He has in mind for us.

Obviously, God's people must line up to His holiness.[1] Holiness is not optional. It is a state that hates sin, and insists on personal righteousness before God. Ultimately, it sets people apart in attitude and conduct, distinguishing them as followers of the true God of heaven.

How is holiness established in our lives? To understand the pattern of personal holiness, we must consider those who were considered holy to God in the Old Testament: the priests. God chose these individuals out of one family, Aaron. He ordained these priests to minister between Him and man. In a sense, they ministered before God in the tabernacle, as well as interceded for others. They represented God to man, and man to God.

Since believers are born into the family of God and serve as the New Testament temple of God, they also make up a lively priesthood to minister before God and stand in the gap for others. The Apostle Peter confirmed this in 1 Peter 2:9, "But ye are a chosen generation, a royal priesthood, an holy nation, a peculiar people; that ye should shew forth the praises of him who hath called you out of darkness into his marvellous light."

---

[1] 1 Peter 1:15-17 (To understand holiness in greater ways, see the author's book, *The Christian Life Series,* Book One, the section entitled, *The Ultimate End to a Matter.*

The High Priest was to maintain the integrity of the priesthood. There was only one man who served in this capacity. For example, Aaron served as the first High Priest until his death. Then, his garments were passed on to his son Eleazar. Once a year, the High Priest would go into the Most Holy Place to offer a sacrifice on behalf of Israel.[2]

Jesus Christ is the one who now serves as the High Priest over the New Testament priesthood. However, He does not serve after the order of the Levitical Priesthood, but of the Melchizedek. There are some important differences between these two priesthoods. The Levitical priesthood had to be passed on, but the priesthood Jesus holds is unchangeable. Only He will hold this priesthood for ages to come. The priests from Aaron had to continually execute their duties. This meant constantly offering up sacrifices and ministering in the Holy Place, by maintaining the bread, oil, and incense. Jesus, who offered the ultimate sacrifice, sat down on the right hand of God, confirming that the work of redemption was completed.[3]

This brings us to the work of holiness. There are two parts to holiness: that of consecration and sanctification. Consecration is man's responsibility in holiness. This means that man separates himself from unholy influences and exposures. Such separation points to total abandonment from that which is unholy in order to become abandoned to God's work and purpose. Once a person separates from the unholy, then he or she must walk out the work of sanctification in his or her life. This also points to a form of consecration, especially in one's lifestyle.

Sanctification is God's part. Each person of the Godhead is involved in this work. For example, God, the Father places a person in the position of sanctification, while Jesus serves as the place of sanctification. Although Christians are positionally sanctified in Christ, they must be established in a state of holiness in attitude and conduct. The Holy Spirit is the one who does the inward work of sanctification by setting a person apart for the sole purpose of God's use and glory.[4] The Apostle Paul makes reference to this in 2 Timothy 2:21, "If a man therefore purge himself from these, he shall be a vessel unto honour, sanctified, and meet for the master's use, and prepared unto every good work."

In order to understand both consecration and sanctification, we must consider the procedures in the lives of the Old Testament priests that distinguish them from the rest of Israel. These procedures were established, so the priests could avoid judgment, while ministering before God. A good example of this judgment can be found in the incident of Aaron's sons when they offered strange fire. God distinctively gave the priests instructions as to what was acceptable to Him. Aaron's sons became flippant about what they offered to Him. They ended up offering

---

[2] Leviticus 16; Numbers 20:23-29
[3] Hebrews 7:11; 9:7-14; 10:11-13
[4] 1 Corinthians 1:2, 30; Hebrews 10:10; 1 Peter 1:2; Jude 1

something strange or perverted to God, which means it was foreign to His nature. His judgment quickly fell upon them, costing them their lives. To reinforce the seriousness of their disrespect, God instructed Aaron not to mourn for them as long as he was executing his duty as High Priest.[5]

Is there any situation where the New Testament priests could experience judgment for not being properly prepared to offer up that which is required before God? The answer is yes. Improper handling of the ordinance of Communion can bring judgment. As a result, Christians must examine themselves as to whether they are prepared to partake of communion.[6]

Every step that the priests executed was a means of preparing themselves to enter into the Holy Place to minister before God. God designed each step. Since God designed these procedures, they served as a means of sanctification. As these priests adhered to each step of sanctification, they were also consecrating or distinguishing themselves as holy or set apart for God's use.

It is important to realize how these priests set themselves apart to fulfill God's plan and purpose for His people. God had established the position of priest to ensure that there would be individuals who possessed the authority to stand in the gap for His people. Ezekiel 22:30 says, "And I sought for a man among them, that should make up the hedge, and stand in the gap before me for the land, that I should not destroy it: but I found none."

We know that very few people are able to stand in the gap. Most people never consider if they are prepared to meet with a Holy God, let alone have the authority to stand in the gap for others. In fact, saints are forever reminded that the only man prepared and capable of standing in the gap was and is Jesus. He is the High Priest who now stands as the only mediator in the courts of heaven between God and man. He has the authority and position to intercede on behalf of His people. No doubt, He has stayed judgment for His people in many ways. Even though Jesus is the ultimate intercessor, saints are still called to make supplication for all saints. They must also be prepared to offer up spiritual sacrifices acceptable to God by Jesus Christ.[7]

To set the priests apart, God designed glorious clothing. This clothing would not only set these individuals apart from nominal religion, but also represent the reality of God and their heavenly mission.

The Apostle Peter talked about the one article that sets apart the New Testament priests in 1 Peter 5:5, "…be subject one to another, and be clothed with humility: for God resists the proud, and giveth grace to the humble." There is nothing as glorious in this arrogant world or in self-

---

[5] Leviticus 10:1-7

[6] 1 Corinthians 11:23-34

[7] Ephesians 6:18; 1 Timothy 2:5; Hebrews 7:25; 1 Peter 2:5

righteous religion as a saint who is clothed in humility. Not only can God exalt this person, but he or she will also edify the Body and stand as a light in this dark world.

There were eight parts to the priest's clothing. The priest's wardrobe was made up of the breastplate with Urim and Thummim, shoulder stones, ephod, a robe with the girdle or belt, girdle of needlework, the broidered coat (linen coat), mitre, golden crown, and linen breeches.[8] "Eight" represents new beginnings. New beginnings point to a new life. It is the evidence of a new life that distinguishes believers from both the world and carnal Christians who still struggle with the flesh and live on the fringes of the world.

The first two objects to be designed were the ephod and girdle of needlework that was upon the ephod.[9] Both were made of gold, blue, purple, scarlet, and fine twined linen. These colors were important in their representation.

"Gold" represented God's divinity. This reminds us that everything must begin with God to ensure separation. He alone determines what is holy. The gold was beaten into thin plates and cut. The beaten gold is symbolic of Jesus' submission as a suffering servant. In fact, Jesus left two examples for His followers: that of servitude and suffering.[10] Servitude points to attitude. This same attitude is developed in Jesus' servants when they become identified with Him in every aspect of their Christian life.

Suffering is the means of maturity or perfection brought forth through faith and obedience. Hebrews 5:8-9 confirms this with Jesus' example, "Though he were a Son, yet learned he obedience by the things which he suffered; And being made perfect, he became the author of eternal salvation unto all them that obey him." Gold also reminds us of Jesus' redemption and how He secured the New Testament priesthood.

The gold was worked in the thread of the ephod and girdle. The picture that is emerging here is how the life of Jesus must be worked into the lives of His saints. It is His life that serves as the source that maintains the believer's well-being. It is also His life in His Church that binds His Body together.

The blue in the different articles was symbolic of the heavenly. This color reminded the priests that their work before God was of a heavenly nature and not of earthly significance. Their work was ordained by God and served as a means to represent Him to man. In order to present this heavenly perspective, they had to separate themselves from the earthly attachments, get beyond the dictates of self, and the demands of the world to gain this perspective.

---

[8] Exodus 29
[9] Exodus 29:5-8
[10] John 13:13-17; 1 Peter 2:21

The color "purple" represented royalty. The Old Testament priests were associated with their future King and Promised Messiah, Jesus Christ. Revelation 1:6 makes this statement about the New Testament priest, "And hath made us kings and priests unto God and his Father; to him be glory and dominion for ever and ever. Amen." The New Testament priests have been translated into a royal state that is headed by the King of kings and the Lord of lords. They make up a kingdom that is eternal and unseen, but can be realized and experienced in the humble heart.

"Scarlet" pointed to humanity and sacrifice. It reminds us that as the Man, Jesus, became the Lamb of God who would take away the sin of the world. The priests had to be covered by their priestly garments, but the saint must be covered by the blood of Jesus to ensure sanctification.[11]

"Fine linen" was symbolic of righteousness. This means a person is considered upright before God. To be upright, New Testament priests must get past self and the world, to follow after righteousness.[12] Righteousness is vital because God can only meet His people at this point.

The next articles that we must consider are the shoulder pieces. They enfolded two onyx stones that bear the names of the children of Israel. Priests were entrusted with burdens. The burden of stones reminded God's representatives that they were not here to represent themselves nor live for themselves. They were here to live for God and represent Him to those they served on His behalf. The other part of this burden is that God is the One who determines the burden and empowers His servants to faithfully fulfill their duties. No doubt the priest was aware of these stones at different times, but these two burdens were equal in weight, and did not hinder him in his responsibilities.

The New Testament priests have one commission that has a two-fold responsibility: To preach the Gospel and make disciples for Christ.[13] Sadly, many Christians refuse to carry these two burdens. They choose burdens that are unrealistic or have no eternal significance. The main reason they fail to shoulder these two burdens is because they do not love God in the way they need to. Therefore, they lack eternal vision.

The next part of the clothing is the breastplate. It is also referred to as the "breastplate of judgment." This breastplate symbolizes the glory and wisdom of God. This article reminds the New Testament priests that they are to bring glory to God through committed, holy service.

Stones were used to keep the names of the tribes of Israel ever before the priests. The two stones in the shoulder pieces hid the names of Israel, while the individual stones with their names were visible. These

---

[11] Hebrews 10:10-14
[12] 1 Timothy 6:11; 2 Timothy 2:22
[13] Matthew 28:18-20; Mark 16:15-16

stones reminded the priest that it was God's people, not works or rituals that were close to His heart. For the New Testament priests, these stones pointed to the fact that they are lively stones that not only make up a holy priesthood, but also are close to God's heart. Another important point about stones was brought out in Revelation 2:17, "He that hath an ear, let him hear what the Spirit saith unto the churches; To him that overcometh will I give to eat of the hidden manna, and will give him a white stone, and in the stone a new name written, which no man knoweth saving he that received it."

There were three parts of the holy garments of linen. Each of these garments pointed to different areas of our lives as Jesus' living priesthood as to where holiness must be in operation to ensure separation unto God. First, there was the broidered coat with the linen girdle. The "coat" represented holiness of heart, while the "linen girdle" represented holiness of service. The "mitre" represented holiness of thought, and the "undergarments", holiness of the flesh. The undergarment was made of fine linen that kept the priest from sweating. This was symbolic of the fact that salvation does not entail personal sweat. Jesus accomplished the complete work of redemption. Zechariah 4:6 puts it in this perspective, "…Not by might, nor by power, but by my Spirit saith the LORD of hosts." Personal sweat in God's kingdom only produces self-righteousness.

This brings us to the crown. There was a banner on the mitre that made this proclamation, *"Holiness to the LORD."* [14] Everything about the priest must be holy. The work of consecration and sanctification would uphold this state in the priest's life.

As you consider these articles, we must note how they started with the outward garments of the priest. Again, we are reminded of how God starts from within and works out, while man begins from outside and works in. It is at the point of Jesus' redemption that both will meet in spirit and fellowship.

Before the priest could put these garments on, he had to be consecrated. He started with the laver. This is true for the New Testament priest. The Word of God is like a washing machine, but before it can cleanse us, we must obey it. Sadly, many believers try to put this life on without being cleansed. As a result, they pervert their life in God, rendering them ineffective. Jesus confirmed this in his example of a person trying to put a piece of new cloth unto an old garment. The garment is made worse, and must be destroyed. [15]

Once the priest was washed, the garments were put upon him. This shows that our life in Christ comes from above. It also points to us putting on the Lord Jesus Christ. The Apostle Paul confirmed this in Romans 13:14, "But put ye on the Lord Jesus Christ, and make no provision for the flesh, to fulfill the lusts thereof."

---

[14] Exodus 28:36; 39:30
[15] Matthew 9:16

After the priest was clothed, a ram was taken and slain. Its blood was applied as a means to set the priest apart.[16] The blood was applied to the priest's ear, thumb, and toe. This application reminds us of the blood of Jesus. When the blood is applied to the ear, we are enabled to hear what the Spirit is saying to carry out God's will. The thumb pointed to service. Service means nothing, unless it is according to God's plan. The toe represented the walk and conduct. Our life must be holy to keep from being considered a hypocrite. To maintain holiness, we must line up to the heart, mind, and will of Jesus Christ.

How about you? Do you understand that your life must be holy? Are you following the pattern of holiness as a New Testament priest, or are you serving the god of this world with your heart, attitudes, and conduct?

---

[16] Exodus 29:19-20

11

THE SHADOW OF REDEMPTION

Although we have been following various patterns, the patterns surrounding the tabernacle present a complete, glorious picture of Jesus. Since this pattern started with the tabernacle, it is clear that God's people must establish a place for Him to dwell within to ensure His presence and communion.

The next pattern has to do with the priest. God's people are chosen to be holy. They are to stand distinct from the world and nominal religion in service and conduct. They must minister to God, and stand as intercessors on behalf of man.

The pattern that follows the priests is the one found in the sacrifices. Sacrifices were the means used to confront and deal with sin, as well as state intentions and devotion towards God. These offerings do not point to nobility, but to the harsh reality of what sin costs, and what must take place for there to be peace between man and God. These sins cost the lives of innocent animals, an act that God did not take pleasure in.[1] Sin costs others who are hurt or robbed by it. It costs man his soul, and most of all, it cost God His Son.

This is why sin is an offense against God. Since He is holy, He cannot tolerate it or look the other way. God had to provide the means by which to satisfy both His holy character and the Law. Such an act was necessary for God to accept man's reaching up to Him in relationship and devotion. To open a way for man to have peace with his Creator, God established sacrifices.

God outlined the type of sacrifices that would be acceptable to Him. They had to be from the best stock. In other words, the sacrifice had to personally cost the one who was offering it. These offerings had to be without blemish and in excellent physical condition.[2] This points to a state of holiness since the sacrifice had to be undefiled. By contrast, the sacrifice had to be the opposite of the offense committed against God.

Sadly, people have an improper concept about sin. Many think that sin is a matter of wrong actions, but it goes deeper. Sin is the essence of man's character. All people are born in a fallen condition. This means they naturally give way to sin, as well as have the tendency to ignore,

---

[1] Hebrews 10:8
[2] Exodus 12:5; 29:1; Leviticus 4:23; Numbers 19:2

cover, up or justify sin. People often walk in deception towards the seriousness or extent of their sin. Their attitudes show contempt towards God and His Law. Spiritually, sin is a blatant affront against God's authority. As a result, sacrifices were instituted to bring a reality check as to how serious sin is. If people were honest in confronting sin as they chose the best substitute for their offense, they would get a glimpse into the depths, costs, and affects of sin.

Unless sin is properly confronted and covered or taken away, there will be no forgiveness or communion with God. In fact, man will hopelessly stand condemned in his sins. There must be a covering that somehow hides sin or a sacrifice that takes it away, so that man can truly come into that place with a Holy God.

Offerings or sacrifices were a means of giving a visible picture of what sin costs. The priests were offering daily sacrifices. Blood flowed and death reigned at the Altar of Burnt Offering. Each sacrifice gave a glimpse into fallen man. Personal sin was being visibly confessed and covered through some of these offerings. Sin ultimately declared that the real consequence of it is separation from life. For man, it is total separation from God.

Separation produces isolation. The greatest cause of isolation for man is vain imaginations. These imaginations come in the form of assumptions, suspicions, and arrogant conclusions. As people give way to these imaginations, they begin to accuse and abuse others, and push people away. After all, sin is self-serving, self-promoting, and arrogant as it claims the right to be rude, inconsiderate, demanding, and self-exalting. It will justify anger, hatred, and unforgiveness, while sacrificing others for its purpose. Since sin is deceptive, it often does these acts in a state of delusion.

At the heart of sin is treachery. In other words, it has no qualms about betraying and sacrificing others for the sake of self. Is it surprising that God would require a sacrifice that was beyond reproach? This sacrifice would be pure instead of treacherous. Although it would cost the life of innocent animals, it would still be a personal cost to the offender, rather than others.[3]

God is forever trying to make sin a personal reality. Due to the pride of people, they become indifferent to personal sin, while crying against the injustice of others' sins. They refuse to see how their sins cost others. Sadly, even what many would consider small infractions that have no significance, such infractions often end up hurting many as the domino effects of sin begin to ripple throughout the fiber of mankind.

This principle was made evident in the case of Achan in Joshua 7. Before the glorious victory at Jericho, the army of Israel was commanded to not take any loot from outside the city's crumbled walls.[4] Nevertheless,

---

[3] Hebrews 9:11-15
[4] Joshua 6:18

Achan's eyes landed on valuable articles. He gave way to the temptation, took the loot, and hid it in his tent. His one simple action brought defeat on Israel, and resulted in his death, along with his family and livestock.

Today, the repercussions of sin vibrate in homes, churches, communities, nations, and the world. It may start out small or insignificant in the eyes of those who justify it, but as Paul stated, "...a little leaven leaveneth the whole lump" (1 Corinthians 5:6).

Sin is a contagious disease of the soul. It invades our perception, making us spiritually dull. It deceives us about our personal condition, making us indifferent towards its work of death in our lives. It operates within the confines of vain imaginations, creating ignorance and superstition towards God. It makes our hearts hard toward truth, our necks stiff with arrogance, and our knees diseased with independence. As a result, man is forever walking in the ways that seem right to him, but they lead to destruction.[5]

As we can see, sin will usually cost others before the offender will taste the bitterness of its consequences. This can be seen in the fact that it cost God dearly. In His holiness, God could not overlook, downplay, or tolerate our sin. He had to provide the means by which our sin would be properly dealt with. We know the story. He provided the ultimate sacrifice.

The animal sacrifices made atonement for sin. This means the shed blood covered the sins. However, God provided a sacrifice that would take away our sins, satisfy the Law, and reconcile man back to Him. This sacrifice came by way of Jesus Christ, the Lamb of God, who took away the sins of the world.[6]

God took it upon Himself to pay for our sin. It cost Him His best. It cost Him something that was not only dear to Him, but also part of Him. It cost Him His Son. It cost Jesus His all, as He offered up His life. On the altar of the cross, Jesus redeemed us with His blood. He gave way to death, so we could receive life. He gave it all, so we could have an eternal inheritance.[7]

It is vital that we see our sin in light of the great cost. It is our tendency to downplay sin in our life, but we must not give way to this tendency. We must learn to hate our sin to ensure that we are sober about confronting it in our own lives. We must overcome our personal sin or we will betray God, cause others to taste the bitterness of our own indifference, and face ultimate judgment.

For the Christian, God provided His Son. However, for Israel, He established different offerings. These offerings would cast a shadow of

---

[5] Proverbs 14:12 (And, if you want to understand how sin works, see the author's book, *The Anatomy of Sin*, in Volume 1 of her foundation series.)

[6] John 1:29; Hebrews 9:26; 10:10-12

[7] Ephesians 1:11-14

the ultimate sacrifice of Jesus. This shadow would give an outline or image of the work Jesus accomplished on the cross. In fact, He served as a completion to all of these sacrifices.[8]

There were five sacrifices. "Five" represents grace. God's grace provided the means by which sin and man's relationship with Him could be honestly confronted. For example, mercy is a product of grace. God actually refrained from showing judgment on sin. Out of mercy comes longsuffering. God will never be tolerant towards sin, but He will be longsuffering towards the sinner. He is not willing that any perish, but that all come to repentance. Therefore, He is longsuffering towards people, giving them ample time to repent.

If man repents, then God is able to bestow on him an act of grace by way of the cross: That of eternal life. The cross is a visible manifestation of grace, while grace is channeled through mercy at the point of repentance. Mercy allows God the opportunity to show His grace through deliverance or salvation, as He gives man space to repent. People who do not understand how sin works will often show contempt towards God by abusing His grace. God shows grace with one goal in mind—to save people. In fact, mercy and judgment came together on the cross to produce the outward evidence of grace that results in eternal life for all who will come to Jesus. To toy with sin, while hiding behind a perverted concept of grace, is to put God to a foolish test.

God's grace is not a ticket or license to do as we desire, but a means that enables a person to do that which is right. We are saved by grace through faith.[9] In other words, grace can only be discovered through the response of faith. Until faith activates the revelation of grace, this virtue of God's longsuffering silently gives people the gift of time to make things right. Ultimately, it gives them the space to find Him, reach their potential, and experience His life. Everything about grace comes down to God wanting His people to discover real life and purpose in Him.

It is important to see Jesus in these sacrifices. Each sacrifice addresses certain aspects of our lives that sin clearly disrupts and destroys. Ultimately, these sacrifices unveil Christ and reveal how complete His work of redemption was on our behalf. All five of these sacrifices are thoroughly discussed in the first six chapters of *Leviticus*. These offerings are the burnt offering, meal offering, peace offering, sin offering, and trespass offering.

There were two types of sacrifices: The voluntary and mandatory sacrifices. God required the mandatory sacrifices, while the voluntary offerings pointed to devotion, intent, and desire of the one who offered the sacrifice.

---

[8] Hebrews 9:11-14

[9] Ephesians 2:8 (If you would like to learn more about grace see the author's book, the *Christian Life Series,* Book One, the section entitled, *It is a Matter of Grace.*

The first types of offering we are going to consider are the mandatory offerings: the trespass and sin offerings. The trespass offerings addressed the sins that trespassed or broke God's Law or covenant. They pointed to the treachery of man that had defied the authority and rule of God.[10] This often meant that the person knowingly trespassed into forbidden areas. Trespass offerings were also offered in cases such as concealed sins, of touching unclean things, and even for sins done in ignorance.

Jesus paid the price for all of our trespasses on the cross. His blood was shed to cleanse us from all unrighteousness. This reality is the foundation of our salvation. It is because of Jesus' sacrifice that we can be forgiven, regardless of how much we have trespassed the Law, which reveals how rebellious man shows utter contempt towards God

The next offering was the sin offering. This offering also pointed to Jesus' death on the cross. He fulfilled both of these offerings when He offered His own body. Although these offerings were mandatory, Jesus' death on the cross was a choice. His sacrifice finished what the other sacrifices could not accomplish.[11]

The trespass offering dealt with man's rebellious actions, but the sin offering addressed man's fallen, unregenerate disposition. It was the condition of sin and death operating within man that separated him from His Creator. This condition is expressed in outward actions of rebellion.

The blood of the sin offering was applied to the horns of the Altar of Burnt Offering. The rest of the blood and fat of the animal were poured at the bottom of the altar, and the bullock burned outside of the gate. Once a year, on the Day of Atonement, the priest would offer up the sin offering of a goat on behalf of Israel. He would apply the blood to the horns of the Altar of Incense and then carry the rest of it into the Most Holy Place. The priest also took another goat and laid all of the sins of Israel upon it. This scapegoat was then taken into the wilderness where it was left.

Jesus Christ served as our sin offering. His blood was applied to the altar of the cross. This all took place outside of the camp or gate where He paid the complete price for our redemption. As the scapegoat, all our sins were laid upon Him. He was then laid in the barren place of the grave where He was left.[12] Hebrews 9:12 tells us that by His blood, He entered the Holy Place.

It was not just the outward sin of humanity that cost Jesus. Man's fallen condition required Him to become the ultimate scapegoat. He would be the One who would bear every sin in His body. It is hard for people to make sin a matter of an inward condition, rather than just an outward manifestation. The reason for this is because they can conform

---

[10] Leviticus 5; Hosea 6:7
[11] Leviticus 4; Hebrews 10:9-21
[12] 2 Corinthians 5:21; Hebrews 13:10-13

the outward man, but they are void of the power to change the inward man. Jesus had to become the sin offering for man, in order for man to be made in the righteousness of God.[13]

The next offerings we are going to consider are the voluntary offerings. These offerings were not required like the mandatory offerings, but were to be offered up with other sacrifices to show the validity of man's intentions and commitment towards God. As a result, they were to be freely offered up to signify consecration, blessings, and devotions for the glory of God. The first offering we will consider is the burnt offering.[14] Aaron, the High Priest, had to offer this offering for himself to be consecrated as priest. The burnt offering had to be washed, showing the complete cleansing or separation. This separation pointed to consecration. Consecration is when something is set apart for God's use and glory. In the case of Aaron, he was setting himself apart to become God's priest.

The burnt offering served as a perpetual offering. In fact, each of the voluntary offerings represented a perpetual sacrifice before God. Such offerings were not offered solely for the purpose of man, but also for the good pleasure of God. These offerings were consumed by fire. Fire represented judgment upon sin to produce that which is holy and acceptable to God. Therefore, the fire was symbolic of all residues of sin being properly judged and destroyed, so that God could receive the offering. For example, the smoke that was released from the burnt offering served as a sweet savor to God. God not only accepted this type of savor, but it brought pleasure to Him.

As New Testament priests, we must present our bodies as the offering. Our lives must first be cleansed by the washing of the Word and consumed by the reality of Jesus Christ.[15] This is the way Christians consecrate themselves to God. They must abandon their own life to embrace the new. Such a life points to the old man giving way to the transforming work of the Spirit, while being consumed by the revelation of the Person of Jesus.

Consecration is necessary to seek and do God's will. Jesus set His life apart to do the Father's bidding. He did nothing unless the Father ordained it. In the end, He submitted His total will and being to the Father by allowing Himself to be offered up on the cross.[16] Therefore, consecration always leads to self-denial and the cross. Ultimately God's will, will be done, bringing Him deserved glory.

The meal offering was where the first fruits were dedicated and offered up to God.[17] The priests were required to pour a mixture of fine

---

[13] 2 Corinthians 5:21
[14] Leviticus 1
[15] Romans 12:1-2; Ephesians 5:26
[16] John 5:19; Philippians 2:6-8
[17] Leviticus 2

flour, oil, and frankincense on the offering. This offering was considered the most holy to the Lord that was made by fire. The possible reasoning behind it is that this offering had nothing to do with man. It was devoid of man's spiritual condition.

The wafer had to be unleavened, pointing to the Bread of life that came down from heaven, Jesus Christ. The Bread of heaven was without sin. This bread had to be seasoned with salt that served as a covenant. The salt pointed to the risen Christ who established an everlasting covenant. Salt also implied authority or the ability to make an impact. The reason Christians have authority is because of the New Testament covenant that was brought forth through Jesus' redemption.[18]

The meal offering was to serve as a memorial. A memorial is a way of remembering God's greatness, intervention, and His abiding work among His people. For Christians, the ordinance of Communion serves as an ongoing memorial.[19]

In the burnt offering, the smoke served as a sweet fragrance to God. After all, the fire had consumed all residues of sin. In the meal offering, it is the frankincense that reaches the throne of God. This sweet-smelling fragrance draws because of its purity and attracts because of the beauty it represents, pleasing God and honoring Him.

For the Christian, our sweet fragrance is the life of Jesus coming forth. Jesus is the firstfruits of every devoted believer. His life coming forth honors God, edifies the Church, and serves as a mirror to the unsaved. Needless to say, this points to a life of service. As Christians, we cannot serve unless we have come to terms with sin and consecrated ourselves totally to God. A visible memorial, or reminder of Jesus Christ in our lives, will come out of unfeigned service. His presence will verify that we have partaken of His nature. If Jesus' life is present, God requires that this life be offered up to Him and imparted to others.[20]

The meal offering reminds us of the ordinance of Communion, but when you put the voluntary offerings together, a pattern emerges about what it requires to be in communion with God. The burnt offering reveals that you must first examine self to ensure that there is nothing standing in the way between you and God. The meal offering requires you to remember who you are honoring, and the final offering represents the product of communion: that of peace.

The mandatory offerings were symbolic of the work of redemption. The voluntary offerings pointed to the purpose of redemption: To establish a life in God that will bring Him glory.

The burnt offering was totally consumed by fire, producing a smoke that pleased God. After all, nothing remained of the old man, thereby allowing God to accept such a sacrifice.

---

[18] Matthew 5:13; John 6:32-35; Hebrews 4:15; 9:15-18
[19] 1 Corinthians 11:23-33
[20] 2 Corinthians 2:15-16; 2 Peter 1:4

In the meal offering, the fire produced a fragrance that pleased God. This fragrance was pure, and had no indications that man had any influence in it other than to offer it to God for His good pleasure. This fragrance pointed to the life of Jesus in us.

In the peace offering, fire was applied once again to the sacrifice. This time, it was applied to the fat. All the fat of this particular offering belonged to God.[21] Fat pointed to the strength of man, but it also pointed to the inward part of man, his affections. In this offering, we see where all personal strength must be submitted to God, and all affections must be directed towards Him. Therefore, God will serve as our strength, as well as hold all of our loyalties and allegiance.

The reason personal strength must be submitted to God is because it serves as a place of reliance for us and a point of contention with God. To have peace with God, we must submit all points of strength to the Holy Spirit, to ensure complete dependency on God. Dependency of this nature comes down to putting our faith in Him, believing His Word, trusting His guidance, and walking in obedience and confidence according to His ways.

Affections that are not directed totally at God will produce divided loyalties and idolatry. God is a jealous God.[22] He will not share our hearts or devotion with another god. He alone must be God. Needless to say, this type of division causes strife in our relationship with God.

For the Christian, the peace offering pointed to the reconciliation wrought by the cross of Jesus. However, reconciliation is far from those who are striving with God due to personal reliance and misdirected loyalties. This is why the fire must be put to the strength and affections of our lives. The fire will allow a person to give way to the work of the Holy Spirit. Personal strength will be replaced with the Holy Ghost's power, and affections with resolution and authority. It is the Spirit's work of sanctification that will make us acceptable to God.

Reconciliation walks hand in hand with the peace of God. It points to fellowship. It was Jesus on the cross who closed the gap between man and God. As a result, Jesus is the One who serves as the Prince of Peace.[23] Therefore, it is not what we have done that brings peace between our Creator and us. Rather, it is what Christ accomplished on the cross. However, we can only receive this peace in humility.

Are you striving in your spiritual life? Follow the pattern of redemption. It begins with confronting sin and looking to Jesus to solve the problem. Once you come to terms with God's provision of His Son, you need to consecrate yourselves in order to give way to the life of Jesus. It is His life that bridges the gap between man and God. Once you come into a right relationship with God, you will have inner peace of the

---

[21] Leviticus 3:15-16

[22] Exodus 20:5

[23] John 14:27; Colossians 1:20

soul.[24] Keep in mind that consecration first requires you to offer your body as a sacrifice. You must partake of the Bread of life, allow the risen life of Christ to impact others with His truth and grace, cease from striving against the Holy Spirit, and submit to the fire. If you do, the life of Christ in you will become the fragrance that will please God and bring honor to His name.

---

[24] Matthew 5:9

12

SET APART FOR HIS WORK

We have been considering the pattern surrounding the tabernacle. There are five significant patterns to examine to receive a balanced picture of the complete life in Christ. As you study these patterns, you can see that the purpose of these designs was a means of establishing a state of holiness in God's people. Out of this state of holiness, righteousness would be defined and the end result would be a godly representation of Jehovah God. For the Christians, this godly representation manifests itself in godliness.

The purpose of establishing this representation in the Old Testament was to bring a distinction between Israel and paganism in the midst of grave ignorance about God. The presentation of the children of Israel's God was to bring a contrast between Jehovah God and the many idols that dotted the dark reality of paganism.

This contrast between God and paganism exposed the emphasis of the attitude and practices that revealed much about the identity and nature of Israel's God and the silent idols. For example, Jehovah God's dwelling place was a tent that was unattractive to the naked eye. It was simple in outward presentation, but inwardly, it was adorned with beauty beyond description. The temples of the pagans were often adorned with the beauty of the world, but they stood dead spiritually as followers exercised idolatry. The tabernacle represented to believers the type of character within a person that determines his or her attitudes towards that which is being worshipped.

Another area of contrast was the priest. The pagan priests might be in elaborate dress, but their real display of devotion or show of penance was through show of suffering and penance, such as cutting themselves, while inwardly, they contained the dark ways of death and destruction. The priests of Jehovah God wore clothing that pointed to His holy character. However, the real point of piousness in their lives was not displayed by suffering. Rather, it was by inward cleansing of heart and mind. Inward piousness was upheld by separation that clearly could be seen in dress, conduct, and attitude. For the Christian, it simply means we are to put on the Lord Jesus Christ.[1]

---

[1] Romans 13:14

The sacrifices or offerings were distinct as well. For Israel, they had to be without spot and blemish. All of the firstborn and firstfruits automatically belonged to God.[2] In other words, sacrifices came from the best the children of Israel had to offer. It showed them that God was the provider and deserved the best to ensure integrity and purity in sacrifices. After all, the sacrifices addressed sin or showed devotion and desire in regard to God. These sacrifices not only dealt with the different aspects of the children of Israel's spiritual lives, but also allowed them to enjoy the gift of life and the freedom to worship God. Such enjoyment brought true rest to their souls and pleasure to God. It is in this environment that there was peace, life, and the freedom to properly worship God.

Pagan sacrifices had to do with a means to show piousness or obtain favor. These gods were creations erected in the minds of people or constructed with their hands. Pagans simply worship the creation rather than the Creator.[3] In some of these pagan beliefs, superstition was so great and sinister that people lived in a world of dreaded fear and tormenting oppression. Whenever deviance occurred in the area of their superstition, harsh consequences could be administered. Human sacrifice was not an unusual means to appease an "angry god."

The sacrifices that Jehovah God instituted, as well as the place and the procedures in which they were to be offered, prevented idolatry. God's heart was to prepare and keep His chosen people distinct from those around them, so that He could bless them. His people would also be a representation of light in the midst of great darkness. This distinction pointed to holiness.

This brings us to the next stage of establishing holiness among His people. The tabernacle was erected, the priest prepared, and the sacrifices designated, but it still was incomplete. The tabernacle was established, but it sat silent. The priests were ready, but they were in limbo. The sacrifices were marked, but remained still. What was missing? The presence and power of God were still missing. Without His presence and power, there was no substance.

It is the presence of God that makes the ultimate distinction in His people. However, before God could grace the tabernacle with His presence and power, everything had to be set apart by anointing it with special anointing oil.[4] Jesus summarized the purpose of anointing in Luke 4:18-19:

> The Spirit of the Lord is upon me, because he hath anointed me to preach the gospel to the poor; he hath sent me to heal the brokenhearted, to preach deliverance to the captives, and recovering of sight to the blind, to set at liberty

---

[2] Exodus 13:2; Deuteronomy 15:19; 26:10
[3] Romans 1:20-25
[4] Exodus 30:22-33

them that are bruised, To preach the acceptable year of the Lord.

Isaiah 10:27 talked about how the anointing breaks the yoke of oppression. As you consider these two scriptures, you begin to realize that anointing pointed to the work of God. It is only as God is given liberty to work in and among His people that there will be healing, deliverance, restoration, and liberty.

The anointing sets people apart for God's purpose. The very nature of anointing also reveals that it can only come from God. Sadly, people touch God's glory by taking personal credit for this anointing. They glory in it as they perceive it as God showing favoritism to them.

Another important representation of the anointing oil pointed to separation unto God. It designated something or someone for His purpose, use, and glory. For example, the tabernacle with all of its furnishings and the priests were anointed. The anointing stipulated that these vessels and objects belonged to God, and must be used for His service. Such a separation pointed to sanctification. What has not been sanctified does not belong to God.

To understand the significance behind anointing, all you have to consider is the purpose of the tabernacle, the priests, and the sacrifices. The tabernacle represented fellowship with God. Do you realize that fellowship with God results in healing? However, the priests were powerless to do what was required by and acceptable to God unless anointed. By being anointed, they had power and authority in their service before God, and in their intercession on behalf of the people. Sacrifices that do not have the approval of God will not bring forgiveness, restoration, and liberty. Therefore, everything had to be anointed, including the tabernacle, furnishings, priests, and even certain sacrifices before God could ensure His presence and power among His people.

It is not enough to be prepared to stand distinct through acts of consecration where you would be separated from the unholy. You must be separated unto God through sanctification. To signify that something was sanctified unto God, anointing oil was used to seal the article or person. As Christians, we know that we have such a seal. The Holy Ghost serves as the seal to an eternal inheritance. He is the one who brings the anointing to the believer's life, while His heart and work are to designate God's people for His use and glory as vessels and instruments.[5]

In order to understand the purpose of anointing, we must consider the makeup of this oil which involved four spices: myrrh, sweet cinnamon, sweet calamus, and cassia.[6] The number "four" points to the function of the world, but when you include the fifth ingredient of oil, you have the number "five", which points to grace. Therefore, the number

---

[5] Ephesians 1:11-14; 1 John 2:20, 27
[6] Exodus 30:23-24

four reminds us of the work Jesus did on the cross on behalf of man. This work took place on earth. It was complete, signifying that His redemption encompasses the four corners of the world. Even though this work was accomplished on earth, it was an act of grace on God's part. Without grace freely offering salvation, redemption would mean nothing.

Grace can be seen in these Old Testament patterns. Often when people consider the Old Testament, they fail to see His grace. When they consider the New Testament, they fail to see His holiness and commandments. You cannot understand grace unless you do so in light of God's holiness and judgment. The necessity of seeing grace in this light is because many fail to see the need for it. In fact, many people hide behind grace, but few properly apply it to their lives. Applying grace means seeing both the spiritual poverty and the desperate need for salvation. Grace is applied when God's provision for salvation is properly embraced by faith.

Sadly, in some arenas, grace is missing or abused because spiritual work often becomes self-centered instead of Christ-centered. It becomes about man's attempts, instead of God's work. Yet, without the application of God's grace, man remains miserably lost and hopeless.

The spices in the anointing oil pointed to Jesus. In fact, they give us insight into His character and work. Like Jesus, these spices also had healing qualities that brought restoration. They also came from different regions of the world. This represented the reality that God's intervention and work are not limited to one group of people or area, but are universal in nature.[7]

These spices came from a variety of plants, showing that if God sets something apart for His work it stands unique. Although the Church is made up of various people, each individual stands unique in God's sight, no matter what his or her background may be.

Another important aspect of these spices is that they had to go through a process to be used. Jesus went by way of the cross, so that His Spirit would produce an abundant life that could make you and me whole. Christians have to go through a process in order to be brought to spiritual maturity. It is a hard, trying process to deny the existence of the former life, to embrace a new life with an eternal purpose.

The anointing oil encouraged the presence of God in the midst of His people. With this in mind, let us now consider the uniqueness of these different ingredients. The first ingredient was myrrh. This word comes from a word meaning "bitter." It is actually extracted from a gum that comes from the stem of a tree. This tree grows in Arabia and East Africa. It is low, thorny, and ragged. As you consider this tree, it would have no

---

[7] Much of the representation and information about these spices were obtained from Ruth Specter Lascelle's book, God's Dwelling Place, pgs. 343-345

real attraction. This was indicative of Jesus on the cross who had no form or comeliness that was attractive to the naked eye.[8]

Although myrrh is sweet, it tastes bitter. The bitterness is symbolic of the bitter cup Jesus had to partake of that became sweet to us as believers. The Christian life is glorious, but it is also intertwined with harshness that crushes believers and brings them to low points of bitterness. Again, bitterness allows us to taste and enjoy the sweetness of Jesus and His Word. In fact, John said of God's words, that they were sweet to his mouth, but bitter to his stomach.[9]

The sweetness of Jesus must be real, so that His people can present this sweetness of heaven to others. When people encounter Jesus, it can prove to become sweet to the seeking heart or bitter to those who are rebellious.

Myrrh was brought to Jesus by the wise men and was used in preparation for his burial.[10] Obviously, myrrh was worthy of a king. It was used not only to purify, but also to designate. The example that Jesus gives us is that there cannot be the sweetness of life or the new birth until there is separation that comes by way of death. Many Christians are surface and weak in their faith because they refuse to taste the bitterness of identification through death, to embrace the sweetness of life. Have you experienced this purification and sweetness?

The next ingredient is sweet cinnamon. This spice comes from the bark of a small evergreen tree. This tree grows in Ceylon and the islands of the Indian Ocean. Evergreen is one of the trees that never change color, regardless of the seasons. Such character points to Jesus who never changes, no matter what the circumstances.[11]

The actual bark of the tree pointed to erect, as in "upright rolls." Apparently, this bark could be rolled up and stood in an upright position. Jesus, as man, stood upright in the midst of depraved humanity. He was lifted above all on the cross, and three days later, the grave had to give way to His resurrection power.

Cinnamon was used for favoring. It also emitted a fragrance that counteracted the stench of the sacrifices in the tabernacle. After all, there is a smell to death. The stench pointed to sin-laden man enfolded in a death sentence, but the fragrance pointed to the resurrected Christ, standing distinct, anointed, and erect in man. It is Jesus' life in us that counteracts the reality of sin, death, and decay. He is the only source that will bring flavor to our lives and emit a sweet fragrance.[12] Can this flavor and fragrance be identified in you?

---

[8] Isaiah 53:2
[9] Matthew 20:22-23; Revelation 10:9-10
[10] Matthew 2:11; John 19:39
[11] Hebrews 13:8
[12] 2 Corinthians 2:15-16

The next ingredient used was sweet calamus. This spice comes from a cane that is highly prized. It grows in the miry soil in Arabia and India. It comes from a word meaning "to stand upright." In His humanity Christ grew up in the miry soil of earth, and stood upright by remaining sinless in the midst of the miry condition of fallen man. He was not influenced by the muddy waters of fleshly compromise, or sucked down into the quagmire of this world. He was not dirtied by the muddy filth of man's anger, hatred, and self-righteousness.[13] He stood upright, in spite of all that He encountered. As a result, He is able to give eternal life to those who come to Him. This should make Him highly prized by all people, but sadly, they trod underfoot His work and invitation in rebellion, mockery, and rejection.

Jesus' followers have the same means to stand apart from the influence of self and the world by the power of the Holy Ghost. Like Jesus, they will also experience the same type of rejection from those who belong to this present age.[14]

The more the bark of the cane was beaten, the sweeter the fragrance it produced. Christ greatly suffered on our behalf, but great were the deliverance, healing, and fragrance that came forth from His suffering and death. If Jesus truly becomes our passion or prized possession, storms, challenges, and persecutions of life will make Him sweeter to us and in us.

Cassia was the next ingredient used. This spice comes from a root word meaning "to split." The concept of splitting refers to rolls being split to retain this spice. This spice comes from a shrub that grows in various parts of the east. It only grows at the great heights of 8000 feet elevation above sea level. Needless to say, this plant flourishes where other plants would never grow. This reminds us that Christ was lifted up by the height of the cross for all to see. From this barren point, He produced fruits unto eternal life. No other person or being could flourish at the point of the cross. It meant finality for mere man. However, Jesus was no mere man, He was and is God Incarnate.

The cassia was bitter to taste, but used as a means to purge man for the purpose of healing. There is no doubt that man must be purged, and anything that would be pure would initially become bitter and unacceptable to him. Christ tasted the bitterness of the cross, the grave, and death, to bring spiritual healing and wholeness to man. However, this wholeness is not possible until each person is willing to taste the bitterness of total identification with Jesus. It is God's heart to see us taste such bitterness, so we can walk in complete wholeness before Him.

This spice also reminds us that all great things come from above. James 1:17 confirms this, "Every good gift and every perfect gift is from above, and cometh down from the Father of lights, with whom is no variablenes, neither shadow of turning." Sadly, man looks within or

---

[13] Hebrews 4:15
[14] John 16:18-20

around for great things, but how many of us look beyond the pinnacles of man, the heights of religion, and the mountains of this world to find and see God's incredible works and gifts? Are you walking in holiness because you have embraced the life from above?

The final product is pure olive oil. It took six quarts of oil to produce the right combination of anointing oil. The number "six" points to imperfect man, but he can be made distinct by the presence of the unchanging Christ. Jesus' work pointed to redemption, and the bitterness of His suffering symbolized the sweetness of life. His life in us represents the only fragrance that will be considered sweet and acceptable to God.[15]

The four spices had to be mixed with the oil. The oil served as a catalyst to bring these ingredients together. Without the oil, the spices remained unique, but had no anointing quality. The oil was vital in many ways. It lubricated, healed, energized, and aided in giving light. All the spices pointed to Jesus' humanity and work on earth, but the oil pointed to the Spirit bringing the life and work of Jesus together within His Body, the Church.

It was the Holy Spirit who anointed Jesus, and who continues to anoint His followers.[16] He serves as the oil for the light and the fire in the hearts of believers. He distributes gifts, and brings forth healing and restoration. For example, "myrrh" represents the Holy Spirit working through Christ, while the Christian serves as His instrument to bring about eternal results.

Cinnamon counteracted the stench of the sacrifice. This represented Christ as the sacrifice with the sweetness of the Holy Ghost. It is the Holy Ghost who attracts others to the Lamb of God.

Sweet calamus is symbolic of the fact that it is the Holy Spirit who anointed both the Man, Christ Jesus, and anoints the believers to go forth in power. This anointing enables people to do the will of God.

Cassia represented Calvary towering above all other religious attempts. It also pointed to the baptism of the Holy Spirit from above. It is the Father who sends this gift of the Spirit, but it is Jesus who baptizes a believer with the Spirit to carry out His commission. It is important for Christians to realize that all they need to live this life can only be obtained from above.

In conclusion, without the anointing of the life of Christ and the seal and power of the Holy Ghost, no Christian will stand distinct or make an impact on others. What about you? Do you have this powerful combination of the spices (the life and work of Jesus) and the oil (the Holy Ghost), or are you like the five foolish virgins in Matthew 25:1-13? They lacked both the life of Christ and the fire of the Holy Spirit.

---

[15] 2 Corinthians 2:15-16
[16] John 1:32-34; Luke 4:18-19

13

PATTERN FOR LIFE

We have been dealing with the patterns of the Old Testament. Each pattern represented different aspects of the Christian life. Each model showed how Jehovah God and His people were distinct among the pagan nations. God designed each pattern as a means of sanctification. These patterns not only set His people apart from the unholy, but also revealed the complete life that is found in Him. For example, the tabernacle pointed to fellowship. It outlined God working from within through transformation, while man works from the outside by way of sacrifice and cleansing.

The priests represented ministry. It showed how they were consecrated to stand in the gap by ministering before God and interceding on behalf of man. Their dress and cleansing revealed total abandonment to God for His purpose.

Sacrifices revealed man's sin and God's provision. They served as a means for making atonement for man, so that he could stand acceptable before God. These sacrifices were designated to ensure forgiveness and create a memorial. Their purpose was to ensure reconciliation.

The anointing oil was symbolic of healing, deliverance, restoration, and liberty. It pointed to wholeness of the soul. It also was a form of sanctification. Whatever the oil touched, it was set apart for God's use and purpose. This ensured the abiding presence of God. It is being in the presence of God that produces fellowship, effective ministry, cleansing, and anointing. Together, this combination summarizes an effective relationship with God.

The final pattern that we will consider is found in the Holy Perfume.[1] Just as the tabernacle pointed to fellowship, the priests to ministry, the sacrifices to reconciliation, and the anointing oil to wholeness, the perfume represented two more aspects about the Christian life.

The first meaning of the perfume pointed to new life coming forth. Before the anointing oil was applied, the tabernacle stood lifeless, the priests idle, and the sacrifices devoid of meaning. The tabernacle, priests, and sacrifices had no significance until God's presence came down to sanctify all that He ordained. God is life, and only He can give

---

[1] Exodus 30:34-38

life to that which He calls forth. The type of life or quality of life is based on the quality of a person's relationship with God.

Life points to Jesus' ministry. He is the way, the truth, and the life.[2] The first two patterns of the tabernacle and priests pointed to Jesus as the way. After all, the tabernacle reminded us of the way to fellowship, while the priests represented the way of prayer that leads to intercession and worship.

The sacrifices pointed to Jesus as the truth. They showed man's hopeless depravity in light of God's holy character. They also revealed God's desire to restore man back into fellowship, but man often rejects it because of his arrogance, ignorance, and delusion. As you study sacrifices in light of the cross, this wooden object becomes the pivotal point of all truth. This truth is summarized in the word "hope." The hope of man rests solely on coming back to the Father, and Jesus is the only bridge to this relationship. He is the only way of salvation and rest for the wandering, lost soul.

The last two patterns of the anointing oil and perfume symbolized Jesus as the life. There are five distinct patterns related to the tabernacle. Once again we are reminded that the number "five" points to grace. The life of Christ in us is the work of grace. Everything God does in regards to man's redemption is an act or an extension of the incredible favor He desires to bestow on man.

God's life only comes out of anointing. When the yoke of bondage is broken, healing, restoration, and liberty can take place.[3] For this life to come forth, the old must be done away with, so that the new can be resurrected. The anointing brings liberty, so the new life can be brought forth in power and glory.

The perfume actually represented the new life coming forth. And, what a life! There are four ingredients in the Holy Perfume. They are stacte, onycha, galbanum, and frankincense. Each of these ingredients is a spice, but frankincense at this stage is no longer a spice, but a perfume that is pure in content. The three spices represented the Godhead.[4] The sweetness that God brings to our lives when He reigns in them in authority, power, and glory is beyond description. It is made obvious by His love, revealed by His grace, and experienced in communion. The perfume also pointed to the work of the third Person of the Godhead, the Holy Spirit. He is the One who combines the character, mind, and work of Jesus with the means to transform Jesus' Church into the Lord's image.

---

[2] John 14:6

[3] Luke 4:18; 24:49; Acts 1:8; 2 Corinthians 3:17-18

[4] The majority of my information about the representation and location of these spices was taken from the book, A Dwelling Place For God, By Ruth Specter Lascelle, pgs. 347-348

The measure of these four ingredients is equal. Equal measurements symbolize equal standing before God. He is not partial, and at the cross, each humble person stands equal, as redemption is made available to all who come, seeking hope, forgiveness, and life. This life produces a fragrance that will reach the throne of God. 2 Corinthians 2:15 states, "For we are unto God a sweet savour of Christ, in them that are saved, and in them that perish."

Like the ingredients in the anointing oil, the ingredients of the Holy Perfume came from a variety of sources. Again, we are reminded about the diversity that God uses to bring forth His work and uniqueness in Jesus' Body. God so desires to use each of us. He clearly knows how to bring forth the fragrance of Jesus in us.

It is also important to point out that this perfume was used on the Altar of Incense.[5] This altar reminded us that our life is about service that involves ministry before God and ministry on behalf of man. The Altar of Incense is also representative of the fact that the life of Christ is ongoing, as long as there are holy fire and incense. God's people can stop His life any time by putting out the fire with sin, personal agendas, and self exalting goodness. When the fire goes out, the fragrance will cease because it will cease to be about Jesus. Obviously, the Christian life should be all about Jesus.

The first ingredient in the perfume was stacte. This spice came from a gum of a storax or balsam tree found in the East. The spice was formed from a substance that oozes forth spontaneously from a growing tree. We are reminded of how Jesus' blood came forth out of His side and continues to cleanse those who are seeking its flowing virtues at the cross from all unrighteousness.[6]

Cleansing allows those who have obtained forgiveness to walk in the light, enjoying fellowship with God and others. This is how the Christian life is expressed. It also allows one the boldness to come to the throne of grace to seek mercy because of Jesus' work on the cross.[7]

Stacte spontaneously came forth in a growing tree. The tree had to be healthy. Its spontaneity pointed to the second representation of this perfume: that of worship. Godly fellowship and ministry are a form of worship. Real worship can only come out of a living Body, the Church. A living Church is identified by spiritual growth. Spiritual growth will take place where aspects of Jesus' characteristics are being perfected in a person's life. It is all about Jesus.

Life that is about Jesus becomes a form of worship that is acceptable to God. We are here to worship God in such a way that it will bring Him glory. Such worship will be natural, spontaneous, and free flowing. Does your worship display such characteristics?

---

[5] Exodus 31:11

[6] 1 John 1:9

[7] Hebrews 4:15

Onycha comes from a crab that lives in the depth of the Red Sea, and is also found in the Indian Ocean. The crab actually had to give up its life to be part of the perfume. This reminds us that like Jesus, we must give up our right to self or our present life to be an effective part of God's kingdom. Self-denial allows the life of Jesus to be worked in and expressed through each of us. Such self-denial results in obedience and worship, ultimately bringing God glory.

This spice increases the fragrance of other perfumes and serves as the base for perfumes in the East Indies. We know that Jesus gave up His life, and He now serves as the base or foundation for our spiritual lives.[8] He is the source behind all that is precious and beautiful in His Church. Since this spice comes from a crab in the depths of the Red Sea, it also pointed to the fact that believers' level of commitment must be sincere. Sincerity comes from the depths of a person's heart. The reality of Jesus must reach greater depths into our being to bring us higher. We can witness this sincerity and depth of Jesus' heart on the cross. He so loved He gave. He reached out to everyone in an equal manner. He allowed His heart to be broken, so that life could flow from His very side.

Christianity is a matter of the heart. Jesus' life must go deep into our beings, so it can become a visible expression of Him in us. We can only worship God from the depths of a sincere heart. It must be personal and real with God. How deep does your Christian commitment go? Your fruits will tell on you.[9]

Galbanum is a gum resin from two Persian plants. These plants are related to the carrot family. This spice actually comes from the juice of a shrub that grows in Arabia, Persia, and Africa. First, we have a spice that spontaneously comes forth from a growing tree. Next, we have a spice that comes from a crab. Now, we have a spice that comes from the juice of a shrub that is related to a vegetable. All of these spices represent some form of movement or life. Movement points to both process and growth.

In order to bring galbanum forth as a spice, the leaves of the plant had to be crushed. As Christians, we must be crushed to experience the Christian life. This process reminds us that to ensure God's nearness, we must have a broken heart and a contrite spirit.[10] Real life only comes out of brokenness and contrition that symbolize humility. Christ walked in meekness and humility right to the cross. For the Christian, humility must be present to produce real worship. Is there humility in your life, or are you walking in pride and self-confidence? If so, the life of Christ will never come forth.

---

[8] 1 Corinthians 3:11
[9] Matthew 7:20
[10] Psalm 34:18; 51:17

Frankincense is the last ingredient. It comes from a tree that grows abundantly in India. As stated, it is also a spice, but in this case, it is in perfume form, and used to combine all of the other ingredients. This shows us that, as believers, we must begin with the reality of the One who serves as our perfume, Jesus Christ.

Frankincense is an important aromatic gum, and is regarded by itself to be a precious perfume. Do you regard Jesus in this manner? He so much wants to impart His life so that we may experience a complete life. However, is He precious enough that you will sell all to gain Him?

The actual symbolism of frankincense is that of white or pure. This refers to the free-flowing, liberal giving forth of its fragrance. Is this not the way of Christ's life in us? It is pure, free-flowing, and giving. Is this not what the new life in us should be towards others as well?

As open vessels, Jesus' life should be pure and flowing freely in us, through us, and out of us. The secret of its preciousness is that it is coming from a pure heart, and it is benevolent and giving. After all, it is Jesus' life and not ours. No person has the right to maintain or keep Jesus' life to him or herself.

The tree has to be pierced in order to extract the frankincense from it. Jesus was pierced, and what came forth was both water and blood. These serve as a witness to the validity of what Jesus accomplished. The Holy Spirit is the One who confirms the witness of this water and blood, as well as makes it a revelation to the hearts of men.[11]

Saints are also born of the water of the Word and of the Spirit. The blood of Jesus cleanses them.[12] This is necessary for a person to enter the kingdom of heaven. Being born of water and of Spirit will identify believers to Jesus and His redemption. Ultimately, Jesus must be our focus, passion, and pursuit.

Frankincense is also used as a medicine and an antidote to poison. Jesus is the antidote to the perversion, poison, and death caused by sin, the world, and Satan.

Predominate in the frankincense flower is the number five. It has five petals and stamens. Its fruit is five-sided, and there are five spices that come from it. Once again, the number "five" points to grace. Grace is predominate and all-encompassing in salvation. If you understand the significance of grace, it will produce humility and worship.

As Christians, we need to worship God in purity, praise Him for salvation, and be in awe of His beauty and holiness. We need to possess Jesus' life to offer up an acceptable fragrance to Him. Experiencing Jesus' life will cause us to rejoice over His beauty, as we allow His fragrance to flow through our life in fellowship, service, and worship. In the end, God will be glorified.

---

[11] 1 John 5:6
[12] John 3:5; 1 John 1:7

A final note, gold, myrrh, and frankincense were brought to Jesus by the three wise men.[13] Some have questioned why these three gifts were brought to the new King of Israel. Some reason that it is because all three of these substances made up a big part of the tabernacle and worship. These men were not only recognizing Jesus as the King, but in all likelihood, they were pointing back to the fact that He was a fulfillment of the types and shadows cast by the Old Testament. This made Him the one true God, who made His entrance as man, and came as the Promised King of Israel. In spite of modern-day speculations, God was in it. In their gifts to this new-born king, the three wise men were recognizing and worshiping Jesus for who He was, God Incarnate and the promised King.

Keep in mind, the gold represented Jesus' deity. He is God who came in the flesh. He opened up the kingdom of God to man as hearts are open to the true God. He closed the spiritual gap as He became the way of fellowship between man and God. He now serves as the High Priest who continually intercedes for us, showing His followers the true way of ministry. He is also the sacrifice who revealed the truth about sinful man and served as the reflection of a righteous God.

Myrrh points to the anointing oil. Jesus was the Anointed One, the promised Messiah, the Christ. He was anointed to bring healing, deliverance, restoration, liberty, and rest to man's wandering soul.

Frankincense reminds us of the Holy Perfume that graced man's life with a bit of heaven, and became a sweet fragrance in heaven. The perfume pointed to Jesus' life that would be offered upon the cross, but also a life that would be resurrected. From the point of resurrection, He would serve as a fragrance through His Body, the Church. This fragrance would reach the throne of God through the flow of worship from the hearts and lips of His people.

As the New Testament priests, may we stand before the Altar of Incense, knowing full well that we have the power and authority to enter through the veil of Jesus' sacrifice into the Most Holy Place. There, we can fellowship with, worship, enjoy, and honor the One who is worthy of all adoration.

What about you? Is the life of Christ coming forth through you, stirring up the lives of those in darkness? Are you serving as a pleasing fragrance to God, or is your life a stench, devoid of true service, fellowship and worship?

---

[13] Matthew 2:11

14

PATTERNS OF OVERCOMING

We have considered some of the Old Testament patterns. They point to Jesus and the Christian life that must be embraced and applied. However, the New Testament is full of patterns that reveal the overcoming life of Jesus being manifested through those who are experiencing His victory in their lives. Overcoming in the kingdom of God is not an option. Revelation 21:7 says, "He that overcometh shall inherit all things; and I will be his God, and he shall be my son."

When you study the concept of overcoming, you must consider the pattern that is found in the overcomers, as well as consider the warnings towards those who fail to do so. One of the first examples of overcoming is John the Baptist. The first aspect of him overcoming is that of focus. He knew his place and responsibility in God's kingdom. He was the voice that came to prepare the way for The Way or the Messiah. He was the best man who came to support the bridegroom. And, when the bridegroom came, he gave way to the Way. In fact, he gladly decreased in order for Jesus to increase.[1]

Jesus said of John the Baptist that there was no one greater born among women than he was. However, those who became less in His kingdom would be considered greater than John. As you consider John the Baptist, you realize that overcoming occurs when one truly gives way to Jesus. As Christians, we are here to prepare the way for The Way. We must simply point to and support the work of Jesus. The more He is exalted, the greater we become in His kingdom.[2]

The Apostle Paul is another example of an overcomer. Here is a man that opposed The Way. He took religious pride in persecuting the new Church. He was going the wrong way when He actually encountered The Way on the road to Damascus. From that point, Paul's life changed. He brought his body into subjection to keep from being a castaway. He counted all things of his past life and of this present world, as dung. He became crucified to the world, as he maintained his course, fought a good fight, and kept the faith that was first delivered to the saints. He summarized his goal in Philippians 3:10, "That I may know him, and the power of his resurrection, and the fellowship of his sufferings, being made conformable unto his death." The Apostle Paul

---

[1] John 3:30
[2] Matthew 11:7-11; 20:25-27; 1 Peter 5:5-6

was willing to offer up all of his attachments to the old life and the world to possess Christ. [3]

Between John the Baptist and the Apostle Paul, we have a simple picture of overcoming. John showed us that we must give way to Jesus in order to overcome. The Apostle Paul left us with the example of losing all to possess Him and all that He has for us. As you study the two patterns of these men, you can begin to understand why many fail to overcome. They lose sight of what is important. We can see this in the destructive pattern of the churches in Revelation 2-3.

The Christians of Ephesus took their focus off of Jesus and left Him behind. As a result, they had a religion without the heart. Those at Pergamos were into heretical doctrines. These Christians had stood in the midst of Satan's seat, while holding fast to both Jesus' name and their faith. However, they were giving way to idolatrous practices. Obviously, they were not maintaining the truth in their midst.

The Christians of Thyatira possessed various aspects of the Spirit, but they had allowed a wrong spirit into their midst. As a result, they had a mixture, and were committing spiritual harlotry as they gave way to that which was contrary to God. The people of Sardis were dead to the things of God. There was no stirring in their midst to possess all that Jesus had for them. In the end, they would fail to finish the course because they were not running the race. Christians at Laodicea were considered lukewarm. The mixture of the world and Christianity blinded them to their real spiritual condition. They had given way to the philosophy of the world, while maintaining a religious cloak. Ultimately, they had become useless to Jesus, and posed no opposition to Satan.

There were also the two churches that Jesus commended. The Christians at Smyrna were being refined in persecution. His instruction to them was to be faithful even unto death and they would be given a crown of life. For the weary Christians of Philadelphia, He told them that since they kept the word of His patience, He would keep them from the hour of temptation.

The Apostle John established the solution to all spiritual challenges in Revelation 1:1, "The Revelation of Jesus Christ..." The Christian life must begin with a revelation of Him in His glory. This brings us to the pattern of Jesus. Jesus is truly an example of an overcomer. As you study His example, you see where He overcame each enemy of the soul. He overcame the flesh, the world, and Satan.

For the world, He overcame it in separation and obedience. The world is made up of the lust of the flesh, the pride of life, and the lust of the eyes. In His temptation in the wilderness, Satan tried to use the platform of the world to cause Jesus to disobey what He knew was right.[4]

---

[3] Acts 9; Philippians 3:7-14; 2 Timothy 4:6-8
[4] Matthew 4:1-10; 1 John 2:15-16

Regardless of the temptation coming from Satan, Jesus would have no part of the world. As a result, He was able to declare in John 16:33, "These things I have spoken unto you, that in me ye might have peace. In the world, ye shall have tribulation: but be of good cheer; I have overcome the world."

Satan had attacked Jesus in various ways. However, Jesus had the authority to overcome. Where is that authority found? It is found in the Word of God. In His humanity Jesus knew the Word and quoted it. He lived by it and used it as a sword of offense. This is vital because Satan uses lies or half-truths to strip people's authority in God. Authority is found and realized at the point of believing the Word instead of Satan's warped, perverted presentation of the Word. Such belief has to do with faith. Jesus made this statement, "...It is written, Man shall not live by bread alone, but by every word that proceedeth out of the mouth of God" (Matthew 4:4b).

Jesus overcame the flesh by giving way to the will of the Father. This was brought out in the Garden of Gethsemane. Jesus was about to embark on His greatest ordeal. He knew the spirit was strong, but the flesh was weak. He knew the spirit could endure, but could the flesh sustain the ordeal? There was much on the line. Jesus knew the cup would be bitter in ways that no mere man could fathom. As He wrestled with the harsh reality of the weak flesh, he came to the same place of submission: Not His will, but the Father's will be done.

The flesh is strong as far as the will, but unable to carry out the impossible. At heart, the flesh is a coward. It wants to be noble, but refuses to be sacrificed. It wants to be exalted, but it will not give way to that which is worthy. Jesus overcame the flesh in the Garden of Gethsemane, and secured salvation on the cross. He finished the course so you and I could have everlasting life.

What will it take for us to overcome? John tells us how to overcome the world in 1 John 5:4, "For whatsoever is born of God overcometh the world: and this is the victory that overcometh the world, even our faith." The key to overcoming the world is to be born again. This means you will have a new disposition that is no longer inclined to go with the rest of the world. As this new disposition is developed to manifest Christ, a person becomes more and more crucified to the world as Jesus becomes a greater reality.

The Apostle John tells us how to overcome Satan in Revelation 12:11, "And they overcame him by the blood of the Lamb, and by the word of their testimony; and they loved not their lives unto the death." The blood of the Lamb reminds Satan that we belong to God, and that he must receive permission from God to sift us. And, when he is given such permission, it is not only to test us, but to also enlarge us in our faith. Although some allow Satan to rob them of their place in Christ, those who choose to believe that nothing is happening in their lives unless God has permitted it, hold onto the fact that they have a High Priest in heaven who is able to make intercession on their behalf. [5]

Christians have their testimonies to overcome Satan.[6] Testimonies involve two elements: the Word of God and experiences. The Word of God reveals Christ to us to establish our testimony of Him as being true. Experiences point to revelations of Christ that are walked out in a relationship with God. Godly experiences simply agree or are reaffirmed by what God's Word has already declared about Jesus.

The Apostle John made this statement in 1 John 2:13, I write unto you, fathers, because ye have known him that is from the beginning. I write unto you, young men, because ye have overcome the wicked one. I write unto you, little children, because ye have known the Father." Notice how the fathers and the little children have a testimony of God. The fathers know Him because of the Word and experiences in their lives, and the children know the Father because of His love. However, notice how the young men overcame Satan.

1 John 2:14 gives us this insight about the young men, "…I have written unto you, young men, because you are strong, and the word of God abideth in you, and ye have overcome the wicked one." The young men overcame Satan because the Word abided in them. The fathers were in a *state* of abiding, rest, and confidence because they *have* overcome much and knew God. The children were in the place *of* overcoming because of the Father's love, but the young men were *in* the process of overcoming.

Experience has to do with character. Character determines strength or endurance. Faith in the Word of God during trying times is what enlarges one, establishing character. Such processes are never enjoyable, but they do refine one's faith in God in greater ways.[7]

Finally, how does a person gain victory over the flesh? Jesus answered this question. He instructed His disciples to deny self, pick up the cross, and follow Him.[8] Death to self is how one begins to let his or her present life go.

Life consists of personal identity, rights, dreams, and pursuits. Life of this nature represents vanity, but many will sell their life in God to maintain this temporary life. They have to compromise what is true and righteous to protect this existence. Such a life serves as a platform for the world and pride to determine values and priorities. Jesus posed the thought that if you gain the whole world, but lose your soul, you have gained nothing.

---

[5] Job 1:6-12; 2:1-6; Luke 22:31-32; Romans 8:28; 1 Peter 1:6-9

[6] If you would like to know more about testimonies, see the author's book, *The Power of out Testimonies,* in Volume 6 of her foundation series.

[7] Romans 5:2-5; John 1:2-4; 1 Peter 1:6-9

[8] Matthew 16:24-26

What many people fail to realize is that the flesh is the biggest avenue by which Satan gains access to a person. This is why John tells us that those who overcome do not love their lives unto death.

We can see the consistent patterns of overcoming. Each overcomer pursued their new life in God through obedience to the Word of God. They understood their position in God because of Jesus' calling and works. And, they did not love their present life or the world. As a result, they were free to pursue a new, eternal life.

On judgment day, there will be no excuse for not overcoming. We not only have the many examples of overcoming, but we have the means and power of the Holy Ghost to overcome. Let's consider the benefits of overcoming.

If we overcome, we will eat of the tree of life in the midst of the paradise of God. Overcoming means that I will not be hurt by the second death, and that I will eat of the hidden manna, as well as given a stone with a new name written on it. To overcome means that I will have power over the nations. I will be clothed in white raiment, and my name will not be blotted out of the book of life. I will be made a pillar in the temple of my God, as well as sit with my Lord in His throne.[9]

The question about overcoming comes down to whether I have an ear to hear what the Spirit is saying. He is the One who leads me into all truth by bringing wisdom and revelation to my spirit. He is the One who identifies me to Jesus, calls me from the world, and sanctifies me from the dictates of the self-life.[10]

As stated, overcoming is not an option. It is not a partial occurrence. Overcoming must take place in every area of our lives. However, the key to overcoming comes down to whether we are following the patterns of God's Word. After all, each pattern leads us away from the flesh, the world, and Satan into a glorious life in God.

Therefore, are you following God's patterns?

---

[9] Revelation 2:7, 11, 17, 26-27; 3:5, 10, 13, 21
[10] John 16:13; Ephesians 1:17

15

EMBRACING THE IMAGE

Patterns are important in discovering something new and better. As I have been revealing in this book, the Old and New Testaments are full of patterns. These patterns give followers of Jesus valuable insight into what to look for in order to recognize the fulfillment of the pattern, as well as walk out a godly productive life. The Apostle Paul confirmed this in Titus 2:7, "In all things shewing thyself a pattern of good works: in doctrine shewing uncorruptness, gravity, sincerity."

The patterns that God gave foreshadow a bit of heaven. Hebrews 8:5 confirmed this, "Who serve unto the example and shadow of heavenly things, as Moses was admonished of God when he was about to make the tabernacle: for, See, saith he, that thou make all things according to the pattern shewed to thee in the mount." These patterns were a way to give man a means to recognize the finished product.

Some patterns served as a design or model as to how men must walk out their lives before God. The Apostle Paul made reference to the concept of such patterns in 1 Timothy 1:16. He stated, "Howbeit for this cause I obtained mercy, that in me first Jesus Christ might shew forth all longsuffering, for a pattern to them which should hereafter believe on him to life everlasting." However, many patterns were a shadow of something greater. In a way, these patterns served as mere outlines as they formed an incredible image.

To the Jews this indelible image was of their soon and coming Messiah and King. For the Gentiles, this pattern would be manifested in their Savior and Lord. Although many or most Gentiles did not know about the patterns of the Old Testament, they were drawn by the Spirit to embrace the fulfillment of many of these patterns. It would be later that they would examine the image veiled in the patterns of the Old Testament to discover that Jesus, the Son of God, was a true fulfillment of the shadow that was cast centuries earlier.

The saints of old had to accept the patterns of the Old Testament by faith. Although they adhered to the patterns by faith, they always looked forward with great expectancy as did Abraham to the unveiling or fulfillment of these patterns: "For he looked for a city which hath foundations, whose builder and maker is God" (Hebrews 11:10).

Hebrews 11:13 reiterated that the Old Testament saints never witnessed the fulfillment of God's promises, but they had the vision and foresight to see the fulfillment of these promises, and were persuaded to believe them. This persuasion caused them to embrace these promises, making them strangers and pilgrims in the land.

For the New Testament saints, they must look back at the fulfillment of these great promises. By faith, they must embrace the One who fulfilled them. They live not in expectancy of seeing a promise fulfilled, for in their hearts, it already is a reality. Rather, they live in expectancy of seeing the One who fulfilled it face to face. Each saint has already seen Jesus, but it has been through a dark glass.[1]

Jesus must be more than a shadow or an outline to His followers. They must experience the different aspects of His character. They must taste the sweet grace of His salvation in greater measure, behold His majesty in truth, encounter His touch in healing, hear His voice in the dark night of their souls, and know His mercy in the midst of great failure.

Even after experiencing the different aspects of Jesus' character, saints will be aware that there is so much more to discover about the depths of His character. At first, Jesus started as a mere shadow, obscured in the midst of curtains, altars, priests, sacrifices, spices, oil, and perfume. His examples were hidden in the names of places, disguised by insignificant objects or examples, and marred by the sin of man. He had remained a mystery, concept, hope, or idea until He intruded into the midst of history and into the lives of ordinary men to forever change the course of humanity.

The elements that cast the heavenly shadow became beggarly in contrast to Jesus Christ's intrusion into history to reveal God to lost, hopeless men, and to fulfill the many promises of God.[2] These elements faded in the background as the Son of the Living God became real.

The Old Testament representations could only cast a shadow as God illuminated His heavenly plans. However, when Jesus came, the shadows gave way to the uncompromising light of the world.[3] There was no more shadow, because the mystery was unveiled to reveal the identity of Jesus Christ. Therefore, the shadows could no longer remain in the consistent light of the Christ.

I do not study the patterns to find Jesus, for I have already found Him. I study the patterns, so the Holy Spirit can bring greater dimension to Jesus' infinite character. I do not follow the patterns because they are interesting. I follow the patterns to discover greater truths and a more abundant life in Jesus.

The truth is I want to discover as much about Jesus as I can. My desire is not noble or religious. My need to know and possess Jesus not only takes on a sweetness, but an urgency. There is no doubt in my mind

---

[1] 1 Corinthians 13:12
[2] Galatians 4:9
[3] John 1:1-5

that I need the reality of Jesus in my life to stand and withstand in the times I am living.

What about you? What are you doing about your life in Jesus? Are you trying to discover Him in greater ways or are you assuming that He will accept you because you know of Him and use His name?

The quality of your life will depend on whether you seek out and follow the patterns that God has so graciously given His followers for their edification. The patterns are many and inexhaustible. Although we as believers may catch glimpses of some patterns, and come to terms with others, there is one constant reality that we must keep in mind. Like all patterns, they are outlines or serve as preludes to the real source.

The Apostle Paul summarized it this way in Ephesians 2:7, "That in the ages to come he might shew the exceeding riches of his grace in his kindness towards us through Christ Jesus." Consider and examine this truth and promise in light of your life in Christ. The depths and possibilities found in each pattern are as far-reaching and infinite as the One who became the living expression and fulfillment of these incredible glimpses into the heavenlies and the eternal.

In what way have you experienced these bits of heavenly revelations in your own life?

Bibliography

Strong's Exhaustive Concordance of the Bible; Word Bible Publishers

Webster's New Collegiate Dictionary, G. & C. Merriam M. Co © 1976

A Dwelling Place for God, Ruth Specter Lascelle, © 1990 by Hyman Israel Specter

The Riches of Watchman Nee, © 1999 by Living Stream Ministry

Born after Midnight, A. W. Tozer, ©1989 by Christian Publications

Whatever Happened to Worship, A. W. Tozer, © 1985 by Christian Publications

A.W. Tozer On Worship and Entertainment, © 1997 by Christian Publications, Inc.

Christ, the Sum of All Spiritual Things, Watchman Nee, © 1973 by Christian Fellowship Publishers, Inc.

Jewish Faith and The New Covenant, © 1980 by Ruth Specter Lacelle

Smith's Bible Dictionary, William Smith, L.L.D., Thomas Nelson Publishers

Vine's Expository Dictionary of Biblical Words, © 1985 by Thomas Nelson, Inc. Publishers

Great People of the Bible and How They Lived, © 1974 The Reader's Digest Association, Inc.

In the Footsteps of Jesus, © 1997 by Bruce Marchiano

Bringing Sons Into Glory & Making All Things New, © 1990 by Oswald Chambers Publications Association

Daily Thoughts for Disciples, ©1990 by Oswald Chambers Publications Association

Bible in the News, February 1999 Issue

God's Will: Our Dwelling Place, Andrew Murray

The Thompson Chain-Reference Bible, © 1988 by the B. B. Kirkbridge Bible Company Inc.

Lectures on the Book of Acts, by H. A. Ironside, 18th printing 1982

Guardians of the Grail, J. R. Church, © 1989 by Prophecy Publications

The Song of Moses, J. R. Church, © 1991, Prophecy Publications

My Utmost for His Highest, Oswald Chambers, © 1935, Dodd, Mead & Company, Inc. Copyright renewed 1963 by Oswald Chambers Publications Association, Ltd.

Number In Scripture, Ethelbert W. Bullinger, Kregel Publications

The Companion Bible, E. W. Bullinger, Kregel Publications

Finding the Reality of God, Paris W. Reidhead, © 1989

Other books by Rayola Kelley:

Hidden Manna (Original)
Battle for the Soul
Stories of the Heart
Transforming Love & Beyond
The Great Debate
Post to Post: (1) Establishing the Way
Post to Post: (2) Walking in the Way
Post to Post: (3) Meditations Along the Way

Volume One: Establishing Our Life in Christ
My Words Are Spirit and Life
The Anatomy of Sin
The Principles of the Abundant Life
The Place of Covenant
Unmasking the Cult Mentality

Volume Three: Developing a Godly Environment
Godly Discipline
Prayer and Worship
Don't Touch That Dial
Face of Thankfulness
ABC's of Christianity

Volume Four: Issues of the Heart
Hidden Manna (Revised)
Bring Down the Sacred Cows
The Manual for the Single Christian Life
Parents are People Too

Volume Five: Challenging the Christian Life
The Issues of Life
Presentation of the Gospel
For the Purpose of Edification
Whatever Happened to the Church?
Women's Place in the Kingdom of God

Volume Six: Developing Our Christian Life
The Many Faces of Christianity
Possessing Our Souls
Experiencing the Christian Life
The Power of Our Testimonies
The Victorious Journey

Volume Seven: Discovering True Ministry
From Prisons and Dots to Christianity
So You Want to be in Ministry

Devotions:
Devotions of the Heart: Books One and Two
Daily Food for the Soul: Books One and Two

Gentle Shepherd Ministries Devotion Series:
Being a Child of God
Disciplining the Strength of our Youth
Coming to Full Age

Gentle Shepherd Ministries Series:
The Christian Life Series
What Matter Is This?
The Challenge of It
The Reality of It

The Leadership Series
Overcoming
A Matter of Authority and Power
The Dynamics of True Leadership

Nugget Books:
Nuggets From Heaven
More Nuggets From Heaven
Heavenly Gems
More Heavenly Gems
Heavenly Treasures

Books By
Jeannette Haley
Books co-authored with Rayola Kelley:
Hidden Manna (Original)
The Many Faces of Christianity (Volume 6)
Post to Post 3: Meditations Along the Way

Other Books:
Rose of Light, Thorn of Darkness (Volume 7)
Interview in Hell (Volume 7)
Interview on Earth (Volume 7)
The Pig and I
Reflections of Wonder (Devotional)

Children Books:
Little Stories for Little People
Traveler's Tales
The Adventures of Zack and Mira
The Adventures of Paul and Dana
(A House on the Beach)
The Monster of Mystery Valley

www.ingramcontent.com/pod-product-compliance
Lightning Source LLC
Chambersburg PA
CBHW031231090426
42742CB00007B/148